THE POLITICS OF
NUCLEAR
BALANCE

THE POLITICS OF NUCLEAR BALANCE

AMBIGUITY AND CONTINUITY IN STRATEGIC POLICIES

William H. Baugh
UNIVERSITY OF OREGON

Longman
New York & London

THE POLITICS OF NUCLEAR BALANCE
Ambiguity and Continuity in Strategic Policies

Longman Inc., 1560 Broadway, New York, N.Y. 10036
Associated companies, branches, and representatives
throughout the world.

Copyright © 1984 by Longman Inc.

All rights reserved. No part of this publication may be
reproduced, stored in a retrieval system, or transmitted
in any form or by any means, electronic, mechanical,
photocopying, recording, or otherwise, without the prior
permission of the publisher.

Table 2.2 (p. 59) is from *MRIV and the Arms Race* by Ronald
L. Tammen (1973). Reprinted with permission from
Irvington Publishers, Inc., New York.

Figure 4.3 (p. 150) from *U.S. Intelligence and the Soviet Strategic Threat* by Lawrence David Freedman. Copyright © 1977 by Lawrence David Freedman. Reprinted by permission of Westview Press and Macmillan, London and Basingstoke.

Figures 4.4 (p. 151) and 4.5a and 4.5b (p. 153) are from
Modeling the U.S.-U.S.S.R. Strategic Arms Race, Ph.D.
thesis, Indiana University, 1982. Reprinted with permission
of Michael L. Squires.

Developmental Editor: Irving E. Rockwood
Editorial and Production Supervisor: Ferne Y. Kawahara
Manufacturing Supervisor: Marion Hess

Library of Congress Cataloging in Publication Data
Baugh, William H.
  The politics of nuclear balance.
  Includes bibliographical references and index.
  1. Strategy. 2. United States—Military policy.
3. Atomic weapons. 4. Atomic warfare. I. Title.
U162.B38 1983   355′.0217   82-24995
ISBN 0-582-28214-4
ISBN 0-582-28423-6 (pbk.)

Manufactured in the United States of America
Printing: 9 8 7 6 5 4 3 2 1   Year: 92 91 90 89 88 87 86 85 84

To My Parents

Contents

List of Tables and Figures   ix
Acknowledgments   xi

Introduction   1

1 Contemporary Dilemmas of Strategic Policy Management   4
    Viability and the Nature of "Strategic" Weaponry   4
    Strategic Weapons Regime Management as a
        Game of Strategy   10
    Constraints on the Political Process   12
    Strategic Policy Issues for the 1980s   24

2 Strategic Doctrine as Problem and Solution   35
    Introduction   35
    The Elusive Concept of Deterrence   36
    Deterrence Theory and Strategic Doctrine   41
    The Evolution of Nuclear Strategic Doctrine   43
    A Plethora of Doctrines   71
    What Drives Doctrine?   77
    The Future of U.S. Strategic Doctrine: Trends and
        Scenarios   80

**3 Strategic Doctrine, Weapons Acquisition,
and Arms Control: Politics and Process**   86
    Introduction: Overview of a Political-Technological
        Process   86
    Influences of the Interactive Environment   93
    The Processes of Intelligence and Assessment   103
    The Roles of Technology   107
    Institutionalized Arms Control   115
    Other Influences on Strategic Program Decision Making   118
    Concluding Remarks   120

4 Assessing the Strategic "Balance": Tools for Policy Analysis   122
    Introduction   122

A Typology and Assessment of Strategic "Balance"
   Measures   123
An Examination of Three Nuclear Exchange Models   136
Using "Balance" Measures to Assess Strategic Weapons
   Programs   146
Using "Balance" Measures in Managing Strategic
   Weapons Programs   154

5 **ICBM Vulnerability and Its Solutions**   156
   Introduction   156
   The Problem: Accuracy Implies Vulnerability—
      And Perhaps Instability   157
   Some Proposed Solutions to ICBM Vulnerability   161
   Assessing the Problem and Proposed Solutions: Measuring
      the Strategic "Balance" in the 1980s   166
   Evaluation of Theoretical Attack Scenarios   170
   Implications of Alternative Solutions to the ICBM
      Vulnerability Problem   187

6 **A Future for Arms Control? Structure, Indicators, and
   Prospects for the 1980s**   192
   Introduction   192
   Structural and Systemic Constraints on Arms Control   196
   Post-World War II Arms Control Accomplishments   204
   Political Patterns in Arms Control Agreements   210
   Scenarios and Indicators for Arms Control in the 1980s   214
   Concluding Remarks: The Prospects for Arms Control   225

References   226
Glossary   239
Index   269

List of Tables and Figures

Figure 1.1 Strength/Distance Function for a Conventional Weapons Regime *6*
Figure 1.2 Strength/Distance Function for a Nuclear Weapons Regime *7*
Figure 1.3 Strength/Distance Functions for Several Types of Weapons Systems *8*
Figure 1.4 The Incentive to Develop New Weapons Technologies *16*
Figure 1.5 Timelines in Development and Deployment of Minuteman ICBMs *20*
Table 1.1 Major Strategic Issues for the 1980s *25*
Figure 2.1 Major Developments and Doctrines in the U.S.—Soviet Strategic Weapons Regime *44*
Figure 2.2 Quantities of U.S. and Soviet Bombers *52*
Figure 2.3 Quantities of U.S. and Soviet ICBMs *53*
Table 2.1 Abbreviations for Strategic Doctrinal Positions *57*
Table 2.2 Expected Soviet Losses in a Countervalue Retaliation *59*
Figure 2.4 Dimensions of Strategic Doctrines *72*
Figure 2.5 U.S. and Soviet Movements in Strategic Doctrine *74*
Figure 3.1 Overview of the Strategic Weapons Acquisition Process *88*
Table 3.1 Themes in the Arms Expenditure Literature *94*
Table 4.1 A Typology of Measures of the Strategic "Balance" *124*
Table 4.2 Three Problems in Aggregating and Distributing ICBM Lethality or CMP *132*
Table 4.3 Functions in Nuclear Exchange Modelling *137*
Table 4.4 Comparative Properties of Three Nuclear Exchange Models *139*
Figure 4.1 Structure of the Arsenal Exchange Model (AEM9) *142*
Figure 4.2 A Schematic of U.S. Strategic Weapons Program Management *147*
Figure 4.3 Actual Numbers of Soviet ICBMs Versus U.S. Projections *150*
Figure 4.4 U.S. and Soviet ICBM Warheads, 1954–1979 *151*

Figure 4.5a U.S. Total ICBM Warheads and ICBM Warheads Expected to Survive a First Strike, 1959–1979   *153*
Figure 4.5b Soviet Total ICBM Warheads and ICBM Warheads Expected to Survive a First Strike, 1959–1979   *153*
Table 5.1   Facilities Lists Used in Assessing a 1981 Soviet Anti-ICBM Strike   *167*
Table 5.2   Allocation of Weapons and Assessment of the Attack   *169*
Figure 5.1   Expected Percentages of ICBMs Destroyed in First Strikes   *171*
Figure 5.2   ICBM RVs Expected to Survive a First Strike Under SALT Limitations   *172*
Figure 5.3   ICBM RVs Expected to Survive a First Strike; Additional Minuteman IIIs Deployed by the U.S.   *175*
Figure 5.4   ICBM RVs Expected to Survive a First Strike; Some Minuteman IIIs Deployed in MPS   *176*
Table 5.3   LoAD, Trident Counterforce, and Fractionation   *181*
Figure 6.1   Behavioral Surface for War Policy   *195*
Figure 6.2   The Decision to Reduce Existing Arms as a Prisoners' Dilemma   *202*
Table 6.1   Major Steps in Contemporary Arms Control   *205*
Table 6.2   Features Commonly Seen in Arms-Control Agreements   *210*
Table 6.3   Some Scenarios and Indicators of Policies Pursued   *215*
Figure 6.3   Scenarios in Arming and Disarming   *216*

Acknowledgments

In recent years a minor fad has appeared, according to which authors suggest that the erudition of those who have read and commented on their manuscripts is so great that they themselves should be absolved of responsibility for any remaining errors. While the progress of this work over the past two years has benefited from a number of insightful readings, for which I extend sincere thanks, I will still accept an old-fashioned responsibility for the result. Any researcher is fortunate to have friends and colleagues who are intensely interested in the subject of study. At the very least, both researcher and research will benefit from the interaction; hopefully the friends and colleagues will also benefit. This writer is indeed fortunate to have had the aid of three individuals who gave far more than the usual readings and comments to this project. Professor Dan Caldwell and Dr. Dean Ing each provided extensive and penetrating reviews of very large portions of the manuscript, thereby contributing markedly to the accuracy and comprehensiveness of the volume. My colleague Harmon Zeigler is due special thanks for having been the first to encourage using book form to summarize and extend the results of some ten years' research into questions of strategic weapons management and arms control.

Helpful readings were also provided at a number of stages during the writing by my colleague John Orbell, particularly in the early stages, and by my mother, who applied the practiced eye of a teacher of English to the manuscript. My Indiana University colleague and sometime co-author on arms transfer issues, Michael L. Squires, is to be thanked for reading portions of the manuscript, for sharing data on strategic weapons quantities utilized in preparing several of the figures, and for engaging in a vital, informative, challenging, and ongoing dialogue about strategic weapons issues that already spans most of a decade. Irv Rockwood has been both patient and encouraging in his role as executive editor at Longman. A number of my students in several classes offered comments on portions of the manuscript and the materials that went into it, thereby helping me both to reach new insights and to refine the methods of presentation. Vital research computing resources were provided by the University of Oregon.

The merits of this work belong in significant measure to the many persons who have helped, read, and commented, including both those identified above and those who could not be mentioned individually. I express my deep thanks to them all for having helped make possible the challenges and joys of this project.

William H. Baugh

Introduction

... arms alone cannot provide the security within which our values and our interests can flourish. Our foreign policy must be directed toward greater international stability, without which there is no prospect for a lasting peace. Thus, our strength in arms—very important—must be matched by creative, responsible, and courageous diplomacy.

We have as a nation that strength and that courage now to present clearly to potential adversaries as well as to our allies.

President Jimmy Carter (1980)

Unfortunately what was once true is no longer so. The United States is slipping. The overall strategic balance is tilting in favor of Moscow.

Our deterrent force is only as persuasive as its ability to survive a first strike in sufficient numbers, and to respond effectively. But the capacity of our strategic force to survive is now coming into question. The relentless Soviet strategic and naval buildup poses a serious threat not to just one, but to all three of the elements of our strategic deterrent—ICBMs, bombers, and Polaris/Poseidon.

Senator Henry Jackson (1971)

The Soviet Union is effectively looking after its own defense, but it does not and will not seek military superiority over the other side. We do not want to upset the approximate equilibrium of military strength existing at present ... between the USSR and the United States. But in return we insist that no one else should seek to upset it in his favor.

Leonid Brezhnev (1977)

Today, in virtually every measure of military power, the Soviet Union enjoys a decided advantage.

President Ronald Reagan (1982)

At the outset of this study, the underlying political or decision-making thesis of this volume may be stated in highly condensed form as follows: The nuclear strategic "balance" is ambiguous because there is no agreement either within or between governments on how it is to be measured. The lack of agreement arises in part from technical and methodological issues in policy assessment, but it arises much more strongly from the fact that doctrines for the use of strategic weapons are themselves ambiguous. These ambiguities, in turn, exist because we have never fully resolved the political questions about what to do with the weapons we already have, let alone with the weaponry we can envision. Severe disagreements exist about both means and ends. Such disagreements are not new phenomena in time and space—they are traditionally the very quintessence of politics.

Moreover, the management of strategic policy is becoming an increasingly important issue in U.S. foreign and domestic politics. While public attention to strategic policy grew during the SALT II debate, it was intensified by the 1980 "shelving" of SALT II ratification efforts (Walsh and Goshko, 1980) and the 1980 Presidential campaign. The summer of 1980 saw charges and countercharges about whether a supposed shift in U.S. strategic nuclear targeting doctrine was making nuclear war more probable or less likely. The entire 1980 campaign was filled with discussions of asserted U.S. strategic inferiority to the Soviet Union, a charge that seemed quite new to the political scene, although it was to be carried forward after the campaign by President Reagan. These and other campaign events appear to reflect a breakdown of the "bipartisan" foreign policy that dominated U.S. foreign relations since the end of World War II. Yet, upon closer examination, we find that the strategic policy issues that became so prominent in 1980 had been clearly drawn for considerably more than a decade. Nonetheless, it is increasingly apparent that we are entering an era in which the strategic "balance" is perceived as being both uncertain and of vital importance, and in which there is a great deal of ambiguity concerning the doctrine to be employed should deterrence fail.

While ambiguity of doctrine may sometimes be used as a bargaining tactic, there is also a lack of clarity about the processes by which strategic doctrines are established and arms acquisitions are dovetailed with arms controls. Although this fundamental area of foreign-policy management features a fairly well-developed set of analytic tools for determining the impact of selected policies, there is a paucity of underlying theory. Quantitative aids to policy assessment are limited in impact, both by the extent to which agreement can be achieved on the input data and by political constraints on the acceptability of suggested policy outcomes. In short, as we begin to build agreement on the technical questions of security assessment, without which no policy movement is feasible, the crucial questions increasingly become those concerning the political management of the perceived strategic balance.

The problems of political management are mounting. After more than a decade of SALT negotiations, the strategic arsenals of both the United States and the Soviet Union are larger, more powerful, and yet more vulnerable than they were in 1969 at the opening of the first formal SALT session in Helsinki. There are growing concerns that the once-assumed stability of the deterrent system has been undermined; that the position of the United States relative to that of the Soviet Union has declined; that perceptions of strength have greater political import than the realities of strength; and that the range of uncertainty about strategic weapons and the strategic "balance" has been widening.

Choices of strategic weapons and the doctrines for their use are influenced by existing arsenals and historic trends in their growth; by arms control agreements; by prior strategic doctrine; by technological feasibilities and limitations; and by both domestic and international political considerations. Moreover, many of these factors are themselves interactive. In addition, dramatic advances in technology offer the promise of new weapons that might, even within the decade, provide the "breakout" from strategic parity and stalemate so feared yet so sought after by strategic planners. Among the new weapons possibilities are truly effective Anti-Ballistic Missiles (ABMs), whether land-based or from a variety of mobile launchers, and Directed Energy Transfer (DET) weapons, both lasers and particle beams, either land-based or space-based. In a time of political uncertainty and rapid technological development, the ambiguities of the strategic "balance" are compounded.

This volume is therefore addressed to the manifold problems of political management of the ambiguous nuclear strategic balance in the 1980s and, to the nontrivial extent we can foresee, beyond. Major themes considered include the following: which weapons, policies, and strategic doctrines are technologically feasible; which are politically acceptable and which are likely; the merger of technological and political feasibilities into strategic doctrines; the policymaking processes that eventuate in those doctrines, including both arms acquisitions and arms limitation decisions; alternative methods that have been used and that might be used for policy assessment; and projections for strategic weapons systems, doctrines, and political developments over this decade, including assessments of the promises and threats posed by the host of new technological possibilities.

FIGURE 1.1 Strength/Distance Function for a Conventional Weapons Regime

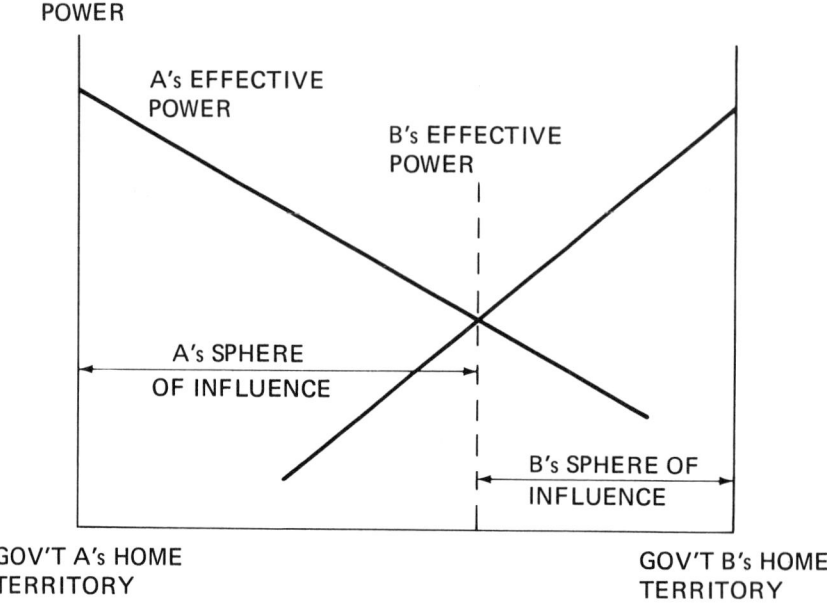

In a regime in which governments possess only conventional (nonnuclear) weapons, effective or usable power declines with distance from its base in a manner described by the Strength/Distance Function (SDF). As one moves further and further away from Government A's homeland, eventually a point is reached at which Government B's power equals A's. Beyond that point, B's effective power will exceed A's. While it may be difficult to locate that point precisely, the fact that it must exist underlies the traditional concept of the division of the world into spheres of influence. Such a regime rests upon the critical assumption that the SDF is fairly steep, so that each government is viable on its home territory.

Consider now an alternative situation, diagrammed in Figure 1.2. Here the SDF is fairly flat, and each government is still very powerful at the other's home territory. If each side's power exceeds some critical deterrence level, a regime of mutual assured destruction may exist. "Assured destruction" is simply the capability to absorb an attack with the assurance that sufficient forces will remain to mount an overwhelming retaliation, a situation in which it is presumed that a rational would-be attacker will be deterred. If both sides have such a capability, the regime is one of *mutual* secure conditional viability. Yet, if governmental decision makers prefer unconditional viability to the uncertainties and dependence on a would-be opponent inherent in even secure conditional viability, it is likely that such a regime will be less stable and more susceptible to upset by changes in military technology than the regime of Figure 1.1.

The modern dichotomy between nuclear and conventional weaponry is readily described in terms of the differences sketched in Figures 1.1 and

FIGURE 1.2 Strength/Distance Function for a Nuclear Weapons Regime

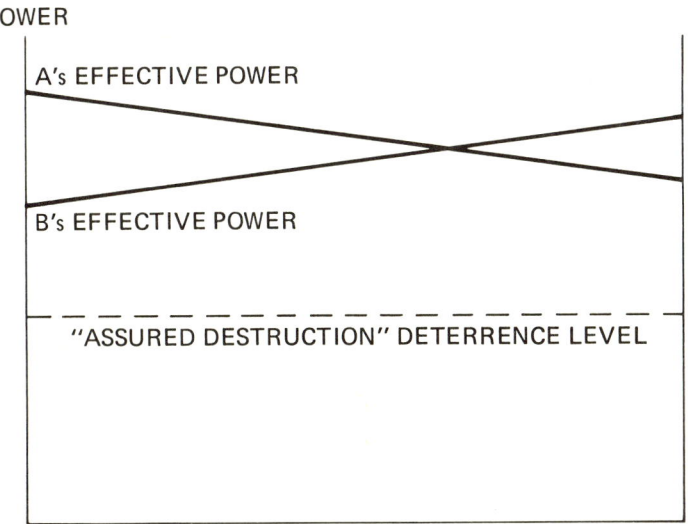

In a regime in which governments possess strategic nuclear weapons, effective power declines only slowly with distance, primarily because of the very great losses to be suffered even if only a tiny fraction of attackers is able to penetrate defenses. Since no government is unconditionally viable, strategic nuclear weapons do not divide the world into spheres of influence, although such spheres may still be defined by conventional (nonnuclear) and tactical nuclear weapons. According to Mutual Assured Destruction doctrine, governments should refrain from initiating attack so long as the destruction they would expect to suffer in retaliation would exceed some maximum acceptable level.

1.2. The class of conventional (nonnuclear) weapons exhibits the behavior of Figure 1.1. Such weapons are now more powerful than at any prior time, and they have significant capabilities for projection over great distances. Yet, such projection takes time and effort, often including considerable difficulties in coordinating the logistics of transport. Moreover, these weapons can be defended against. The Strength/Distance Function therefore exists and is of nonnegligible steepness. Very few aircraft have intercontinental range without aerial refueling or intermediate airfields for staging; the transport of tanks overseas is extremely difficult and expensive by air, and thus cannot be carried out on a large scale; and large numbers of troops and their supplies are most readily moved by sea, which is a very slow means of transport. Every one of these classes of weapons and transport is subject to considerable attrition by defenders. Conceptual SDFs for several types of weapons systems are shown in Figure 1.3.

The decline of power projection capability with distance is clearly seen

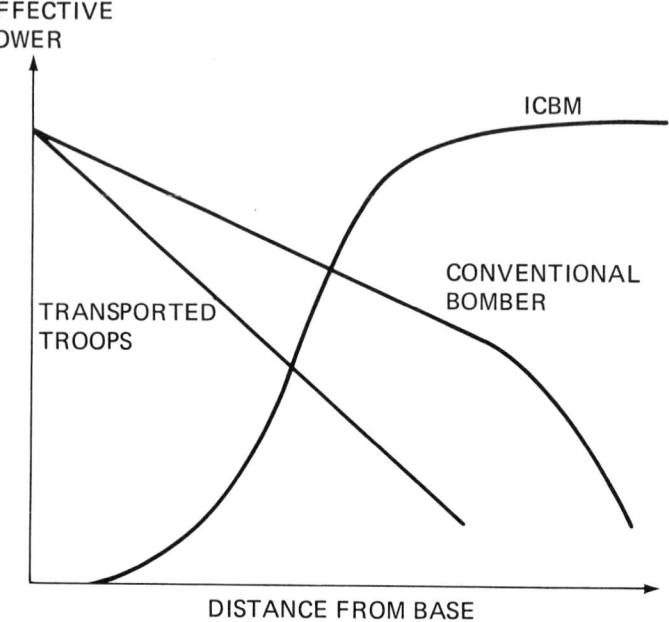

FIGURE 1.3 Strength/Distance Functions for Several Types of Weapons Systems

Conceptual Strength/Distance Functions (SDFs) for several types of weapons systems represent the manner in which their effective power changes with distance from the basing point, but do not represent their relative power. While troops may be the most effective weapons system at very short ranges, the SDF of transported troops shows a steady decline with distance, primarily because transport by any means takes time and is subject to attack throughout, with such attacks intensifying as the target is approached. Conventional manned intercontinental bombers reach their targets in a matter of hours but may require refueling; their SDF curves downward because they are subject to intense attacks as they enter the target zone. ICBMs are designed to be fired over distances of some thousands of miles; the need to burn or dispose of fuel precludes their use at short distances, so that their SDF only begins to rise from zero at intermediate ranges. The present lack of a significant terminal defense means that ICBMs reach their maximum effective power at long range; deployment of an effective ABM system would lead to a downward-curving SDF at long range.

in the 1980 U.S. attempt to infiltrate a commando group into Iran to rescue the embassy hostages. Similarly, studies of capability to counter a Soviet invasion of Iran projected that, by maximum effort, the United States could land over a period of 16 to 30 days perhaps a quarter of the troops the Soviets could move overland, and even less armor (Burt, 1980, 4; Middleton, 1980). Conventional weaponry may be more sophisticated and more powerful than at any earlier time in history, but its capabilities still decline significantly with distance from the homeland, so that great powers may remain viable against such weapons.

A considerably different situation exists with nuclear weapons. Although the boundary between the most powerful conventional explosives and the smallest nuclear devices is blurry, the larger nuclear devices and their associated delivery systems exhibit an SDF more like that of Figure 1.2 than that of Figure 1.1. These are weapons designed expressly for intercontinental projection, with Strength/Distance Functions that vary among delivery systems, but that generally have quite shallow slopes. Intercontinental bombers have a moderate SDF and are subject to terminal defenses. Submarine-Launched Ballistic Missiles (SLBMs) are subject to a slight SDF, mainly reflecting the time required for the submarines to travel from their home bases to operating areas closer to the opponent's homeland. As the ranges of SLBMs are increased, this SDF becomes steadily shallower, both because of reduced travel time and because the submarines may more readily be defended close to home shores. Finally, Intercontinental Ballistic Missiles (ICBMs) cannot be fired readily over short ranges and thus are essentially ineffectual near their bases. Being designed for true intercontinental range and not subject to any significant terminal defenses at this time, they have an almost perfectly flat SDF at long ranges. Of course, if effective terminal defenses are developed, this situation could change, and one could at least envision a race between numbers of attackers and numbers of defenders.

At this point one runs headlong into a major dilemma of defense: ideal stable security has traditionally been thought to require unconditional viability in the home territory. As Boulding has put it,

> . . . for national defense as a system to possess any kind of equilibrium and for nations to be unconditionally viable under a system of national defense, each nation must be able to preserve an area of peace within its critical boundaries even if it has to maintain this area of peace by fighting wars outside it. (1962, 267)

A crucial development in twentieth-century international politics is that for the first time in history it has become at least possible, if not probable, that no more than one state can be unconditionally viable at any given time—and then only if it has a monopoly on the highest military technology. While Boulding's condition can be met today with conventional weapons, the intercontinental nuclear weapon without an adequate defense implies a loss of even conditional viability, unless a deterrent regime can be maintained. Moreover, the rise of such deterrence doctrines as Mutual Assured Destruction has not changed the desire of governments for stable viability. In this light, we can describe all of the major nuclear weapons programs about which policy questions face us in the 1980s as directed toward achieving one of two contradictory goals: (1) to preserve a stable deterrent system based on mutual secure conditional viability; or (2) to "break out" from that system to a regime of unilateral unconditional viability.

Seen in the broadest sense, strategic issues would include an enormous range of aspects, such as the number, makeup, strength, and cohesiveness of alliances; the degree and duration of political support a government could expect to win in the world at large under varying conditions; anticipated political and military support in times of crisis; assurance of the availability of crucial military bases for far-flung operations; assurance of the availability of such essential resources as oil, manganese, and chromium; the capability to project conventional military power overseas in support of any of these objectives; monetary and technological resources to support the programs necessary to sustain such capabilities; and the ability to command the internal political support and cohesiveness required to see such programs through. We turn now, however, to further consideration of the structure of central strategic weapons "regimes," consisting of the opponents, their weapons systems, and the doctrines for utilization of those weapons.

STRATEGIC WEAPONS REGIME MANAGEMENT AS A GAME OF STRATEGY

The development of a strategic weapons regime through all of its stages, including (a) assessment of risks based upon estimation of the possible and probable intentions of an opponent; (b) evaluation of technological possibilities for weapons development; (c) program planning, funding, and implementation; (d) research and development of the actual weapons systems; (e) deployment and eventual retirement and/or replacement of weapons; and (f) consideration of negotiated arms reductions, constitutes a highly complex interactive process that can be described as a "mixed-motive game of strategy" between governments. Games of strategy are characterized by interaction and rules for management of interaction; by choices from among sets of options; by costs and benefits (or payoffs) associated with each possible outcome; and by outcomes jointly determined by the choices of all parties. The rules of interaction, sets of available options, and payoffs associated with each outcome may be said to form the "structure" of the game, and some important behavioral generalizations have been drawn about the implications of major classes of game structures. (Poker and chess are two of the more popularly known games of strategy.)

For our purposes, a strategic weapons regime is an interactive structure involving two or more governments, a structure within which certain action choices are available to each party at any given time. The pattern of such choices planned out over time by a single government in a game is referred to, somewhat confusingly for our present purposes, as a strategy. The interaction outcome at a point in time is determined jointly by the parties' strategy choices and cannot be determined by a single party acting alone. Such an interactive choice situation with jointly determined outcomes clearly qualifies as a game of strategy (Luce and Raiffa, 1957; Rapoport, 1966, 1970).

Moreover, the game we are interested in is a *mixed-motive* game, which makes the strategy choices by the parties particularly complex and difficult to predict. In such a game there are both conflictual and cooperative motivations, making the prediction of an optimal strategy especially problematic. It has become common to refer to choices under such circumstances as involving elements of paradox (Brams, 1976; Howard, 1971). In the game of managing strategic weapons policy, the conflictual motives include drives for power and influence, as well as the desire to best the other party for personal, governmental, and ideological gain. Cooperative motivations include the desire to minimize costs, avoid risks, reduce uncertainty, and avoid catastrophic war. The choices that must be made are further complicated by the fact that information is seldom as complete or as reliable as decison makers could wish. If we knew all the choices previously made in the game of strategy, we would be said to have "perfect information" (Riker, 1962, 34). However, that degree of information is difficult to obtain in face of the secrecy endemic to the strategic weapons regime.

A game of strategy implies a number of other significant features of the decision-making situation facing governments. Since outcomes are jointly determined, one can never be completely certain of winning. Because the game is played under structural and situational constraints, even a player who makes the best available choices with consummate skill will lose in situations characterized by unfavorable structures (Luce and Raiffa, 1957, 64–65). Recall that, in the arena of conventional weaponry, even a great power has a sphere of influence within which it is at an advantage and outside of which it is at a disadvantage. Moreover, one cannot invariably play one's most-preferred strategy. To do so every time, at least in certain interaction structures, would cause one's play to become predictable and thereby enable an opponent to counter it. Steven Brams has called this the "paradox of inducement," noting that,

> . . . despite the equilibrium properties of an outcome, or the fact that a strategy associated with it is dominant, the anticipation of this strategy choice by the other player(s) may motivate the first player to choose another (dominated) strategy that leads to a preferred outcome for himself. A paradox of inducement occurs when a player must choose an apparently irrational dominated strategy to avoid a less-preferred outcome that is induced by the anticipation that he will choose his dominant strategy. (1976, 114)

The paradox of inducement occurs because of the paramount need to maintain credibility; a threat that has never been carried out under any circumstances may eventually evoke only complete disbelief. Thus, if a situation repeatedly arises in which one always chooses a dominant strategy, an opponent will come to count on such a choice and will play so as to counter it. A nondominant strategy may then be induced in order to confound the opponent. One may suggest, for example, that the dominant strategies of both the United States and the Soviet Union in the 1962 Cuban missile crisis were to limit confrontation in order to avoid a major war. Yet President Kennedy precommitted the United States to a strategy of confrontation by insisting that the Soviet missiles be withdrawn from Cuba. In so doing, he confounded Soviet expectations based on previous interactions, including the Bay of Pigs invasion and his Vienna summit meeting with Khrushchev, that he would back down under pressure. He also left the Soviets the last clear choice between yielding and escalating the level of conflict.

There may also be a "paradox of disincentive" in the theory and practice of nuclear deterrence. For, if deterrence rests on the idea of assured destruction, defined as the capability to destroy the "hostage" cities of an opponent who has attacked your military forces, and if that assured destruction is mutual (MAD), then to carry out a retaliation implies a consequent trading of city destructions on both sides, ending with the mutual destruction of all that both societies hold valuable. In such a strategic weapons regime, such retaliation is thus irrational, so that deterrence ought not work. The logic of this argument implies that we must find some regime other than MAD to ensure that "first strikes" against military targets do not occur; the problem is discussed further in Chapter 2.

CONSTRAINTS ON THE POLITICAL PROCESS

Central strategic weapons regimes have significant relations to both domestic and foreign stakes and issues, which tend to act as constraints on the political process. Domestic stakes include large numbers of jobs in the supply and operation of military hardware; opportunities for career advancement or career destruction in the political, military, and bureaucratic sectors; promotion of the fortunes of companies and even whole industries; and deeply felt concerns about national security on the part of millions of individuals throughout the political–military system. Foreign stakes include political and military support, both directly, on strategic weapons issues, and less directly, concerning issues such as those previously discussed. The political process regarding strategic weapons has an enormous number of constraints that define and limit policy options and channels of action. Let us consider some of the more important classes of constraints.

Technology as Constraint or Limiter of Possibilies

Just as the set of possible outcomes is constrained by the structure of options available to the players of the strategic game and the patterns of their previous choices in similar situations, the possible policy options are themselves constrained by the available technology. Whatever is physically unworkable or undeveloped cannot be politically feasible. This is yet another reason why governments cannot always pursue their most-preferred strategies. Consider two examples in which technological developments have turned the unworkable and politically unacceptable into the workable or possible: aerial–spatial reconnaissance to verify compliance with arms limitation agreements, and Anti-Ballistic Missile (ABM) systems.

President Eisenhower's "Open Skies" arms control proposal of 1955 would have allowed the United States and the Soviet Union to overfly major portions of each other's territory to verify that no unsuspected war preparations were underway (Barton and Weiler, 1976, 77). Resting on the need for numbers of aircraft to operate over foreign territory in the same airspace as those of the nation-state under surveillance and to operate without any malfunction that might endanger life below or require a forced landing, the plan lay at the edge of what was technologically reasonable. While the plan was technically feasible, there was no sufficiently compelling political reason to require that it be implemented, and it was quickly rejected. Seventeen years later, however, in the SALT I negotiations, there was a politically compelling need to establish a system to verify compliance with arms control terms without requiring on-site inspection of foreign installations. By that time, a new technology sufficient to the task was available, in the form of photographic reconnaissance satellites that were already highly developed. The principle adopted was that such "national technical means" of verification would be allowed to operate unhindered (U.S. Department of State, 1979, 53). It seems clear that in the face of Soviet insistence that on-site inspections could not be allowed (which thus saved the U.S. delegation from having to deal with the question of whether its government was really any more enthusiastic than the Soviets about such inspections), the availability of a workable verification technology was crucial to achieving a SALT agreement.

It may also be argued that one of the major reasons that we were able to achieve an ABM Treaty in SALT I, under which we essentially banned ABMs for the indefinite future, was that the ABMs of around 1970 were so problematic as to be unworkable on a major scale (Chayes and Wiesner, 1969). Yet by 1980 it appeared that several types of effective anti-ballistic missiles might be built (Snow, 1980, 288). Among these are ground-launched or air-launched missiles of more advanced capabilities than those tested a decade earlier; high-powered laser weaponry, both ground-based and space-based; and beams of charged or neutral high-energy particles, most likely from massive ground installations. As these technologies have developed, calls have been heard with increasing frequency for the U.S. government to abrogate the SALT I ABM Treaty and proceed with development and deployment of a massive ABM system. The rationale for such calls is generally cast in terms of responding to Soviet strategic arms building programs that have placed the land-based ICBM deterrent of the

United States at risk (see the assessment in Chapter 5). Regardless of the rationale offered, such calls would not be likely to be put forward unless there was the promise of an available and effective technology with which to carry them out.

Given the promise of a workable ABM technology, we are confronted with the political problem of deciding whether or not to exploit that possibility. The 1972 SALT I ABM Treaty set a limit of 200 ABMs per side, divided between two sites, and the 1974 Protocol halved that limit to a single site of no more than 100 ABMs per side. In addition to those limits on land-based ABMs, any space-based deployments appear to be prohibited by article V, section 1 of the ABM Treaty, which states that "Each Party undertakes not to develop, test or deploy ABM systems or components which are sea-based, air-based, space-based, or mobile-based" (Barton and Weiler, 1976, 369). Directed Energy Transfer (DET) weapons for ballistic missile defense, such as particle beams or lasers, may not technically be ABMs, but as John Newhouse points out, it was clearly the intent of the SALT I negotiators to ban such systems.

> Perhaps more important . . . was the discussion on August 9 (1971) of futuristic ABMs. Strictly speaking, these are not ABMs because the interceptors would not be ballistic missiles but other more exotic devices, like lasers, charged particles, or electromagnetic waves . . . While it would take many years, certainly more than a decade, to develop, test, and deploy any one of the exotics, heading them off during SALT was priority business; happily, it was largely accomplished. (1973, 230)

Despite this apparent clarity of purpose in the SALT I ABM negotiations, by 1980 a number of calls had been heard either to abrogate or circumvent the ABM Treaty. On June 10, 1980, Representative Ron Paul of Texas introduced House Joint Resolution 566, calling for U.S. withdrawal. In his first major argument in that resolution, he asserted that "the Treaty and its related Interim Agreement, Protocol, and Agreed Interpretations have thwarted the development of an anti-ballistic missile system necessary to defend the American people from an attack, thus jeopardizing the supreme interests of the United States," and in his fifth argument he asserted that "the program of massive militarization by the Soviet Union that has resulted in an imbalance of power with the United States of America is an extraordinary event that jeopardizes the supreme interests of the United States" (House Joint Resolution 566, 1980). On July 1, 1980, Senator Malcolm Wallop of Wyoming rose in the Senate to urge that the United States proceed directly to the development of a space-rated laser system, bypassing a ground-testing phase, and, by being the first to deploy such a system, attempt to deny the Soviet Union the capability to orbit similar weapons (Congressional Record—Senate, 1980, S9074–S9080). While Paul's resolution was referred to committee for burial and Wallop's amendment was voted down on the Senate floor, on March 23, 1983 President Reagan called for study and definition of "a long-term research and development program to begin to achieve our ultimate goal of eliminating the threat posed by strategic nuclear missiles," and called upon "the scientific community" to "give us the means of rendering these nuclear weapons impotent and obsolete." (Cannon, 1983a). While administration officials were quick to point out that the study directive did not imply any violation of the ABM Treaty in the near future, the fact that such a proposal was made publicly reflects the new possibilities opened by the advance of technology; by changes in perceptions of the U.S.–Soviet military balance, which will be more fully assessed in Chapter 5; and by continuing ambiguities and controversies about an appropriate strategic doctrine for the rest of this century, an issue which will be examined in Chapter 2.

Technology as Drive: The Prisoners' Dilemma

The limitation of the politically feasible options to (at most) the set of physically workable alternatives has an obverse side: a natural incentive to develop and deploy the weapons that *are* conceivable and believed to be workable, out of fear that if one exercises restraint an opponent may proceed with the development and gain a significant advantage. The structure of options and payoffs may be represented in the classic game known as the prisoners' dilemma. Consider Figure 1.4, representing the choice situation when two governments must each decide what action to take regarding a possible new weapons project. In this highly simplified game of strategy, each side must choose either to develop the new weapon (strategy 2 for us, strategy B for our opponent) or to refrain from that development (strategy 1 for us, strategy A for our opponent) in hopes of reaping some benefits. For each government, the risk-averse strategy is to proceed with the new development, and the risky strategy is to refrain. For if one government refrains while the other proceeds, and the new weapon proves to be significant, the government that has begun the development might gain a major strategic advantage.

The fear of such an outcome (cell 2A or 1B in Figure 1.4) is likely to drive both governments to proceed with the new weapons development. Yet this is very much a mixed-motive game, and its central paradox is that if both governments choose the strategy dictated by individual risk-averse rationality, they will find themselves at a joint socially worst outcome, in cell 2B. For if both governments develop the new weapon, the arms race will be escalated, both in monetary costs and in the destruction to be incurred in the event of war. If the new weapon proves to be significant, a preexisting deterrent system may be destabilized, depending on the weapon's characteristics and the other properties of the strategic weapons regime existing between the two governments. A socially preferable outcome, that is, one under which both governments would be better off, is found in outcome cell 1A. There, the costs and risks associated with the

FIGURE 1.4 The Incentive to Develop New Weapons Technologies, Represented as a Prisoners' Dilemma Game of Strategy

	Opponent's Choices	
Our Choices	(A) Do Not Develop (Risky)	(B) Develop (Risk Averse)
(1) Do Not Develop (Risky)	(1A) Global "Best" Outcome. Costs minimized. No New Uncertainties Are Introduced. Arms Race Not Escalated into New Weapons Types	(1B) We Lose Advantage. Opponent Gains. Possible Strategic "Breakout"
(2) Develop (Risk Averse)	(2A) We Gain Advantage. Opponent Loses. Possible Strategic "Breakout"	(2B) Minimax. Globally Dangerous Outcome. Arms Costs and Risks Rise. Costs of War May Increase. Deterrence May Be Destabilized or Modified. New Weapon May or May Not Prove to be Significant

This set of choices exists with respect to any new weapon or technology. The risk-averse strategy is to "hedge one's bets" by pursuing the development, choice (2) or (B), perhaps reserving a decision about deploying the weapon until later. If both governments make this choice, the globally least-desirable outcome (2B) results. Achievement of the jointly best outcome (1A) requires that both governments make the risky choice (1) or (A) to refrain from the development, thus also foregoing any chance of advantage.

new development are avoided, no escalation into the new weapons type occurs, and the uncertainties inevitably associated with change are avoided. In order to reach that outcome, each government must give up the hope of gaining an advantage through the introduction of the new weapon. However, even that goal-modification is not sufficient to overcome the fear that the other side may not be so reticent. The prisoners' dilemma has been expressed strongly, if turbidly, in one of Colin Gray's many critiques of U.S. strategic doctrine:

> In the matter of strategic posture, *it is more important to do what is seen to be correct unilaterally than it is to do what is really undesirable jointly.* In short, the consequences of holocaust through deterrence failure or irrelevance are so severe that a range of desirable strategic postures should not be dis-

missed solely because they are believed to be nonnegotiable with the Soviet Union. (1974b, 1154)

It should be remarked that the prisoners' dilemma originated as a description of the motivations and actions of rational, self-interested individuals. Strictly speaking, one cannot assume that even the decisive group of decision makers in any government will behave as a unitary purposive actor. However, it is routine to consider the policies of governments as resulting, at least as a first approximation and especially at the strategic level, from rational selection by unitary actors (Allison, 1971, Chapter 1). Concerns about falling behind in a technological race have been frequently cited as a rationale for arms racing (see, for example Gray, 1974a, 227–231), and those concerns clearly have the structure of the prisoners' dilemma game of strategy. A great deal of policy negotiation does take place within governments, and as Riker (1980) points out, the preference orderings of collectivities cannot readily be predicted even when we know the preference orderings of the individuals who make up those collectivities. Still, individuals and agencies can use that prisoners' dilemma fear as an argument in their policy bargaining.

Indeed, we can see the prisoners' dilemma at work in the original U.S. government decision to launch a nuclear development program in World War II. Prominent scientists approached President Roosevelt through the good offices of Albert Einstein, suggesting that it *might* be possible to build a nuclear explosive that *should* be one or more orders of magnitude more powerful than any previously envisaged bomb. Possession of such a device might significantly shorten the war and reduce overall loss of life, particularly for the side in possession of the weapon. Moreover, prior to the rise of the Nazis, Germany had been virtually *the* world center of modern physics research, and it was believed that Germany still had some sort of nuclear research program. This structure of motivations and possibilities is precisely that of the prisoners' dilemma: a potentially strong advantage if one acquires the weapon first, and a potentially dire peril if the opponent obtains it first. In addition, there was little doubt that the Hitler government *would* use the new weapon if it was developed, so that the United States could be seen as having no real choice so long as it was seriously believed that Germany might develop a nuclear bomb before she could be defeated.

Reaching a cooperative outcome between governments requires either the development of trust or the establishment of mechanisms of control which enable each side to verify that the other is complying with an agreement to restrain the new development; otherwise, either government may yield to the desire to seek an advantage. The dynamic of the prisoners' dilemma is central to the problem of arms development and arms control, and in the past it has almost always proved easier to follow the noncooperative strategy than to establish verification mechanisms. In the strategic weapons regime, the stakes are far too high to proceed on trust in the absence of reliable mechanisms of verification, so that the actual choices reduce to either proceeding with the new development or devising credible control regimes. In practice, the strategic weapons regime always features some mix of trust, control, and arms racing.

Other Rationales for Arms Racing

States may also engage in arms racing for a variety of reasons other than the prisoners' dilemma fear of destabilizing impacts from new technologies, as suggested by Colin Gray (1974a). Governments may choose to build up military strength in the hope of deterring attack. They may also engage in arms races in order to attain a more favorable outcome should war occur, particularly if they believe that war is likely, and that deterrence will ultimately fail. A state may engage in arms racing in order to increase its diplomatic weight, either through direct use of military force in coercion or by extracting political concessions through the threat of such coercion. Arms racing may serve the vested interests of domestic military–industrial complexes and their political allies. States may engage in arms races in order to preserve or enhance a degree of dignity or prestige believed appropriate or necessary to the state's position in the world; an example of this may be found in the contribution of France's nuclear "force de frappe" to national "grandeur." And a state may engage in an arms race because an external "pacer" serves deeply entrenched bureaucratic and programmatic interests, as discussed below.

Bureaucratic and Programmatic Pressures

Strategic policy choices occur within the framework of significant bureaucratic and programmatic constraints of funding, timing, and jobs. New weapons programs may imply the growth of the agencies that carry them out. At the very least, those programs contribute to the maintenance of the agencies' employment, responsibilities, and influence. Note, for example, that in 1972 when the Nixon administration put SALT I forward for ratification of the ABM Treaty and congressional approval of the Interim Agreement, the arms limitation agreements were quickly followed by a package of programs for new building in all of the unconstrained areas, notably including the B-1 bomber, new Trident missile submarines, the second ABM site allowed under SALT I, and cruise missile development. Indeed, even at the time there were reports that the Nixon administration had struck a bargain with the Joint Chiefs of Staff under which the new programs were traded for the Chiefs' approval of the SALT agreements. Subsequent reports confirm the earlier stories. As John Newhouse notes in describing the Verification Panel meeting of April 28, 1971, less than a month before the formal signing of SALT I,

> . . . the meaning of the exchange between Kissinger and (Admiral Thomas H.) Moorer was clear to those who heard it: The Navy would have Trident,

assuming congressional approval, and the President would have the support of the Chairman of the Joint Chiefs of Staff (Moorer) for an SLBM deal that gave the Soviets nearly half again as many missile-carrying submarines as the United States. (1973, 246)

A particularly revealing exchange took place between Senator Jacob Javits and Secretary of Defense Melvin Laird (1972, 94–95) when the Secretary testified before the Senate Foreign Relations Committee.

> Javits: You are said to have answered a question on linkage as follows: "I could not support the [SALT] agreements if the Congress fails to act on the movement forward of the Trident system, on the B-1 bomber and on the other programs that we have outlined to improve our strategic offensive systems during this five-year period."
>
> On the other hand, Dr. Kissinger said, and I quote from the published statement of his briefing: "Therefore, our position is that we are presenting both of these programs on their merits. We are not making them conditional. We are saying that the treaty is justified on its merits, but we are also saying that the requirements of national security impel us in the direction of the strategic programs and we . . . hope the Congress will approve both of these programs as it examines each of them on its merits."
>
> What is the President's policy? Does he link the approval of the weapons systems to the approval of the agreements or does he not?
>
> Laird: Well, I think that the President would want the Congress to consider them on a separate basis. . . . As to my support for the treaty and my support for the interim agreement on offensive weapons, my support for these particular agreements does anticipate that we will go forward with the requests of the President in the 1973 budget which he has submitted. . . . I would only add that the President has stated that these are all equally essential . . .

Evolutionary Development

Whatever changes are made to strategic weapons systems must also occur under another quasi-technological constraint—that of the evolutionary development of major sociotechnical systems. The strategic weapons regime is too large and costly to change significantly in a year or two. Planning, securing funding, developing, and testing a new weapons system takes years, and the costs of manufacturing and deploying the weapons must be spread over still more years. The systems may then undergo waves of rebuilding and/or upgrading in an evolutionary manner and over a considerable period of time. Moreover, the systems must be evolutionary in yet another way: what is newly deployed today cannot be incompatible with what has already been deployed.

New weapons thus enter into the strategic weapons regime in parallel with older weapons. Only occasionally will they be somewhat different in kind from the older weapons, e.g., first introductions of SLBMs or cruise missiles. Even then, the personnel are likely to be the same and the command and control structures will be the same, quite similar, or at least

FIGURE 1.5 Timelines in Development and Deployment of Minuteman ICBMs

Year	Key Management Decisions	MM I	MM II	MM III
1958	Decision to develop. Discontinue building earlier first-generation missiles.			
1960		Tests		
1962	Decision to stop building at 1000 Minutemen.	150 IOC		
		190		
1964		600		
		800		
1966	1000 total reached. Open MIRV debate.	800	80 IOC	
		700	300	First
1968		600	400	MIRV
		500	500	tests
1970		490	500	10 IOC
		390	500	110
1972		320	500	180
		150	500	350
1974		21	450	529
		Phased out	450	550
1976			450	550
			450	550
1978	Upgrading of 300 MM III with Mk12A RVs begins.		450	550
			450	550
1980			450	550
			450	550
1982			450	550
1984			.	.
1986	Earliest likely IOC of MX.			

SOURCES: SIPRI, 1974, 1980, 1982; Squires, 1982b.

parallel to the previously existing structures. Existing equipment *does* constrain new possibilities. One example is seen in the SALT limitations on increases in the size of ICBMs; a more fundamental example can be seen in the fact that increasing the range of SLBMs to intercontinental distances required size increases that in turn necessitated a new generation of nuclear missile-carrying submarines (SSBNs), or would have required major retrofitting of the earlier Polaris/Poseidon generation of submarines.

Examples of all the evolutionary development constraints are reflected in the history of the Minuteman ICBM series, as summarized in Figure 1.5. The decision to develop a series of solid-fueled ICBMs was made early in 1958 (Raymond, 1958), before we had even successfully completed development of the first generation of liquid-fueled ICBMs. First tests of the Minuteman I occurred in 1960, about the same time the decision was made essentially to discontinue production of the first-generation ICBMs.

An Initial Operational Capability (IOC) was reached with 150 missiles two years after testing began. Over the following three years the stock was rapidly built up to a high of 800 Minuteman I missiles, and beginning in 1967 these missiles began to be phased out in favor of the improved Minuteman II. Yet the decision to limit the total number of Minutemen to 1,000 had already been taken in January of 1963 (Bottome, 1971, 83). The Minuteman I remained a part of the U.S. arsenal for some 13 years from IOC to final phase-out. By 1966, the Minuteman II had reached IOC and the following year the Minuteman I missiles began to be phased out. Only two years later, in 1968, the United States began testing Multiple Independently targetable Reentry Vehicles (MIRVs), and by 1970 the MIRV-enabled Minuteman III had reached IOC. Minuteman I missiles remained in the arsenal until 1975, however, gradually being removed as Minuteman IIIs were deployed. Minuteman IIs were built up to a high of 500, then held constant at that number from 1969 through 1973. They were then cut back to 450, as a total of 550 Minuteman IIIs were deployed. As of the early 1980s, quantities were still being held at 450 Minuteman IIs and 550 Minuteman IIIs, and the earliest anticipated IOC for the follow-on MX missile was 1986.

To say that 1980 was already 14 years after Minuteman II IOC and 10 years after Minuteman III IOC, while true, would be highly misleading. In the interim, both Minuteman II and III were subject to significant improvements in the blast resistance (hardness) of their basing silos, and to major improvements in warheads and guidance systems. For example, in 1979 the Mk12A reentry vehicle (RV) began to be deployed on a significant fraction of the Minuteman IIIs (SIPRI, 1980, xxxv); the new RV featured a warhead with about twice the explosive yield of its predecessor, and guidance accuracy improved to about half the previous circular error probable (CEP). In the Soviet Union improvements of this magnitude would be more likely to be designated as new models. Thus the Minuteman ICBM series has demonstrated very long lead times but also very long operational lifetimes and a major capacity for evolutionary upgrading of performance capabilities.

This attribute of slow and evolutionary change is exhibited by many of our major sociotechnological systems, resulting from the same economic and compatibility requirements seen in the Minuteman missile program. For example, telephone switching systems must generate and transfer compatible signals even though several generations of equipment are in operation at any given time, ranging from simple multimotion mechanical switches through the latest fully electronic exchanges utilizing large-scale integrated circuits. Any instrument connected to the system must be capable of generating compatible signals and receiving them from any other instrument. Moreover, the system is highly capital intensive, and any major change in equipment must be phased in slowly in order to spread the costs over time. Other telecommunication systems exhibit some of the same properties. When the frequency range allocated to FM radio broadcasting was changed in the 1940s, every existing tuner was rendered useless. Television systems operate within the framework of a set of basic technical specifications for picture resolution and signal frequencies established decades ago. Changes such as color, UHF broadcasting, stereo sound, and closed captions must be fitted into that framework to avoid making all the existing equipment obsolete. Color, for example, is transmitted in a compatible scheme that yields no degradation in signal when received by a black-and-white set.

Finally, similar attributes of capital intensiveness and slow change are seen in transportation systems. Faced with a national need to reduce dependence on imported petroleum, Congress passed laws requiring improved average fuel economy in new vehicles. The slow phase-in can be interpreted in a number of ways—as reducing the political costs of passing the requirements by deferring their full impact; as allowing time for manufacturers to develop means for meeting the new requirements; as providing an opportunity for individuals' vehicles to wear out and be replaced with more efficient units in an orderly manner; as allowing time for public tastes to be equilibrated to the new order in style and performance; and as spreading the inevitable costs of the change over a long period. It is clear that some case can be made for each of these purposes, and that it took a decade for annual gasoline consumption to begin to fall in the United States.

Ideologies and Values

A very different type of constraint on politically acceptable options in the management of strategic weapons policies and programs is that exercised by the ideologies and values of the relevant political actors. That influence has become much debated over the past few years. Soviet declaratory policy verges on questioning the seriousness of a U.S. government that cannot ratify the SALT II agreement; and within the United States an extensive and varied debate about Soviet intentions is carried on. It may be debated whether claims about the favorable or evil ideological bent of an opponent precede and bias interpretation of intent, or are offered up after assessment of that intent in order to render unpleasant policy prescriptions more palatable. Within the U.S. strategic policy debate, there is a very high correlation between those who assign great significance to Soviet communist revolutionary ideology and those who advocate major strategic weapons building programs to counter a dire Soviet threat.

William Zimmerman (1974) distinguished three alternative positions advocated in U.S. interpretations of Soviet policy, and labeled them "essentialist," "mechanistic," and "cybernetic." The essentialist position describes Soviet foreign-policy behavior as "flowing logically from the nature of totalitariansim," so that "it is not what the country . . . does but what it is which is the source of conflict" (1974, 91). Some of the notable figures whose statements illustrate this position include John Foster Dulles, Alexander Solzhenitsyn, and Richard Pipes. The mechanistic approach may best be described as a traditional power balance political view; foreign-policy behavior is based not on ideology and declaratory policy, but on the interests of a government as a world power. A notable interpretation of Soviet foreign policy from this perspective is George F. Kennan's famous *Foreign Affairs* "X" article (1947), setting out the concept of a policy of "containment." More recently, Henry Kissinger and Zbigniew Brzezinski have evinced views that are variants of this perspective. Finally, the cybernetic view holds that we may be able to evoke desired responses from the Soviet Union by carefully sending the appropriate signals. Yet as Zimmerman notes,

> A cybernetic or organismic imagery of a state's foreign policy . . . not only (a) presupposes a reactive propensity on the part of those who act in the name of the state. It also presupposes that (b) external events have an impact on attitudes and produce structural adaptation, and that (c) attitudinal divergence and political conflict are persistent attributes of the political process even within rigidly hierarchical command systems. (1974, 96, 99)

Notable figures who have advocated such a position in recent years include Herbert Scoville and Paul Warnke.

Clearly, individuals holding these various positions will tend to prescribe very different strategic policies. An adherent of the cybernetic view may be likely to stress the possibilities for arms control, building mechanisms for verification to allow a mutually cooperative solution to the prisoners' dilemma of new arms. An adherent of the mechanistic school may still favor arms control, but is likely to place greater stress on bargaining from a position of strength, and may well become involved in urging contemporary versions of confrontation and brinkmanship in times of heightened international tension. Finally, an adherent of the essentialist view is quite unlikely to hold that arms control is a good idea, and may be more likely to argue for major new arms programs in order to counter the dire plans of the Soviet opponent. Diverse views of U.S. policy comparable to Zimmerman's three categories may be found on the Soviet side.

All these analysts have access to essentially the same information about the acts and the declaratory policy of the opponent, but the theory held about the nature of the opponent's political system acts as a filter biasing the interpretation of that information. To the Center for Defense Information, the MX missile program is a "quantum jump in the arms race," a waste of money, not needed for any legitimate defense purpose, and likely to evoke a fearful reaction from the Soviet Union (*Defense Monitor*, 1977, 1, and 1980). To the Committee on the Present Danger, the MX is "critical . . . (to) . . . reverse the unfavorable trends in the U.S.–Soviet nuclear balance which would otherwise continue unchecked" (1978, 21–22), is thus vitally needed to counter a present threat of overwhelming Soviet attack against the United States, and may well come too late unless other interim measures are taken.

The role of such perceptual and interpretational filters in the political processes for deciding strategic weapons policy is more fully examined in Chapter 3. At this point, however, it should also be remarked that values may also constrain policy more directly by ruling out some objectively conceivable options. For example, during the 1950s and 1960s the United States held a unilateral nuclear advantage over the Soviets sufficient to ensure at least secure conditional viability, but there is no serious evidence to suggest that any significant consideration was ever given to exploiting that advantage. While it may be argued that the United States' strategic advantage was used to permit limited war operations in such cases as the 1962 Cuban missile crisis and the 1958 Lebanon occupation, only a few decision makers were willing to entertain discussion of a preemptive nuclear strike against the Soviet Union—even though some of those same decision makers today assert that the Soviets would use a comparable opportunity to strike the United States.

There are thus many different types of constraints on the political process for making strategic weapons decisions, including limited options and complex countervailing motivations in the game of strategy that characterizes the strategic weapons regime; limitations on the available weapons technology; drives to develop new weaponry out of a prisoners' dilemma fear about the possible consequences of restraint; a need to make any changes in major sociopolitical systems evolutionary; an ever-present bureaucratic/programmatic pressure for expansion; and the roles of values and of selective perceptions in limiting the perceived options. All of these types of constraints act on (1) the development of strategic doctrine, as set out in Chapter 2, and (2) the fuller political process, as discussed in Chapter 3. We turn first, however, to a review of the major strategic weapons policy issues which may be anticipated in the 1980s.

STRATEGIC POLICY ISSUES FOR THE 1980s

Earlier, the strategic policy program decisions to be made in coming years were categorized as being intended either (1) to restore and/or preserve stability in a deterrent system based on mutual secure conditional viability, or (2) to break out from that regime to a condition of unilateral conditional viability. Presumably either type of program could be put forward under the belief that an opponent was (or might be) striving for a breakout. The discussions of specific programs that follow in this section are organized according to classes of strategic weapons—the familiar "triad" of ICBMs, SLBMs, and bombers, plus possible new types such as DET weapons. Within each class both offensive and defensive weapons are considered. Options upon which decisions must be taken are set out, together with the related political issues and strategic doctrine issues. In every case, it

TABLE 1.1 Major Strategic Issues for the 1980s (and Possibly Beyond)

Options in Deployment/Hardware/R & D	Related Political and Doctrinal Issues
Triad Segment 1: Land-based Missiles	
Deploy MX	Is strategic weapons regime stable without
In what form?	SALT II limits on RVs?
With what basing scheme?	Effects on START, other future arms limitation talks?
Deploy "Midgetman" single-warhead light ICBM	Can strategic weapons regime be returned to single-warhead missiles? Possibly stabilizing change
Build ABMs	Abrogate SALT I ABM Treaty?
Land-based	Who benefits most?
Silo-based	Details of action?
Air-launched	
Space-based	
Build SICM	Abrogate SALT I Interim Agreement?
Triad Segment 2: Aircraft	
Deploy new manned bombers?	Revise triad concept?
B-1 version	
Stealth bomber	Deploy multiple new types?
Stretch FB-111	
Used as penetrator?	Buy off USAF with ABMs and new
Used for ALCM standoff?	space-weapons missions?
ALCM/Carrier aircraft	
Triad Segment 3: SLBMs	
Trident SSBN deployments	Keep to SALT I and II limits?
Trident II (D-5) SLBM development	Sea-based silo-killer?
Seek high accuracy	Doctrinal revision for SLBMs with
Seek larger size?	hard-target kill capability
Non-Trident options, e.g., SUM	Move to a dyad, phase out ICBMs?
New Segments for the "Triad"	
Space-based weapons systems	"Breakout" possibility
Lasers	Denial of one side or the other
Particle beams	Possible supremacy
Missiles	New arms race
Air-launched ABM	Abrogate Outer Space Treaty?
	Abrogate SALT I ABM Treaty?
Air-launched anti-satellite missiles	

appears clear that the technology to carry out these developments either already exists or can be predicted with sufficient confidence to make a reasonable program feasible. Therefore, some decision will be taken in each case, even if it is only the "nondecision" to delay. The author's intent in this section is not to settle these issues, only to raise them for detailed consideration later. The key issues are summarized in Table 1.1.

ICBMs and Ballistic Missile Defense

Land-based missiles of intercontinental range have been a crucial part of the U.S. strategic arsenal for some two decades. Often considered the backbone of that arsenal, they have been prized for an accuracy that gives recent models great destructive potential, for purchase and operating costs that are low relative to those of SLBMs and bombers, and for simple and rapid channels of command and control that permit great flexibility in their potential uses. For technical reasons, an early plan to shuttle Minuteman ICBMs around the country on railroad cars as a means of deceptive mobile basing was abandoned, and ICBMs have been deployed only in hardened launch silos in fixed locations. (See Chapter 5.) It was perhaps natural, therefore, that the SALT negotiators would place limitations not on missiles themselves, but on missile launchers. The wisdom of that choice has come under considerable question in recent years. As the accuracies of ICBM warheads have increased, it has become theoretically possible to destroy, with a high degree of confidence, almost any hardened target in a known fixed location, using only one or two warheads.

Taken together with the fact that SALT I limited missile launchers but not the number of warheads that can be placed on an individual missile, this accuracy makes a disarming first strike against ICBMs theoretically possible, since the number of attacking warheads can easily outnumber the other side's launch silos. Major uncertainties remain, however, about either side's ability to carry out a massive "disarming" first strike against ICBMs. Chief among those uncertainties are the facts that there is absolutely no data on the use of large numbers of such weapons under wartime conditions, and that some degree of interference or "fratricide" is expected when many nuclear explosions occur close together in time and space, degrading the theoretical performance capabilities of ICBMs. Yet these uncertainties, which are discussed in more detail in Chapter 5, seem not to have entered very influentially into the strategic debate.

A further complicating factor is the possibility of "cold launch" capabilities, in which a missile is ejected from its launch silo by a blast of compressed gases before the engines ignite, making it relatively simple to reload the still undamaged "cold" silo with a new missile in a matter of hours. Thus an attack could be launched and another readied within a day, even if all launchers were used in the initial strike. The United States has even demonstrated that no launch silo is actually required to fire an ICBM (Robinson, 1979a, 24), which fundamentally undermines the national technical means (NTM) of verification assumed in the SALT negotiations and effectively forces greater reliance on more traditional means of intelligence gathering.

Against this background of growing theoretical vulnerability of fixed land-based ICBMs, a number of steps have been taken and others have been proposed. In SALT II, the United States agreed with the Soviets to limit not only the numbers of missiles and bombers, but also the numbers of warheads that could be carried on an individual missile. This implies that if some fraction of the ICBM force could be given multiple launch points, the ratio of warheads to possible missile locations would not be great enough to permit a disarming first strike. SALT II, however, has not been ratified by the United States, and in 1982 President Reagan moved to reopen negotiations, bypassing SALT II to seek a new and presumably more favorable agreement. The new talks were designated START, for Strategic Arms Reduction Talks, to emphasize the Reagan administration's break from the SALT process. Only projected Soviet fear of a new arms race has been offered as an explanation of how the USSR is to be induced to participate seriously in such negotiations after the effective failure of seven years of SALT II bargaining (Washington Post, 1980).

Within the time period of the SALT negotiations, both the United States and the Soviet Union have also carried out extensive programs to upgrade the technical capabilities of ICBMs, most particularly in the improvement of accuracy, which compounded the problem of ICBM vulnerability. Such improvements have played a major role in the ongoing debate over strategic doctrine, as discussed in Chapter 2. The specific U.S. answer to the ICBM vulnerability problem has been the proposal to develop and deploy an advanced new missile, the MX, using—at least in the Carter administration's proposal—a multiple deceptive basing scheme (MPS, for Multiple Protective Shelter) designed to make a would-be attacker's task prohibitively difficult while still allowing cooperative verification of the number of missiles deployed. The Reagan strategic weapons announcements of October 2, 1981 (Lescaze and Wilson, 1981) represented a *nondecision* on the MX basing issue—what former Defense Secretary Schlesinger called "a decision to punt" (Getler, 1981), in that MX development was to be continued and some initial deployments begun, while reserving a decision on the ultimate basing mode until 1983 or 1984. Congress, however, was not happy about funding MX production until the basing mode issue was settled. By mid-1982 the Reagan administration was leaning toward clustering the MXs in a "dense pack," relying on the interference or "fratricide" effects between multiple incoming warheads to provide partial protection (Halloran, 1982a), the plan ultimately announced by President Reagan on November 22, 1982 (Cannon, 1982). Once that announcement had been made, however, new congressional opposition quickly built, primarily on the ground that dense pack basing did not solve the ICBM vulnerability problem. Within a month Congress had rejected MX deployment funds, pending settlement on a basing plan, and in April of 1983 a presidential study commission (the Scowcroft Commission) recommended deploying 100 MX missiles in existing Minuteman III silos, despite their vulnerability (Cannon, 1983b). This plan was given some chance of passing the Congress (Hornblower and Wilson, 1983), but was accompanied by another recommendation for development of a new, single-warhead light ICBM, possibly to be mobile-based, for IOC in the early 1990s; the proposed new missile was promptly dubbed the "Midgetman."

On the offensive side of the triad's ICBM leg, the key question facing the United States thus remains whether to proceed with major MX development and deployment, and what sort of basing scheme to develop. Proposals have been made for air mobility of MX, and many in Washington believe that the "racetrack" basing scheme is unworkably complicated (Robinson, 1979c). The 1981 Reagan announcements left air mobility, some variant of MPS, and some new variation on ABM defense of ICBMs as the possibilities for the eventual decision. By mid-1982 the continuous airborne patrol option was dropped without explanation after having provoked intense disagreement between Secretary of Defense Weinberger, who favored it, and the Air Force, which opposed it (Halloran, 1982b). Dense-pack basing and ABM protection remained favored options until rejected by Congress. As we shall see in Chapter 5, however, none of the MX basing schemes proposed thus far will solve the problem of being vulnerable to a disarming strike unless there is also some limitation on the number of warheads available to shoot at those basing points, as proposed under SALT II. If there is a breakdown in the SALT/START process, the impetus for a basing scheme suitable for cooperative verification may vanish, and other basing schemes and/or ABM schemes may gain favor. (See Gray, 1977, 18–24, for nine forms of mobility.)

It appears that opponents of the MX are more likely to propose new weapons in a different leg of the triad in order to offer both lower costs and greater anticipated security. On the defensive side of the ICBM leg, we face a wide-open range of ABM options, including land-based ABMs of advanced capabilities (Klass, 1980), and "pop-up" short-range ABMs based in or near the missile silos they would defend. Such a Low-Altitude Defense (LoAD) system received key House Armed Services Committee support in 1980 (Aviation Week, 1980a). If the MX is deployed in dense-pack basing, some form of ABM protection is likely. Given a single MX base, a limited system of up to 100 ABMs would be possible without violating the SALT I ABM Treaty. Other missile defense possibilities include air-launched ABMs and the whole range of DET weapons, whether land- or space-based. Since most of these represent technologies far newer and less highly developed than those to be employed in the MX, the range of options is considerably wider, and the range of uncertainty about what might finally result is correspondingly greater.

Perhaps the chief political and doctrinal issues raised in connection with ICBMs at this time are whether any development can make ICBMs stable against a preemptive attack in the absence of SALT II-type limits on the number of warheads per missile, and whether it is better to retain or retire a class of weapons the vulnerability of which can be asserted to be an invitation to attack. Most of the ABM schemes proposed would require that the United States abrogate the SALT I ABM Treaty, which might well end any possibility of a further SALT or START process for many years. Moreover, there is reason to question who would benefit most from such a development; as we will see in Chapter 5, the theoretical degree of U.S. ICBM vulnerability in the mid-1980s would be greater without SALT II than with it. Finally, the concern about ICBM vulnerability has prompted a number of suggestions for changes in U.S. strategic doctrine in order to reduce that vulnerability. The nature of those changes, and their political and strategic costs, will be considered in Chapter 2.

SLBMs

While ICBMs were once almost invulnerable because of the combination of hard silos and inaccurate missiles, and while that essential invulnerability might be restored by making ICBMs mobile, the safety of SLBMs has *always* depended on mobility. Assessments of the ease with which a deployed SSBN (submarine) may be detected and attacked wax and wane over the years. While in the early 1970s it was said that submarine detection capability was "on the edge of a precipice" because of impending technological breakthroughs (Kupperman, 1975), current confidence in the relative safety of SSBNs seems to be high. On the other hand, U.S. capability to track SSBNs using hunter–killer submarines is so great that by 1980 the Soviets had stopped deploying many SSBNs outside the Barents and Greenland Seas. Both the United States and the Soviet Union have moved steadily to SLBMs of longer range, which offer larger reaches of ocean within which to operate while still remaining within range of their targets, and also reduce the proportion of time SSBNs spend sailing between their home ports and their on-duty stations. The ultimate extension of this concept is the SSBN that cruises above the continental shelf of its home state, within range of extensive protective air cover, and relies on an SLBM of intercontinental range. This is the logic of the U.S. Trident generation of SLBMs and SSBNs. The facts that the Soviet SS-N-18 SLBM already has a range of 7,000 km (about 3,800 nautical miles) (SIPRI, 1980, 226) and the SS-N-8 a range of 9,000 km (*Aviation Week*, 1980b) suggest that the Soviets will pursue a parallel development.

One question faced by the United States is how many Trident submarines to deploy. The first reached IOC in late September 1982 (Portland Oregonian, 1982), and was to be followed by a basic building rate of one SSBN per year through 1984 and three ships every two years thereafter (Brown, 1980, 131). By late 1981 the Reagan administration had cut back the planned building rate to one Trident per year (Wilson, 1981, A12). During 1980 and 1981 the 10 oldest Polaris SSBNs were retired and by 1982 the first four Poseidon SSBNs had already been converted to carry Trident I missiles, with another six scheduled for early conversion (SIPRI, 1982, 274). During the early 1980s the number of operational U.S. SLBMs was allowed to fall below the limits allowed under SALT I and II. The ultimate size of the U.S. SLBM arsenal is yet to be decided, based in part on assessments of the size and capability of Soviet strategic forces (Brown, 1980, 131). If those assessments show the United States at a disadvantage, particularly because of ICBM vulnerability, pressures to accelerate the Trident program can be anticipated. Yet such pressures would be slow acting, because of the long lead time necessary to build additional SSBNs. Increasing the number of Tridents to be built would not raise major political and doctrinal issues in U.S.–Soviet relations unless the number of missiles were to exceed SALT ceilings. (See also Chapter 6.)

Far more serious questions are raised by programs to improve the payload and accuracy of the Trident I missile or the new Trident II missile. By some projections of anticipated accuracy in the next generation of U.S. SLBMs, the Trident II or Trident D-5 missile would become a sea-based silo-killer, possessing an accuracy sufficient to destroy the hardest land-based silos even with its relatively small warhead (Gray, 1977, 11; Downey, 1976). Such a development is already underway (Brown, 1980, 132; *Aviation Week*, 1980c) and threatens to confront the Soviets with at least as large an ICBM vulnerability problem as that now faced by the United States. (See also the assessment in Chapter 5.) In fact, the drive to acquire a hard-target kill capability with SLBMs through accuracy improvements can be traced as far back as 1968 (Ball, 1977). Such a capability could be seen as provocative and dangerously destabilizing, likely to lead to an escalation of arms competition both in SSBNs and SLBMs and in Anti-Submarine Warfare (ASW) capabilities to counter the improved submarines. Alternatively, a relatively secure sea-based deterrent force with antisilo capability could be seen as an ideal answer to the problem of ICBM vulnerability, perhaps even allowing the phasing out of land-based missiles entirely, or making it possible for the United States to forego development of the MX missile. In his 1981 strategic weapons announcement, President Reagan called for continued development of the Trident D-5 missile while continuing development of the MX and other systems (Lescaze and Wilson, 1981). In any event, putting a hard-target kill capability at sea represents a significant revision of strategic doctrine. SLBMs also present far greater difficulties in maintaining rapid, reliable, and secure channels of command and control than do land-based missiles.

Some nonTrident SLBM options have also been posed, both to solve the problem of ICBM vulnerability and to anticipate and help overcome some of the difficulties of making submarines themselves relatively safe against future ASW developments. Perhaps the most interesting of these are the schemes proposed by Drell and Garwin for a large number of small submarines that would cruise over the continental shelf near U.S. shores, each carrying perhaps two missiles of intercontinental range. This scheme, designated "SUM" for Small Underwater Missile, has been argued to have significant cost advantages over both the MX and the very large Trident submarine (Drell, 1979; Drell and Garwin, 1981; Office of Technology

Assessment, 1981). It would also address another Trident difficulty: in a wartime environment, the 24-missile Trident submarine would be hard put to launch all its missiles before falling prey to an enemy's ability to track the submarine through observation of its missile launch points. By moving from the Polaris/Poseidon SSBN's 16 launch tubes to 24 launch tubes, the designers of the Trident have compounded this difficulty.

Strategic Aircraft

Far different options and vulnerability problems are presented by the aircraft leg of the strategic triad. The bomber was the first strategic weapons carrier of intercontinental range and was the mainstay of U.S. strategic forces until the mid-1960s. Given sufficient warning of an impending attack to allow takeoff, the manned bomber may be the most secure leg of the triad in the 1980s. While slow, it has the advantage of being recallable. It is subject to a variety of terminal and area defenses, including both ground-launched and air-launched missiles, although there has been a continuing development of aids to penetration of enemy airspace. In addition to aids in evading defenders, penetration aids may feature air-launched cruise missiles and Short-Range Attack Missiles (SRAMs) that give the bomber an ability to "stand off" outside the range of its target's defenders. Under the Carter administration, the United States engaged in a major program to develop and deploy air-launched cruise missiles (ALCMs), and to move away from the traditional bomber toward a "cruise missile carrier"; neither program would be much constrained by SALT II limits. Both bomber and ALCM forces, of course, would be subject to counterattack by a variety of antiaircraft means, including "look-down, shoot-down" aircraft/missile systems.

A number of programs for "new" manned bombers have been put forward, either singly or in combination. In 1981 President Reagan called for production of the already developed B-1 and for continuing development of a new bomber incorporating more of the "stealth" technology for reducing radar detectability and thus promoting penetration capability (Lescaze and Wilson, 1981). Other proposals, usually seen more as interim measures but apparently dropped for the time being, include increasing the range and payload of the existing FB-111 aircraft by rebuilding them to include a "stretched" fuselage (Robinson, 1979B).

Critics argue that defensive capabilities are now so great that any role for the manned bomber is based more on sustaining the role of the United States Air Force than on a realistic assessment of strategic military needs. Defenders of the manned bomber stress the survivability of the bomber force, given adequate warning of attack, and its control flexibility; they also suggest that maintaining this leg of the triad forces the Soviets to devote resources to air defense that would otherwise be freed up for investment in other weapons. Following President Reagan's announcements on October 2, 1981, Secretary of Defense Weinberger asserted that the B-52 could no longer penetrate Soviet airspace, while the B-1 would be able to do so for a few more years; both assertions were substantially modified in the Secretary's congressional testimony the next month, to assert B-52 penetrability lasting into the mid-1980s and B-1 penetrability lasting into the early 1990s, with even greater capabilities for the follow-on "stealth" bomber (Weinberger, 1981). As discussed in Chapter 2, any revision of the concept of a strategic triad, even though that structure arose through historical accident, would be a radical step. With a view to bureaucratic dynamics, one could suggest that the Air Force might be bought off from its commitment to manned bombers if offered a major new mission to operate space-based weapons.

Exotic Weapons

The possibility that the traditional triad might be expanded to include space-based weaponry opens up even greater ranges of uncertainty. Almost any such program would violate the 1967 Outer Space Treaty, which prohibits orbiting "weapons of mass destruction" about the earth—presumably including nuclear warheads on space-based ABMs, and possibly including space-based laser ABMs. There is the possibility that the central focus of strategic war could be moved off the face of the earth, reducing some of the dangers that have haunted humankind for a generation. It is almost certain that a substantial new arms race would result, but there are genuine uncertainties about which side would be most advantaged. The Soviet Union has pursued a steady and substantial program to learn about and exploit opportunities to place, and maintain, humans in near-earth space. The United States space effort, ever prone to the fits and starts of a succession of major programs each aimed at a significant technological leap forward, and in a state of relative inactivity following the Skylab program of the early 1970s and the Apollo–Soyuz joint mission of 1975, took a quantum jump ahead of Soviet space technology when the space shuttle became fully operational in 1982. While follow-up programs are characteristically vague and speculative, the space shuttle is expected to cut the costs of placing objects in orbit by a factor of ten under previous launchers, which will give the United States the capability to mount a massive near-earth space program at a bearable cost. A large but minority fraction of the planned shuttle flights is to be explicitly military, with Air Force launches planned from Vandenburg Air Force Base in California (Covault, 1981). (See also Helman, 1983.)

A major U.S. program for space-based weapons beginning in the mid-1980s thus appears to be quite feasible. Lasers and particle beams in orbit offer the promise of being able to shoot down missile warheads during the higher portions of their trajectories. Given the presumed capabilities of such weapons to change aim rapidly and to track a large number of targets quickly, they appear to offer the promise of the first highly effective ballistic missile defense. With that promise, however, comes a considerable threat, for the laser that can shoot down an ICBM warhead can also shoot down a spacecraft entering orbit to begin setting up an opponent's ABM laser. It is this possibility that gives the first government to implement a major space weapons program the chance to effect a breakout that cannot be matched by an opponent. Senator Wallop, while claiming that the space-based laser weapons he proposed in 1980 "are by their nature purely defensive weapons" because they "cannot harm anything on Earth and are fit only to destroy the weapons of mass destruction that travel in or on the edges of space," also carried on the following revealing bit of dialogue with himself:

> The question might well be asked: Is the Senator from Wyoming suggesting that we build space laser weapons before the Soviets and then prevent them from putting up any?
> My answer is yes, I am suggesting that if we do not build them before the Soviets do, we will not have that choice. They will have it in their power to decide whether or not to let us join them. (Congressional Record–Senate, 1980, S9074–S9075)

Other analysts have suggested that widespread development of space-based anti-ICBM weaponry would simply drive strategic weapons competition into new areas of weaponry operating within the atmosphere, where they would be shielded from lasers and from some particle beams based in orbit (Ravenal, 1980), a prediction that seems quite plausible in view of the historically demonstrated dynamics of arms competition. All such developments are, of course, highly speculative. Yet it seems clear that (1) a major move into the space-based weapons field entails costs, risks, and potential benefits of enormous magnitude, and (2) none of these factors may be predicted easily or with any great degree of confidence at this time.

Steps in space weaponry beyond ballistic missile defense are not difficult to envision. Even in the later 1970s we saw real concern about antisatellite weaponry, with evidence that the Soviets were somewhat ahead of the United States in such developments. The potential of antisatellite weapons is evident, since we rely heavily on satellites for early warning of missile launches and for communication channels as diverse as military command and control, intercontinental television links, and the Washington–Moscow "Hot Line." Recent reports suggest that the United States is already developing an antisatellite weapon of simple design and low cost, to be launched from a high-altitude aircraft (Covault, 1980); preliminary studies on such a weapon were conducted as much as two decades ago, very early in the space age (Ing, 1981).

The antisatellite capabilities of lasers or particle beam weapons in orbit are obvious, but those same weapons could also attack manned spacecraft. The combination of space-based weaponry and relatively inexpensive means of launching humans into orbit, such as the space shuttle, opens the possibility of a whole new arms competition, the costs and end of which are indeed difficult to foresee. As already noted, the possibility that the first power in orbit can deny that space to any opponent has been recognized, and it both tempts and induces fear. Faced with the very real possibility that a breakout from the present deterrent regime might be made through a major move into space weaponry, both the United States and the Soviet Union may initiate major new programs within this decade unless effective control mechanisms are worked out and accepted. The prospects for such agreements do not appear very favorable at this writing, because of the general climate of U.S.–Soviet relations and because of very real uncertainties and ambiguities in the applicable strategic doctrines, the subject to which we turn in the next chapter.

2
Strategic Doctrine as Problem and Solution

INTRODUCTION

Strategic doctrine has been defined by former RAND Corporation analyst Fritz Ermarth as "a set of operative beliefs, values, and assertions that in a significant way guides official behavior with respect to strategic research and development (R&D), weapons choice, forces, operational plans, arms control, etc." (1978, 138). Strategic doctrine has also been characterized as "the theology of the specialists in the nuclear age" by John Newhouse (1973, 8), a journalist who wrote the history of SALT I "authorized" by Henry Kissinger (although it does not present the SALT delegation's perspective) and was then asked to take a position in the United States Arms Control and Disarmament Agency (ACDA). Like other theologies, strategic doctrine has evolved over time and in response to a variety of forces both internal and external to the body of specialists. The doctrine purports to set out what major weapons systems are required and how they would be used in time of war. It therefore comprehends both a technical and a political role. The technical aspect consists of statements about how particular weapons would be used under particular sets of wartime conditions. This aspect is potentially very complex and highly detailed, in order to deal with the widest possible range of contingencies. In particular, the technical aspect must include details and options for the targeting of strategic weapons. The political aspect of strategic doctrine, however, consists of statements and assumptions about the sorts of conditions under which war might occur and the sorts of general goals that might be undertaken, whether of deterrence, dominance, or victory in war.

Although strategic doctrine purports to set out what major weapons systems are required and how they would be used in time of war, uncertainties, ambiguities, and apparent irrationalities of U.S. doctrine have existed since the advent of nuclear weapons, and seemed to grow throughout the 1970s. The evolution of that doctrine is sketched in this chapter, from nuclear monopoly in the late 1940s, through "massive retaliation" (MR) predicated on nuclear superiority in the 1950s, through "mutual assured destruction" (MAD) based on the notion that a potential but rational attacker will be deterred by the threat of a very-likely irrational retaliation, on through the battle between MAD and "damage limitation" (DL) or "warfighting" which has flared periodically since the late 1960s, and into the more recent controversies over a "countervailing" strategy. Other possible doctrines, including first strike, minimal deterrence (as practiced, for example, by France and China), launch on warning, and their variants are considered. Although it is asserted that weapons are acquired in order to carry out a doctrine, there are disturbing signs that doctrine may also be evolved to justify weapons acquired for other reasons. The current insistence on the need for a triad of land-based and sea-based missiles plus bombers provides a clear example that doctrines tend to be continued beyond the point indicated by a careful needs assessment, since the triad arose incrementally and almost by historical accident.

Much of current strategic doctrine is ambiguous and disputed. Such threats as launch on warning or nuclear escalation in response to an invasion of Western Europe rely on ambiguity for much of their (putative) force. The roots of strategic doctrine lie in theories of deterrence and the political management of power balances. Foundations for the present doctrine were laid in the late 1940s and early 1950s (see, e.g., Brodie, 1946), and although waves of renewed interest can be discerned, there has been relatively little serious work on deterrence theory since then. Despite these glaring weaknesses, the continuing debate over strategic weapons programs and arms control attempts has frequently been phrased in terms of a debate over strategic doctrine and the requirements of that doctrine.

The sections which follow are devoted the nature of deterrence, patterns in the evolution of contemporary U.S. deterrence theory, relations between deterrence theory and strategic doctrine, the historical evolution of U.S. nuclear strategic thinking, and some alternative doctrines. Attention is then directed to the factors that give rise to strategic plans and to the interplay between the resulting doctrines and other elements of the political processes of strategic decision making. The final section of the chapter is an assessment of some alternative futures for U.S. strategic planning in the 1980s and beyond.

THE ELUSIVE CONCEPT OF DETERRENCE

Because the roots of strategic doctrine lie in theories of deterrence and the political management of power balances, deterrence theory underlies many of the apparent paradoxes of strategic doctrine and practice, including the following examples:

- Some acts are apparently paradoxical or irrational under one strategic doctrine, but not under another.

- Intent is usually inferred from capability, an inference with highly questionable foundations in logic.
- Governments may appear to take actions that are objectively against their best interests measured in terms of potential gain.
- Agreement between declaratory policy and actual working strategic doctrine is relatively rare. Massive retaliation, for example, was declaratory policy during part of the 1950s without ever being operational policy. Yet when the United States had a first-strike capability against the Soviet Union, roughly from the mid-1950s to the mid-1960s, it was not used.

Although these observations appear somewhat perverse, deterrence theory at first glance seems fairly straightforward. Most of the complications arise from the fact that deterrence combines threat with promise and, possibly, reward. While it is a largely deductive theory (George and Smoke, 1974, 61–71), these several facets lead to complex and often conflicting motivations on the part of those who would practice deterrence, and from the conflicts many confusions arise. Perhaps the greatest uncertainty lies in the realm of what the practitioners of deterrence will actually accomplish. Writing in 1960, Thomas Schelling, one of the best-known early theorists of deterrence, commented that,

> What is impressive is not how complicated the idea of deterrence has become, and how carefully it has been refined and developed, but how slow the progress has been, how vague the concepts still are, and how inelegant the current theory of deterrence is. (1960, 7)

Twelve years later Morton Halperin was to write that,

> ... deterrence depends on influencing the decision of other governments. We have a very poor understanding of how our force structure is perceived by potential adversaries and how it affects their decisions. (1972, 75)

Halperin went on to note that even after the experience of SALT I "we still have no real basis for determining how our strategic force decisions affect the probability of nuclear war" (1972, 81). In that same year Colin Gray noted that "we do not know with any confidence (a) what will deter the Soviet Union, and (b) whether the Soviet Union needs deterring" (1972, 123–124).

Granting that the perceptions and expectations of others are at least difficult to measure or predict, such is clearly the aim of deterrence. And if we can accept so difficult an aim, we can agree with Richard Brody's admirably straightforward definition of deterrence.

> Deterrence refers to the attempt by decision makers in one nation or group of nations to restructure the set of alternatives available to decision makers in another nation or group of nations by posing a threat to their key values. The restructuring is an attempt to exclude armed aggression (resort to war) from consideration. (1968, 130–133)

In many works, the concept of deterrence has been broadly applied to international interactions (e.g., George and Smoke, 1974; Russett, 1963) and not limited to grand strategy. Here, however, its use will be restricted to applications at the nuclear strategic level.

Limiting deterrence to this level still leaves room for several distinctions about what sort of deterrence is sought. Herman Kahn early on distinguished three types of deterrence according to the kinds of threats faced and goals sought. Type I is the deterrence of direct attack: under certain strategic doctrines it would call for automatic response. Type II is defined as "using strategic threats to deter an enemy from engaging in very provocative acts, other than a direct attack . . ." while Type III is graduated or controlled deterrence, referring to acts that "are deterred because the potential aggressor is afraid that the defender or others will then take limited actions, military or nonmilitary, that will make the aggression unprofitable" (Kahn, 1960, 126).

A useful propositional treatment was given by Patrick Morgan when he sought to reduce "immediate" deterrence, roughly equivalent to Kahn's Type I, and "general" deterrence, which seems to embrace Kahn's Types II and III, to their underlying assumptions. Morgan's assumptions for immediate deterrence are as follows:

(1) In a relationship between two hostile states the officials in at least one of them are seriously considering attacking the other or attacking some area of the world the other deems important.
(2) Key officials of the state that is to be the target of the attack must realize this.
(3) The target state, realizing that an attack is a distinct possibility, must threaten the use of force in retaliation in an attempt to prevent attack.
(4) Leaders of the state planning to attack must decide to desist primarily because of the retaliatory threat(s) of the opponent. (1977, 33–35)

Similarly, the general deterrence situation is characterized as follows:

(1) Relations between opponents are such that leaders in at least one would consider resorting to force if the opportunity arose.
(2) The other side, precisely because it believes the opponent would be willing to consider resort to force, maintains forces of its own and offers warnings to respond in kind to attempts to use force contrary to its interests.
(3) The decision makers at whom the general deterrent threat is aimed do not go beyond preliminary consideration of resorting to force because of the expectation that such a policy would result in a corresponding resort to force of some sort by leaders of the opposing state. (1977, 40–41)

Morgan's propositions relate the concept of deterrence to the concrete situations in which it is relevant and to the behavioral responses which are sought and offered by the decision makers. While continuing to restrict our attention to the nuclear strategic level, we can accept his immediate deterrence as descriptive of central war threats and general deterrence as descriptive of situations in which nuclear strategic war may be threatened over issues arising outside the heartland of either party.

An alternative but complementary approach is to describe deterrence in terms of Boulding's (1962) concept of viability. *Classical deterrence theory is then seen as describing situations in which mutual insecure conditional viability obtains.* (See Figures 1.1 and 1.2.) Presumably no government can be deterred by threats to any of its interests lying within a zone of unconditional viability, although it may be influenced by threats to interests lying outside that sphere of influence. As suggested in Figure 1.2, when neither side has secure conditional viability, there may still be a level of expected retaliatory damage so great as to deter attack. The situation pictured in Figure 1.2 would obtain if there were stable deterrence under a doctrine of mutual assured destruction. Before turning to an examination of strategic doctrine, however, let us consider the development of contemporary deterrence theory.

Robert Jervis (1979) has identified three "waves" of contemporary theory about deterrence. The first wave came immediately after World War II, in the work of such writers as Bernard Brodie, Arnold Wolfers, and Jacob Viner, and grew out of a desire to examine the consequences of the advent of nuclear weapons. Most of this work attracted little attention and remained to be rediscovered some 10 years later, after international developments forced greater attention to national security matters. By the late 1950s, a second wave that included the works of Brodie, Herman Kahn, Thomas Schelling, Glenn Snyder, and Albert Wohlstetter had grown and received considerable attention. This second wave exploited the heuristic value of game theoretic treatments and explored the implications of deliberately "irrational" behavior in a rational model framework. Part of the attention the second wave received was searching criticism, some of which contributed to the eventual third wave. Although there is no logically necessary tie, the second wave was strongly identified with the foreign policy of containment. Second-wave deterrence theory offered little or nothing about how to modify the motivations of opposing players; it tended to be focused on interactions of high conflict potential, or immediate deterrence situations, to the exclusion of general deterrence. Attention was directed to threat and promise to the near-exclusion of rewards. Deterrence theory has also been criticized as biased in favor of status quo powers: it asserted that most of the literature is written from the standpoint of the state resisting change; that status quo powers are more likely to fear that backing down from one confrontation may provoke a domino effect in later confrontations; that defending powers are better able to argue that any losses they suffer would redound to the benefit of third parties; and that defending powers are likely to have greater credibility because of greater experience in the system (Jervis, 1979, 297–298).

The second-wave theorists were also accused of being ethnocentric in presuming that there was a single correct analysis of the conflict situation, and that eventually the other side must come to realize it (Jervis, 1979, 296). This criticism has taken on new relevance in the debate over Soviet intentions which has ensued since SALT I. The first round of SALT I sessions has been characterized as a "seminar in strategic theory" (Barton and Weiler, 1976, 180), and the eventual agreements were once hailed as representing an acceptance by the Soviets of mutual assured destruction (MAD) doctrine. Newhouse, for example, notes that after those first sessions "Moscow had come more than halfway toward accepting the favorite apothegm of Washington's assured destruction school of strategy: 'offense is defense, defense is offense'" (1973, 176). Yet, faced with the massive Soviet MIRV buildup in the ensuing years, even many liberal analysts have come to question whether the Soviets have ever accepted mutual assured destruction doctrine in anything like the sense held by U.S. negotiators. Indeed, it might be argued that the Soviets have managed strategic weapons with the Maoist axiom that "political power grows out of the barrel of a gun" firmly in mind. Still, it is instructive to note the recent comments of Raymond L. Garthoff, Executive Officer and Senior Advisor to the SALT I delegation, formerly of the State Department's Bureau of Political–Military Affairs (PM), the section chiefly responsible for SALT, and later U.S. Ambassador to Bulgaria:

> The record indicates that the Soviet political and military leadership accepts a strategic nuclear balance . . . as a fact, and as a probable and desirable prospect for the future. They are pursuing extensive military programs to ensure that they do not fail to maintain their side of the balance, which they see as in some jeopardy given planned American programs.
> In Marxist–Leninist eyes, military power is not and should not be the driving element in world politics. With "imperialist" military power held in check, the decisive social–economic forces of history would determine the future of the world. In their view, the United States has come to accept mutual deterrence, and some strategic arms limitations, not because it is our preference, but because we have no alternative given the general world "relation of forces," and Soviet military power in particular. (1978, 146)

The third wave of deterrence theorists gained some prominence in the 1970s by raising these and other criticisms, and by seeking to plug some of the previous gaps in theorizing and testing. Morgan points out that under the doctrine of mutual assured destruction, deterrence ought not work; at the heart of the rational theory of deterrence is the assumed irrationality of incurring one's own destruction in order to retaliate. For,

> . . . anything that gives governments greater confidence in their ability to . . . understand, control, and manipulate deterrence situations is counterproductive. *But this is precisely what classic deterrence theory set out to do*, and these are exactly the terms McNamara used to describe the position the U.S. government felt it had achieved by applying the best deterrence theory had to offer. (1977, 121)

Other third-wave theorists such as George and Smoke (1974) and Russett (1963) have sought to test general deterrence theory through examinations of historical cases, although their tests are at best preliminary. Morgan and Kahn have directed attention to things that can go wrong, the causes and consequences of deterrence failure. Other analysts have sought to take the possibilities of rewards into account and to broaden the theory to include risk management, recognizing that neither victory nor defeat will necessarily or even usually be total. George and Smoke (1974), for example, emphasize both positive inducement and the psychological dimension of deterrence. Kahn and others have stressed the role of perceptions in successful deterrence, a stress that has been echoed in recent years by such analysts of the strategic balance as Colin Gray and William Van Cleave, who lay great stress on perceived political will. Others have emphasized the roles of domestic and bureaucratic politics as constraints on the management of deterrent systems, the necessity to build commitment on a sound (and traditional) foundation of intrinsic and strategic interest, and they have just begun to address the relative lack of political content in deterrence theory. The persistent criticisms about the "apolitical" nature of deterrence theory (see, e.g., Jervis, 1979, 322–324) and the concrete scenarios of Morgan's immediate and general deterrence serve as reminders that war is always simply one of a range of options, and that strategic doctrine, while perhaps primarily aimed at effective deterrence, must provide for many more contingencies. We therefore turn next to examinations of the relationship between deterrence theory and strategic doctrine, and of the evolution of contemporary U.S., and, to a lesser extent, Soviet nuclear strategic doctrines.

DETERRENCE THEORY AND STRATEGIC DOCTRINE

As noted in the introduction to this chapter, strategic doctrine comprehends both a political and a technical aspect. Both aspects are quite indispensable. The technical aspect includes the details of carrying out political goals and the technical assessment of whether particular goals are or are not possible, given one's available weaponry and the state of an opponent's forces. The political aspect, however, includes not only the setting of goals compatible with internal and world political circumstances, but also assessment of the opponent's political goals and the range of means considered acceptable to accomplish them. From these two radically different aspects of strategic doctrine arise many of the confusions and ambiguities that have plagued the strategic debates of recent years, for the methods of assessment appropriate to the two different aspects may be fundamentally at variance.

There are, as Barton and Weiler (1976, 123) note, no nuclear strategic "experts," only "theoreticians." Yet the technical questions about numbers of weapons available and characteristics of their performance are knowable within specifiable ranges of uncertainty that are themselves an essential part of the technical analysis enterprise. The assessment of political intent and acceptable means, however, is an entirely different sort of process, fraught with great uncertainties and differences of interpretation. As if this state of affairs were not uncertain and difficult enough, the technical and political aspects are often intermingled in the debate over policy. The interpretation of a piece of technical information can be colored by the political perspective of the analyst, and given greater or lesser weight or even totally conflicting interpretations by different analysts. There is little disagreement, for example, that the Soviets have pursued a substantial buildup of land-based ICBMs with multiple warheads since the mid-1970s. To Raymond Garthoff, former member of the U.S. delegation to SALT, this is evidence that the Soviets are worried about U.S. potential and seek to stabilize their side of a deterrent balance (1978); to the Committee on the Present Danger it is evidence of a Soviet grand design to shift the world political balance permanently in their favor, utilizing strategic warfare if necessary (1978). While leaving aside an attempt to resolve this disagreement for several chapters until more foundation has been laid, we must note that such differences in interpretation of the known objective information are not new. The political and technical management of the strategic weapons regime is itself a game of strategy between governments: the governments are inextricably members of an interactive system; outcomes cannot be controlled by one party but are jointly determined by the actions of all; and no move can be taken without consideration of the options available to the opponent and the opponent's likely reaction. Strategic doctrine therefore must be seen as a "strategy" in the game-theoretic sense. Therefore it must be formed in light of an opponent's capabilities—and of what is known about that opponent's strategic doctrine.

Because of this role as strategy in an interaction, strategic doctrine will tend to change over time in ways that may be complex and difficult for any government to predict far in advance. In fact, one might at first be surprised that the number of doctrinal shifts over the years has not been greater, and that the issues fought over in doctrinal wars are generally sketched far in advance and tend to produce controversies that survive over many years. That persistence is aided, of course, by the long lead times and lifetimes characteristic of strategic weapons systems, as discussed earlier. It is also helpful to those who would attempt to assess doctrine.

Strategic doctrine may be assessed in a number of ways. As in any intelligence function, it is common to give considerable weight to the capabilities of an opponent's forces in being or forces known to be planned. Declaratory policies must also be examined, although they may well be misleading. The ideal sources would be internal documents such as actual strategic planning directives, targeting orders, contingency plans, and National Intelligence Estimates (NIEs). Unfortunately, the stakes in this business are so great that only a handful of individuals in any government will have access to such documents, and very great efforts indeed are expended to prevent the leakage of such information to other governments. Those who would work as analysts in the open literature, therefore, will not have access to the documents. One readily available source is historical or "insider" accounts, although they tend to lag behind the interesting events by unpredictable but often considerable periods of time, depending in part on elections, policy disagreements, and other causes of personnel movement. Another and more timely source is provided by the "leaks" of information that are so much a part of relatively open governments in which agencies and individuals fight over policy and often seek the support of others outside official lines of authority. While nuclear weapons date only from 1945 and fine detail is often frustratingly limited, the broad thrust of doctrine was quite clear in the early years. Since the mid-1960s, it has become somewhat less clear, although the issues fought over within the U.S. government, at least, have been clearly drawn. Considerably less detail is available about Soviet strategic doctrine.

THE EVOLUTION OF NUCLEAR STRATEGIC DOCTRINE

The discussion that follows in this section is keyed to Figure 2.1, which sets out some of the major developments in the strategic weapons regime, along with descriptive labels for U.S. and Soviet strategic doctrines, and some measures of the U.S.–Soviet nuclear strategic balance. (See also the discussion of such measures in Chapter 4.) The evolution of doctrine and doctrinal issues will be sketched through a number of stages over the period 1945–1980ff. Only the U.S.–Soviet strategic weapons regime is considered, on the ground that the actions of third parties had little or no impact on the strategic plans of either superpower.

1945–1949: U.S. Supremacy and Restraint

The period from the closing stages of World War II until 1949 was one of a U.S. nuclear monopoly, although little was done to exploit it. Both the United States and the USSR substantially reduced their total military efforts in the immediate postwar years, and the United States did little to acquire either a significant stock of nuclear weapons or any effective means of delivering them to targets over intercontinental distances. Actual production capability at the end of the war was only a few nuclear weapons per month, and no intercontinental bombers yet existed, although the United States had some B-29s based in England and Japan. It appears that early in 1948 there existed only 32 modified B-29s capable of carrying nuclear bombs, and that in July of that year there were only some 50 nuclear bombs in stock (Rosenberg, 1979, 64–65). Additionally, personnel specially trained for nuclear weapons were quite scarce; by early 1947 the

FIGURE 2.1 Major Developments and Doctrines in the U.S.–Soviet Strategic Weapons Regime

Year	Nuclear Strategic Balance	Major Developments	U.S. Strategic Doctrine and Policy	Soviet Strategic Doctrine and Policy
1945	U.S. nuclear monopoly	First nuclear weapons	Targeting of cities	Consolidation of WWII gains; narrow, continental mission
1946				
1947		Baruch and Gromyko plans NSC-20 and Containment	Containment of Soviet/Communist expansion	
1948				
1949	U.S. monopoly of intercontinental delivery vehicles	First Soviet nuclear weapon B-36 deployment approved	Rearmament Engagement in Europe and Asia	Stalin sees nuclear weapons as adjunct to conventional forces
1950		NSC-68 & military buildup Decision to build H-bomb	Targeting extended to include both industrial and military targets	Western Europe effectively held hostage, as USSR is faced with U.S. monopoly on intercontinental bombers
1951				
1952				
1953		First U.S. H-bomb (Nov.) First Soviet H-bomb (Aug.)		
1954		Massive Retaliation announced 12 Jan.	Massive Retaliation, militant posture	Ambiguous doctrine and posture
1955	Developing symmetry in delivery capabilities	First Soviet bombers able to reach U.S.		
1956				
1957		Gaither Report First Soviet ICBM test (Aug.) Sputnik I launched (Oct.)		
1958				
1959		First SIOP		Apparently minimum deterrence, not first strike

44

Year			
1960	ICBM "gap" favors U.S.		
1961		"Missile gap" fears in U.S. Soviet Strategic Missile Forces organized McNamara's Ann Arbor speech (16 June)	Evolution of deterrence theory, flexible response	"Speak-softly-while-getting-a-big-stick" (Kolkowicz, 1971, 437) Massive Retaliation doctrine Inflexible posture Strategic inferiority
1962		Cuban Missile Crisis Minuteman I IOC	Second Strike Counterforce targeting begins (and continues until about 1974)	
1963		Limited Test-Ban Treaty Hot-Line agreement		
1964		Chinese nuclear bomb (Oct.)	Soviet intentions under-estimated AD & DL seem to be on equal footing	Moving toward invulnerable second-strike force
1965			Greater-Than-Expected threat considered	
1966	854 U.S. ICBMs, 304 Soviet	Minuteman II IOC Soviet ICBM buildup starts	Both sides developing deterrence capability, flexible response, global posture.	
1967	U.S. levels off at 1054 ICBMs	Outer Space Treaty	Enthoven to Congress: U.S. seeks AD + SUPER	
1968		NPT signed Safeguard ABM approved		
1969	Effective parity established by now	SALT negotiations open	U.S. AD capacity > necess (Enthoven)	
1970		IOC of first U.S. MIRV		Long-term, sustained military buildup begun
1971		Poseidon IOC (Mar.) Biological Warfare Convention (Apr.)		
1972		SALT I agreements	Strategic Sufficiency	
1973		Accelerated Trident program		
1974		Indian nuclear bomb (May)	Retargeting (Ikle & Schlesinger); graduated escalation options	

FIGURE 2.1 (continued)

Year	Nuclear Strategic Balance	Major Developments	U.S. Strategic Doctrine and Policy	Soviet Strategic Doctrine and Policy
1975				
1976				
1977				
1978				
1979		SALT II signed but not ratified by U.S.		
1980		PD59 signed 25 July	Countervailing	
1981	"Window of (U.S.) ICBM vulnerability" begins to open	Major new U.S. strategic weapons effort		
1982		START negotiations open		

46

Strategic Air Command had 20 trained air crews and only six weapons assembly specialists (Friedberg, 1981, 40).

Such nuclear doctrine as existed was exceedingly primitive; given the secrecy of the Manhattan Project development, a Presidential directive for first use of nuclear weapons was required. As some of the scientists who worked on the project discovered to their horror, military plans called for the new weapon to be exploited like any other—this one simply happened to have very great destructive power. A movement within the small scientific community involved in developing the bomb to call for a demonstration explosion rather than first use against a city was stillborn, both because the requirements of secrecy militated against the movement's gaining real political force, and because serious technical questions were raised about whether such a demonstration could even be conducted. (Observers could hardly verify the force of the explosion without being told in advance what to expect, so as to know what instruments to emplace and where.) In any event, there were not enough bombs to spare for demonstrations. While some experts involved in the development project recognized that mere awareness that the bomb worked was at least half of what other governments needed to know to become nuclear powers, the prevailing opinion seems to have been that the United States could look forward to a long period of nuclear monopoly. Strategic doctrine of the period seems hardly to have developed beyond expectations that nuclear bombs could be used against cities with military potential or production complexes, as had been done in Japan, and that such a threat should pose a highly credible deterrent. Friedberg (1981, 40 and 45) argues that this period saw closer U.S. adherence to a doctrine of attacking only cities than has any subsequent period, on the grounds that nuclear monopoly implied that there were few "time-urgent" military targets in the Soviet Union, and that air power had the capability to shape the outcome of any war very early in the hostilities. Thus,

> Cities were targeted because it was believed they could be found and hit from the air, because their destruction was thought the best way to weaken Soviet military might and because no other logical target set existed.

1949–1955: Monopoly of Intercontinental Delivery Vehicles

U.S. expectations of a lasting nuclear monopoly were rudely shattered in 1949 with the explosion of the first Soviet nuclear device. Moreover, that explosion came against a background of growing confrontation between the always somewhat uncomfortable allies of the late war. Europe had seen the imposition of Soviet domination in the east, establishment of the Iron Curtain, economic devastation that prompted the Marshall Plan, and pressures on Greece and Turkey that prompted the Truman Doctrine; the Soviet Union had been subjected to considerable pressure from President Truman to bring about the withdrawal of her troops from northern Iran;

China had seen the final mainland victory of the People's Republic; and governments and publics had begun to ponder the meaning of cold war. Whereas the United Nations had been founded on the official principle of collective security based on a multipolar post-World War II power distribution, we now perceived a tightly bipolar world calling for a doctrine of containment (Kaplan, 1957; Barton and Weiler, 1976, 124). In 1949 the deployment of the 10,000-mile range B-36 bomber, which had been designed during the darker days of World War II as a means of bombing Germany from the continental United States, was approved (Bottome, 1971, 3)—and with that approval the United States moved to acquire the first truly intercontinental means of delivering nuclear weapons.

Faced with mounting international pressures and growing Soviet capabilities, U.S. planners began to expand and subdivide their lists of targets. As stated by Henry Rowen, former Deputy Assistant Secretary of Defense for International Security Affairs and once president of the RAND Corporation,

> The designated ground zeros were almost entirely (1) industrial facilities; (2) "retardation" targets, e.g. transportation links whose destruction was intended to slow the westward movement of Soviet forces; and (3) counterforce targets, the bases of the small and concentrated Soviet long-range air force. (1975, 222)

From this period until about 1960, both economic and military targets were designated for sizable attacks (Friedberg, 1981, 45). Development of thermonuclear weapons was also authorized, after a major but secret fight within the military–scientific establishment, in the well-placed fear that the Soviets would proceed directly from nuclear to thermonuclear development. In this instance the prisoners' dilemma fear that the other side would proceed with the new development (whether as an attempt to gain advantage or simply out of fear) proved to be correct.

However, from the advent of nuclear weapons until his death in 1953, Stalin viewed nuclear weaponry as essentially adjunct to conventional forces. The Soviet Union concentrated on rebuilding from World War II and consolidating her recent gains, and Soviet military policy was "characterized by a basic reliance on massive conventional forces deployed in an active defense posture with a narrow, continental mission" (Kolkowicz, 1971, 432–433). It may also be argued that during this period Western Europe was held hostage to the threat of a Soviet conventional invasion. Faced with an effective U.S. nuclear monopoly because of the Soviet Union's lack of intercontinental delivery vehicles, Soviet leaders could hardly make a more serious countering threat.

Partly because of the developments in Europe and China, this period of effective U.S. nuclear monopoly was also a period of considerable U.S. fear, a situation reflected in the political decisions to develop the thermonuclear bomb and deploy the B-36 bomber, and in the strategic doctrine of the time. Although the first wave of deterrence theory had already passed and this period saw the rise of the second wave, the body of strategic theory was still not highly developed, nor had it been subjected to a period of searching criticism. With the advent of the thermonuclear bomb still several years away, nuclear weapons had not yet come to dominate strategic thinking. The year 1950 saw the preparation of the highly secret National Security Council paper NSC-68, with its evaluation that a worldwide communist threat existed. It also saw the acceptance of an official policy of containment, and the outbreak of the Korean War, testing the limits of containment and the willingness of the United States to resort to using nuclear weapons—the quantities of which were still far too small to employ them extensively in Korea while we feared a greater threat to Western Europe. While the actual doctrine adopted is unclear, following Stalin's death in 1953 some Soviet military leaders urged that one component of Soviet strategic planning be a strike against U.S. strategic forces before they were launched (Barton and Weiler, 1976, 125). This was a time of alliance building and of preparation on both sides for the eventual possibility of a global war that would involve the extensive use of nuclear weapons.

The early 1950s saw several other major developments. The first thermonuclear weapons were tested by the United States in November 1952 (Walz, 1952) and by the Soviet Union in August 1953 (Lawrence, 1953). With those first hydrogen bomb explosions, the stage was set for the new superweapons to begin to dominate strategic thinking, and serious reaction was quick in coming. In an October 6, 1953 speech President Eisenhower made some stunning observations:

> While our homes have witnessed scarcely any of the horrors of the battlefield that are so familiar to citizens of Western Europe, we know that their unique physical security has almost totally disappeared before the long-range bomber and the destructive power of a single bomb.
> ... we are forced to concentrate on building such stores of armaments as can deter any attack against those who want to be free.
> ... the paramount alternatives of our day [are] ... first ... a wasteful and devastating contest in the production of weapons of inconceivable power. The other alternative is a world ever advancing in peace and prosperity through the cooperative effort of its nations and peoples. (*The New York Times*, 1953)

Eisenhower's speech is notable for posing the decline of national viability resulting from the combination of the new weapons' destructive capability with intercontinental means of delivery, and also for posing the "paramount alternatives of our day" as being set by the choice between arms racing and arms control. Yet arms control was not seriously foreseen, at least as a short-range option.

The year 1954 saw the announcement of the doctrine of massive retaliation, (MR) and an Indo-chinese peace settlement that already indicated that massive retaliation would fail under at least some circumstances. The announcement on January 12, 1954 of the policy which came to be termed massive retaliation was the event which first caused widespread semipublic attention to be devoted to the concept of deterrence. In a speech before the Council on Foreign Relations, Secretary of State John Foster Dulles set out the basics of the new policy.

> The Soviet Communists are planning for what they call "an entire historical era," and we should do the same.
>
> We need allies and we need collective security. And our purpose is to have them, but to have them on a basis which is more effective and on a basis which is less costly. . . . The way to do this is to place more reliance upon community deterrent power, and less dependence upon local defensive power.
>
> We want for ourselves and for others a maximum deterrent at bearable cost.
>
> Local defense will always be important. But there is no local defense which alone will contain the mighty land power of the Communist world. Local defense must be reinforced by the further deterrent of massive retaliatory power.
>
> [For] if the enemy could pick his time and his place and his method of warfare—and if our policy was to remain the traditional one of meeting aggression by direct and local opposition—then we had to be ready to fight in the Arctic and the tropics, in Asia, in the Near East and in Europe; by sea, by land, and by air; by old weapons and by new weapons.
>
> . . . the President and his advisers, represented by the National Security Council, had to take some basic policy decisions.
>
> And the basic decision was . . . to depend primarily upon a great capacity to retaliate instantly by means and at places of our own choosing. (*The New York Times*, 1954)

Even at the time, this policy was seen as prompted by desires to lower the costs of defense and to adopt a policy somewhat less defensive than containment and less likely to leave the initiative to the communists (Kaufmann, 1954, 2–3). The new policy rested on four crucial assumptions: that communist actions around the world originated in and were controlled from Moscow and Peking; that although the Soviet and Chinese leaders had far different goals from the United States, they shared very similar calculations of the costs and benefits accruing to particular policy gambits; that actions on the periphery of the communist world could therefore be forestalled by demonstrating that the costs of expansionary moves would greatly outweigh the benefits (Kaufmann, 1954, 5); and that the United States had a preponderance of force and of the means to deliver it sufficient to deter rational would-be aggressors. The first three assumptions have been substantially disproved in the intervening years. The last is more problematic.

The United States still had an effective monopoly of intercontinental means for nuclear weapons delivery. Yet despite Dulles' own reinterpretation and refinement of his policy intent (Dulles, 1954), the experiences of Korea and Indochina clearly indicated that containment and massive retaliation had limits, and that the communists were quite willing to probe those limits. As Kaufmann noted even in 1954:

> During the Korean war . . . we not only tried to prevent the enemy from reaching his objective; we also attempted to punish him for his audacity by removing North Korea from his sphere of influence. Liberation and medium-weight retaliation actually became components of our policy at that point. But when we computed the costs attached to them, and discovered in addition that our antagonist was quite willing to play the game in this more expensive arena, we settled for our original objectives and the stalemate of Panmunjom. In fact, so poignant was the lesson of Korea that in Indo-China we did not intervene directly at all. (1954, 9–10)

It was thus realized in at least some quarters that even when it was enunciated, the policy of massive retaliation was bankrupt at its core; we might credibly threaten such retaliation in the event of a threat to one of our core interests, presumably including a major Soviet move against Western Europe, but U.S. behavior already demonstrated that the threat would not be carried out to counter a move against a low-stakes peripheral target. Moreover, the policy could be seen as inviting just such probes of the periphery as occurred in Korea and Indochina. The inability of the United States to arrange credible nuclear or conventional responses to the 1956 Soviet invasion of Hungary clearly demonstrated that massive retaliation would not work on important targets within the opponent's sphere of influence. Still more ominously for its long-term prospects, MR policy rested on the United States' sole capability to project nuclear power over intercontinental range. Clearly that monopoly could not persist indefinitely, and when its inevitable end came, it would be obvious to all that a more sophisticated and realistic policy was required. That end was not long in coming; the Soviets demonstrated the Bison and Bear intercontinental bombers in 1955 Moscow flybys. There were indications that both bombers were available in reasonable quantities (Daniel, 1955), and both sides were already beginning to develop long-range ballistic missiles.

During 1954 and 1955 several proposals for pure counterforce targeting appeared, although the concept was not to gain much acceptance for another eight years. In 1954, for example, former Secretary of the Air Force Thomas K. Finletter wrote that "the old counter-industry concept . . . should be given up" in favor of planning attacks on nuclear and conventional forces, command control and communication (C^3) systems, and supply lines (Futrell, 1971, 551). While the expanded forces necessary to perform such a mission undoubtedly would have been attractive to the Air Force, they were not available in that time of MR doctrine and budget stringency. Moreover, the necessary detailed target information would not become available until better reconnaissance systems were deployed. To guarantee the success of a pure counterforce strategy would have required massive, accurate and virtually simultaneous attacks on the entire Soviet nuclear force, a task that was not yet technically feasible.

1955–1962: Long-Range Bombers and First-Generation ICBMs

The last half of the 1950s was a period in which intercontinental bomber forces were built up, along with massive continental air defense capabilities, and in which the first moves were made toward an eventual new generation of strategic weapons, the intercontinental ballistic missiles (ICBMs). Additionally, as Friedberg (1981, 47) notes, by the end of the 1950s the concept of an all-out "spasm war" appeared to dominate the strategic planning process. There is now evidence that each side more than once attempted to minimize its investment in then-current technologies in order to concentrate on the next generation of weapons under development; and it appears that the Soviets limited their deployments to substantially fewer than those of the United States. The Soviets never deployed more than a fraction of the number of U.S. intercontinental bombers; in 1955 they had 40 compared to 1,150 for the U.S.; in 1957, 90 to 1,515; in 1959, 175 to 1,540; and in 1962, 140 to 1,515 (Squires, 1982b; see also Figure 2.2.). Although the losses to be incurred from even a low penetration rate of nuclear bombers through defensive lines were expected to be very great indeed, throughout this period it was assumed that a defense was possible and that considerable warning of an attack could be obtained. Accordingly, substantial efforts were expended on missiles and aircraft for continental air defense. One reason the Soviets gave for reject-

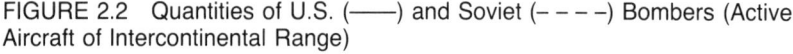
FIGURE 2.2   Quantities of U.S. (———) and Soviet (– – – –) Bombers (Active Aircraft of Intercontinental Range)

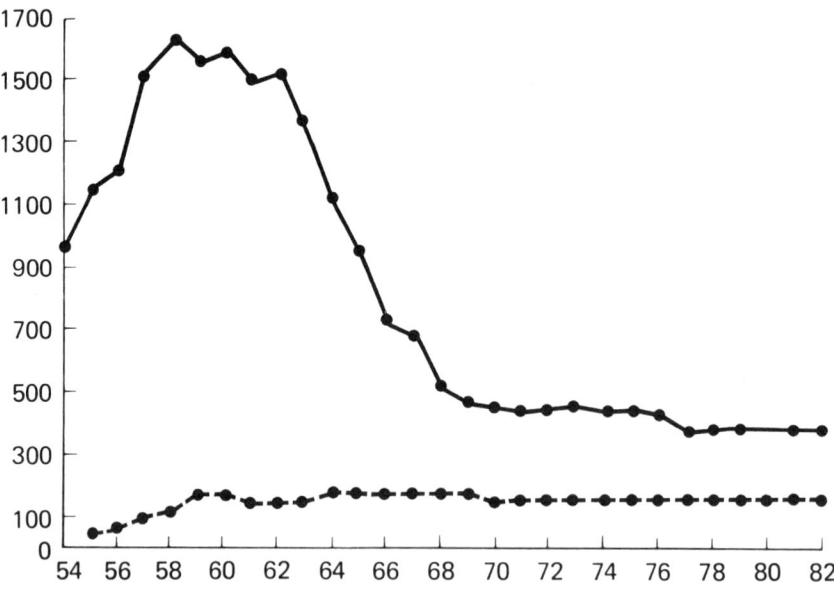

SOURCES: Squires, 1982; SIPRI, 1982.

ing the "Open Skies" proposal was that improved knowledge of their basing would have deprived bombers of part of their invulnerability to attack. Except for the announcement of massive retaliation, however, relatively little attention was directed to strategic doctrine. U.S. bombers were still targeted in part for Soviet cities; whether the Soviets reciprocated in their targeting doctrine is less clear (Barton and Weiler, 1973, 127). At minimum, however, the United States hedged its bets by defending some cities with Bomarc A9B antiaircraft missiles, as well as interceptor aircraft.

During this same period, though, the foundations for later massive ballistic missile developments on both sides were laid—and those developments forced much more attention to be paid to doctrine. First signs of the new technology were not auspicious for the United States. The Soviets had successfully tested their first ICBM in August 1957, and their tests were conducted far from public view. In contrast, the United States, having publicly committed itself to launching an earth satellite for the 1957–1958 International Geophysical Year, was subjected to the dual embarrassments of having the Soviets launch the first such successful satellite in October 1957, and of having its own highly publicized Vanguard satellite launcher blow up on the pad in its first attempt two months later. This period also saw a number of spectacular public failures in tests of early U.S. ballistic missiles. These unexpected and interrelated failures

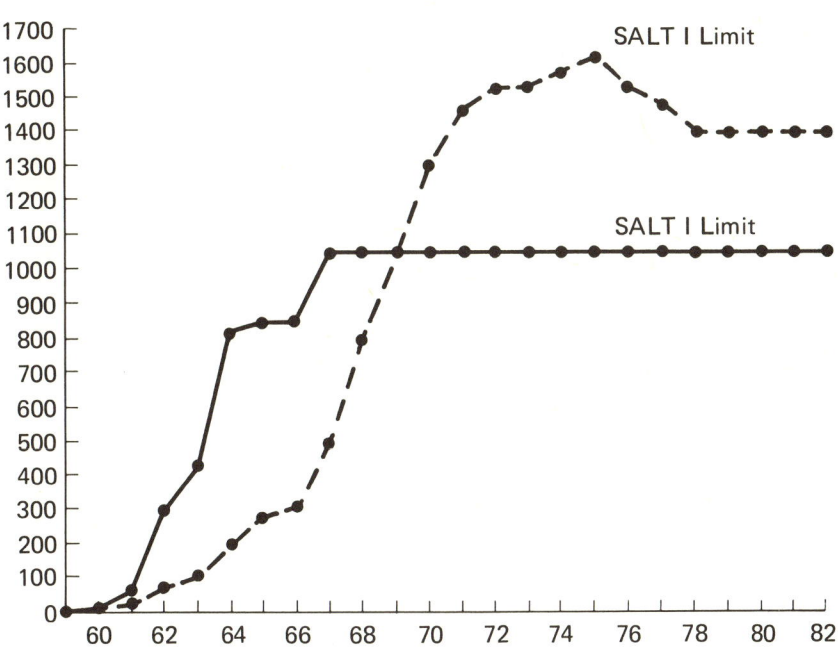

FIGURE 2.3 Quantities of U.S. (———) and Soviet (- - - -) ICBMs

SOURCES: 1982; SIPRI, 1982.

undoubtedly contributed to deep concern, manifest by the time of the 1960 election campaign, about a "missile gap" detrimental to the United States. We now know that in 1960 an ICBM gap indeed existed—but like the bomber gap of the 1950s, it was in favor of the United States rather than the Soviet Union, although the Soviets did have more IRBMs and MRBMs. (See Figure 2.3.) In 1961 the Soviets had four SS-6 and 20 SS-7 ICBMs, while the United States had 54 Atlas ICBMs, nine Titan I ICBMs, and 96 Polaris SLBMs; a year later the Soviets had four SS-6s and 75 SS-7s, while the U.S. had 90 Atlas, 54 Titan Is, 150 Minuteman I ICBMs, and 124 Polaris (Squires, 1982b). In actuality, though, both sides already had decided to limit deployment of their first-generation ICBMs in favor of later models expected to be available within two years.

Although these first ICBMs were not very accurate, could not be launched quickly, and were terribly vulnerable while on their launch pads, some reconsiderations about strategic doctrine were forced because they could move thermonuclear warheads of considerable size over thousands of miles in about a half-hour, and because there was at the time simply no defense against a warhead once it was successfully launched. This was a period of some doctrinal confusion. If there was no defense against the latest weapons, either deterrence had to work, or one had to be able to deny targets to the opponent through "hardening" or evacuation; the only remaining option was preemptive war, striking the opponent's missiles in their vulnerable stage prior to launch. Attention began to be directed to the distinction between "counterforce" (CF) and "countervalue" (CV) strikes. A counterforce strike is one directed at the military stocks and weapons of an opponent, designed to remove military capabilities, including the capabilities to retaliate or to exploit a victory. A countervalue strike, on the other hand, is one directed at cities, population centers, means of production and distribution, and other elements of infrastructure, designed to deprive an opponent of the necessary means for a working modern society. The bombing missions of World War II had had both CF and CV aspects; counterforce was seen in strategic bombing of targets believed vital to the war effort, such as ball bearing plants and oil refineries, and CV aspects were seen in the terror bombings of London, Tokyo, and Dresden. Against those bombing raids, no fully effective defense short of victory on the ground was ever found.

Yet the new world of ICBMs promised to be different. Fear of CV retaliation would presumably cause an initial attack to be counterforce, directed at an opponent's missiles. If those missiles could be sufficiently "hardened" (protected) against blast and radiation from attacking warheads, the surviving missiles could be used in a CV retaliation. Nonetheless, the first-generation ICBMs promoted great and rather reasonable fears that they could destabilize deterrence, for although they were not very accurate, they were accurate enough to destroy an ICBM located above ground in the prelaunch phase, or to do great damage to a city or a bomber base. These first-generation ICBMs were thus very insecure weapons, capable of either CF or CV strikes, but unlikely to survive CF strikes against them. This implied that they were best suited to making first strikes, which appeared to threaten the stability of deterrence once enough such missiles had been built. Small wonder, then, that a missile gap appeared so fearsome.

Strategic doctrine was adjusted only rather slowly to these changes. While it was natural to look for a defense in the form of ABMs, and while they were easily visualized, they quickly proved to be a highly problematic sort of defense, and one that could not be available for at least several years. A doctrine not based on defense would have to be found, at least for the mid-1960s. Examination of the numbers of missiles and bombers available to the two sides during this period (see Figures 2.2 and 2.3), together with awareness of the large Soviet conventional military forces, strongly suggests that the Soviet doctrine was actually one of minimum deterrence (Bottome, 1971, 42). If faced with anything short of all-out nuclear onslaught, they could protect their land mass from conventional attack and deter any U.S. nuclear strike by threatening not the certainty, but the possibility of destruction to some North American population centers. The political aspect of a strategic doctrine of minimum deterrence (MD) would assert that the Soviets need not possess enough deliverable nuclear weapons to create an absolute certainty of being able to destroy U.S. cities: that certainty would constitute an assured destruction (AD) capability. Rather, under MD doctrine, the Soviets need only have the capability to create some uncertainty among key U.S. decision makers to deter any attack. Such a doctrine, of course, can only be inferred from Soviet actions as we now know them, while Soviet declaratory policy of the time, emphasizing the nonexistent missile gap and trumpeting Soviet space and rocketry "firsts," can be seen both as intended to camouflage the true situation and as having caused a sizable U.S. overreaction. Yet if Soviet doctrine around 1960 actually was MD, it still made sense for them to proceed with ICBM developments, both to avoid the possibility of a later technological gap in missilery and to hedge against the constant improvements being made in air defense against bombers. In such hedging we can see some of the roots of the eventual development of nuclear "triads" of bombers, ICBMs, and SLBMs on both sides.

Soviet strategic doctrine has tended to shift significantly at the rare and unpredictable times of internal leadership transitions, and the severity of doctrinal shifts has probably been increased by the lack of institutionalized procedures for handling those transitions. Leadership changes have usually been followed by periods of several years during which political power was consolidated before any major changes in strategic doctrine were made. From Stalin's death in 1953 until about 1960 both strategic doctrine and military posture were ambiguous because they were undergoing major changes. By 1960, the old reliance on conventional forces had been ended and those forces sharply reduced. A global deterrent mission was assigned to the Air Defense Forces, subsurface Navy, and the newly created Strategic Missile Forces. During the period 1960–1964, ending with Khruschev's ouster, the Soviets appeared to recognize their strategic inferiority, although they were able to mask it well with an aggressive declaratory policy in the instance of the "missile gap." Indications are that the USSR had sufficient strategic nuclear forces to actually possess a credible minimum deterrent (MD), and that they planned to use it to its utmost in the event of war. Kolkowicz, who has written an excellent treatment of Soviet doctrinal and political shifts up to 1970, argues that their doctrine in the early 1960s was massive retaliation (MR) (1971, 433–434). While Soviet forces were in fact a good deal smaller than those of the United States, most U.S. interpretations at the time could hardly have disagreed more. As Bottome has noted:

> The apparent fact that the Soviet Union had adopted a minimum deterrent strategy was not believed by those responsible for formulating American military policy. The basic assumption throughout the period of the missile gap was grounded on the belief that the Russians were utilizing the maximum capability credited to them by U.S. intelligence. This assumption was changed only when "hard" information became available which indicated that the Soviet Union was not using its maximum capability, and even then it was not adopted by all agencies of the intelligence community. (1971, 42–43)

While Bottome interprets the Soviets' limited strategic forces as indicating that they adopted MD doctrine, most other analysts (e.g., Kolkowicz, 1971, 439) tend to stress the point that Soviet strategic war plans in the early 1960s called for the use of all available forces, making their doctrine closer to massive retaliation. Khrushchev appears to have held strongly to concepts of deterrence and assured destruction, and to have expected any nuclear war to be massive. In any event, it is almost impossible today to read into actual Soviet missile and bomber deployments up through the mid-1960s any first-strike capability, let alone intent.

The 1950s and 1960s saw repeated cycles of overestimation and underestimation of Soviet deployment plans by the United States, and Figures 2.2 and 2.3 dramatically demonstrate that the result up until 1970 was generally a U.S. arsenal far larger than that held by the Soviets. (See Bottome, 1970; Bottome, 1971, Chapter III; and Freedman, 1977.) The first Single Integrated Operational Plan (SIOP) for the conduct of all U.S. forces in a strategic nuclear war was adopted in 1960. Following a study completed late in 1959, a Joint Strategic Target Planning Staff (JSTPS) was formed to coordinate planning between the services, prepare a National Strategic Target List (NSTL), and write the SIOP (Ball, 1974, 11). The plan called for a single massive attack against an "optimum mix" of "high priority military, industrial and government control targets" (Rowen, 1975, 225). At the beginning of the 1960s, official Washington clearly did *not* hold that the Soviets were pursuing MD. Given the fears of a missile gap, the slowly speading recognition that massive retaliation had never been fully credible, and the dawning realization (spurred by DeGaulle's move to develop an independent French MD "force de frappe") that as Soviet nuclear strength grew, a U.S. "nuclear umbrella" deterrent threat in support of Western Europe became less and less credible, new (and presumably countering) developments in both hardware and doctrine were not long in coming.

1962–1968: Second Strike Counterforce and Assured Destruction

The new developments in U.S. strategic doctrine and hardware in the early 1960s centered around three key events: the advent of the first Minuteman missiles, with an IOC in 1962, providing the first reasonably secure ICBMs that could be expected to "ride out" a first strike and then retaliate; the beginnings of a continuing clash between AD and damage limitation (DL) doctrines, both espoused in varying mixes and degrees at different times by then-Secretary of Defense Robert McNamara; and McNamara's June 16, 1962 University of Michigan commencement speech at Ann Arbor, which marked the announcement of a doctrine of second strike counterforce (SSCF). To help translate the growing alphabet soup of abbreviations and acronyms for elements of doctrine, a summary is presented in Table 2.1, and discussion in the following sections will be keyed to it. A fuller treatment, of course, is presented in the Glossary.

TABLE 2.1: Abbreviations for Strategic Doctrinal Positions

AD	Assured Destruction
CD	Civil Defense
CF	Counterforce
CV	Countervalue
CVL	Countervailing
DL	Damage Limiting
DM	Doomsday Machines
FR	Flexible Response
FS	First Strike
LOA	Launch On Assessment
LOW	Launch On Warning
LTA	Launch Through Attack
MAD	Mutual Assured Destruction
MD	Minimum Deterrent
MR	Massive Retaliation
PAR	Parity
PPW	Prepositioned Weapons
PRE	Preemptive War
SS	Second Strike
SSCF	Second Strike Counterforce
SUF	Sufficiency
SUPER	Superiority

Note: See also the definitions in the Glossary.

The controversy between partisans of AD and DL has characterized the strategic debates of almost 20 years, although each doctrine has been subjected to manifold variations. Ironically, as John Newhouse notes, Robert McNamara is the "prophet of record for both schools," (1973, 11) and his record demonstrates considerable vacillation and frequent mixes of variations on both AD and DL doctrines. Among his key utterances are a modified DL position as enunciated at Ann Arbor in 1962; a clearly stated AD position in 1967; and the DL-supportive announcement in 1967 of plans for a limited city-defense deployment of ABMs. To maintain as Newhouse does (1973, 11) that McNamara shifted clearly from DL to AD is difficult, given a careful reading of his many statements. (See also Tammen, 1973, 111–112.) Head (1978, 549) argues convincingly that McNamara always emphasized "programming forces separately for deterrence through assured destruction and defense through damage limitation," and both AD and DL aspects appear to have been present in U.S. doctrine throughout his tenure. As one example, both aspects are reflected in the structure of the AEM9 nuclear exchange model which was programmed during this time period and is discussed in Chapter 4, in the section, "The Arsenal Exchange Model." Friedberg has summarized this duality in U.S. strategic doctrine as follows:

> At the risk of oversimplifying, it seems clear that U.S. strategic doctrine, such as it is, has always contained two different strands. One is "assured destructionist" in coloration and emphasizes the importance of the countervalue deterrent, the dangers of regarding nuclear forces as ordinary weapons of war, the risks of threatening the enemy's nuclear capabilities, the value of stability and the necessity for indices of "sufficiency." The other strand is more traditional, arising as it does from some universal and time-honored principles of military action. It focuses on war outcomes, on the importance of preparing to achieve sensible objectives should deterrence fail and therefore on the necessity for defeating the enemy by denying him his objectives and destroying his willingness and ability to wage war. At times these two sets of ideas have come into open conflict. In certain areas one strain or the other has clearly been dominant. But often they have simply co-existed with one another. (1981, 39)

AD requires the capability to ride out or survive an initial attack, presumably a CF attack against one's weaponry, with confidence that enough weapons would survive to wreak overwhelming CV retaliation on the attacker's cities in a second strike (SS). Any first strike would thus be irrational, and presumably would be deterred. The attacker's first strike (FS) would logically be directed against weaponry (CF), in order to minimize the scope of the retaliation. The term "assured" destruction, of course, is something of a misnomer, since all such calculations are based on probabilities and have ranges of uncertainty, a point rarely recognized in the literature. (But see Steinbruner and Garwin, 1976.) We might better speak of "expected" destruction, still referring to the expectation that one

TABLE 2.2 Expected Soviet Losses in a Countervalue Retaliation*

1 MT Equivalent Delivered Warheads**	Total Population Fatalities		Industrial Capacity Destroyed (percent)
	Millions	Percent	
100	37	15	59
200	52	21	72
400	74	30	76
800	96	39	77
1200	109	44	77
1600	116	47	77

* SOURCE: Tammen (1973, 113). All values are as of 1972, assuming a total Soviet population of 247 million, of which 116 were urban population.
** See the discussion of this measure in the section "Composite Measures" in Chapter 4.

could ride out a first strike and expect to mount an attack that would destroy the fabric of modern civilization on the side that initiated attack. The proponents never seriously addressed the question of what would happen if the side that initiated the war still had some weapons left over for a CV counterretaliation. McNamara went so far as to attempt to quantify U.S. expectations of the amount of AD required to deter a rational would-be attacker; by 1968 the expectations of CV damage that would be done to the Soviet Union were as shown in Table 2.2, and McNamara generally held that losses of roughly 25 percent of their population and 45 percent of industry should be sufficient to deter the Soviets (Newhouse, 1973, 18). Table 2.2 indicates that roughly 300 missiles should be sufficient to accomplish the levels of destruction believed necessary to make assured destruction work. Yet as noted in the section "Evolutionary Development" in Chapter 1, and in Figure 1.5, the decision to build a force of 1,000 ICBMs was taken in 1963. It appears that that decision to build several times the minimally required number should be attributed to some combination of factors including (a) allowance for some fraction of misfires and malfunctions, (b) allowance for losses in absorbing an initial CF attack, (c) bureaucratic pressures for still larger numbers, which Kennedy and McNamara hoped to head off, and (d) the political saliency of the number 1,000. (See, for example, Ball, 1981.)

Assured destruction doctrine has the somewhat uncomfortable corollary that one is committed to the concept of hostage cities. Presumably, if both sides have an AD capability, based on secure retaliatory forces capable of riding out a first strike, one has a stable system of mutual assured destruction. In 1961 McNamara spoke of the need for a capability to ride out an attack and carefully control the retaliatory response.

> In this age of nuclear-armed intercontinental ballistic missiles, the ability to deter rests heavily on the existence of a force which can weather a massive nuclear attack, even with little or no warning, in sufficient strength to strike

a decisive counterblow. This force must be of a character which will permit its use, in event of attack, in a cool and deliberate fashion and always under the complete control of the constituted authority. (1961)

Yet opponents labelled the system of mutual assured destruction by the acronym MAD, largely on the basis that cities were required to be left vulnerable. As Newhouse put it, AD doctrine asserts that,

> ballistic-missile defense of population is immoral because it may degrade your adversary's ability to destroy your own cities in a second strike. His confidence undermined, he might then be tempted in a crisis to strike preemptively; in short, knowing that you are effectively protected from his second-strike assault and fearing your intentions, he may choose to strike first. (1973, 9)

In contrast to these basic tenets of AD doctrine, the adherents of DL have protested against the concept of renouncing the means for limiting damage to one's society, have challenged the morality of a policy that contemplates circumstances for killing millions of innocent people, and have called for deployment of offensive forces able to significantly degrade an opponent's military capability through CF strikes, and/or defend metropolitan areas, for example, by an ABM defense. This conflict between the AD and DL schools was to characterize the strategic doctrinal debates from the early 1960s on.

By the time of his 1962 Ann Arbor speech, however, McNamara had shifted from pure DL doctrine embracing both CF and CV retaliation, to a variant calling for the counterattack to be directed almost solely against military targets—second strike counterforce, or SSCF.

> The U.S. has come . . . to the conclusion that basic military strategy in a possible general nuclear war should be approached in much the same way that more conventional military operations have been regarded in the past. That is to say, principal military objectives, in the event of a nuclear war stemming from a major attack on the Alliance, should be the destruction of the enemy's military forces, not of his civilian population. (1962, 4)

SSCF was a part of the Kennedy administration's attempt to come to grips with the need to have credible options for different levels of threat, to face the problem that lay at the core of massive retaliation—that heavy nuclear retaliation against threats to peripheral areas and interests was not believable, particularly as the capabilities to prosecute a devastating central war mounted. The answer was believed to lie in flexible response (FR), a doctrine calling for responses appropriate to the degree and kind of challenge, embracing both limited and major conventional war capabilities (for which funding had been deliberately reduced during the Eisenhower years under MR doctrine) and nuclear prowess. It was perhaps a natural corollary that one might also be able to limit the nuclear options to a carefully controlled ladder of escalation as suggested by Kahn (1965) among others. In a December 1962 interview, McNamara expanded on his views of these options.

I believe myself that a counterforce strategy is most likely to apply in circumstances in which both sides have the capability of surviving a first strike and retaliating selectively. This is a highly unpredictable business, of course. But today, following a surprise attack on us, we would still have the power to respond with overwhelming force, and they would not then have the capability of a further strike. In this situation, given the highly irrational act of an attempted first strike against us, such a strike seems most likely to take the form of an all-out attack on both military targets and population centers. This is why a nuclear exchange confined to military targets seems more possible, not less, when both sides have a sure second-strike capability. Then you might have a more stable "balance of terror." This may seem a rather subtle point, but from where I'm sitting it seems a point worth thinking about. (Alsop, 1962)

The strategy of a flexible response rested on a number of assumptions, most of them arguable. It was assumed (1) that deterrence would not necessarily work under all circumstances; (2) that the numbers of lives lost in war would depend significantly on the types of targets attacked (i.e., on whether nuclear strikes were CF or CV); (3) that limiting damage to the United States and its allies would be a major goal, best sought through CF attacks against the enemy and through civil defense (CD) measures; (4) that providing for CD and holding some forces in reserve would provide incentives for the enemy to limit attacks to CF; and (5) that such a war would not really destroy civilization so thoroughly that the United States would have no interest in the post-attack environment; hence, "sufficient forces should be available to eliminate or neutralize residual enemy capabilities, bring the war to a conclusion, and provide a measure of protection thereafter" (Kaufmann, 1964, 52).

As implied in McNamara's 1962 interview with Alsop, SSCF and FR doctrines had another and perhaps more ominous implication: U.S. second strike (SS) capabilities effectively exceeded the first strike (FS) capabilities of the Soviet Union, a point explicitly recognized by Undersecretary of Defense Roswell Gilpatric in 1961 (Loftus, 1961, 6). Forces so great as to offer such advantage might well actually offer the United States an FS capability to destroy Soviet weaponry in a CF attack. The United States, in short, was still seeking and was close to achieving nuclear superiority (SUPER), regardless of the officially declared doctrine. Inspection of the weapons quantity balances shown in Figures 2.2 and 2.3 for the early 1960s supports this interpretation. This period of U.S. advantage was relatively short, however, since by 1964 there was evidence that the Soviets, like the United States, were moving toward a second strike capability expected to be invulnerable to attack, through hardening of land-based missiles and through putting some missiles at sea in SSBNs (Newhouse, 1973, 67). The McNamara years saw considerable vacillation and many conflicting signals in U.S. strategic doctrine, as we sought to cope with the problems of low-level threats and our loss of nuclear superiority. In 1963 Congressional testimony, McNamara denied that nuclear war could be "won" in the normal sense of the word, but indicated that "we would win in the sense that their way of life would change more than ours because we would destroy a greater percentage of their industrial potential and probably destroy a greater percentage of their population than they destroyed of ours" (McNamara, 1963, 340–341). Yet, in the 1964 posture statement, he seemed to put AD and DL on an equal footing:

> . . . a damage limiting strategy appears to be the most practical and effective course for us to follow. Such a strategy requires a force considerably larger than would be needed for a limited "cities only" strategy. While there are still some differences of judgement on just how large such a force should be, there is general agreement that it should be large enough to ensure the destruction, singly or in combination, of the Soviet Union, Communist China, and the Communist satellites as national societies . . . and, in addition, to destroy their warmaking capability so as to limit, to the extent practicable, damage to this country and to our allies. (1964, 31–32)

As already noted and as seen in Figure 2.3, the Soviets were about to begin a massive buildup of ICBMs, and the period of U.S. nuclear superiority was winding to a close. As Newhouse argues, "by 1964, the recognition that the United States was in the autumn of its strategic supremacy had set in. A number of things seemed to empty damage limitation of its credibility, if not desirability" (1973, 67). Thus the McNamara years saw frequent shifts and mixes between SSCF, FR, DL, and AD as declaratory policy. These doctrines were to be followed by the apparent ascendancy of AD doctrine for a period of some five years, capped by the negotiation and ratification of the SALT I agreements.

Yet despite the continuing debate and shifts in declaratory policy, throughout this period there was little change in *operational* policy as embodied in strategic targeting. Much of the reason lies in the political role of the declaratory policy, as summarized by Henry Rowen:

> The primary purpose of the Assured Destruction capabilities doctrine was to provide a metric for deciding how much force was enough: it provided a basis for denying service and Congressional claims for more money for strategic forces . . . However, it was never proposed by McNamara or his staff that nuclear weapons actually be *used* in this way. (1975, 227)

Rather, throughout the period from 1962 to 1974, U.S. strategic targeting corresponded fairly closely and consistently to the requirements of Second Strike CounterForce (SSCF).

During roughly this same period, from 1964 through 1969, Kolkowicz has argued that

> . . . the Soviet Union came into phase militarily with the United States. It also adopted a flexible-response doctrine, achieving strategic parity with the United States, and placed its strategic and conventional capabilities in a global configuration. (1971, 439)

For the Soviet Union, of course, these changes came in the wake of

Khrushchev's ouster, and involved a massive building program in strategic weaponry. Kolkowicz has described the new regime's policy as one of "restraint, prudence, and continuing detente" and as a "speak-softly-while-you-are-getting-a-big-stick" policy (1971, 437). Once rough strategic parity had been achieved, both sides faced increased incentives to limit strategic arms. It is therefore notable that the SALT I negotiations began in 1969, with the agreements being signed in 1972.

Throughout this same period there was also a vigorous debate over strategic doctrine within the Soviet Union. The conservatives argued that "an *a priori* rejection of the possibility of victory is harmful" and leads to "moral disarmament . . . fatalism and passivity," and that nuclear war need not necessarily pose "a threat to the physical survival of nations and states." At the same time the moderates argued that "no superiority can save the aggressor from retaliation. Any efforts of an aggressor to achieve relative nuclear superiority are neutralized in advance by the fact that the other side possess absolute power which guarantees the destruction of the aggressor" (Kolkowicz, 1971, 447). This Soviet debate is entirely analogous to the U.S. debate between the partisans of AD and of DL doctrines. A cause for some concern is the more recent assertion that the conservatives gained greater influence under Brezhnev than they had had under Khrushchev, and that their influence increased throughout the 1970s.

1968–1973: SALT I and the Heyday of Assured Destruction

As late as 1968 Alain Enthoven, then running the Systems Analysis group in the Pentagon, stated that "we do not intend to allow our policy of basing the size of our forces on assured destruction to result in the Soviets overtaking us or even matching our strategic nuclear capability" (1968, 118), a statement which appears to indicate that even while recognizing the loss of superiority and while embracing AD doctrine, the Johnson administration still sought some measure of advantage. The ratification of the SALT I agreements represented a brief period of clear ascendency for AD principles, at least in Washington. For a time, many even believed that the Soviets had accepted AD, although that view has been vigorously challenged in more recent years. In an objective sense, SALT I represented an acceptance on both the U.S. and Soviet sides that after the massive buildup of the late 1960s, Soviet nuclear forces had reached some sort of rough parity with the United States. Given different design philosophies in the two nation-states and different historical patterns of development for their strategic arsenals, it would have been unreasonable to have expected precisely equivalent sets of weapons, even if both sides had accepted exactly the same strategic doctrines.

Coming out of a long period of strategic superiority and numerical leads over the Soviet arsenal, the U.S. decision makers were loath to accept the idea of "parity," and sought a more attractive term to describe the state of the strategic balance. The Nixon administration settled on "strategic sufficiency," a term which partly covered the larger numbers of some classes of weapons allowed to the Soviets under the SALT I agreements. Several conditions were laid out for strategic sufficiency at different times. They included the following: (1) deterring an all-out surprise attack on U.S. strategic forces by maintaining an adequate second-strike capability; (2) maintaining forces adequate to prevent the United States or its allies from being coerced; (3) denying any incentive for the Soviets to strike the United States first in a crisis (i.e., maintaining crisis stability); and (4) preventing the Soviet Union from gaining the ability to cause greater CV urban industrial destruction than the United States could inflict on the USSR in the event of nuclear war (Kintner and Pfaltzgraff, 1973, 428; Willrich and Rhinelander, 1974, 229). These conditions were taken collectively as a statement of the general goals of U.S. strategic doctrine in the early Nixon administration. As embodied in the SALT I agreements, they did not necessarily require numeric equality, let alone superiority. Contrasted against the desire for numeric equality as expressed in the Jackson amendment to the SALT I instrument of ratification, and later calls, as heard in the 1980 presidential campaign, for a "margin of safety" (read numerical superiority), SALT I and the concept of strategic sufficiency indicate the high-water mark of AD doctrine.

SALT I established some quantitative but very few qualitative limitations; under a five-year Interim Agreement the numbers of launchers were limited, but the number of warheads or reentry vehicles (RVs) that could be placed on a single missile was not limited, and no restraints were placed on testing or upgrading of RVs. Under an ABM Treaty, ABM defenses were almost banned, with each side being allowed two sites of no more than 100 ABMs each, one site to protect the national capital and one to protect an ICBM field; and those limits were cut to one site per side by the 1974 Protocol to the Treaty. By setting such stringent limits in the ABM Treaty and Protocol, the SALT negotiators appeared to have written "finis" to the long period of wrangling over whether or not to build an ABM system, a debate that had occupied Washington since the middle-1960s. By 1967, McNamara had been compelled to accept a thin ABM deployment for city defense in order to forestall pressures for wider deployments. Although the configuration of the planned ABM system changed somewhat from Johnson's to Nixon's administration, it was still supported when SALT I negotiations began, and by the time the agreements were finalized both sides had small ABM sites either operational (around Moscow) or nearing IOC (near Grand Forks, ND). Yet, several times during SALT the United States had proposed a total ABM ban. (See, for example, Gerard Smith, 1980, especially Chapters 3 and 6.) Such a ban, of course, was directly contrary to DL doctrine but entirely consistent with the desire, under AD doctrine, to leave hostage cities on both sides. Moreover, the limitation of numbers of launchers under the terms of the Interim Agreement was also consistent with AD doctrine, since it promised to stabilize the mutual AD regime.

Yet in the pattern of limitations set and limitations foregone in SALT I, together with the characteristics of the arsenals of the two sides, lay the roots of the AD doctrine's loss of potency over the decade of the 1970s. SALT I had limited launchers, not missiles, which meant that the reloading of launchers was possible in principle; and far more critically, launchers had been limited without limiting the numbers of RVs that could be placed on a single missile. Limiting the numbers of launchers without capping the number of warheads made the eventual problem of "ICBM vulnerability" inevitable; as warheads became more and more accurate, it would ultimately become possible to attack even the hardest target having a known location with virtually complete confidence of destroying it, and there could be more than enough warheads to destroy all the opposing side's missiles. The possibility of this development had been realized at least by the middle-1960s, and details of its implementation and severity are assessed in Chapter 5. Given the degree of concern expressed in 1974 and after, it seems somewhat surprising that no more thought was devoted to this development while the SALT I agreements were being hammered out. The problems later found with the framework of the strategic weapons regime as it emerged from SALT I were to lead to renewed calls for ABM deployments and to the reemergence of DL doctrine in the ICBM "retargeting" debates that began in 1974.

1974 *ff.*: MIRVs, Retargeting, and the SALT I Aftermath

The debate between proponents of AD and of DL doctrines was rejoined with vigor following SALT I and has been with us off-and-on ever since. In fact, as we have already seen, the roots of that debate go back at least to the early 1960s, and both AD and DL elements have been seen in U.S. strategic doctrine since the 1950s. The debate gained strength and publicity in 1974 in the form of heated exchanges over the so-called "retargeting" of ICBMs from cities (favored by AD doctrine) to military targets (favored by DL doctrine). In actuality there were few or no changes in missile targets at that time; what was new was that small subsets of the target list could be attacked selectively, and this caused greatly increased political attention to be directed to strategic targeting doctrine. Secretary of Defense James R. Schlesinger correctly indicated (Barton and Weiler, 1976, 143) that the change, if indeed there actually was a change, would be better labelled "flexible targeting" or "limited strategic options." For Friedberg (1981, 45), 1974 marked the point at which the United States finally shifted from SSCF to a new strategic targeting policy. It is known that the changes announced in January 1974 by Schlesinger resulted from a full interagency review conducted over the period 1972–1974 (Davis, 1976, 3–4). In the following discussion the "new" doctrine will be denoted FT, for flexible targeting. Schlesinger (1974, 7) indicated that the aims of the change were to emphasize "flexibility and selectivity," so as to "shore up deterrence across the entire spectrum of risk" and thereby reduce the likelihood of nuclear war and, should such a conflict nevertheless come, "keep that conflict at as low a level of violence as possible . . . in terms of the violence of the weapons involved."

These aims sounded laudable, but they rested on a number of significant assumptions about the size, composition, performance characteristics, and targeting of U.S. and Soviet strategic forces. In fact, several issues were rolled together in the "retargeting" debate, comprehending (1) the setting of strategic force sizes, including proliferation of MIRVs and working out the implications of the SALT I agreements; (2) flexible targeting itself; and (3) improvements in the accuracy of nuclear warheads. Schlesinger (1974, 2–3) argued before the Congress that following the signing of SALT I the Soviets had launched a legal but massive program to test and deploy new missiles, demonstrating an "ongoing development program" that was "staggering to us in its size and depth, though not its pace." It was perceived that SALT I limited the "potential Soviet advantage by breaking the momentum of their ongoing development programs, especially the ICBM program," and that the Soviets were now pacing the arms "race" (Schlesinger, 1974, 7). Schlesinger went on to assert that "once the Soviet Union built up a counter-deterrent, assured destruction became a logically incredible kind of threat" (1974, 14), although the threat might still work, and therefore "a targeting doctrine which stresses going only against cities is not an adequate deterrent for most purposes . . ." (1974, 8). What was called for, then, was not a change in ICBM targets but in the set of target options to be made available to the National Command Authority. At the same time, however, funds were requested both for improving the flexibility of Command and Control (C&C) systems and for increasing the accuracy of our ICBMs (Schlesinger, 1974, 8).

Recognizing the long lead times required for ICBM development (see Figure 2.3), it is clear that the Soviets had new missiles under development at the time SALT I was signed, whereas the United States did not. One consequence was a rapid increase in Soviet missile stocks up to the SALT I ceiling, which they reached in 1975. Another consequence was significant improvement in the quality and aggregate throw-weight of Soviet missiles. As the payload or throw-weight of a missile is increased, the number and/or explosive yield of warheads that can be launched increases. Since only the numbers of missiles had been frozen under SALT I, the Soviets were free to deploy large numbers of MIRVs, and their throw-weights made an arsenal with large numbers of sizable warheads possible. The combination of warhead numbers and sizes raised the spectre of ICBM vulnerability, since, as accuracies were slowly increased, a hard-target kill capability might be developed. As Schlesinger (1974, 2, 36) indicated, U.S. advantages in warhead totals at the time of SALT I were much more transitory than Soviet advantages in numbers of launchers and their traditionally larger missiles; as a consequence "the potentiality for a perceived major first-strike capability against our ICBMs is built into the weapons that they have under test at the present time, plus the throw-weight and numbers they have as a result of SALT I." While strongly implying that the United States might have to engage in deliberate arms racing to induce the Soviets to agree to meaningful limitations in SALT II (1974, 7), Schlesinger asserted that "neither side can acquire a high-confidence first-strike capability" even in the future (1974, 17), so that there "will never be a powerful incentive for a strike against land-based strategic forces taken by themselves" (1974, 37). He even went so far as to assert (1974, 50) that U.S. "operational counterforce capabilities" might well exceed those of the Soviet Union at that time.

In part, Schlesinger was simply expressing his position in a doctrinal debate that had long preceded SALT I. DL doctrine was hardly new, nor were fears about the eventual and theoretical possibility of ICBM vulnerability. What was new was simply the political opportunity to use objections to the consequences of SALT I as an opening wedge to argue the case for DL doctrine. Nor were all the arguments without weight. In the European context, MR doctrine had long been incredible and AD doctrine's call for nuclear escalation in support of Europe seemed similarly incredible now that the Soviets had their own AD capability. Schlesinger (1974, 9) asserted that under the former doctrine of "massive preplanned strikes" one actually "would not have had blast damage in the cities," which clearly implies that the actual targeting was CF rather than CV, regardless of the amount of collateral damage to civilians and societal infrastructure that would be sustained. Pronouncements in support of FT were produced from the annual posture statements of Secretaries of Defense as far back as Robert McNamara's FY 1963 report. (Schlesinger, 1974, 26–27). Thus the desire for flexibility in targeting was hardly new. The high degree of political attention had come because Schlesinger openly called for planning the actual operating procedures that would be required to implement those desires.

> . . . in order to have that kind of (FT) capacity one has to do the indoctrination and the planning in anticipation of the difficulties involved. It is ill-advised to attempt to do that under the press of circumstances. Rather one should think through the problems in advance and put together relevant, small packages which a President could choose under the circumstances in which they might be required. (1974, 9)

In the familiar language of theories of bureaucratic politics, Schlesinger was calling for the development of Standard Operating Procedures (SOPs) for FT options, recognizing that it would be very difficult to carry out Presidential orders for limited strategic options under wartime conditions without such preexistent procedures. While the development was primarily a matter of planning, funds were also asked for the supporting Command Data Buffer, which allows changes to be made in the targets of the entire ICBM force in about a half-hour. Yet the new command and control channels could hardly be used to implement FT options that had not been preplanned.

Implementing the new doctrine in an actual wartime environment raised some profound questions, however. The idea of limited nuclear options rests on concepts of rational leadership, and under those concepts a clear communication of intent becomes supremely important. As Schlesinger (1974, 13) noted

> ... if we were to maintain continued communications with the Soviet leaders during the war, and if we were to describe precisely and meticulously the limited nature of our actions, including the desire to avoid attacking their urban industrial base, . . . political leaders on both sides will be under powerful pressure to continue to be sensible.

Serious concerns remained, however, about whether nuclear war could in fact be limited, whether the channels of communication could be maintained, whether decision makers would act rationally, and whether a limited nuclear attack would trigger general revulsion with a consequent termination of the war, or escalation that could not be stopped short of a massive nuclear exchange. Ultimately, these are questions about the behavior of key decision makers under stress and in times of crisis. There is very little data available, but the studies of perception and expression of hostility by key leaders prior to the outbreak of war in Europe in 1914 give little cause for complacency; almost to a man, those leaders perceived that they were engaged in an arms race and that the race would lead eventually to war, but that their side could not back down. (See, generally, Holsti and George, 1975, and, more narrowly, Holsti, North, and Brody, 1968, and Zinnes, 1968.)

In his congressional testimony, Schlesinger (1974, 10) also attempted to separate the issue of FT doctrine from the related issue of programs to increase ICBM warhead accuracies. Clearly, if one seeks to destroy military targets with assurance and precision, it can be done both with greater confidence and with smaller warheads when those warheads are more accurate. Additionally, the "collateral damage" to civilian and other unintended targets will be reduced, although we know rather little about how badly the test-range accuracy of missiles would be degraded under wartime conditions. (See Steinbruner and Garwin, 1976.) A substantial increase in accuracy could also lead, at least in theory, to a first strike (FS) capability; even rather small warheads would then have a high probability of destroying a hardened missile silo. (See also the assessment in Chapter 5.) The United States, which at SALT I had depended on its larger numbers of warheads to offset the Soviets' larger numbers of missiles, would now depend on its higher technology to produce warheads that could outperform the Soviets', even when launched from smaller missiles. By this means "essential equivalence" might be maintained; there would be "some degree of equivalency" between the "gross characteristics of the [strategic] forces" of the two sides (Schlesinger, 1974, 41). Nonetheless, as Air Force Colonel Richard G. Head has noted (1978, 549), the requirements for maintaining essential equivalence "are much more complex and subjective than were those of assured destruction," and Secretary Schlesinger himself made a particularly revealing comment about the concept of sufficiency:

> David Packard once observed that sufficiency was an ideal word because everybody thought he knew what it meant, yet it didn't mean a thing. He was always rather outspoken about these things, but there is certainly a latitude in interpreting what sufficiency means. (1974, 56)

In fact, the supposedly new FT doctrine was subjected to attack on a number of grounds. Increasing ICBM accuracy might well enable the United States to offset Soviet advantages in numbers and throw-weight. But it might also represent a simple bureaucratic drive to maintain and expand programs, or it might represent a technological drive, perhaps fueled by prisoners' dilemma-type fears, to actualize whatever weapons could be conceived. And despite Secretary Schlesinger's many protestations to the contrary, it might also represent a hidden agenda to achieve a major CF capability against the Soviet Union. It was asserted that the "new" FT doctrine, by promoting such a CF capability and thus making Soviet ICBMs vulnerable, might make nuclear war more likely; that consideration of "small" nuclear strikes would lower the threshold of nuclear war; that some strategic planners might be carried away and seriously consider such options as likely rather than merely possible in extremis; that arms competition with the Soviets would be encouraged by launching new programs; that attaining a CF capability would impede a number of arms-control options such as qualitative limitations on MIRVs; and that the military services might want to push the new programs far beyond what Schlesinger officially sought (Baker and Berman, 1974).

In retrospect, it seems clear that many forces influenced the FT doctrine, which was not really new in 1974. The implications of failing to include a MIRV ban in SALT I were not adequately thought out by the full hierarchy of decision makers until two years or so later, as ruefully admitted by Henry Kissinger. (See also Gerard Smith, 1980.) Both the U.S. and Soviet sides were fearful of developments during the 1970s. With respect to such new developments as the spread of MIRVs and major improvements in ICBM accuracy, a situation having the structure of a prisoners' dilemma seems clearly to have existed, whatever other bureaucratic and technological motivations may have impelled the new programs. Regardless of the fate of those new programs, implementation of FT clearly did require the development of appropriate SOPs. The debate over what was termed retargeting thus comprised several major issues, each having deep roots. That debate has remained with us ever since, surfacing again publicly in the 1980 presidential campaign in the form of a debate over a "countervailing" strategy.

1980 ff.: Countervailing

A limited public debate over the supposedly new "countervailing" strategy added a bit of life to an otherwise rather dispirited 1980 presidential campaign, but added nothing to the debate over strategic doctrine—for the simple reason that the debate was merely a replay of the issues of retargeting and FT. The old arguments about force sizing, accuracy, MIRVs, new Soviet missiles, ICBM vulnerability, shoring up deterrence, and making nuclear war more likely were raised once again, but no new solutions were offered. A few excerpts from Secretary of Defense Brown's FY 1981 Annual Report suffice to make the point.

> What has come to be known as assured destruction is the bedrock of nuclear deterrence, and we will retain such a capacity in the future. It is not, however, sufficient in itself as a strategic doctrine. Under many circumstances large-scale countervalue attacks may not be appropriate—nor will their prospect always be sufficiently credible—to deter the full range of actions we seek to prevent.
>
> It has never been U.S. policy to limit ourselves to massive counter-city operations in retaliation . . . For nearly 20 years, we have explicitly included a range of employment options—against military as well as non-military targets—in our strategic nuclear planning.
>
> I am not at all persuaded that what started as a demonstration . . . could be kept from escalating to a full-scale thermonuclear exchange. But . . . there are large uncertainties . . . and . . . it should be in everyone's interest to minimize the probability of the most destructive escalation and [to] halt the exhange before it reach[es] catastrophic proportions.
>
> [In general, the U.S. aims] . . . to make a Soviet victory as improbable (seen through Soviet eyes) as we can make it, over the broadest possible range of scenarios. (Brown, 1980, 65–67)

The label "countervailing" had in fact been used by Brown in his 1979 Annual Report for FY 1980 without attracting much attention. Yet FT has always seemed frustratingly slow to implement. According to one official, even by 1980 the desired flexibility was "more an aspiration than a reality now. But unless at some point somebody decides to do it, the problem never gets solved" (Getler, 1980). Some news stories openly noted that little was new in the countervailing strategy, and linked the supposed change to the retargeting debate and Schlesinger's 1974 statements (Wilson, 1980b). It seems likely that the entire debate was heated up primarily in response to election campaign attacks on President Carter's defense policies as inadequate to meet the Soviet challenge.

At the end of three and one-half decades of the nuclear age, therefore, U.S. strategic doctrine appeared to call both for an AD capability as a deterrent in some extreme situations and for an FT–CF capability to deter attack or provocation under a wider range of circumstances. In a broad sense, this may be taken as a description of actual, if not always professed, U.S. strategic doctrine over the previous two decades, despite the apparent ascendency of AD doctrine under SALT I. The FT component, however, has proved difficult to implement, due to public opposition from some quarters and, one may assume, certain bureaucratic inertias. Nonetheless, it appears that the shape of U.S. strategic doctrine has remained relatively stable, despite fairly vigorous public debates over what that doctrine ought to be and whether or how it should work. That stability appears all the more surprising in light of conflicting public statements by such leaders as McNamara and in light of the many alternative possible strategic doctrines.

General trends in U.S. strategic doctrines over the first 35 years of the nuclear age are schematized in Figure 2.1. The United States held clear nuclear superiority from 1945 until about 1960, and less clear superiority through the 1960s, although it may be argued that the superiority was never easy to translate into political victories. The short-lived doctrine of massive retaliation (MR) was announced in 1954 and was generally recognized as dead by around 1960, a year that marked a major turning point. From that time forward the two contending themes of assured destruction (AD) and damage limitation (DL) characterized the strategic doctrinal debates. AD became more or less dominant at the time of SALT I in 1972, but lately has come to be seen as less and less a part of U.S. doctrine. DL was expressed in the form of second strike counterforce (SSCF) in 1962 and was later joined by the doctrine of flexible response (FR), first enunciated in 1963. Later labels included flexible targeting (FT) in 1974 and countervailing (CVL) in 1980. Both AD and CVL remained components of U.S. doctrine at the beginning of the 1980s, but with CVL evidently dominant. Nonetheless, a number of significant alternative doctrines has been suggested over the years without ever being adopted by the United States, and we turn next to an interpretation which integrates the doctrines already adopted together with those as yet only conceived.

A PLETHORA OF DOCTRINES

All of the strategic doctrines listed in Table 2.1 have been organized in three major dimensions in Figure 2.4. Each of the three dimensions represents a continuum, so that each placement of an acronym for a doctrine represents the central tendency of a distribution. The front-to-right dimension represents a continuum from response (to an attacker's option) to attack initiation, or from riding out an attack to engaging in preemptive war. The front-to-left dimension represents the continuum extending from pure CF strikes to pure CV strikes. Finally, the up–down dimension represents the range from massive to limited strikes. In each case doctrines comprehending a range of options or otherwise difficult to classify on a dimension are placed in the center on that dimension; for example, doctrines not calling solely for either massive or limited attacks are placed midway on the up–down dimension.

At the front edge of the cube are the doctrines calling for riding out

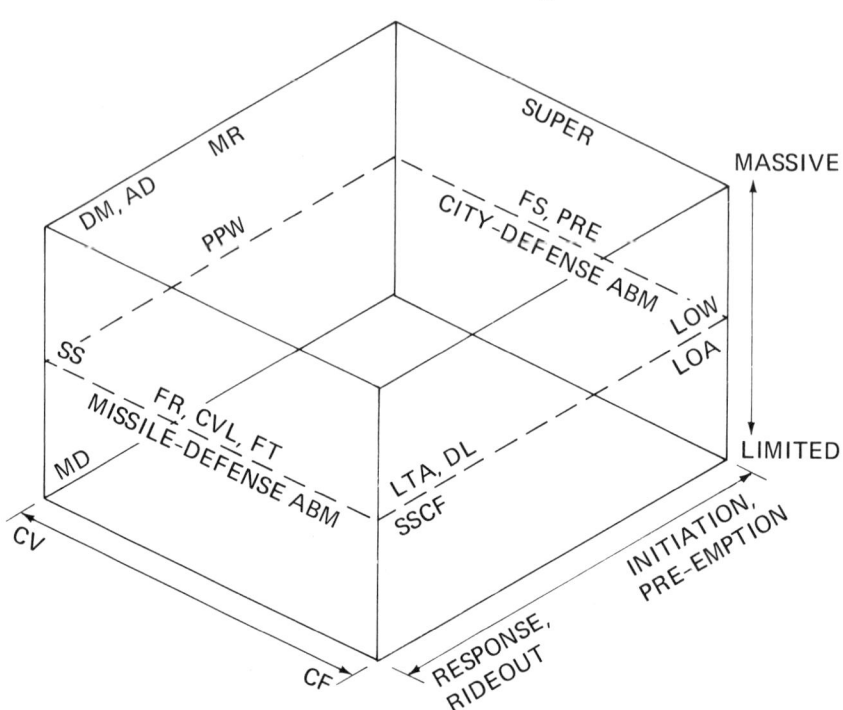

FIGURE 2.4 Dimensions of Strategic Doctrines

In this conceptual organization of strategic doctrines, the front-to-right dimension represents a continuum from response to attack initiation; the front-to-left dimension represents a continuum from pure CF strikes to pure CV strikes; and the up–down dimension represents the range from massive to limited strikes. Doctrinal abbreviations are given in Table 2.1 and in the Glossary.

an attack and responding (CF) against military targets: DL, SSCF, and LTA embracing a range of possible counterattack magnitudes. Of these doctrines, only the last has not already been discussed in the previous section. LTA is launch through attack, under which some missiles would be launched without waiting for an attack to be fully ridden out, due to a concern that too many missiles might be lost and inadequate retaliatory forces result. This option is distinguished from the variants at the front right corner, launch on warning (LOW) and launch on assessment (LOA), both of which call for preemption rather than rideout on the part of the attacked party (Garwin, 1979). The problems of all these variations on LOW were considered in a classic and devastating critique by Paul Wolfowitz (1970), and are discussed later. Several other doctrines embracing possible attack initiation are grouped on the right rear face of the cube; each could include both CF and CV strikes. These doctrines are first strike (FS), preemption (PRE), and the potential use of superiority (SUPER), which could include a massive attack. Use of ABMs to defend cities is also included here, since such usage could be an important adjunct of a PRE strike, in order to deny the other side hostages against whom a retaliation could be mounted. This is, of course, a worst-case evaluation of an opponent's capability, and more benign motivations for deploying city-defense ABMs surely can be envisioned.

At the left rear face of the cube are AD and MD, both doctrines that would generally involve CV targeting, but could be used either in response or in preemption: massive retaliation (MR), and prepositioned weapons (PPW). The latter is the cheap way to destroy cities, for example, by thermonuclear devices shipped to key points as ordinary freight in anticipation of possible use and detonated by remote control. At the left edge of the cube are two doctrines generally considered to involve CV targeting and both of which are responsive in nature: second strike (SS) and use of "doomsday machines" (DM). This last is a family of hypothetical devices envisioned by Kahn (1960, 145 ff.). In simple form, they could consist of three elements: a device capable of destroying all human life, perhaps a network of large and "dirty" thermonuclear bombs; an invulnerable computer to control their detonation; and a program instructing the computer to actuate the bomb network whenever a published "behavioral code" was violated, say by a Soviet attack on the United States. At the center of the left front face are three other doctrines that assume rideout but could involve both CF and CV retaliations: flexible response (FR), flexible targeting (FT), and countervailing (CVL). Use of ABMs for missile defense is also placed there, because defense of retaliatory missiles is consistent with any doctrine calling for rideout. Finally, parity (PAR) and sufficiency (SUF) are not located in the figure because they do not stipulate any particular use of weapons, whether CF or CV, massive or limited, responsive or initiatory.

In Figure 2.5 the same structure is applied to the doctrinal movements of the United States and the Soviet Union over time, as discussed in the previous section. Starting from a position of nuclear monopoly and clear superiority (SUPER) in 1945, the United States moved to massive retaliation (MR) in 1954, then quickly changed to AD, DL, and FR in the early 1960s. Both AD and DL elements remained, with various names, through the 1970s. The Soviets, having joined the nuclear club in 1949 and not having attained a true intercontinental delivery capability until 1955, appeared to have adopted MD doctrine by 1959. By the mid-1960s, they showed some signs of having adopted AD, and more recently of having adopted a general warfighting (DL) or FR posture, possibly with some capability to preempt. As with the United States, both AD and DL elements are present, and Soviet declaratory policy has always included warfighting.

These movements by the two superpowers seem quite reasonable if interpreted as mutual responses. Given the initial U.S. monopoly, the Soviets could hardly enter the nuclear club by any other gateway than

FIGURE 2.5 U.S. (——) and Soviet (– – –) Movements in Strategic Doctrine

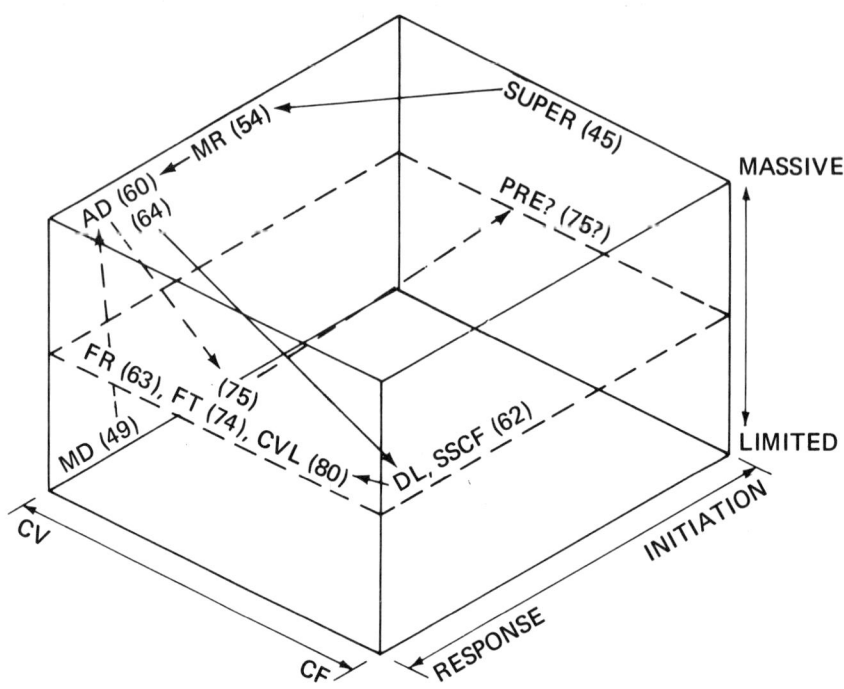

Major positions in U.S. and Soviet strategic doctrines are plotted in the same three-dimensional conceptual space established in Figure 2.4, with years the doctrines were first announced or assumed in parentheses. The United States entered the nuclear age with a monopoly or superiority; thus the Soviets could hardly enter except with a minimal deterrent. Massive retaliation was announced in 1954. In the early 1960s U.S. doctrine shifted to assured destruction (AD), second-strike counterforce (SSCF), and flexible response (FR); since that time U.S. doctrine has always included both AD and DL or FT elements. By about 1964 the Soviets had acquired an AD capability, and by the mid-1970s they had moved to variants of FT. By some other analysts' interpretations, by the mid-1970s the Soviets had begun to acquire a capability for preemptive war initiation.

minimum deterrence (MD). They would then logically move to acquire the means to deter U.S. attack (i.e., to effectuate AD). Having attained that capability, they might then embrace more ambitious and aggressive doctrines. In this evaluation, having reached what is generally regarded as rough nuclear parity, the two superpowers have gravitated to the same region of doctrinal space. With the disappearance of the freedom to initiate attack under SUPER or MR doctrines, which rested on monopolies of nuclear weapons and, later, of intercontinental delivery capabilities, it was necessary for the United States to move to more restricted, responsive doctrines. Since perhaps 1970, a number of analysts have perceived what

Kolkowicz (1971, 440) termed "a form of progressive strategic convergence of the superpowers." It is important to note, however, that Kolkowicz was writing at the time of the SALT I negotiations. In the more pessimistic times that have followed, one might be more inclined to note that Soviet achievement of essential strategic parity could serve as a base either for continued parity or for an effort to achieve SUPER or breakout.

Among the doctrines not yet used, both DM and the LOW/LOA/LTA group deserve further comment. Kahn (1960, 145 *ff.*) did an excellent job of demolishing his own thought experiment, the class of doomsday machines, for if either side seriously entertained the prospect of building such a machine, there would likely be both great public revulsion (especially in the affected but unconsulted countries) and a race between the superpowers to be first to place one in operation. The race would come about because the most likely first item in either side's published behavioral code would be that the other side could not build a doomsday machine. A number of other serious problems can be envisioned, including the exceedingly great costs of coding or computer errors. Finally, as we enter an age in which space colonization is beginning to be considered, the base premise of DM doctrine, that total destruction can be assured in a single act, is undermined.

Problems of implementing any of the LOW/LOA/LTA set of doctrines were summarized by Wolfowitz (1970), who categorized them under the four headings of (1) dangers of false alarms and accidental war; (2) calling for total retaliation in response to limited attacks; (3) weakening the deterrent; and (4) provoking the attacker. Any LOW decision would have to be made under severe time constraints, on the basis of early radar or infrared satellite warning signals. Infrared detection satellites over the Soviet missile fields could provide at most 30-minutes warning time, radars even less. Such time hardly allows for sending word to the President and receiving a response, let alone for assessment, analysis, queries to other decision makers, and adjustment of our target set in light of the assessment. Worse yet, an attack by means of SLBMs would offer at most about 10-minutes warning time from launch to impact, although it may be argued that no massive attack would be made using SLBMs because of their slow rate of fire.

Most of the alternatives suggested for overcoming the response-time problem seem unworkable. Waiting for the first explosions or for enough explosions to clarify the full nature and scope of the attack (thus adopting LOA) can be ruled out because those initial explosions could be used to create such atmospheric turbulence over our missile fields that launches would be difficult or impossible (a "pindown" effect) and those missile fields would thus be left in the more vulnerable position of having to ride out a full attack. Arming or disarming missiles in flight by means of coded signals is subject to the dangers that signals might not be received in a wartime environment and that the opponent might discover the code.

Accidental wars could also become much more likely under a hair-trigger LOW system. All retaliatory deterrent systems must be designed with two conflicting goals in mind: to ensure that an attack is launched *when* doctrine calls for it, and to ensure that no attack is launched *unless* doctrine calls for it. Maximizing the chance of meeting either goal minimizes the chance of meeting the other. In particular, under LOW the actual launch decision might well be made by comparatively junior military officers.

The problem of warning time implies that LOW doctrine would have to call for a major retaliatory strike even in response to what might prove to be a light or unauthorized attack. Even the rapid target changes made possible by the Command Data Buffer system could hardly be made for the entire ICBM force within the warning time available, so that few options could be implemented, even if there were adequate time to consider them. A major attack might well first appear to be a light attack, perhaps because of a planned pindown of missiles. And any attack on our means of receiving warning, such as an antisatellite strike, would have to be interpreted as the prelude to a potential all-out missile attack. Thus, even a light attack or a strong sign that an attack might be planned could call for a total retaliation.

The deterrent effectiveness of the "quick trigger finger" implied by LOW is subject to conflicting interpretations. Schelling (1960, especially chapter 2) would argue that a restriction on our own freedom to bargain strengthens our bargaining position. By implication, then, LOW should be a highly credible threat, and we should be comforted by its inflexibility. Yet we have long since abandoned MR doctrine's call for all-out response to limited threats as incredible. In contrast to the Schelling position, Wolfowitz (1970, 2282) argued that "the very inhumanity of the 'launch on warning' threat weakens its credibility as a deterrent." If the credibility of our deterrent is indeed questioned, it may even prove to be an invitation to attack us. Alternatively, LOW policy might prove to be a provocation to attack us preemptively, in the belief that our hair trigger would otherwise be touched off in some later time of crisis. Thus, on several accounts, LOW doctrine appears to be unwieldy or unworkable, very possibly dangerous and potentially destabilizing. LOA can be dismissed on grounds of fear of a possible pindown of missiles; and LTA is subject to the same objection, and the concern that while it allows greater decision-making time, it also would result in losses that would reduce the available forces. There is, of course, a continuum shading from early LTA through later LTA to full rideout of an attack. Given the dangers and difficulties of the LOW class of doctrines, it appears that rideout is likely to remain a more reasonable policy. Nonetheless, in 1982 there was a report that the Soviets might be considering adoption of LOW (Doder, 1982). We turn next to some further considerations of the processes which bring about strategic doctrines and changes in such doctrines.

WHAT DRIVES DOCTRINE?

Strategic doctrine is but one element in an extremely complex political–military system considered in some detail in the next chapter. As noted in the introduction to this chapter, strategic doctrine comprehends both a technical and a political role. In its technical aspect, doctrine includes statements about how particular weapons would be used under particular sets of wartime contingencies. These statements may include option sets from which the President and other National Command Authorities (NCA) would make choices, and highly detailed plans for the implementation of each of those options, including missile target lists and details of the order and rate of firings. In its political aspect, doctrine encompasses statements and assumptions regarding the conditions under which wars would be fought and the general goals to be sought; this aspect includes the decision rules by which the President and NCA would make choices from among the available options.

In both its technical and its political aspects, strategic doctrine is constrained by the available technology, and lies at the interface of technology and politics. These constraints imposed by the available technology are double-edged. Sometimes they rule out desired options as impractical, as in 1970, when it was not possible to promise a highly effective large-scale ABM system. At other times, however, the availability or possibility of a new technology forces serious consideration to be extended to a new development. The decision to develop the thermonuclear bomb in the early 1950s was such a case; theory showed that it ought to be possible to build and that its explosive yield would vastly exceed that of existing weapons, and fear sealed the case for building it. In such cases the logic of the prisoners' dilemma seems to play a major role: new developments believed to be possible are pursued out of fear of the consequences should the opponent be the only one to proceed with development. The prisoners' dilemma, of course, originated as a description of the motivations and actions of rational, self-interested individuals, as described earlier in the section "Technology as Drive" (Chapter 1). Yet it is routine to consider the policies of governments as resulting, at least as a first approximation and especially on the strategic level, from rational selection by unitary actors (Allison, 1971, Ch. 1). Agencies, moreover, can still use the prisoners' dilemma fear as an argument in their policy bargaining within governments.

These observations strongly imply that whatever weaponry can be envisioned will, in the absence of generally accepted constraints, be built—and that doctrine for the utilization of the new weaponry must then be developed. An example may be found in the series of technical developments during the 1970s which made ever greater accuracy possible for ICBMs. These included inertial navigation improvements such as better gyros, the AIRS (Advanced Inertial Reference Sphere) system, and position sensors such as star trackers (about which we have learned much from the space program) and the NAVSTAR system to allow worldwide positioning to within 20–30-foot accuracy in three dimensions through radio triangulation on a system of satellites. On-board computers such as the NS-20 system have allowed both more sophisticated MIRVs and increases in accuracy; they will also make terminal guidance of reentry vehicles possible, allowing super-accurate maneuverable reentry vehicles (MARVs). Even without MARVs, it was generally accepted that the new Mk12A RV being installed on Minuteman III missiles had a 1980 accuracy value (CEP) of 600 feet or better (SIPRI, 1980, xxxv). Attainment of such accuracies implies that even relatively small warheads have a true silo-killing hard-target capability. The result is a technologically driven increase in the role allocated to precision CF strikes, closely associated with the rise of FT and CVL doctrines and a general shift to a stronger DL component in strategic doctrine. (See Shapley, 1978.) Concerns that such doctrines might be more the product than the source of programs for accuracy improvement were raised early in the retargeting debate (Schlesinger, 1974, 17, 22).

Increased accuracy also leads to the problem of ICBM vulnerability, according to which no fixed-location missile is safe because even a small warhead can be delivered so close to it. This case seems to be an instance of a general trend under which new technological possibilities lead to the building of new weaponry and subsequent changes in strategic doctrine so as to accommodate the new weapons, and the combination of new weaponry and new doctrine leads to newer problems, which give rise to still newer programs as solutions. In the case of ICBM vulnerability, one proposed solution is missile mobility, which in turn leads to major difficulties in verifying the numbers of missiles for arms control purposes. (See also the more thorough discussion of the ICBM vulnerability problem in Chapter 5.) New problems may also open up possibilities for new weaponry. The problems of anticipated eventual ICBM vulnerability and the instabilities associated with the fragility of the earliest ICBMs led to desires for creation of an essentially invulnerable second strike deterrent in the form of SLBMs, which implied an entire new "leg" to what we have since come to know as the strategic weapons triad. Once the triad was established, it became subject to all the pressures of bureaucratic preservation of programs, stakes of key personnel in the program, and so on. Yet, once again a new problem seems to be in the making because of the combination of capabilities generated under apparently disparate programs. Combining SLBMs, built to provide an invulnerable deterrent, with MARVs, built to provide maximal CF flexibility and capability, implies that we may soon see a true silo-killing hard-target capability based at sea (Ball, 1977); that end clearly was never envisioned by those who originally set up the U.S. SLBM program (Kuenne, 1966).

Air Force Colonel Richard G. Head has argued that U.S. military missions definitions are typically broad, general, and not highly detailed (1978, 547), which would logically lead to a certain degree of generality or even vagueness in strategic doctrine. Head has also argued that Soviet and American military doctrines diverge on the matter of quantitative superiority, that "American R&D style has traditionally emphasized qualitative superiority, with smaller numbers, and U.S. military doctrine, while appreciating the value of mass, has adjusted accordingly." One of the results of this tendency to substitute technological sophistication for large numbers of personnel and weapons has been "a certain tendency for technology to drive both strategy and doctrine" (1978, 550). As Kolkowicz (1971, 451) has phrased it,

> The problem lies in certain asymmetries between politics and technology: Politics is essentially conservative, intuitive, present-oriented; technology is innovative, autonomous, and future-oriented. The mating of the two in the nuclear context creates a tense and unstable union.

There thus exist very strong ties between the nominally technical and the nominally political sides of the strategic doctrine formation process. The discussion thus far has focused primarily on drives that start on the technical side. Yet if the technical side is constrained by what is known and believed possible, the political side is equally constrained. Some conceivable strategic goals simply are not politically acceptable. Ignoring the problem of ICBM vulnerability has been mentioned as a possibility, but relatively few politicians would take that suggestion very seriously. Solving the vulnerability problem by scrapping ICBMs entirely has even fewer adherents. Selling the concept of strategic sufficiency proved to be difficult for the Nixon administration at the time of SALT I. The idea that we might be quite well protected under our own doctrine while having fewer ICBMs and fewer SLBMs than the Soviets did not sit well with the Congress, and was not acceptable without the Jackson amendment which effectively instructed the SALT II negotiators to come up with a formula providing for equal numeric limits. In this instance, as in others, the idea that we may be inferior on some measure of the strategic balance (see also Chapter 4) is not politically acceptable. Similarly, giving up the major programs and missions of the past is exceedingly difficult; witness the continued vitality of the manned bomber in the face of ever-improving air defenses, and the durability of the strategic triad concept in an age of ICBM vulnerability.

A number of general tendencies of the political process are also noteworthy. Capability is almost always taken to imply intent, but only as long as we are talking about an opponent. This tendency is yet another instance of the relationship between trust and power discussed earlier under the rubric of the prisoners' dilemma, and it is a clear example of worst-case analysis. Another example is provided by the verification debate in SALT; the entire discussion of verification problems and the possibilities for working out cooperative measures to assure that neither side was violating the agreements was conducted in terms of the hypothetical most-effective possible attack, rather than in terms of what was believed to be probable. There is also a major problem of political gain seeking, under which defense programs may be put forward more for expected popularity than out of a belief that they are greatly needed. The 1980 presidential and congressional campaigns saw what appeared to be a consensus that military spending should be increased while all other government spending should be reduced and taxes cut. Moreover, open statements by many candidates including Ronald Reagan indicated that arms racing was to be preferred to maintaining a status quo under which the United States perceived itself as weaker than the Soviet Union (Washington Post, 1980).

One might ask if there can be such a thing as "too much defense," and one clear answer is that there is indeed too much if one cannot afford it or if one scares an opponent into a major arms race. Deciding whether one of these cases applies depends critically on the deciding politician's model of the U.S.–Soviet confrontation. In the section "Ideologies and Values" in Chapter 1, three general models for interpreting Soviet intentions were introduced: cyberneticist, mechanist, and essentialist views. Adoption of one or another of these views is almost a matter of ideology, about which most writers and strategic analysts are silent. The assignment of any writer of strategic doctrinal prescriptions to one or another of these three schools of thought is usually fairly straightforward, and the 1980 campaign may be interpreted as having been fought, in part, to change the general perception of the U.S.–Soviet confrontation and what needs to be done about it. We thus saw a shift from 1972 to 1980 in the national consensus about how to interpret Soviet behavior.

Finally, the evolution of strategic doctrine is constrained by what is believed to be credible, effective strategy. Yet interpretation of the credible is again very strongly influenced by both technical and political considerations. In deciding questions of effectiveness, we are forced to consider both aspects: first, what technologies offer credible promise of performance; and second, what model of what is politically acceptable—and of what the opponent intends—is held by the decisive group of political leaders? Given these constraints, what lies ahead in the development of U.S. strategic doctrine for the 1980s?

THE FUTURE OF U.S. STRATEGIC DOCTRINE: TRENDS AND SCENARIOS

In light of the above analysis, two very different general aims might be sought in strategic doctrine: rideout or breakout. Consider first a rideout scenario. Perhaps the strongest argument for rideout is that no high-confidence first strike capability can be attained (Schlesinger, 1974, 17).

If one does not have an FS capability, it is most illogical to contemplate initiating an attack. As indicated in the section, "A Plethora of Doctrines" and in Figure 2.5, while both the United States and the Soviet Union have gained massive deterrent forces, and as doubts have grown about the ability of either side to carry out a disarming first strike, their strategic doctrines have tended to converge on the DL/FT/CVL set. The ever-increasing size of the two strategic arsenals tends to push both superpowers toward damage limitation, threat analysis, riding out any attack, assessing the scope and nature of an attack before deciding on an appropriate retaliation, and flexible targeting. Since neither side has a significant defense against missiles and each has assured destruction, it is impossible either to overwhelm the opponent or to mount a realistic defense. Thus, the only logical alternatives are to ride out any possible attack or to work toward some combination of breakout (to change the regime to one of advantage) and arms control (to stabilize the deterrent regime). While it cannot be proven that arms control or limitation will ultimately work, they are almost certain to be preferred to the war alternative when AD exists, and are likely to be far less costly than seeking a breakout that one plans not to exploit fully. Under this scenario, governments logically tend toward DL, FT, CVL, and a stress on flexibility and response.

This set of arguments has strong programmatic implications, and is itself influenced by ongoing programs. It is the "business as usual" set of arguments, and implies no threat to major ongoing and projected research, development, and deployment programs. Under this scenario one would expect to see a continuation of the triad during the 1980s; a new manned bomber, whether the B-1 or a derivation; a new land-based ICBM, presumably the MX in some deceptive basing mode; and a new and improved SLBM, the Trident II or Trident D5. Each major ongoing program would thus be maintained and updated. Within its first year the Reagan administration moved to pursue each of these programs.

In 1982 the Reagan administration unveiled its initial START proposals, which had the avowed general aim of imposing new degrees and dimensions of symmetry on the U.S. and Soviet arsenals. Under those proposals, in a Phase I agreement both sides would agree to equal limits of 850 ballistic missiles (a reduction of about half for the United States, and two-thirds for the Soviet Union), a total of 5000 reentry vehicles (down from about 7200 per side), a maximum of 2500 RVs on land-based missiles (requiring substantial Soviet reductions but no U.S. cuts), and no change in current bomber levels (on balance, an advantage to the United States). In a Phase II agreement, rough equality in total missile throw-weight would be sought, a change that would allow U.S. deployment of new heavy missiles but would require Soviet cuts. The throw-weight proposal would reverse the result of several decades in which the two sides have followed differing doctrinal thrusts and asymmetric technological capabilities and biases. Thus it has been attacked as an unrealistic proposal designed to offer the appearance of arms control while provoking Soviet rejection, which could then be used as an excuse for a massive new arming program (Fred Kaplan, 1982).

For the United States to pursue the initial Reagan START proposals seems to offer little promise of any early substantive agreement, and to pursue the Reagan administration's arms-building plans implies that the same set of strategic problems seen in recent years will continue. FT doctrine will remain difficult to implement because its requirements are much more open-ended than are those of AD. ICBM vulnerability will continue and grow more acute, at least in theory, unless solved either by combining ICBM deceptive basing (through some form of mobility) with limits on the number of RVs per missile or by deploying a substantial ballistic missile defense (ABM) system. Given the United States' failure to ratify SALT II, and the slow beginning of the START talks in 1982, renewed stability for the ICBM regime appears unlikely. Some sort of new ABM effort does appear likely (see, for example, *Aviation Week*, 1980a), particularly if the MX is deployed in the dense-pack basing mode or in Minuteman silos. Any ABM effort threatens the continuance of the SALT/START process, but offers some promise of reducing the incentive to proliferate further MIRVs, and thus of limiting the degree of ICBM vulnerability. Overall, however, the prospect under this scenario is for a continuation of the old set of problems, extended to still higher levels of weaponry, cost, destructive potential, uncertainty, and potential instability.

An alternative scenario or set of programs exists, aimed at a breakout from the effective stalemate that has characterized the central strategic weapons regime for almost two decades. This scenario involves exercising one or more options, each tied to some program based on new or significantly improved technology. Each such program thus indicates the drive which technology exerts on strategic doctrine and the prisoners' dilemma fear of an opponent's possible breakout. Land-based ABMs, such as those planned under the LoAD program (*Aviation Week*, 1980a) offer some significant improvements over the designs of the 1960s, although it is questionable whether they offer a true breakout potential. The family of space-based laser or DET ABMs, however, has such a potential. Either set of programs will generate major pressure to abrogate the SALT I ABM Treaty. If the defense they offer is good enough, as it may be with the space-based systems, it could end the need for rideout as an element of strategic doctrine.

A fairly detailed set of such proposals was put forward in 1982 by Daniel O. Graham (1982), a retired Army Lieutenant General and the head of a Heritage Foundation project called High Frontier. The High Frontier concept calls for a comprehensive program for military and industrial exploitation of outer space, including a major strategic defense mission supported in part by the other space capabilities. It has been asserted that the entire program could be funded over its first decade for some 40 billion dollars, roughly the cost of the MX-MPS scheme discussed in Chapter 5. Ballistic missile defense would be built in layers, with quick deployment of a terminal point defense of missile silos to be followed in stages by two later layers of space-based defense using nonnuclear projectiles and DET weapons. A major doctrinal underpinning of the project is the goal of ending reliance on deterrence (always referred to as MAD) and substituting strategic defense (labeled "Assured Survival"). The intent in building such a defense is not to achieve perfection in the form of zero enemy penetration, but to reduce enemy penetration to the point that any attack is deterred by uncertainty about its effects. As Graham notes:

> Given the drastic consequences of a failed nuclear attack on an opponent, the critical military task is to keep a potential aggressor *uncertain of success*, if not certain of failure. In the absence of defenses, the Soviet military planner has a rather straightforward arithmetic problem to solve to be quite sure of the results of a disarming strike . . . simply to ensure that he can deliver two warheads of current size and accuracy against each target. If, on the other hand, [he] must consider the effects of a strategic defense . . . he is faced with a problem full of uncertainties . . . *Such uncertainties are the essence of deterrence.* (1982, 4)

High Frontier's preferred approach to point defense of ICBM silos is to use large numbers (perhaps 5,000–10,000) of small (up to several inches in diameter) "swarmjet" rocket projectiles against each incoming warhead, fired from a radar-guided hardened launch tube near the silo. This supersonic shotgun approach would be designed to achieve roughly 85 percent kill probability for interceptions under 40,000 feet, relying on the kinetic energy of the moving projectile to disable the incoming warhead. While the High Frontier program does not require putting any nuclear warheads into space, and thus would not violate the Outer Space Treaty, its conformance with the SALT I ABM Treaty is much more problematic. Graham argues his case for creative interpretation thus:

> The High Frontier spaceborne defensive systems fall into the category described in the treaty as "systems based on other principles" which are "subject to discussion" with the Soviets. Point defense systems can be selected which are so different from ABM systems as defined in the treaty, that they too could be considered as outside the treaty. Indeed, some silo defense systems can be considered "dynamic hardening"—a substitute for reinforced concrete—rather than an ABM. Further, the current ABM Treaty is scheduled for review in 1982, and the United States could propose any amendments deemed necessary to accomodate strategic defensive decisions. (1982, 10)

While Graham interprets the swarmjet point defense as an instance of "dynamic hardening," it seems difficult to find evidence that such an interpretation would have been accepted by the framers of the ABM Treaty. If one were to count individual projectiles rather than launchers, not even a single swarmjet launcher could be deployed under the 100-ABM limit.

It appears that the bottom line for this proposal, as for other ABM proposals, is a willingness to abrogate the attempt in the SALT I ABM Treaty to ban all but a small number of *any type* of ballistic missile defenders.

The total High Frontier program of ballistic missile defense and space military capability could also be viewed as a U.S. program for achieving strategic breakout. The United States, having begun the nuclear age in a position of absolute superiority, entered into development of thermonuclear weapons in the 1950s, and into many of its subsequent strategic weapons programs out of fear that the Soviets might otherwise achieve a breakout. Yet a number of U.S. programs over the decades have had such breakout potential themselves—for example, the Minuteman missile and Polaris SSBN/SLBM programs, and particularly the Trident D5 program. Since the middle-1960s, however, we have lived with a growing sense that rough parity has been achieved in the strategic weapons regime, and that a breakout by either side was becoming less and less likely. Can we confidently predict, however, that a large price may not be offered—by either side—for a reasonable hope of breakout? As Axelrod (1979, 244) notes, "when stakes get very large, a great deal of surprise can be expected." Previously unexpected and unacceptable risks might then be taken to achieve breakout. President Reagan's March 1983 call for serious study of the long-term potential of strategic defense programs of the type proposed in the High Frontier program only intensified the debate over stability and breakout.

As we consider the implications of changing national administrations for decisions between rideout and breakout scenarios, the shift from the Carter to the Reagan administrations may be interpreted as a shift from a set of decision makers who were dominantly either cyberneticist or mechanist in their interpretations of Soviet strategy to a new set who ranged from mechanist to essentialist. (See Zimmerman, 1974, and the section "Ideologies and Values" in Chapter 1.) Compare, for example, the statements of Secretary of State Muskie or Secretary of Defense Brown (1980) with those of Reagan's advisor Richard Pipes, who demonstrates a distinctly essentialist position in his commentaries on Soviet global strategy (1980, 31ff.), and Defense Transition Team member William R. Van Cleave (Van Cleave and Barnett, 1974). In general, President Reagan early surrounded himself with defense policy advisors who were inclined to urge higher military spending (Wilson, 1980a). As a group, these individuals tend to favor a "stronger" defense (see the assessment of measures in Chapter 4) and U.S. superiority; they tend to distrust the Soviets intensely, and evaluate the chances of reaching cooperative accommodation with the Soviets as relatively small unless approached from a position of U.S. superiority, and, in a few cases, they seek outright U.S. breakout. During the 1980 campaign, President Reagan asked, "Since when has it been wrong for America to aim to be first in military strength?" and urged that the United States "restore true essential equality for our own security and for the political perceptions of our adversaries, our allies, and Third World countries" (Reagan, 1980).

In summary, the prospects for U.S. nuclear strategic doctrine during the decade of the 1980s appear to include the following: a continuation of rideout plus FT or CVL doctrines, combined with new programs to maximize the flexibility in FT, with a concomitant increase in DL capability; some sort of land-based ABM program, such as LoAD, with a resulting increase in DL capability; and at least some initiation of programs with a breakout potential, such as space-based laser ABMs. The breakout possibilities, of course, hinge on the probabilities of success in developing new technologies, but offer the threat and promise that the strategic weapons regime we have come to know over the past two decades may be significantly destabilized. Moreover, each of these programs may be pursued in parallel with some continued SALT or START effort toward limited arms control. Several of the specific programs anticipated for the 1980s will be analyzed in detail in later chapters, but in Chapter 3 we turn to the political processes for implementing such strategic programs and doctrines.

3

Strategic Doctrine, Weapons Acquisitions, and Arms Control: Politics and Process

INTRODUCTION: OVERVIEW OF A POLITICAL–TECHNOLOGICAL PROCESS

At any given moment the United States possesses an arsenal of strategic weapons in place, a series of research and development programs which may lead to new weapons for that arsenal, and sets of doctrines specifying how and under what conditions the weapons may be used. The evolution of U.S. strategic doctrine was sketched in the previous chapter, from its origins in nuclear monopoly following World War II, to parity, to superiority jitters, to institutionalized arms controls in the 1970s, and into the post-SALT era of the early 1980s. As noted in that sketch, strategic doctrines are inherently subject to historical and technological constraints imposed both by the number and capabilities of available weapons in the arsenals and by the often widely divergent technological development paths chosen by competing governments.

Nonetheless, weapons stocks, development programs, and strategic doctrines are all merely parts of a multifaceted and highly interactive political–technological system, the end product of which is that complex of weaponry and doctrine referred to earlier as the "strategic weapons regime." That regime is characterized by a tremendous number of interactions, including those between available weapons, doctrines for their use, and programs to develop new weapons; those between the U.S. and Soviet governments and, occasionally, other governments; and those among all of the significant actors within the nominally "domestic" political systems of the member governments. With so complex a series of interactions, apparent contradictions and unresolved conflicts may be expected almost routinely.

Consider the problem of "ICBM vulnerability" as an example. It was realized early on that the *potential* problem was inherent in the technology itself: if missile warhead accuracies were increased sufficiently, and as long as no fully effective defense could be devised, no target in any known location could survive attack. An initial solution was to place missiles on virtually unlocatable submarines, thus ensuring the security of the missiles and the stability of rideout deterrent doctrine. Yet when the hypothetical increase in accuracies began to be actualized as a product of the two superpowers' continuing research and development programs, the political clout of those individuals charged with administering existing programs—and their desire to maintain evolved (triad) doctrine—became powerful biases against phasing out the land-based ICBM. Given the developing vulnerability problem, proposals for new technologies of land-mobility were developed, only to run headlong into opposition from those who saw the new programs as too complex to be reliable, as threats to fiscal stability, as threats to land and environmental interests, or as the probable triggers of a new round of Soviet strategic weapons building in response to U.S. programs, and thus as (at the least) threats to the already limited attempts to institutionalize strategic arms control.

This single problem of ICBM vulnerability, already spanning two decades from its theoretical formulation to its emergence as a pressing current policy dispute, exhibits interactions between the U.S. and Soviet governments; among weapons, development programs, and doctrine; and among major domestic political and bureaucratic actors. Predicting the impact of policy shifts under realistic options for dealing with problems of this type requires an ability to fathom the myriad operating complexities of the strategic weapons regime. Toward that end, an overview of that process or regime is presented in this chapter. Organized into successive "snapshots" of increasing resolution or detail, the presentation begins with Figure 3.1, in which the broad influences determining the stock of strategic weapons in the U.S. arsenal are set out. Several of the major segments of Figure 3.1 are then explored in greater detail in the later sections of this chapter.

Figure 3.1 is a highly simplified sketch of the political–technological system by which U.S. strategic weapons stocks and strategic capabilities are produced. Because of the complexity of the process, even this first schematization is organized into a number of constituent processes. The figure is divided horizontally according to the conceptual "columns" of basic process, primary feedback interactions between different parts of that process, and constraints limiting the process. The process "column" is then organized vertically into a five-step sequence of (a) intelligence gathering, to garner information about the external environment; (b) interpretation and assessment to determine probable needs; (c) program option generation, including selection and funding of program options in light of

88 / *The Politics of Nuclear Balance*

FIGURE 3.1 Overview of the Strategic Weapons Acquisition Process

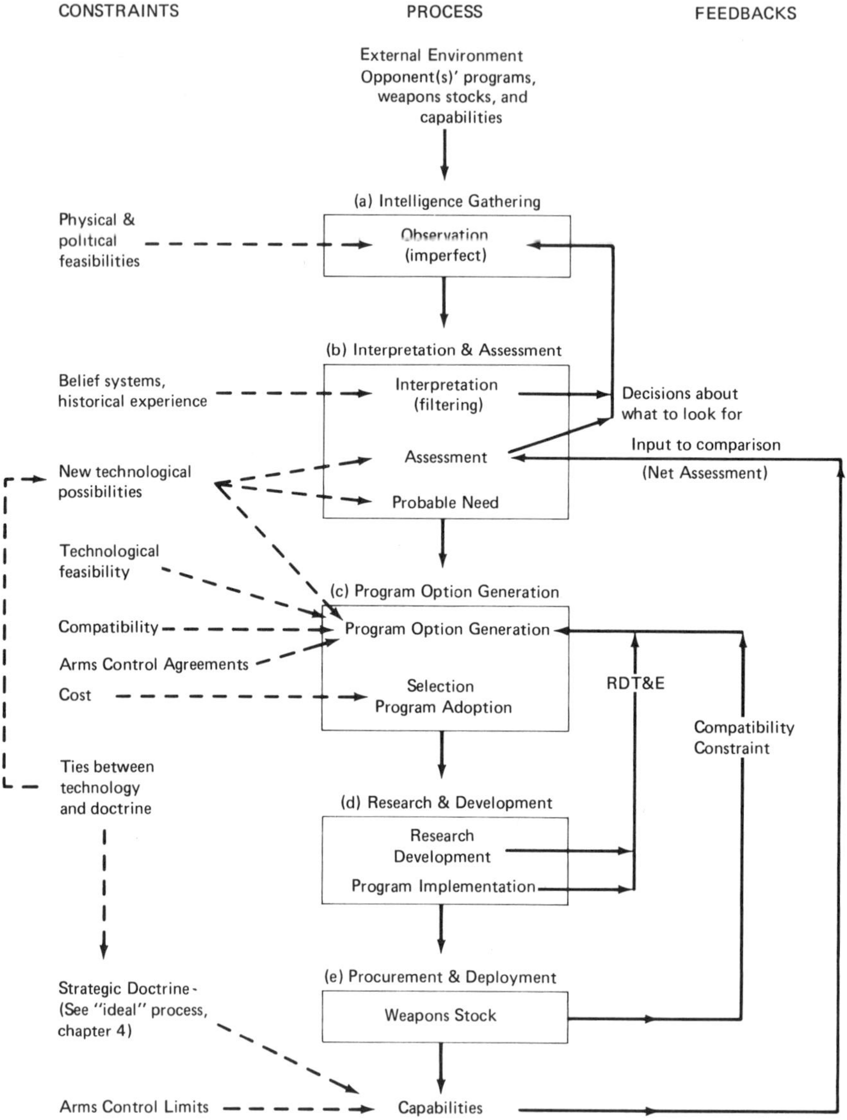

CONSTRAINTS	PROCESS	FEEDBACKS

External Environment
Opponent(s)' programs, weapons stocks, and capabilities

↓

(a) Intelligence Gathering

Physical & political feasibilities — — — → Observation (imperfect)

↓

(b) Interpretation & Assessment

Belief systems, historical experience — — → Interpretation (filtering) → Decisions about what to look for

New technological possibilities → Assessment ← Input to comparison (Net Assessment)

→ Probable Need

↓

(c) Program Option Generation

Technological feasibility — — →
Compatibility — — — — → Program Option Generation ←
Arms Control Agreements —
Cost — — — — → Selection Program Adoption

RDT&E

Compatibility Constraint

Ties between technology and doctrine

↓

(d) Research & Development

Research Development
Program Implementation

↓

Strategic Doctrine - (See "ideal" process, chapter 4)

(e) Procurement & Deployment

Weapons Stock

↓

Arms Control Limits — — — → Capabilities

expected needs, existing programs and capabilities, and a myriad of constraints; (d) research and development; and (e) actual production of weapons and their deployment and incorporation into the arsenal.

Like any schematization, this one involves some simplification and idealization. Each of the general steps is subject to constraints, and each is influenced by the feedbacks of information received from steps further along in the sequence. It should also be remembered that even after weapons deployment, strategic capabilities depend on several other key factors, including (1) inherent performance capabilities, reliability, and state of readiness of the weapons; (2) strategic doctrine(s) for their use, subject to the limitations that any use or threat of use is part of an extremely complex n-person game (in the technical sense of that term set out in Chapter 1) and that the exact conditions under which use of the weapons is appropriate may not have been foreseen; (3) agreements by treaty or in other forms calling for specific uses or nonuses under particular conditions; (4) the actual time, place, and circumstances of possible use; and (5) "political will" or readiness of key actors to countenance actual use. Let us now turn to slightly closer looks at each of the five general steps sketched in Figure 3.1.

The external environment of programs, weapons stocks, and the capabilities of potential allies and opponents is a central focus of intelligence-gathering efforts. All such observations, however, are imperfect, being limited by the unwillingness of any government, even an ally, to share *complete* information. Governments may attempt to deceive by such means as camouflaging construction efforts or deployed weapons; encoding telemetry from missile tests; testing weapons in concealed or limited modes; keeping weapons, production locations, and deployment points away from public view; and understating or hiding expenditures. They may also engage in quite elaborate programs of deliberate disinformation, aiming either to overstate capabilities (as seen in Khrushchev's claims about Soviet missile accomplishments in the late 1950s) or to hide or understate capabilities (as seen in the actions of most of the potential but unavowed nuclear states). Intelligence gathering is also subject to both physical and political constraints. Collection of information from satellite imagery is limited not only by the resolution or seeing capability of orbited cameras, but also by the number of launches one can afford and the speed with which orbit changes can be accomplished in order to bring satellites over the areas of greatest interest under favorable light and weather conditions. And while political constraints sometimes promote intelligence gathering, as in the accepted practice or noninterference with orbiting satellites, more often they impede that gathering of information, as in the refusal of any right of on-site inspection by foreign nationals, or recurring controversies over whether reconnaissance aircraft violate national airspaces.

Moreover, while the gathering of intelligence is constrained and imperfect, the interpretation and assessment of that information is even more problematic. Decisions on what to look for in the first place are limited by one's expectations about what is probable. Further, interpreting the information that *is* collected is inevitably a "filtering" process in which truly meaningful information (or "signal") must be separated from noninformation or disinformation ("noise"). Such filtering relies heavily and necessarily upon past experience as a guide. It also typically, if less necessarily, relies upon belief systems which condition our expectations about probable events and our interpretations of their meaning. (The section "Ideologies and Values" in Chapter 1 covered some of the ways in which our interpretation of received signals is influenced by basic patterns of expectation concerning an opponent's probable intent.)

Additionally, in any evaluation there remain some elements of uncertainty, thus allowing a range from optimistic to pessimistic interpretation. In such situations it is routine to evaluate the performance of an opponent's weaponry more generously than that of our own ("worst-case estimation") and to infer others' *intent* from their *capabilities*. We may well believe, for example, that in most situations the United States would not be the first government to employ nuclear weapons in some new war even though it possessed the requisite nuclear capability; yet we are quite reluctant to ascribe a comparable reticence to the Soviet Union or even to the People's Republic of China despite the long-standing Chinese formal pledge of no first use. Finally, accurate interpretation and assessment are doubly threatened by new technological possibilities, which we may both fear lest they be discovered first by an opponent, and tend to overlook because they are by nature unexpected.

In principle, assessment of needs should lead to the generation of program options designed to meet those needs. In practice, however, program options are generated more or less continuously, as natural products of the ongoing research and development process and as routine outputs of every organization. Indeed, it is central to the argument for the existence of "technological creep" (about which more later, in the section "The Roles of Technology") that evolutionary increases in capability will be generated as routine R&D outputs. It is thus difficult to determine categorically whether program options precede or follow doctrine and needs-assessment; instances of both sequences are all too easily found. Let us therefore assume for the present that program options are generated both as routine organizational outputs and as responses to assessments of risk.

Nonetheless, the generation of program options is subject to an enormous number of constraints, both physical and political. If appropriate technology is not well in hand or susceptible to ready development, a program may lag far behind schedule and greatly exceed cost estimates without ever yielding a workable weapon suitable for quantity production and deployment. The unsuccessful attempt to develop long-range cruise missiles in the 1950s clearly demonstrates this phenomenon (Perry, 1979, 18). Yet new technological possibilities may either suggest new types of weapons or be developed in response to perceived needs expressed in strategic doctrine. In most cases, new weapons must be at least somewhat compatible with those already in the arsenal, as discussed in the section "Evolutionary Development" in Chapter 1.

Beyond the need for evolutionary development in order to allow new weapons to be fitted into the existing regime, the most important aspect of compatibility is often conformability to established doctrine and images of organizational "essence." Halperin, Clapp, and Kanter (1974, 28) have defined an organization's essence as "the view held by the dominant group in the organization of what the missions and capabilities should be." Such an image extends to concepts of the sorts of people who should be members of the team, and to what their skills, experiences, and knowledge should be. Halperin et al. note that the United States Air Force's essence has been "the flying of combat airplanes designed for the delivery of nuclear weapons against targets in the Soviet Union" (1974, 28), and that, with respect to missiles, "sitting in silos just cannot compare to flying bombers" (1974, 30). Note that this is a strictly post-World-War-II mission for an organization that did not become independent until 1947.

Both the Air Force's ICBM mission and the Navy's SLBM mission were very strongly resisted when first proposed, although each grew to involve a major share of its respective service's total effort and budget. The concept of organizational essences helps explain such otherwise perplexing resistance. The Air Force's attachment to maintaining the strategic bomber is reflected in the extremely low priority assigned to ICBMs in the 1950s (see, for example, Perry, 1979, 12–15); in advocacy of the B-70 and later the B-1 as successors to the B-52; in a series of programs through the 1960s and 1970s to upgrade the B-52s in order to continue to keep them operational; and in the Skybolt and later SRAM aircraft-launched missile programs. Each of these programs extended and maintained the essential manned-bomber mission. (Note also the staffing assumption embodied in the phrase "manned" bomber.) Similarly, Tactical Air Command (TAC) support for development of the TFX or F-111 or FB-111 in the 1960s, while justified on grounds of assigned TAC missions, actually led to a weapons system that could carry out the essential anti-Soviet mission and, given improved Soviet antiaircraft defenses, might even offer better chances of doing so successfully than Strategic Air Command (SAC) high-altitude subsonic bombers. Indeed, by 1979 there were proposals to "stretch" the FB-111s to extend their range and payload, giving them an openly admitted strategic bombing role (Robinson, 1979B).

Halperin et al. describe the Navy's essence as maintaining "combat ships whose primary mission must be to control the seas against potential enemies" (1974, 32). Hence, we should not be surprised that the established Navy was reluctant to take on the SLBM mission in the late 1950s and early 1960s, particularly when SLBM funds were taken from other Navy programs rather than being added to the base budget. Once the Polaris SLBM program was well-established, however, the natural bureaucratic push to expand the program led to improved accuracies (lower CEPs) and higher explosive yields, so as to move beyond the purely finite deterrent mission of Polaris and toward a hard-target kill capability as reflected in the Trident program. By such developments the Navy could both continue its own program and challenge the Air Force's ICBM mission in an era of developing ICBM vulnerability.

Organizational essences thus imply extension of existing programs, and the generation of program options is subject to the full gamut of bureaucratic constraints, including the stakes which individuals and agencies have in existing programs, resistance to innovation, fights over budget shares, limitations on the range of options considered, defensiveness over "territories" of assigned responsibility, desires to expand territory, staff, and budgets, and the fundamentally incremental nature of planning and budgeting. (See, for example, Allison, 1971; Braybrooke and Lindblom, 1963; Davis, Dempster, and Wildavsky, 1966; and Peck and Scherer, 1962.) Finally, cost is an ever-present constraint. Typically, as unit costs rise in the development stage, planned production runs are curtailed, sometimes to a level that brings capabilities for performing the originally planned mission very seriously into question. The C-5A transport aircraft provides an excellent, if grim, example of this phenomenon.

Given the impact and continuity of organizational essences, it should not be surprising that the research, development, test, and evaluation (RDT&E) portion of the DOD budget is remarkably constant, generally running about 10 percent of the budget over the past two decades. This effort covers development of strategic weapons, basic research, operation of defense-oriented research centers, and the advanced development of promising systems in aeronautics, flight simulation, intelligence, and biomedical science. The "technological creep" pressures inherent in this DOD function are largely responsible for actualizing the once-potential threat of ICBM vulnerability. In contrast, when need and the availability of suitable technologies combine, outstandingly rapid and efficient performance may result. An excellent example is provided by the development of the Air Force Thor intermediate-range ballistic missile (IRBM) in the late 1950s; it relied on the packaging of available technologies and proceeded from project definition to an initial demonstration in about one year, and to a full-scale operational test in three years. Still, when the match between technology and mission is less propitious, programs may escalate in cost, lag far behind schedule, and yield little usable output. During the same period as the Thor IRBM development, for example, the Navaho long-range cruise missile program fell behind schedule a full year for each year the missile remained under development (Perry, 1979, 18).

If the RDT&E share of the DOD budget has remained relatively constant, the same cannot be said of the procurement share. The long lead times of research and development and the prisoners' dilemma motivation to explore all possibly significant research avenues both provide drives to continue the RDT&E effort as a complex of ongoing programs. Moreover, the desire to retain key personnel and accumulated expertise argues for maintaining a relatively steady level of effort. Yet even successfully developed weapons systems may never see deployment in significant numbers.

Procurement may fluctuate greatly between periods of active hostilities and relative peace, as was demonstrated in the cases of Vietnam and Korea. Such limited wars may also significantly affect the *mix* of weapons to be procured, skewing dollars away from strategic and into tactical weaponry.

The decade of the 1970s saw considerable emphasis placed on so-called "bargaining chips": weapons systems developed with the nominal intention of bargaining them away for offsetting concessions in arms control negotiations. An instructive example is provided by the modern cruise missile. Initially developed as a SALT bargaining chip, it demonstrates the fundamental problem of bargaining chips: once developed, it became too attractive to the potential users for them to allow it to be bargained away. It is not at all uncommon for weapons systems to be caught up in protracted bureaucratic–political struggles before moving from development to procurement and deployment. The long history of efforts to procure a manned bomber as a successor to the B-52, proceeding through the ups and downs of the B-70 and B-1 programs, provides a good example. Here, again, there is a crucial feedback: the availability of a weapon often has significant influences on perceptions and assessments of needs.

The remarks above constitute only the briefest of sketches of the myriad interactions between the complex of factors influencing the size, composition, and possible uses of the U.S. strategic arsenal. Any truly comprehensive treatment is beyond the scope of this volume, and could be at least a full book in its own right. For the reader interested in more extended expositions of these topics, a number of citations have been included in the summary paragraphs above. Nonetheless, while there is well-developed literature on some of these themes, such as budgetary phenomena in general and defense budgeting in particular, the material available on other themes is quite limited. Accordingly, the next several sections are devoted to more detailed considerations of topics chosen in order to summarize and build upon the better-developed parts of the literature, and to flesh out the parts that are less well developed, or in which there have been important recent developments. The general focus of selection is the interaction of politics and technology in the strategic weapons acquisition process. Topics include the influences of the interactive environment; the intelligence and assessment process; the roles of technology; institutionalized arms control; and other influences on strategic program decision making. Empirical evidence about selected aspects of the process is given throughout the chapter, in references to other sections of this volume, and through references to the works of others. The final section provides a brief summary and concluding remarks.

INFLUENCES OF THE INTERACTIVE ENVIRONMENT

There is no isolation in the world of contemporary strategic weapons; every government is in either active or potential interaction with its envi-

TABLE 3.1 Themes in the Arms Expenditure Literature

Central Explanatory Locus	Theme or Process	Principal Authors	Policy Advocates
International			
	(1) Action–Reaction	Ricardson (1960)	McNamara E. Kennedy
	(2) War Mobilization (Ratchet Up)	Russett (1970)	
Domestic			
	(3) Bureaucratic Politics	Allison (1971) Kanter (1972) Ostrom (1977)	
	(4) Political–Business Cycle (Military– Industrial Complex)	Griffin et al (1981)	

ronment. For the superpowers that interaction is complex, consuming, and extremely active; and the fact that essentially every strategic doctrine presumes the existence of some threat external to the home government is only one aspect of the inherently international and interactive character of any strategic weapons regime. That character is fundamental to all strategic interpretation and planning; the manner in which we believe the strategic weapons regime to be organized and to function will influence the ways we interpret data received both from within and without our own government.

Let us approach the question of how the strategic weapons regime functions by focusing on the broader issue about just what mechanisms drive military spending. There is a substantial literature on this topic in political science and economics, and, considering the centrality of the issue, one might be somewhat surprised at the lack of consensus. Four major explanations can be identified, and they need not always be viewed as mutually exclusive. Those explanations and some of their principal expositors are listed in Table 3.1. The action–reaction process (ARP) model has its explanatory locus in international interactions, while in the bureaucratic politics (BP) and political–business cycle (PBC) models we assume that the primary incentives to military spending arise within nation-states, and the war mobilization (WM) model combines interactional and domestic motivations. Let us consider each of these models for what it says about the process of strategic weapons building and for the policy implications a believer might draw from the model.

The Action–Reaction Process (ARP) Model

The action–reaction process (ARP, or action–reaction phenomenon) model is perhaps the best known of the four and is frequently alluded to in discussions of "arms races." As in the prisoners' dilemma, the fundamental motivation is fear—in this case, fear of the possible consequences of failing to have adequate capability for response to the present damage potential posed by an opponent's existing arsenal or the future damage potential implied by that opponent's arms expenditures. If at least one party desires a "margin of strength" or if all parties desire parity but cannot agree on how it is to be measured, the system has the potential for an upward spiral in arms acquisitions limited only by war or the onset of economic limitations. Hence, the "arms race." ARP systems have been the subjects of a small but hardy band of analysts who have explored their implications through mathematical modeling, beginning with the pioneering work of Lewis Fry Richardson (1960) and continuing through the works of Baugh (1977a, 1977b, 1978), Brito and Intriligator (1974, 1977b, 1981, and others), Gillespie et al. (1976, 1977), and Smoker (1963a, 1963b, 1964, 1965), among others. The ARP model has also been adopted by policy analysts who have used it in the interpretation of historical data. Two of the more interesting examples of analysts performing this kind of interpretation are Richardson, who incorporated the ARP concept in his mathematical model of arms expenditures and then applied the model to the World War I case (1960, Chapter II), and Tammen, who applied it to the U.S. decision to deploy MIRVs (1973, especially Chapter 1). Finally, there is abundant evidence that at least some recent political leaders have held the ARP theory, among them Secretary of Defense McNamara (1967b) and Senator Edward Kennedy.

This last point is of more than passing interest, because the ARP model has significant policy implications. First, it predicts an arms race under circumstances that seem much more probable than the conditions required to prevent such racing, for if the motivation to arm is fear of an opponent, domestic economic limits to arming impose the only natural constraint. Political constraints may also be applied, however. It may be possible to freeze arms quantities or military spending if all parties can accept a parity principle. Presuming that no government will long accept a formalized position of inferiority, a freeze on arms or spending requires that each government give up the desire for a margin of superiority and accept the only other politically salient point (i.e., parity). In this connection, it is interesting to note that in Richardson's mathematical model arms spending can be stable only if the product (over both governments in a two-nation model) of "fatigue and expense" coefficients (which reflect the difficulty of a marginal increase in defense spending) exceeds the product of the reaction coefficients. (See, e.g., Baugh, 1978, or Blalock, 1969, Chapter 6.)

A second serious implication of the ARP model is that reaction leads naturally to a bias toward worst-case analysis. As McNamara (1967b) noted:

When calculating the force we require, we must be "conservative" in all our estimates of both a potential aggressor's capabilities and his intentions. Security depends upon taking a "worst plausible case" . . .

Pitman (1969) has noted that in the practical world of strategic weapons the process of action and reaction is exacerbated by uncertainty about a number of points, including (1) performance characteristics of an opponent's weaponry, (2) numbers of deployed weapons, (3) technological innovations, (4) research and development lead times, and (5) attempts to be deceptive about the numbers and characteristics of weapons. Coupling worst-case analysis to any such uncertainty leads automatically to overreaction. If complete information and its accurate assessment would lead to a level of military effort just barefly stable, a nominally "conservative, damage-limiting" assessment in any area of uncertainty will lead to a higher-than-required level of effort, which in turn will trigger a response and destabilize the system.

According to the ARP model, the statement that "There's no such thing as too much defense" is clearly incorrect. "Too much" can be either what one cannot afford or what will scare an opponent either into attacking or attempting to outspend until one side or the other is driven up against some economic constraint. Knowledgeable accounts indicate that part of the first session of the SALT I negotiations was devoted to a U.S. attempt to "sell" the ARP model to the Soviets. Barton and Weiler note that:

> The first session in Helsinki was largely exploratory, amounting almost to a seminar in strategic theory. . . . Among the issues discussed . . . were the action–reaction phenomenon, the concept of deterrence, the effects of ABM, and, in general terms, various alternative approaches to limiting strategic arms . . . (1976, 180)

They further note that "during this first session it became clear each (government) sought unilateral advantages by defining 'strategic system' differently" (1976, 180). Additionally, Newhouse remarks that "parity, it was felt, would serve Soviet purposes, but not necessarily America's" (1973, 166). Key figures in the SALT I negotiations thus demonstrate both belief in the ARP model and policy positions like those the model inferentially warns us against.

An additional implication of the ARP model is that the way to break the cycle of fear and reaction is through communication between erstwhile competitors, a conclusion shared with the prisoners' dilemma model. If one arms because of fear of the consequences of falling behind an opponent, communication offers perhaps the only real chance to become convinced that the opponent's actual intent is not really dire. In the world of political interactions, of course, such trust may be almost impossible to achieve. Communication offers the hope of a lesser but useful achievement; if mutual acceptance of some parity principle is the only politically acceptable stable solution in an ARP system, such acceptance is much more likely to be reached through negotiation than through tacit bargaining without direct contact. We are thus led naturally from the ARP model to institutionalized arms control as a means of limiting the action–reaction cycle.

There is some evidence that key decision makers who adhered to the ARP model were in fact led to seek arms limitation agreements. Newhouse (1973, 46) remarks that "even now, Russian diplomats speak admiringly of McNamara's early initiatives aimed at starting talks." And Richard Nixon, who entered the White House as a skeptic but came to support SALT very strongly, made some interesting observations in his very carefully worded March 14, 1969 announcement of his administration's new plans for ABM deployments. The Nixon administration had inherited the Sentinal ABM program, first announced under Lyndon Johnson as a light city-defense system. In redirecting the system to ICBM defense, the new administration seemed to adhere to assured destruction doctrine. Asserting that the modified system had "been designed so that its defensive intent is unmistakable," Nixon noted that an alternative heavy city-defense deployment "might look to an opponent like the prelude to an offensive strategy threatening the Soviet deterrent" (Newhouse, 1973, 152).

While adherents of the ARP model may be led to seek arms-limitation agreements in order to stabilize the deterrent system and limit expenditures, in the absence of such agreements the model leaves an extremely serious question: how conservatively must "threat" be evaluated, and *which of various competing measures of threat are to be accepted*? A particularly severe problem is posed by the use of a "Greater-than-Expected" Threat (GET). As Newhouse notes,

> The term, or concept, signifies an enemy capability that exceeds the "high end" of the range of threat in the National Intelligence Estimates (NIE's). Acceptance of the concept meant laying down an orderly process of planning to hedge against it. The question was how to hedge . . . (1973, 72)

The only inherent upper limits to GETs are those imposed by the requirements of political and military credibility. Compounding the already grim implications of the ARP model for action–reaction spirals, this concept tends to institutionalize worst-case analysis. And while not often public, conflicts between different Washington factions over the seriousness of threats have occasionally attracted considerable notice. Tammen (1973, 27–28) cites congressional testimony to the effect that in the MIRV debates then-Secretary of Defense Laird frequently cited Soviet threat levels exceeding the NIE, a practice pointed out and roundly criticized by Senate Foreign Relations Committee Chairman Fulbright. An even more public example occurred in the Ford administration, with the "Team A, Team B" case. Having appointed two teams of experts to assess Soviet military effort, with one extending the previous estimates and the other taking a much more conservative and pessimistic view, the administration adopted the more extreme set of evaluations to use in arguing for increases in the DOD budget. A more recent example is found in the debate over "ICBM vulnerability" in general, and U.S. vulnerability to a Soviet first strike in particular, both points to be considered in detail in Chapter 5. We turn next, however, to an alternative model for military expenditures—the War Mobilization (WM) model.

The War Mobilization (WM) Model

The War Mobilization (WM) model asserts that increases in military spending come not so much from direct reaction to an opponent as from permanent escalation during and immediately following any war (Russett, 1970, 2–5). In effect, there is an indirect action–reaction process in which military expenditures, having made a quantum jump during the war, never drop back to their prewar level. That quantum jump, of course, is facilitated by perceptions of threat and need, so that in wartime the defense budget accounts for the greatest proportion of increases in government spending (Crecine, 1970, 32). Military spending is thus said to "ratchet up" in wartime.

Obvious questions occur, however, about whether all *segments* of the military budget are affected equally, and about whether the WM argument should be considered to apply to real (uninflated) or only to nominal expenditures. Regarding the first point, for example, we know that the winding down of the Vietnam war was accompanied both by new strategic weapons programs and by substantial reductions in total military personnel. Suppose we divide the DOD budget into the following four major segments:

Operation and Maintenance (OM)

Personnel

Procurement

Research, Development, Test, and Evaluation (RDT&E)

Since World War II these four categories have accounted for 92–97 percent of DOD expenditures annually. OM expenditures finance operating costs for equipment and facilities, fuel, supplies, and repair parts, and currently account for about 30 percent of the DOD budget. This category tends to fluctuate over time, rising in wartime and falling afterward. Personnel costs cover active and retired military personnel, and tend to ratchet up in wartime, remaining higher after a war largely because of the continuing postwar costs of paying benefits to former military personnel. This effect tends not to be offset by postwar decreases in total active personnel, and personnel costs currently run about one-third of the DOD budget. Procurement covers acquisition costs of all types of durable military equipment. While this segment of the budget has fluctuated considerably, it has also shown a tendency to ratchet up. To some degree the *types* of weapons procured are skewed by war, e.g., toward tactical weapons during the

Vietnam war and toward strategic weapons afterward. Rapidly inflating costs of new weaponry have tended to push the procurement share upward, although this effect has been offset somewhat by delays in acquisitions and by reductions in the total quantities procured. Finally, the RDT&E share of the DOD budget, discussed above in the introduction to this chapter, is generally quite stable, running about 10 percent.

Given the tendency of procurement to ratchet up, we should expect that the nominal cost of strategic weapons programs will rise over time. Yet, with the exception of the Vietnam war peak, the total DOD budget in real dollars has remained relatively constant since the onset of the Korean war, so that the WM argument appears not to apply to the *real* defense budget. Two caveats may be noted, however. First, disagreement about the real levels of U.S. and Soviet defense efforts exists because it is always difficult to determine what precise deflator to apply to military expenditures. (See, e.g., Central Intelligence Agency, 1978.) Second, programs to raise real defense spending announced late in the Carter administration and early in the Reagan administration may lead to real-dollar ratcheting upward in the procurement of strategic weapons. In particular, plans in both administrations to deploy the MX missile and in the Reagan administration to revive the B-1 bomber program could have that effect.

Some empirical evidence about past military spending supports the WM model. While that evidence thus implies something about the actions of military and political leaders, however, it tells us nothing directly about the beliefs that motivate them to those actions. In particular, the WM model is not necessarily inconsistent with the ARP, BP, or PBC models. It does have at least two significant policy implications, however: (1) since nominal spending tends to rise over time, pressures perceived by those leaders who do accept the ARP model may tend to increase; and (2) if we institutionalize arms control, we can expect significant pressures for spending on uncontrolled new and preexistent programs.

The Bureaucratic Politics (BP) Model

The bureaucratic politics (BP) model is widely accepted, and is perhaps best known to international-relations scholars through Allison's summary and application to the Cuban Missile Crisis (1971). The origins of the model, however, lie primarily in the literature of organizational decision making. In brief, the BP model asserts that problems are solved by incremental changes to existing programs, and that organizations have an inherent dynamic of survival and expansion. That dynamic is echoed in the pioneering budgetary analysis of Davis, Dempster, and Wildavsky (1966), who found that the best predictor to current budget was last year's budget times a multiplier for inflation and expansion, plus an increment for new programs. The BP model predicts that any agency will at minimum attempt to preserve its existing programs, budgets, personnel, and areas of responsibility, and will seek to expand them whenever possible. The motivations for such actions assertedly arise from natural human tendencies to seek responsibility, power, and their attendant benefits.

There is a good deal of evidence to support both the incremental decision making and the organizational survival and growth premises of the BP model. In the strategic weapons field, this model provides an explanation for the remarkable persistence of "triad" doctrine, despite the fact that the emergence of the triad was incremental. Once the triad had been deployed, too many agencies had stakes in maintaining each constituent mission. Another example may be found in the quest of some segments of the U.S. Navy, continuing since the end of the Vietnam war, to find some mission to justify pulling a few battleships out of mothballs. That justification appears to have been found by the Reagan administration and accepted by Congress, in the form of a plan to deploy up to four battleships refitted as missile carriers, despite continuing doubts about the Navy's ability to recruit enough qualified personnel to crew the ships. On balance, it appears that the BP model captures at least some aspects of the dynamics of organizational decision making and budgeting.

Furthermore, the implications of the BP model are not necessarily inconsistent with the WM model. War clearly requires expansion of some military-agency missions, and the BP model predicts that the missions less vulnerable to postwar cutbacks will survive at the new, higher levels of activity and funding. Regarding arms control, both models imply that it will be very difficult to curtail deployment programs already under way. The BP model also predicts that decisions *not to deploy* a weapon that has already been developed will seldom be considered final by the developing agencies, which will bring continuing pressure for reconsideration and reversal. The B-1 bomber program is a case in point. With respect to the problem of "arms races," the BP model seems to predict a slow but steady growth in military spending (what Richard Smoke (1975, 152) has termed a "march") rather than an accelerating race or spiral. (Except for a small number of works devoted to BP models, e.g., Charles Ostrom (1977), the majority of efforts to model arms expenditures formally have assumed an ARP phenomenon as their point of departure, a situation which has caused that entire literature to be referred to as "arms race modelling." (For an alternative approach to treating the case of slow growth in arms spending by means of formal mathematical models, see Baugh, 1977b.)

For the U.S.–Soviet system, BP appears superior to ARP as a model of actual aggregate spending patterns. Recently, however, Michael Squires (1982a, 1982b) has found evidence to support an action–reaction process between U.S. and Soviet strategic weapons deployments, according to some very politically salient measures of strategic "balance," a point discussed further in Chapter 4. Finally, to the extent that the BP model implies that organization size and budget are measures of power and influence, the long-range prospects for arms control, an organizational constraint quite opposed to the thrust of the BP dynamic of survival and expansion, might be evaluated by contrasting the Department of Defense with the United States Arms Control and Disarmament Agency (ACDA), which consists of some 200 persons housed within the State Department.

The Political–Business Cycle (PBC) Model

Another alternative to the BP model, and one not totally inconsistent with it, is the political–business cycle (PBC) model. Developed by economists and political scientists mostly in the early 1970s, the PBC model has been reduced by Nincic and Cusack (1979, 104) to a set of propositions which may be paraphrased as follows:

1. The performance of the economy at large influences electoral outcomes for incumbent political authorities.
2. Incumbents therefore attempt to manipulate the economy for their electoral ends.
3. Military expenditures affect overall economic performance.
4. Incumbents therefore attempt to use military spending, at least partially, for political–electoral purposes.

Proposition (1) is supported by the studies of Kramer (1971) and Tufte (1975), both of whom found that relatively modest changes in disposable real personal income induced changes of four to six percent in the congressional vote for the incumbent party. Tufte (1978, 3–28) also found that postwar increases in real disposable income coincided with election years, and that unemployment rates declined in the two years preceding presidential elections, tending to support proposition 2. Support for proposition 3 can be found from economists and political scientists occupying many different positions on a liberal–conservative spectrum, although radical analysts tend to assign greater importance to military expenditures than do their more conservative colleagues. A "mainstream" statement can be found in Hitch and McKean's observation that defense spending "tends to buoy up total spending (and) makes a deficiency of total demand less probable" (1961, 69). John Kenneth Galbraith (1967, 235) assigns a somewhat greater role to defense spending in the "regulation of demand," and, from a more radical perspective, James Cypher (1977, 1) maintains that "postwar stabilization has (for the most part) been achieved by manipulating military expenditures."

While some anecdotal evidence to support proposition 4 can be found in the memoirs of statesmen (see, e.g., Nincic and Cusack, 1979, 106–107), the ultimate acceptance or rejection of the PBC model must rest on empirical tests of that proposition. The model is usually structured to assert that increases in military spending will occur before and during presidential election years, and decreases in the years following such elections (hence a "political–business cycle"), with the changes being consciously manipulated by the incumbent party. "Consciousness" of manipulation, of course, is not directly testable, but the other variables are open to observation. Nincic and Cusack (1979, especially 108) predicted changes in real U.S. defense spending over the period 1948–1976, using an econometric model including variables for (a) the previous year's change, (b) war involvement (a function representing rapid buildup over two years and a smaller exponential decline after the end of the war, the pattern seen in both the Korean and Vietnam conflicts), (c) election timing (a dummy variable calling for increases in presidential election and preelection years, and decreases for two years after such elections), and (d, e) change in private consumption and investment spending. They found that, ceteris paribus, military spending is cut back at a rate of two billion dollars per year after presidential elections, and expanded at a similar rate in the two years prior to those elections. Their overall R-squared was 0.71, and the T-statistics of all but the consumption and investment terms were significant at the five-percent level or better.

This constitutes fairly strong evidence that changes in U.S. military spending are cyclical and that those cycles are correlated with the political calendar. Although the BP model predicts spending that tends to increase slowly and regularly, this evidence could be interpreted as indicating that political leaders and legislators collaborate to time increases for their own political benefit, either with or without the cooperation of the permanent bureaucracy. Given the long-term trend for real military expenditures to be nondeclining, however, that cooperation would probably be forthcoming. Nincic and Cusack's "war involvement" variable, in fact, includes the "ratcheting up" effect asserted by Russett (1970) in the WM model. To the extent that this cycle of spending changes is favorable to military contractors, the PBC model may also be reasonably compatible with the "military–industrial complex" model popular in some of the literature over the past decade. (See, e.g., Sarkesian, 1972, and Rosen, 1973.) While it is asserted to apply only to the United States (see, e.g., Lindbeck, 1976), the PBC model has some intriguing policy implications. Foreign believers in an ARP model might be misled both into excessive pessimism by preelection increases and into excessive optimism by postelection decreases. Otherwise, the PBC model is not necessarily incompatible with either the WM or BP models.

A particularly intriguing instance of political cycling of strategic weapons expenditures may be appearing in the case of the MX missile, although the evidence is not yet all in. Originally announced by President Carter, partly as a domestic bargaining chip to gain Senate ratification of SALT II, MX deployment was strongly supported by President Reagan both before and after the 1980 election. Yet by the fall of 1981, faced with strong opposition to MX deployment in Utah and Nevada and with a desire to limit defense spending increases in hopes of balancing the federal budget by 1984, the Reagan administration was seriously considering proposals to reduce MX deployment to perhaps half the missiles and one fourth the number of shelters originally planned. As will be shown in Chapter 5, under most basing schemes, scaling back the planned deployment would completely vitiate the intended impact of MX on the ICBM vulnerability problem, since by 1981 the Soviets *already* had enough separately targetable warheads to attack each Minuteman, each Titan, and each of 1000 MX shelters with two recent-generation reentry vehicles. By the summer of 1982, plans for MX basing had come full circle, from depending on dispersal and deceptive basing to depending on "close packing" and fratricide among attacking warheads in order to survive (Halloran, 1982a). The subsequent congressional rejection of dense pack basing led to an even more vulnerable basing proposal in April of 1983—deployment of 100 MX missiles in existing Minuteman III silos (Cannon, 1983b). Yet through all the changes in basing plans, the intent to develop MX and deploy it in *some* manner survived.

The four classes of models examined above may be distinguished by whether they assert an action–reaction process between governments (ARP) or assert that changes in military spending arise primarily from causes internal to nation-states (BP, PBC) or from a combination of internal and reactive factors (WM). Especially for ARP believers, and to a lesser extent for those who hold to other models, the action one proposes to one's home government is a function of (a) the way the strategic weapons regime is believed to operate and (b) the information available about the capability and intent of other governments. In the next section, therefore, we turn to the problems of gathering and interpreting information concerning potential opponents.

THE PROCESSES OF INTELLIGENCE AND ASSESSMENT

National Intelligence Estimates (NIEs) are documents which embody the intelligence community's current knowledge about the situation in some specific country or region, or about a particular topic, along with estimates of projected future developments. The Director of Central Intelligence (DCI), as the president's principal foreign intelligence advisor, is officially responsible for each NIE, which is supposed to reflect the DCI's judgment about the known (and knowable) facts and probable developments. While prepared for use at the highest policy levels of the government, NIEs represent the considered judgment of the entire intelligence community; major differences of opinion, where present, will be reflected in the text and footnotes of the NIE document (Fain et al., 1977, 43). Such differences, of course, are common and the attempt to project future developments often ends with a very wide range of disagreement. In the specific area of strategic weapons, NIEs have been prepared for such topics as whether early multiple-warhead tests of the SS-9 missile indicated a Soviet

MIRV program or simply MRVs, or whether the Soviets were attempting to achieve a first strike potential. Projections about such crucial topics as the U.S.–Soviet strategic balance may be prepared at many different times over the years, to reflect changing physical and political conditions.

In preparing and utilizing NIEs, officials must be concerned with a host of actual and potential problems, including the following: (a) Timeliness: Does the estimate reflect the latest available information? How long will it stay timely? Was it prepared and presented in time to have an appropriate bearing on policy decisions? (b) Completeness: Recognizing that truly complete information is only theoretically possible, in part because other governments will strive to limit access to data about their actions and intent, how closely is the ideal of completeness approached within the available time and with available resources? (c) Precision: Given the input data, are the conclusions replicable? (d) Accuracy: Recognizing the other limitations, are the asserted facts correct and do the projected events actually come to pass? (e) Relevance for action: Beyond the question of timeliness, does the NIE raise and answer the questions essential to making policy decisions about projected actions?

Additional potential problems include the following: (f) Bias: Is the estimate biased to reflect the perspective or interests of the department primarily responsible for its preparation, or of the CIA itself? Such biases could take many forms, including promoting particular types of actions (military, diplomatic) or principal reliance upon particular agencies or advancing the interests of one foreign government in preference to another. The 1973 shift to a system of 11 National Intelligence Officers (NIOs), each with staff responsibility to the DCI for intelligence collection and production activities in a geographical or functional specialty, increased the problem of agency bias, since each NIO is primarily identified with a single agency (Fain et al., 1977, 44). Interagency disputes that were previously reflected in the NIE drafting process may now surface only after the draft has been completed and circulated. (g) Filtering: Are particular facts or even completed estimates withheld because their conclusions and predictions contradict known user preferences regarding policy or outcomes? How severely is information distorted in transmission by being "interpreted" by each transmitting individual? (Tullock, 1965, 137–141). (h) Direct pressure: Are estimators pressured to reach certain specific answers or types of solutions, or to avoid others?

Examples of all these types of problems are not difficult to find, given the period of intensive analysis of intelligence failures and abuses that has followed the United States' withdrawal from Vietnam. At the grandest level, we now know that data on hand in Washington would have permitted a realistic assessment of the success probability of policies actually adopted in Vietnam. But while the intelligence-*gathering* system worked, the estimates were not presented or were not acted upon or were biased to reflect the desired "light at the end of the tunnel" (Hoopes, 1969).

Political pressures on the preparers of NIEs may also be found in the strategic weapons field. At the time of the SS-9 MRV-vs.-MIRV controversy in June of 1969, Henry Kissinger called DCI Richard Helms to the White House, argued that the Soviets had been conducting MIRV tests, and asked that a new draft NIE on Soviet strategic forces be rewritten to provide additional evidence supporting the DCI's view that the tests did not actually demonstrate a MIRV capability. Perhaps this case simply reflects necessary feedback between users and preparers; the requested rewriting was done but the conclusion remained unchanged. Those preparers involved, however, later stated that they had felt serious pressure and considered the White House actions to be "a subtle and indirect effort to alter the DCI's national intelligence judgement" (Fain et al., 1977, 46–47).

In another Nixon administration incident, political pressure was rather more heavy-handed and direct. An assistant to Secretary of Defense Laird informed DCI Helms that a paragraph in the draft NIE on Soviet strategic forces contradicted Laird's public position. The offending paragraph began as follows:

> We believe that the Soviets recognize the enormous difficulties of any attempt to achieve strategic superiority of such order as to significantly alter the strategic balance. Consequently, we consider it highly unlikely that they will attempt within the period of this estimate to achieve a first-strike capability . . .

Helms then deleted the nettlesome paragraph. Later, in a move indicative of the fact that reaching agreement on an NIE is actually a bureaucratic battle over ideas, the paragraph was restored as a footnote by the State Department representative on the United States Intelligence Board (Fain, et al. 1977, 47).

The bureaucratic battle over ideas takes place within what we have thus far casually referred to as the "intelligence community." The functionally defined "community," in fact, embraces analysts and officials in a number of agencies, which should lead us to expect all of the traditional sorts of bureaucratic maneuvers to advance the views and standings of particular agencies. Let us therefore review the principal agencies making up that system, drawing extensively on the summary provided by Fain et al. (1977, 24–25):

> The intelligence community is an administrative apparatus composed of specialized agencies with roles circumscribed by both statute and policy control. Some elements of it have evolved somewhat independently (such as the Department of Defense, the State Department, and the CIA) and have overlapping jurisdictions and capabilities. This framework exists and is encouraged to promote a "healthy competition" and "diversity of views" among the various elements of the community. Presided over in theory by a "director of Central Intelligence" and subjected to continuing review by four different coordinating bodies, plus the president's own staff, the various intelligence agencies are supposed to unify on matters of supreme importance. Four

organizations comprise the principal operating elements of the community:

Central Intelligence Agency. Established in 1947, the CIA was to correlate and evaluate foreign intelligence relating to the national security; to recommend to the NSC methods for the coordination of intelligence; and to perform those services that the NSC determined could be more efficiently accomplished centrally. It was authorized "to perform such other functions and duties as the NSC may from time to time direct," language often interpreted to authorize covert action. Police, subpoena, law enforcement powers, and internal security functions were forbidden. . . . The director of Central Intelligence is responsible for all activities of the CIA, but is also the principal intelligence adviser to the president and NSC, and thereby responsible for coordinating the activities of the entire intelligence community.

Bureau of Intelligence and Research. This State Department bureau is devoted to the assessment rather than the collection of intelligence. Serving policymakers in the State Department, INR manages the department's external research and provides departmental policy guidance for intelligence operations conducted by other agencies.

Department of Defense and the Defense Intelligence Agency. The DIA supports the Joint Chiefs of Staff and the secretary of defense with its own intelligence assessments and coordinates Department of Defense involvement in national intelligence. . . . A semiautonomous program within the Defense Department is the Program for Overhead Reconnaissance, which operates overhead reconnaissance programs for the entire intelligence community under the general direction of the DCI and the assistant secretary of defense for intelligence. In addition, it responds to specific requirements determined by a committee of the U.S. Intelligence Board. . . . Each of the armed services maintains sizable intelligence organizations and conducts its own cryptology. All participate in the production of national intelligence but concentrate on the security of installations and personnel and on the weaponry of their counterpart services in other countries.

National Security Agency. NSA is the largest of the intelligence agencies in personnel despite considerable contraction in recent years. It is responsible for monitoring foreign communications and other signals for analysis by other agencies. NSA is also responsible for protecting the security of U.S. communications and is technically part of DOD.

The intelligence units of the FBI, Treasury Department, and Energy Research and Development Administration are also formally part of the intelligence community, contributing specialized foreign intelligence on matters within their jurisdiction. . . .

With so many quasi-independent agencies, the intelligence community should be expected to display substantial internal disagreement on a regular basis. Even if consensus can be achieved, there is still the problem of potential clashes between the "reality" uncovered by the intelligence and assessment process, and the desires of top policymakers. In his testimony before the Pike Committee (1976, 26 January, 13–14), John Huizenga labeled this "a natural tension between intelligence and policy":

. . . the task of the former is to present as a basis for the decisions of policymakers as realistic as possible a view of forces and conditions in the external environment. Political leaders often find the picture presented less than congenial. . . . Thus, a DCI who does his job well will more often than not be the bearer of bad news, or at least will make things seem disagreeable, complicated. and uncertain. . . . When intelligence people are told, as happened in recent years, that they were expected to get on the team, then a sound intelligence-policy relationship has in effect broken down.

Gaining and acting upon accurate assessments of the capabilities and intent of other governments are thus subject to a wide variety of misfires, ranging from the difficulties of obtaining sufficient data, through interpretational disagreements exacerbated by all the forces of bureaucratic politics, to the all-too-frequent unwillingness of leaders to accept an unwelcome message. Moreover, throughout the intelligence gathering and assessment process the questions asked, the data accepted, and the interpretations placed on that data will all be influenced by beliefs about the way the strategic weapons regime functions, as explored in the previous section. In the following section we turn to some considerations of the roles of technology as it interacts with strategic doctrine and the politics of managing the strategic weapons regime.

THE ROLES OF TECHNOLOGY

The relationship of technology to strategy may be symbiotic, with each lending legitimacy to the other. The degree to which either dominates the other may change with circumstances and the character of political leaders.

Pranger and Labrie (1977, 4)

Technology is both a constraint and an incentive in the strategic weapons regime. Constraint arises mainly in that we cannot always achieve the technology to build desired weaponry at the precise times that doctrine may require. Such a constraint was seen in the apparent impossibility of achieving a reliable and sufficient ABM technology in the 1960s and early 1970s. Incentive, however, arises in the normal workings of the scientific research and technological development communities, coupled with the fears that governments have in interacting with one another. What is possible for one government to envision and develop usually can be envisioned (or learned about through espionage) and developed by an opposing government, provided that it has a comparable scientific and industrial base and commits the necessary resources.

Unfortunately, this leads to a very serious instance of the prisoners' dilemma: if one can conceive of a weapons system, either offensive or defensive, that would make a significant difference in the strategic weapons regime, one had best develop it before any opponent can develop and deploy the same system or a counter to it. Even if you intend no offensive use of the new weapon, its mere possession may have significant political payoffs both domestically and in dealing with the opponent and other governments. The advantage conveyed by a new weapons system may be only transient, until the opponent can match or counter it. Yet in the strategic weapons regime (as in other spheres of activity) political leaders are notoriously reluctant to credit opponents with their own level of restraint from exploiting transient advantages.

This prisoners' dilemma incentive extends even into the realm of arms control agreements: a government which believes it can achieve a transient advantage with some new weapon is unlikely to agree to limit its deployment. The refusal of the United States to consider limits on MIRVs at the time of SALT I provides a good example. (Recall Tammen, 1973.) While stringent limits on deploying the unpromising 1960s ABM technology were reached in SALT I, MIRVs were ignored, despite the fact that they were first conceived as a means of saturating and thus overcoming a widespread ABM system. Thus, in the early 1970s the United States, which alone had deployed MIRVs, gained a temporary advantage in total number of warheads. Moreover, Soviet acquiescence in ignoring the MIRV issue in SALT I reminds us that transient advantages often can be reversed, since in the later 1970s the Soviets were able to equip their larger and more numerous ICBMs with MIRVs and thereby present the United States with an ICBM vulnerability challenge. The field of arms control is therefore seen to combine a game of new technological developments with a game of political constraints on the utilization of those developments.

Considering the stakes in those games, it should come as no surprise that the superpowers maintain research and development (RDT&E) efforts consistently representing a significant and relatively constant share of their total defense budgets, as noted in the introduction to this chapter. Granting that some element of probability enters the payoff of any research program, the very existence of massive and continuing military R&D programs cannot help but lead, over the long run, to a continuing technological "creep" or "drift" of ever-improving performance and a succession of new types of weapons. (See, e.g., Shapley, 1978.) That drift will occur not only because of the governments' desires to obtain and/or exploit advantages, but also because of the inherent dynamic of science and engineering: if an improvement can be envisioned, it becomes a challenge that must be realized. New developments are therefore "pulled" along by this dynamic at the same time that they are "pushed" by prisoners' dilemma fears.

Building on that dynamic, Harry Gelber (1974, 523–528) has identified 10 "categories of real or potential advantages" that the superpowers might hope to gain by seeking technological innovations in strategic weaponry. A paraphrasing of Gelber's categories follows, with some comments.

1. The urge to know, to refine understanding of scientific principles

and increase expertise, for improving management forecasts and for deciding what systems to produce and deploy.
2. Production of more effective and efficient weapons than those of the opponent. The problem of ICBM vulnerability, as previously noted, arises because of a technological creep in accuracy improvements. And, as Shapley (1978) notes, that creep was relatively inexpensive. It attracted little political attention beyond the "retargeting" debates of the mid-1970s, discussed in Chapter 2, under the heading, "The SALT I Aftermath."
3. Development of weapons likely to avoid particular sets of legal or political prohibitions. Unfortunately, establishment of limited arms controls increases this incentive, as, for example, the selective and quantitative limitations in SALT I gave impetus to pursue qualitative improvements and to exploit unconstrained types of weaponry.
4. Increasing freedom of maneuver, for example by shortening lead times for new forms of deployment, or by promoting the ability to take rapid advantage of any new technological development.
5. Increasing the possibilities for influencing, or even manipulating, the decisions of an opponent, by possessing technical initiatives and the attendant advantages in lead times. An opponent might be forced to build larger numbers of weapons the effectiveness of which had been threatened, or to spend heavily to develop some counter to a threat that might never be deployed. This incentive is closely related to the never-well-actualized theory of bargaining chips in arms control negotiations.
6. Sustaining the effectiveness of national intelligence efforts. True scientific and technological "breakthroughs" are not easily predictable and tend to result from the serendipitous and synergistic pooling of ideas and research results communicated across national boundaries in a worldwide scientific community (See, e.g., Burke, 1978, and, for some contrasting positions, Gelber, 1974, 512.) Nonetheless, ceteris paribus, the government which has technological superiority can better anticipate where an opponent's technology is likely to move. As Dr. William Foster (1972) testified when he was Director of Defense RDT&E, "In those areas where we acknowledge technological parity or inferiority, we cannot have high confidence in our estimates of Soviet capability, nor can we predict with confidence what their next steps forward will be."
7. Influencing an opponent's strategic perceptions and resource allocations at minimal cost. Since there are tradeoffs between information and deployed weaponry, the side with a technological lead may wish to decrease the opponent's uncertainties in selected respects. Deterrence may be promoted and the oppo-

nent restrained by sharing some information about the capabilities of one's own weaponry. Decreasing the opponent's uncertainties may also reduce ARP effects and lower the feedback on both your own deployments and your own RDT&E efforts. In effect, this is the arms-race-dampening alternative side of the influence incentive suggested above at (5).
8. Pursuing strategic deception and exploiting political advantages that arise from technical possibilities. The skillful use of disinformation about one's own RDT&E program, even if the deceptions were not lasting, could misdirect, confuse, and blunt an opponent's R&D program.
9. Diplomatic effects vis-à-vis allies. Sharing of information from a great power capable of sustaining a large research effort can strengthen allies militarily and tighten political bonds. Sharing research costs also can reduce great power expenditures without impairing security.
10. R&D effort as a domestic program. R&D effort has proved much less vulnerable to domestic political challenges than have actual deployments of new weapons systems. Bureaucratic pressures will therefore dictate support of technological advances to maintain organizations and budget shares, to keep new weapons systems "alive" for possible later deployment, and to maintain a relatively inexpensive "hedge" against uncertain futures.

The confluence of these many incentives seems to ensure a large and continuing military R&D program, with its attendant technological drift. That drift, in turn, implies a fundamental problem in achieving meaningful and lasting arms control: if control agreements are based on specific technologies of (a) weapons and (b) verification, then technological drift will be accentuated toward new types of weapons subject to less stringent constraints, and/or toward developments which may not be verifiable using the agreed means. Both effects are demonstrated over the period from SALT I to SALT II. Following SALT I ratification the United States pursued vigorous development of modern cruise missiles. Unconstrained by SALT I, they were severely threatening to the USSR, prompting the Soviet government to press for cruise-missile controls in SALT II. Yet such controls were difficult to provide under the previously accepted verification formulae. The 1979 SALT II agreements specified deployment delays and quantitative limits on numbers of carrier aircraft, numbers of cruise missiles per aircraft, and range of cruise missiles; but each of these limits was exceedingly difficult to verify with high confidence using available technology.

Cruise missiles are relatively small and may be hidden easily; the Navy Tomahawk can be launched from a submarine torpedo tube, and other cruise missiles are of comparable size. Conversion of large commercial aircraft such as Boeing 747s to cruise missile carriers would be quite difficult to detect and could be carried out quickly; verification of numbers of cruise missiles carried *inside* either bombers or commercial aircraft is essentially impossible by any means other than espionage. Finally, the range of a cruise missile can be extended some hundreds of miles by lengthening the missile two feet or so to provide additional fuel tankage, so that range is exceedingly hard to verify by remote means. In every respect, then, the cruise missile limits agreed upon in SALT II are not susceptible to high-confidence verification without the use of intrusive, close-up means of checking.

Additional severe verification problems were posed by new developments in MIRVing and ICBM mobility following SALT I. The SALT II agreements of 1979 limited the number of independently targetable RVs to a maximum of 10 per ICBM, limited the fraction of missiles that could be MIRVed, and permitted deployment of mobile ICBMs only after 1981. None of these limitations could be verified with complete confidence by remote means. The verification of the limit on RVs per missile relies on the assumption—argued differently by different authorities—that no missile would be deployed with a system of RVs that had not been fully flight-tested. Verification thus relies strongly upon observations of tests. High-resolution radars and satellite photography are capable of determining the numbers and sizes of RVs tested. Additionally, to some extent, tracing reentry paths can distinguish between true RVs and dummies that might indicate additional carrying capacity on the test missile.

Yet missiles have been deployed before with untested RVs—the Minuteman I being one example. As to which missiles are deployed with MIRVs, the SALT II negotiators had to settle on a formula that all missiles of a type that has been *tested* with MIRVs are assumed to be MIRVed, yet the only certain way to verify this would be to conduct on-site inspections of randomly selected missiles. Finally, the introduction of mobility vastly complicates the problems of counting missile launchers, as seen in Soviet concern about the U.S. MX and in U.S. concern about possible conversion of the Soviets' mobile SS-20 MRBMs into SS-16 ICBMs by the addition of a third stage. In the MX basing plans proposed by the Carter administration, considerable ingenuity was devoted to cooperative verification measures which would offer the Soviets assurance by satellite photography that the allowed number of missiles was not being exceeded. (See the second section of Chapter 5.)

In each of these instances, verification has been greatly complicated by new technological developments that strain the limits of the verification means agreed upon in SALT I. As Robert Perry has observed (1977, 1),

> The arms control agreements of 1972 were the products of negotiating initiatives of the early 1960s which acquired form and substance in the late 1960s and were formalized nearly a decade after the weapons they addressed had

been developed and (to some extent) deployed. The means of verification so precisely unspecified in the various agreements were of similar vintage. Thus the verification measures agreed upon in 1972 were those deemed adequate, largely on the basis of experience in the late 1960s, to confirm mutual compliance with agreements limiting the numbers and quality of strategic weapons from the era of the mid-1960s.

There is thus a continuing cycle consisting of technological development, weapons deployment, and arms control, and there is little or no evidence that the cycle is converging on a more stable strategic weapons regime. Arms control agreements have tended to fix the technology of verification, which has acted together with the forms of constraints themselves to guide the directions of future weapons developments. New political formulations have then been required to take account of the new technologies and to bring about acceptance of verification technologies adequate to the changed task. The history of SALT II in attempting to constrain qualitative improvements in missilery by using SALT I vintage national technical means (NTM) of verification is not encouraging, and contributed heavily to some Senators' serious doubts about enforceability when the treaty was put forward in 1979 for ratification. As Perry has observed, "*Assured Detection* is likely to be as fundamental to American concepts of strategic deterrence in the 1980s as was Assured Destruction in the 1960s" (1977, 9). Assurance of detection, like "margins of safety," is likely to be determined as much by the mind of the perceiver as by any external, physical realities.

The continuing game of weapons development, deployment, and arms control may also be greatly complicated by differences between the technological and development "styles" of the two superpowers. Perry notes that

> ... the USSR ordinarily invests in an R&D process that relies on incremental, sequential improvement of previously developed and deployed weapons—with certain important exceptions—and the United States normally prefers technological thresholding—also with some significant exceptions. Though important, the exceptions require departures from normal practices that cannot become "normal" in either country within the next decade or so. (1977, 23)

Despite its substantial scientific establishment, the Soviet Union may be less able to exploit new technology than the United States, and the Soviets have repeatedly expressed interest in U.S. R&D and industrial management processes (Perry, 1977, 23–26).

Differential technological flexibility may pose a real difficulty in achieving arms control agreements, since the agreements tend to skew R&D into new and uncontrolled areas. Such a concern on the part of the Soviets seems to be reflected in Professor Yu. Kulish's comment (1972, 214) that "the reliability of the existing [SALT I] agreements may be considerably reduced if the United States continues its policy of achieving scientific and technological superiority in strategic arms developments . . ." In the history of ICBM developments, U.S. technology has repeatedly leapfrogged that of the Soviets. The USSR built a small early ICBM lead in the late 1950s only to have the United States match it rapidly and move immediately to second-generation solid-fueled ICBMs. The Soviets then moved into their second-generation ICBM program only to have the United States take the initiative in developing MIRVs. Most authorities continued to credit the United States with superior missile accuracy at least up to 1980, and perceptions of an imbalance in ICBM vulnerability (see Chapter 5) are based not on superior Soviet technology but on their larger numbers of ICBMs carrying larger warheads.

Another aspect of differing technological styles is that different development establishments may have fundamentally dissimilar design approaches or philosophies, which may lead to system asymmetries that complicate the process of arriving at arms controls. Soviet heavy ICBMs are a classic example; the United States opted early for smaller missiles on the assumption that it could develop miniaturized warheads and guidance systems. Yet by the time of SALT I, the superior throw-weight of the larger Soviet missiles had come to pose a problem; it was politically difficult to accept the asymmetry that had arisen technologically.

Differences of approach are also clearly seen in other areas at technological frontiers; the U.S. and Soviet space programs provide good examples of contrasting approaches. U.S. manned space efforts have involved a series of distinct programs—Mercury, Gemini, Apollo, and the space shuttle—each building on its predecessors but with no operational time overlap, often having long periods with no space flights at all between programs, and with entirely new hardware for each program. This continuing push for new hardware featuring the latest and highest technology is consistent with Head's observation (1978, 548) that the U.S. weapons acquisition process is dominated by "military preferences for high performance and industry competition for new contracts." The Soviet space program, in contrast, has involved a fairly steady series of launches, fewer generations of hardware, smaller changes from generation to generation, and some overlap between the series of spacecraft in use. Still other differences are seen in the design philosophies of that space hardware. U.S. programs from the first have emphasized astronauts as pilots, highly trained individuals who have a significant role in flying their spacecraft, which tend to be very heavily instrumented in the manner of fighter aircraft or modern jetliners. This trend is accentuated in the space shuttle, which has very extensive on-board computing facilities designed to make it much more independent of ground control than its predecessors. Soviet spacecraft, on the other hand, have emphasized ground control, automated docking in orbit, and a crew status more akin to that of passengers and experimenters.

Still another example of differing U.S. and Soviet technological styles can be found in long-range bomber development. (See Perry, 1979, 16.) Theory that is just being rediscovered by the builders of U.S. jetliners suggests that a turboprop system will make most efficient use of turbine propulsion. Soviet designers applied this principle to a whole generation of strategic bombers at the same time that U.S. and British designers were obtaining superior performance from turbojet bombers while, with the exceptions of re-engined older passenger aircraft and the ill-fated Lockheed Electra, ignoring turboprop propulsion.

The turboprop-versus-turbojet case provides an interesting demonstration that the theoretically most-efficient technology may not prove most amenable to development and use, and the 1950s attempts to develop long-range cruise missiles provide another example. It appears that at any given time only certain problems are amenable to solution, and that it is not always possible to predict the most appropriate technologies. We might thus speak both of appropriate technologies and appropriate problems, where an appropriate problem is solvable by use of technologies either at hand or capable of being developed. In the 1950s the long-range cruise missile mission was not an appropriate problem because the needed technologies did not exist. Two decades later, after further developments in microelectronic circuitry could be applied to guidance systems, and after inertial guidance systems had been further developed, an effective and compact cruise missile could be built.

This case illustrates how important the confluence of nominally unrelated lines of development can be in determining whether technology appropriate for intended missions actually exists. It is tempting to us in the United States to think, although not easy to prove, that the necessary threads of scientific development are more readily brought together in an open society than in one as closed and compartmentalized as the Soviet Union. Technological success may well be related as much to styles of societal organization as to the shares of GNP devoted to research and development. The greater the information flow about R&D within a society, the greater are the chances of "cross-pollinations" between seemingly unrelated lines of research. Secrecy is thus a weapon with many cutting edges: it increases one's own uncertainty of prediction as well as an opponent's uncertainty, and it impedes synergistic connections between different lines of scientific research. It is not unreasonable, therefore, to ask the extent to which high technologies are made available in the general and consumer economies, since widespread availability will tend to stimulate engineers and designers to devise new applications.

Moreover, the question of technological leadership or relative standing has important implications for strategic doctrine. The United States entered the nuclear era with a weapons monopoly which demonstrated the most extensively applied nuclear technology and was grounded on the world's best nuclear physics establishment. Relatively speaking, there was then nowhere to go but downward, since the Hiroshima explosion informed the entire scientific and technical world that a nuclear explosive was possible. For the United States to have maintained nuclear superiority over the Soviet Union and other powers indefinitely would have required a continuously greater level of effort and/or the existence of structural differences between the societies that would enable the United States to stay one generation ahead in technology indefinitely. Structural differences which tend in that direction well may exist; but in nuclear technology as in other areas, they often can be overcome by sheer effort which either (a) adequately accomplishes a goal by use of an inferior technology, or (b) builds technological parity in a limited sector but not in an entire economy. The first effect was demonstrated when the Soviets bypassed the problem of warhead miniaturization for a generation by building larger booster rockets than the U.S.; the second effect is demonstrated in the Soviets' ability to mount major nuclear weapons and space exploration programs while never matching the level of computer technology that has played such a major role in the comparable U.S. programs. It therefore appears that early post-World War II projections of indefinite U.S. nuclear superiority, and later reluctance in the 1960s to admit the Soviets' achievement of nuclear parity, demonstrate misunderstandings both of the ability of focused effort to develop some adequate technology, and of such efforts to overcome structural and societal limitations.

Technology thus plays a crucial role not only in the direct development of the strategic weapons regime, but in the functioning of societies and in determining the sorts of weapons which may be built, the means of verifying arms control agreements, and the set of strategic problems that political leaders must attempt to manage. The ongoing dynamic of scientific research and development dictates that a stream of new developments may be expected to challenge the ingenuity of political leaders in formulating controls, and seems to predict that technological drift or creep will continue to overwhelm any attempts to freeze or forego specific technologies. Some of these possibilities are considered further in the following section, which is devoted to problems of institutionalized arms control.

INSTITUTIONALIZED ARMS CONTROL

The evolution of the nuclear strategic weapons regime since 1945 has rested on two fundamental propositions. First, the combination of extreme destructive capability with prompt and reliable means of weapons delivery over intercontinental distances has meant that in a world of many nation-states, no single state can have unconditional viability in the sense defined in the first section of Chapter 1. Second, the essential irreversibility of the knowledge that such weapons and delivery systems can be built means that we can never return to the relatively more comfortable prenuclear world.

We will use the weapons, continue to live with them, or do away with them, but in any event we are forced by their very existence to do something about *managing* them. Even should we succeed in doing away with the weapons, the knowledge that more could be built would require a continuing management regime. In the second section of Chapter 1, human management of the strategic weapons regime since 1945 was described as a mixed-motive game of strategy between governments, a game characterized both by conflictful and cooperative motives. One way in which the cooperative motives have been actualized (although always tempered by the conflictful motives) has been through the limited establishment of institutions for strategic arms control.

As Barton and Weiler (1976, 9) note:

> Arms control is often said to have three goals: (1) to make war less likely, (2) to make war less destructive if it does occur, and (3) to reduce the economic cost of armaments.

Calls for nuclear arms control have tended to emphasize the first and third of these goals and deemphasize the second. Yet despite earlier and relatively unsuccessful attempts through such channels as the United Nations, the actual establishment of putatively permanent institutions for the pursuit and management of strategic arms control came about only in the SALT era. Not until the signing of the SALT I accords in 1972 was it entirely clear that the two superpowers were ready to establish a "cap" on the numbers of deployed strategic weapons, and in SALT I a permanent Standing Consultative Commission was established to deal with charges of possible violations of the agreements. Perhaps most importantly, both formally within SALT I and informally within the political structures of the two superpowers and the world at large, an expectation of further SALT agreements was established. It may well be that the SALT I establishment of a *process* and *expectation* for further strategic arms control was an even more important developmental step than the movement from such previous agreements as the Limited Nuclear Test Ban Treaty of 1963 and the Nuclear Nonproliferation Treaty of 1968 to agreements explicitly limiting the further deployment of strategic weapons that might already have been developed.

It is difficult to overemphasize the importance of institutionalizing that expectation and process for obtaining further strategic arms control agreements. Before SALT I, arms control agreements tended to cover targets of opportunity, either issues that just could not easily be ignored any longer, such as fallout from atmospheric nuclear tests, or points on which agreements could be reached easily because they ruled out new areas of competition not yet exploited, as in the 1963 demilitarization of Antarctica. Although all signatories to the Nuclear Nonproliferation Treaty made the highly qualified pledge to "pursue negotiations in good faith on effective measures relating to cessation of the nuclear arms race at an early date" (York, 1973, 156), as a rule each of the pre-SALT arms control agreements was *ad hoc* and conveyed no concrete expectations of follow-on agreements. While one could argue that there was indeed a continuing noninstitutionalized process in which ever more serious topics were brought under negotiation and agreement, the process and procedure for further agreements took a quantum leap forward with SALT I. After 1972 it was necessary to consider some arms control institutions, however limited, as a serious and continuing part of the system for managing both U.S. strategic weapons and the broader U.S.–Soviet strategic weapons regime.

It is therefore all the more important to assess the meaning of the apparent breakdown in the SALT process at the end of the 1970s. President Carter's withdrawal of the SALT II treaty from submission for Senate ratification in 1979, candidate Reagan's disavowal and denunciation of SALT II in the 1980 campaign, and President Reagan's slow movement toward the opening of START negotiations in the summer of 1982, all combined to mark at least a partial break in the SALT process which was begun in 1969 and which had engendered such high hopes at the time of the 1972 SALT I signing. Assessing the current viability of the strategic arms control process is thus a difficult but important task.

The development of post-World War II arms control agreements is covered in some detail in Chapter 6, preliminary to assessment of the prospects for further agreements in the 1980s. Interconnections of the arms control process with the broader political processes for managing the strategic weapons regime are discussed in the fourth section of Chapter 6. As examined there, arms control negotiations exhibit many problems common to the political mechanics of any sort of negotiations, from the roles of tacit bargaining and unilateral initiatives to the role of salient points such as "parity" about which agreement may be reached, to the relatively greater ease of reaching agreement when negotiations are carried out in secret, over limited numbers of points, and by few negotiators. The political "prices" of the agreements reached to date have included the tendencies to couple control measures with new building programs in uncontrolled areas, to avoid destruction of existing weapons, to allow programs already funded to run to completion, and to prohibit only acts not yet undertaken.

Finally, a number of technopolitical constraints tend to limit accomplishments in strategic arms control. Because of the fundamental irreversibility of new knowledge gained, almost all introductions of new technology throughout history have proved to be irreversible. New weapons technologies have seldom been supplanted except by still newer ones promising some combination of greater destructive power, higher performance on other measures such as speed and maneuverability, or (all too rarely) lower cost. The few attempts to ban some future technology by specifying the *function* of a weapon rather than its technology have been complicated by the difficulty of foreseeing future technologies well enough to define functions in ways that are proof against future discoveries of loopholes. Setting static limits on the numbers of weapons, as in SALT, tends to provide strong incentives to develop the performance capabilities of allowed individual weapons; and quantitative limits on weapons have proved far easier to verify than qualitative limits, at least with the nonintrusive national technical means of inspection thus far accepted. Finally, some degree of human resistance to change may be heightened by the fact that, in principle, any change may destabilize a previously stable strategic weapons regime.

In light of this discussion, and referring to Figure 3.1, arms control institutions and agreements are seen to influence the process of determining ultimate strategic weapons stocks and capabilities at several points, including (a) determining the political feasibilities of alternative means of observation and verification, (b) setting possible limits on the technological possibilities that must be taken into account in assessing threat and need, (c) limiting available program options, (d) limiting numbers and types of weapons deployed, and (e) at least indirectly affecting the range of options available in the formulation of strategic doctrine. In the following section, brief consideration is given to a few additional influences on strategic program decision making.

OTHER INFLUENCES ON STRATEGIC PROGRAM DECISION MAKING

Still more influences on strategic program decision making, beyond those already discussed in the preceding sections, may be identified. From time to time—though certainly not as often as some Congressional critics might wish—considerations about balances between anticipated costs and benefits enter the evaluation of new weapons programs. If we accept the evidence that bureaucratic pressures tend to keep most segments of the budget constant or nondecreasing in real terms, it is logical that military programs should be prioritized according to benefit/cost ratios, with the most worthy projects being selected first. Exactly what benefits and costs are to be considered, however, and how they are to be measured, tend to be quite problematic. Estimating the feasibility of some proposed new weapons system can be an almost equally difficult task. Here, once again, the dynamic of the prisoners' dilemma tends to cause one to err by considering almost all proposals to be feasible. In fairness to the decision makers, however, it should be noted that technological forecasting is a notoriously difficult task, made all the more difficult by the exponential growth in human knowledge and technological capabilities noted by such analysts as Buckminster Fuller.

Closely related to the difficulties of technological forecasting is the task, already mentioned at several points, of verifying other governments' activities and adherence to arms control agreements. While verification difficulties tend to become convenient tools for opponents of arms controls, they must give some pause to even the most optimistic observer. Important directions for the possible future evolution of arms control efforts may well lie in the development of new, more effective, and more inclusive means of verification, and/or in winning broader acceptance of such means. Since precedent plays such an important role in arms control efforts, as in other spheres of diplomacy, the establishment of any precedent provides an important indicator of progress. Some such indicators that may be particularly significant in the 1980s are discussed in Chapter 6, in the section, "Scenarios and Indicators."

A further criterion applicable both to strategic weapons systems in general and to strategic arms control schemes in particular, is crisis stability. As discussed in Chapter 2 (in the section "SALT I and Assured Destruction"), crisis stability was one of the four criteria established by the Nixon administration for "strategic sufficiency" at the time of SALT I. Briefly put, it requires that the strategic weapons regime be structured in ways that minimize incentives to strike first in some time of crisis. Given the increasing sense in Washington in recent years that the "bolt-out-of-the-blue" strategic strike without warning, so feared in the 1950s, is much less likely than a strike during or immediately following some crisis in which one side has been forced to make significant concessions, crisis stability is an important consideration both in weapons system design and in arms control proposals. A number of U.S.–Soviet agreements, beginning with the "Hot Line" agreement of 1963, tend to promote crisis stability. (See also the third section in Chapter 6 and Table 6.1.)

Finally, the concept of a strategic nuclear "balance" between the United States and the Soviet Union plays a crucial role in the political process, and thus in determining the very weapons programs and deployments that are perceived to determine that balance. Unfortunately, much of the ambiguity of that balance arises from arguments over which crucial quantities are to be measured to determine the balance at any particular point in time. Much of the debate over SALT II hinged on perceptions of both the statics and dynamics of that balance, with a great number of quantities being suggested to measure it. A variety of such measures either used or suggested is classified and discussed in the second and third sections of Chapter 4. Decisions on which measure(s) to use tend to hinge on the interplay between (a) the political saliency of the proposed measure and (b) the strength and centrality of the measure's relationship to the actual functioning of the strategic weapons regime. This author's position, as developed in Chapter 4, is that *effects measures*, that is, measures of the expected effects of using specific aggregates of weapons against specific target sets, tend to provide the technically soundest and most reliable measures. The chief drawback of such measures is that they are seldom transparent as they rely on a myriad of technical assumptions, and thus suffer limited political saliency in comparison to such far cruder measures as the total number of available missile warheads. Chapter 5 provides a detailed example of the use of effects measures for applied policy analysis, in a study of relative U.S. and Soviet capabilities to mount disarming strikes against land-based missiles in the 1980s under a variety of different possible weapons-building and arms control programs. Some thoughts on the possible use of effects measures in comprehensive programs for managing the strategic weapons regime are given in the fourth section of Chapter 4.

Barring closure on some single measure or class of measures, however, the strategic "balance" will tend to remain under dispute and at least somewhat ambiguous. The dynamic of winning political disputes implies that a measure often will be selected because it is salient and its current value supports a position advocated by the individual adopting the measure, rather than because of the measure's underlying soundness. Beyond that dynamic, however, no measure is better than the quality of the data required to calculate it. The quality of intelligence and assessment, expressed as accuracy, precision, and range of uncertainty in estimates, must always set some limit on our knowledge of the strategic balance, just as it limits our ability to forecast future technologies and decisions. Beyond the dynamic of its political uses, therefore, there will always be some degree of ambiguity in the strategic balance.

CONCLUDING REMARKS

The preceding sections set out only a sketch of an integrated, systemic view of the political and management processes which unite the disparate elements of arms control agreements, strategic doctrine, new weapons acquisitions, historical patterns of action, technological possibilities and forecasts, stocks of existing weapons, and major domestic and foreign actors. These are only some of the elements making up a multifaceted and highly interactive political–technological system, the end product of which is that complex of weaponry and doctrine referred to here as the strategic weapons regime. With so many elements, that regime is characterized by a tremendous number of interactions, and routinely exhibits unresolved conflicts and apparent contradictions. One manifestation of such conflict and contradiction is the continuing ambiguity of the U.S.–Soviet strategic nuclear balance, an ambiguity which stems both from the role of that perceived balance in continuing policy debates and from inherent uncertainties in any measure of the state of the system. The beginning of knowledge about any system, however, lies in an understanding of its structure, and in the following chapters we turn to more detailed studies of several aspects of the contemporary strategic weapons regime, each intimately related to the ongoing controversies about strategic "balance." Chapter 4 is a detailed consideration of measures of the strategic balance; Chapter 5 presents an application of the class of effects measures to the analysis of a variety of weapons-building and arms control measures as they may impact on the problem of ICBM vulnerability; and Chapter 6 presents an assessment of the prospects for new arms control agreements in the 1980s.

4

Assessing the Strategic "Balance": Tools for Policy Analysis

INTRODUCTION

The concept of a strategic nuclear "balance" between the United States and the Soviet Union plays a crucial role in the political process, and thus in determining the very weapons programs and deployments that are perceived to determine that balance. Much of the SALT II debate hinged on perceptions of both the statics and dynamics of that balance, and many quantities were suggested to measure it. Among those in frequent use were numbers of missiles, numbers of warheads, size of warheads, payload or "throw-weight" of missiles, and "hardness" of missile silos against blast effects. Some analysts even went so far as to compare the *numbers* of such measures on which one side or the other excelled. For example, Donley (1979, 40) presents a chart of time lines for 13 strategic balance measures, dividing each line into periods of "US Advantage," "USSR Advantage," and equality, and drawing dire conclusions from the fact that the number of indices on which the U.S. leads declines steadily over the period 1960–1983. Such arguments, of course, overlook the fact that any other time-trend would be extremely unlikely, given the historical development patterns of the two arsenals. The United States entered the nuclear era with a monopoly and still held a commanding lead in 1960, by which time the Soviets could muster little more than a minimum deterrent (MD) capability. Presuming that they could eventually match U.S. technology and were willing to commit the necessary resources, it was inevitable that something closer to parity would eventually develop, and most analysts would agree that essential equivalence or parity was achieved by around 1970. Such developments would not be likely to occur without the Soviets gaining an advantage according to at least *some* measures of the strategic balance. Rather than numbers of such measures, we should attempt to determine first, which measure or measures are best, and then what the time-trends are.

The next (second) section of this chapter comprises a typology and assessment of the many measures that have been suggested. The best criterion is found to be an "effect" or outcome measure which assesses the projected impact of strategic weapons under credible doctrines for their use. Such effects may be calculated through the use of a nuclear exchange model, which allows us to test alternative policies through simulation by asking "If a war were fought according to a particular strategic doctrine, using specified arsenals of strategic weapons, what would the effects be?" Such nuclear exchange models are valuable tools for strategic policy analysis. In the third section several such models are outlined, including the Arsenal Exchange Model (AEM 9) developed for the United States Air Force; the Strategic International Relations Nuclear Exchange Model (SIR NEM D12) developed for the United States Arms Control and Disarmament Agency; and a simpler model, NEMATODE 2.2, developed by the author and used for illustration. Such questions as the point at which an increase of detail in such models leads to diminishing returns are considered. In the fourth section the utility of strategic balance measures in assessing weapons programs is examined, taking as an example the problem of cycles of estimation and misestimation in planning ICBM and MIRV programs since the early 1960s. The most important role of the strategic "balance," however, continues to be as a political perception, and the utility of balance measures in the political process of managing strategic weapons programs is examined in the fifth section.

A TYPOLOGY AND ASSESSMENT OF STRATEGIC "BALANCE" MEASURES

The many strategic balance measures that have been put forward are grouped in Table 4.1 and the subsections below into three general types, as follows: Simple counts of weapons and/or their characteristics (first subsection) are the easiest and crudest measures of the arsenals available for use in a nuclear exchange. Composite measures or figures of merit (second subsection) are transformations of, or calculations from, the simple counts, intended to measure more adequately a government's capabilities to accomplish general missions such as the destruction of soft area targets or hard point targets, using the available arsenals of weapons. Finally, outcome or effects measures (third subsection) are the simulated results of nuclear exchanges in actual war outputs, allowing one to estimate such quantities as ICBMs surviving a first strike or numbers of warheads available for a second strike, given specific arsenals of weapons with distinct characteristics, and under specific doctrine and tactics for their use. Advantages and difficulties of the three classes and of different specific

TABLE 4.1 A Typology of Measures of the Strategic "Balance"

Simple Counts of Weapons Characteristics
("Bean Counting"; War Input Measures)

  Numbers of Weapons
    e.g., ICBMs
        SLBMs
        Total Missiles
        Bombers
        Total Launchers or Delivery Systems
        Strategic Nuclear Launch Vehicles or SNLVs
        "Large" or "Heavy" Missiles
        MIRVed Missiles
        ALCMs, GLCMs, SLCMs
  Numbers of Warheads
    e.g., Missile Warheads (Reentry Vehicles, or RVs)
        Bombs
        ALCMs, GLCMs, SLCMs
        Total of RVs and Bombs
  Total Megatonnage (Explosive Yields)
  Total Throw-Weight of Missiles
                        Bombers
                        Missiles plus Bombers
  Characteristics of Weapons
    e.g., Reliability
        Availability (Duty Factor)
        Time-to-Launch after warning
  Performance Parameters (reflective of technology)
    Yield
    Yield/Throw-Weight
    CEP
    Hardness
    Penetration Aids (missiles and bombers)
    MaRV (Terminal Guidance) Capability
  Numbers and Characteristics of Defensive Systems
    ABMs
    Air Defense Aircraft
    Air Defense Missiles

Composite Measures or Figures of Merit
  Total Equivalent Megatonnage (EMT) or Area-Destruction Potential
  Counter-Military Potential (CMP) or "Lethality" (K)
    or Hard Target Kill Potential
  MIRV Potential of Missiles (based on Throw-Weight and RV Yield/Weight)
  Fractionation Potential of Missiles (same bases as MIRV Potential)
  Any of the Above Measures Applied to ICBMs
                                SLBMs
                                Bombers
                                ALCMs, GLCMs, SLCMs
  Equivalent Weapons Index (EW)
  PSI Index

Outcome or Effects Measures
(Simulation Results; War Output Measures)

Expected Surviving Numbers of	Missiles
	Warheads
	Bombers
	Submarines
	et cetera
Expected Surviving or Residual	EMT
	CMP
	or other composite measures
Expected *Shifts in Relative Holdings* on any of the above measures	
Range of Uncertainty in Expected Outcomes	
Relative Force Size (RFS) Index	
Comparisons with Assured Destruction deterrence levels	

measures are discussed in the respective subsections. To use any of these measures in considering a strategic "balance," of course, it is necessary to compare values between governments, whether directly, through ratios or percentages, or through examination of time-trends.

Simple Counts of Weapons and Their Characteristics

The simplest possible measures of strategic weapons systems are direct counts of specific types or classes of weapons, for comparisons between sides. Such counts measure the material resources available as inputs to a nuclear exchange, and are often referred to as "bean counting" measures. One might count numbers of ICBMs, or numbers of SLBMs, or total missiles, combining both ICBMs and SLBMs. Recall, for example, Figures 2.1 and 2.2. One might count bombers separately, or combine them with total missiles to achieve a count of total launchers or total strategic nuclear launch vehicles (SNLVs). One might also count cruise missiles either by type of launch mode (ALCMs, GLCMs, or SLCMs, for air-launched, ground-launched, or submarine-launched cruise missiles, respectively), or as total cruise missiles, or as another component to be included in total SNLVs. Many such counts are rather straightforward and reasonably reliable; ICBM and SLBM launchers are readily verified and fall under SALT limits, at least for the present. Funding for production and deployment programs is known with some confidence; the carrying capacity of aerial and seagoing cruise missile carriers is known and reasonably subject to verification. One might also count weapons in classes that have characteristics of special interest, such as "heavy" ICBMs (those that can carry large numbers of warheads) as used in the SALT agreements, or MIRVed ICBMs. Again, these counts can be made with a fairly high degree of confidence in their accuracy.

Simple counts of some weapons types, such as ICBMs, can be used to give rough measures of the number of significant military targets that could be attacked, and thus how many weapons would be required for such an attack. Beyond this one advantage, however, one cannot be terribly sanguine about this class of measures. To count ICBMs as a class implies that all ICBMs have equivalent characteristics, for example, numbers and yield of warheads, accuracy (CEP), range, throw-weight, reliability, duty factor or availability for time-urgent launch, and so on. Such an implication is misleading enough in relation to the U.S. arsenal, which by 1980 had Titan II ICBMs, Minuteman IIs, and Minuteman IIIs with two generations of RVs having different warhead yields and accuracies. It is more misleading in relation to the Soviet arsenal, which has an even more diverse range of ICBM models and characteristics. The problem is compounded by comparing simple counts of ICBMs between the United States and the Soviet Union, because such a comparison implies that an average U.S. ICBM has characteristics equivalent to those of an average Soviet ICBM. Such an implication contradicts the known missile characteristics, and fails to allow for the historical differences in technology and design that have shaped the evolution of weapons systems in the two arsenals. Additionally, the more inclusive the counts are, the more severe the difficulties become. To count total missiles blurs the differences between ICBMs and SLBMs, and those differences are very large indeed; SLBMs circa 1980 simply lacked the accuracy/yield combination necessary to destroy hard point military targets such as ICBM launch silos. To add bomber and missile quantities in measuring total SNLVs combines weapons with radically different characteristics, launch times, degrees of vulnerability, modes of penetration, and accuracy.

Most of the same disadvantages apply to the use of total warheads as a strategic measure. One might count total missile warheads (reentry vehicles or RVs), total bombs, cruise missiles, ALBMs, et cetera, or combine all such measures into a grand total of available strategic nuclear warheads. That value tells the total number of military and civilian targets that can be attacked. It was a measure much beloved by former Secretary of Defense McNamara (Newhouse, 1973, 77), which makes a good deal of political sense when we recall that during the 1960s the United States far outdistanced the Soviets in numbers of strategic nuclear delivery systems in every class, including ICBMs, SLBMs, and especially intercontinental bombers. In the early 1960s, when Pentagon officials sought major weapons-building programs to implement McNamara's doctrine of second strike counterforce (SSCF), he was able to use U.S. superiority in numbers of warheads to good advantage in arguing for budgetary restraint.

Others of the simple measures move beyond mere counts of weapons to the cumulation and comparison of their characteristics in order to give crude indications of what might be done using the weapons. Total megatonnage (explosive yield) gives a very simplistic measure of the total area which could be destroyed in soft (city) targets. This value was seen as very important in the 1950s and 1960s, when the United States had deployed thermonuclear bombs of 28-megaton yield and the Soviets had tested weapons of up to 58-MT yield, hardly suited for any tasks except threatened (or actual) retaliatory terror attacks against cities. Decades later, total megatonnage was cited by some opponents of SALT II. In recent years, great emphasis has often been laid on the total payload or throw-weight of missiles as a crude indicator of their potential for MIRVing and of the sizes of warheads that may be carried. This measure has received particular attention because of the historically larger sizes of Soviet ICBMs, which at one time compensated for their lower reliabilities and accuracies. Once the missiles were built, however, it was easier to reach agreement that they be retained in the Soviet arsenal than that they be dismantled. Thus, the USSR was allowed up to 308 "heavy" ICBMs under SALT I and SALT II, while that class was denied the United States. No quid pro quo was offered; the agreement simply recognized that previously built weapons constrained negotiating positions and SALT outcomes. Yet those heavy ICBMs contribute markedly toward making throw-weight a measure biased toward the Soviets. A major argument for retaining the small number of obsolescent Titan II missiles in the U.S. arsenal was their contribution to the throw-weight balance, since the rest of the U.S. ICBM stock consisted of the much smaller and lighter Minuteman IIs and IIIs. Gray (1977, 32–33), for example, cites "order of magnitude" throw-weights for the Titan II, Minuteman II, and Minuteman III as 8,000, 1,000, and 2,000 pounds, respectively.

In addition to throw-weight, a number of other missile performance parameters are sometimes compared between arsenals. Many of these parameters do not lend themselves to aggregation, but give some indication of comparative technologies and levels of development. Among these measures are (a) warhead explosive yield; (b) yield per unit weight, which gives indications of miniaturization and of MIRV efficiency; (c) expected accuracy, measured by circular error probable (CEP), the most crucial parameter in determining hard target kill capability; (d) hardness of missile silos or other shelters, in PSI or pounds per square inch of overpressure which could be survived, a crucial parameter in determining the ability of a missile force to ride out a first strike; (e) availability of super-accurate Maneuverable Reentry Vehicles (MaRVs) with a terminal guidance capability; and (f) existence and anticipated effectiveness of penetration aids such as chaff to confuse radars, or decoy RVs to deplete ABM defenses. Given the very limited testing that has taken place, the effectiveness of missile penetration aids in wartime is a highly problematic parameter indeed. In the virtual absence of ABM defenses under the SALT I ABM Treaty, it may not even be an important one. Yet penetration aids are almost imperative for bombers, and comprise highly developed electronic countermeasures (ECM) against aircraft and antiaircraft missiles; about such measures we have a great deal more data. A final set of simple measures one might wish, of course, is counts of defensive systems, such as ABMs, air-defense aircraft, and antiaircraft missiles.

Composite Measures or Figures of Merit

The simple measures discussed above have the advantages that they are readily obtainable and often can be verified with high degrees of confidence. Some also provide useful indications of what might be done in a war, as, for example, the number of independent warheads sets a limit on the number of separate targets that could be attacked. Others, such as performance parameters, may be useful in comparing levels of technology. Still others, however, give only very crude measures, as in the use of total megatonnage to indicate soft-target area destroyable. In the search for more accurate assessments of what might be done under wartime conditions, a number of composite measures has been developed. These are calculations upon or transformations of the simple counts, according to simple theories, in order to overcome some of the difficulties of aggregating the properties of individual weapons across entire arsenals.

One of the best known composite measures is equivalent megatonnage (EMT), used to give a better measure of area-destruction potential than simply counting total explosive yield or megatonnage. A simple calculation shows that the same soft area target can be destroyed with fewer megatons of explosive yield if that force is distributed in several warheads than if it is concentrated in a single one. Suppose that one's aim is to destroy all conventional (nonhardened) structures in a city, which requires about 12 PSI overpressure (Glasstone, 1977, Ch. 5). If the explosive yield of a warhead is visualized as being distributed throughout the volume of a sphere centered on the point of explosion, the overpressure produced will be a declining function of distance from the explosion, and beyond some critical radius the overpressure will be insufficient to destroy the target structures. Imagine a sphere having that critical radius. The surface of the ground lying below the explosion may be thought of as a plane which intersects the sphere, so that within a circular area on that plane all conventional structures will be destroyed. The critical radius of destruction on that plane will be proportional to the critical radius of the sphere, with the proportionality depending on the height of burst above the plane. If the explosive yield of the warhead is increased, the critical radii will be increased. However, the yield must be distributed throughout the volume of the sphere, which increases as the cube of its radius, while the area of a circle is proportional to the square of its radius. Hence, the area of the circle within which destruction takes place is proportional to the two-thirds power of the explosive yield, and there are diminishing returns to scale as yield is increased. This effect is compensated in the calculation of equivalent megatonnage (EMT) as

$$EMT = aY^{\frac{2}{3}} \tag{4.1}$$

where Y is explosive yield and a is a constant of proportionality. Application of this simple formula allows the area-destruction potential of any warhead to be compared fairly accurately to that of a warhead of some reference size, usually one megaton. EMT per warhead may then be aggregated over an entire arsenal of missiles and/or bombs as a reasonably good measure of destroyable soft-target area.

Some analysts have argued that this EMT measure still assigns excessive weight to large blasts. A one-megaton warhead can subject 20 square miles to at least 10 PSI overpressure (Sibley, 1977) while a five-megaton warhead can subject 58 square miles to 10 PSI or above (Richelson, 1980, 783). Yet some major cities cover significantly less than 58 square miles or have highly developed regions along the shorelines of bodies of water. Thus the greater the warhead yield, the greater the probability that at least some destructive capability will be "wasted" outside the perimeters of target cities. One method suggested for further correction of the effective yield of large warheads is to compute EMT as proportional to the square root ($\frac{1}{2}$ power) of yield whenever yield exceeds one megaton (Groover, et al., 1978). This method is also used in the Arsenal Exchange Model described later in this chapter ("The Arsenal Exchange Model"). An alternative correction is to replace EMT with Richelson's Distinct Blasts Index (DBI), in which one counts the number of blasts of one megaton or greater that could be produced by combining smaller warheads into groups large enough to total at least one megaton each. (Richelson, 1980, 784). This correction downweights large warheads even more strongly than does calculating EMT using yield to the $\frac{1}{2}$ power. Both these corrections share two difficulties: the calculated value is discontinuous at the point at which yield equals one megaton, a choice which appears quite ad hoc; and that discontinuity implies the loss of an otherwise linear relationship between EMT and the total area destroyable. Richelson (1980, 784) justifies the ad hoc choice on the ground that "all cities can be either severely damaged or totally destroyed by a one-equivalent-megaton blast at their center." Regrettably, the same could be said of blasts of 500 KT or 350 KT or 170 KT.

While the ability to destroy soft and spread-out targets such as cities depends primarily on the capability to deliver sufficient explosive yield, the ability to destroy hard point targets such as missile silos is much more critically dependent on the accuracy with which warheads can be delivered. Moreover, if accuracy is sufficiently high, warhead yields need not be terribly great, and blast and radiation damage will not be large at great distances from the point targets. These facts are reflected in the equivalent indices Counter-Military Potential (CMP), developed by the RAND Corporation (Collins and Cordesman, 1978, 76–79; Barbieri, R-1314), and Lethality (K), widely publicized by Kosta Tsipis (1974a,b; 1975a,b,c), which attempt to measure the ability of one side to destroy the other's ICBM arsenal. This index turns out to be quite misleading and prone to serious aggregation problems. It has even led different authors, e.g., Tsipis, 1974a,b, 1975a, and Rummel, 1976, to come to mutually contradictory but still incorrect conclusions about U.S. ICBM vulnerability—based on different data than those considered in Chapter 5.

To develop the CMP index, start with the probability that a hard-point target of hardness H will survive attack by a warhead of yield Y delivered with accuracy CEP; that expected survival probability will be

$$P_s = e^{-Y^{\frac{2}{3}}f_1(H)/(CEP)^2} \text{ or } (\tfrac{1}{2})^{-Y^{\frac{2}{3}}f_2(H)/(CEP)^2}, \quad (4.2)$$

where $f_1(h)$ and $f_2(H)$ are functions of hardness, incorporating constants of proportionality derived theoretically and through extrapolation of empirical parameters determined in weapons tests. Many essentially similar forms of this survival probability have been used; see, for example, the incorrect derivation by Tsipis (1974a), brief comments by Richelson (1980, 786), extended comments on different forms by Davis and Schilling (1973, 210–216), and two excellent brief articles by Bellany (1973, 1979). In the NEMATODE 2.2 model the author used the form

$$P_s = (\tfrac{1}{2})^{-9Y^{\frac{2}{3}}/H^{0.8}(CEP)^2} \quad (4.3)$$

This is an adaptation of a widely used unclassified formula (Leestma, 1972), and is intended to apply mainly to hard-point targets, such as missile silos. If we define lethality or CMP as

$$K = CMP = Y^{\frac{2}{3}}/(CEP)^2 \quad (4.4)$$

and note that the probability of destroying the target is one minus its probability of survival, or

$$P_s = 1 - P_s \quad (4.5)$$

then

$$P_k = 1 - e^{-kf(H)} \quad (4.6)$$

The index K or CMP *is* useful for illustrating the relative contributions of yield (Y) and accuracy (CEP) to the destruction of hard point targets. For example, if Y = 1 and CEP = 1, CMP = 1. If we keep target hardness unchanged but double the explosive yield to T = 2, CMP rises only to 1.59. But if we double accuracy, cutting CEP to 0.5, CMP is quadrupled, rising to four. Equation 4.5 must be corrected, however, for extremely high accuracies or extremely low yields. As Richelson (1980, 787) notes, the formula breaks down if yield is so low that a warhead could not destroy its target if detonated at its exact center. For example, if Yexp($\tfrac{2}{3}$) were 10exp(–7) and CEPexp(2) were 10exp(–10), K would be 1,000, which should be more than sufficient to destroy a silo hardened to 5,000 PSI; yet the weapon would produce no more than 300 PSI overpressure. While this case is extreme, it does point out that corrections to the formula become ever more important in a world of smaller yields and increasing accuracies.

Using K or CMP to illustrate the relative contributions which changes in yield and accuracy make to destroying a particular target is straightforward and useful; the difficulties come in attempting to aggregate CMP over an entire arsenal and an entire set of targets. In an actual nuclear exchange, putting a missile silo out of action would require that at least one warhead detonate near enough to disable the missile, silo, control equipment, or controllers by blast overpressure, radiation, thermal effects, electromagnetic pulse (EMP) effects, piling so much debris on the silo door that it jams or cannot be opened without incurring damage to the missile, or some combination of these effects. Each silo has some specific hardness and is attacked by one or more warheads each of which has a specific yield and accuracy, and thus a specific CMP. Yet to use total missile force CMP as an index for strength comparisons or as a measure of capability to destroy an opponent's ICBM force usually leads to one or more of four incorrect assumptions of aggregation and distribution, as seen, for example, in Tsipis's use of the K index (1974a,b; 1975a,b).

First, one must either break the target ICBM force into classes of silos each having the same hardness, or assume some representative hardness value for all silos. The latter choice may introduce substantial inaccuracies. Second, and far more serious, the CMP of large missiles cannot always be distributed over the desired target set. Every target must be attacked with at least one warhead, and the availability of sufficient total CMP to carry out a contemplated attack does not necessarily imply the availability of a sufficient number of warheads. Simply to add CMP in an attacking ICBM force and compare it to the total CMP required to destroy a set of silos neglects the fact that almost any case of missile neutralization—except, possibly, for accumulation of enough debris to block the silo door—will result from the explosion of a single warhead. If, for example, a silo is neutralized by the second of two warheads detonated, it usually means that the first failed to explode close enough. Third, and perhaps still more serious, use of the CMP index has tempted several authors, including Tsipis and Rummel, to overlook the problem of fratricide and add warheads indefinitely until their total CMP value reaches the level required to destroy a silo at some level of probability, say $P_k = 0.97$. While in practice one probably cannot fire more than two warheads at a silo within a short period of time, Tsipis and others have added warheads as if there were no limit to the number which could be fired virtually simultaneously. Finally, adding warheads to achieve a desired lethality may cause neglect of the fact that there is some lower limit to the accuracy/yield combination below which it is not worthwhile to launch a warhead at a given silo, because the warhead either has too low a probability of striking close enough or has too low a yield to destroy the silo even if exploded on top of it.

These technical difficulties in the use of the CMP or K index have led to erroneous policy analyses. By ignoring fratricide, Tsipis was able to add many small U.S. warheads for hypothetical attacks against Soviet ICBM silos, which overstated U.S. capabilities and gave an inaccurate picture of the relative U.S.–Soviet ICBM balance in the mid-1970s. This problem was pointed out by several other analysts, including Thomas Brown (1976, 57). A converse side of this problem of aggregating too many small war-

TABLE 4.2 Three Problems in Aggregating and Distributing ICBM Lethality or CMP

Target ICBM Force to be Attacked
1,000 silos
$P_k = 0.97$ when CMP = 50
To destroy an expected 97 percent of silos requires CMP = 50,000

Problem 1: Lethality cannot be distributed in units of less than one warhead.

Attacking Force: Type	Number	CMP	Total CMP	P_k	Silos Destroyed
M1	500	100	50,000	0.99	0.99(500) = 495
M2	100	50	5,000	0.97	0.97(100) = 97
			55,000		592

Since 408 silos are expected to survive, the attack fails.

Problem 2: Fratricide may be overlooked.

| M3 | 5,000 | 10 | 50,000 | 0.60 | 840 |

Anticipated fratricide effects limit targeting to two warheads per silo; since 160 silos are expected to survive, the attack fails.

Problem 3: Extremely small warheads may have almost no effect against hard silos.

| M4 | 50,000 | 1 | 50,000 | 0.02? | Essentially none |

heads to obtain sufficient CMP to destroy a silo is the problem posed by missiles with large throw-weights: they may have very great lethality, but it cannot necessarily be broken down into sufficiently small units for efficient destruction of a large number of targets, and CMP may thus overstate the contribution of such large missiles to an actual nuclear exchange. Similarly, the random failure of a single high-lethality weapon could lead to a nontrivial loss of strength in an attack. Finally, although the P_s and P_k calculations underlying the derivation of CMP or K are expected values, Tsipis has interpreted them as confidence levels, claiming to have derived the amount of lethality necessary to destroy an ICBM force with, say, 97 percent confidence. Even if all the assumptions about allocation and aggregation were correct, they would not make the mean value of a probability distribution into a confidence level, nor correct the fact that Tsipis has not demonstrated a theory for calculating a confidence interval about that mean.

Some of the difficulties of aggregating and distributing ICBM lethality are illustrated by the three hypothetical missile attacks summarized in Table 4.2. (The first case was suggested by Richelson, 1980, 787–788, with somewhat different numbers.) Suppose that it is desired to attack an ICBM force housed in 1,000 silos and that a CMP of 50 gives a 97 percent probability of destroying one such silo. To destroy an expected 97 percent of the silos thus requires a total lethality of 50,000. The force available to make the strike in Attack 1 consists of 500 M1 missiles with CMP of 100 each, plus 100 M2 missiles with lethality of 50 each. The total ICBM force CMP is 55,000, which appears to be more than sufficient. Yet even though the M1 and M2 missiles have P_ks of 0.99 and 0.97, respectively, against the target silos, they are single-warhead missiles. The "excess" CMP of the M1 missiles cannot be distributed to attack additional silos, and the attack is limited by the number of available warheads. We expect that 592 silos would be destroyed, and the attack fails its objective. Hypothetical Attack 2 also fails. The force available consists of 5,000 M3 missiles of CMP=10 each. However, fratricide prevents assigning the apparently necessary five warheads per target, and each individual warhead has only a moderate probability of destroying its target. With $Pk = 0.6$ per warhead and fratricide limiting the attack to two warheads per target, we expect a total of 840 silos to be destroyed, leaving 160 ICBMs available for retaliation. Hypothetical Attack 3 illustrates still another problem which might be overlooked when using the CMP index. In this case 50,000 M4 missiles are available, each with $CMP = 1$. While this appears to offer sufficient total CMP, even if we neglect fratricide the individual warheads are simply too weak to have any significant chance of neutralizing their target silos.

While EMT has been used as an index of soft area targets destroyable and CMP or K as an index of hard point targets destroyable, several other composite indices have seen at least limited use, and some of these indices were specifically intended to overcome problems with EMT or CMP. Richelson (1980, 789) has proposed a PSI Index of hard-target kill capability, in which one of the problems of using lethality as an index is overcome by taking into consideration the hardness of each target. This correction, of course, requires either that each target be considered separately, or that targets be divided into classes of equal hardness, so that the calculation of the index is made more complex. Neglect of fratricide is still a problem when there are many small warheads. A more successful index is Payne's Equivalent Weapons (EW) index (1977, 109–110), which is an attempt to summarize the capability to attack a complete target system effectively. The EW index of a warhead is defined as follows:

$$\text{EW (per weapon)} = 1/[a/P_{k1} + b/P_{k2} + c/P_{k3}], \quad (4.7)$$

where a, b, and c are the proportions of soft-point, soft-area, and hard-point targets, and the P_ks are the respective probabilities of destroying such targets. The EW index is then the summation of the EW value over all warheads, and represents the expected number of targets destroyed when weapons are randomly allocated with no more than one warhead per target. Yet, like K, the EW index could seriously underestimate strategic capability, since it does not allow for careful nonrandom targeting or for the use of more than one warhead per target.

One could calculate values of many of the composite indices for specific types of weapons, such as ICBMs, SLBMs, or bombers. Particular attention has been directed to the MIRVing and MIRV fractionation potential of missiles, based on missile throw-weights and the yield-to-weight ratio of reentry vehicles. Beyond the development of such limited indices, it is clear that the attempt to refine indices of the overall potential of a strategic arsenal for carrying out a major attack against some other target set has involved ever-increasing disaggregation, with attendant increases in the complexity of calculations. Without taking account of the peculiarities of allocating a particular type of attacker to a particular target, each described by different key parameters, the sorts of problems found in using the lethality index constantly reoccur. It has been in attempting to overcome those problems, as well as in seeking to model more complex, subtle, and realistic scenarios, that the class of outcome/effects models has been developed.

Outcome or Effects Measures

The class of outcome or effects measures is derived from simulations of hypothetical war scenarios, asking in effect "What would the results be if a war were to be fought with this targeting plan and these arsenals of strategic weapons?" The simulations are performed with nuclear exchange models, which are considered in more detail in the following section. Such models involve the use of higher levels of disaggregation to solve the problems of aggregation and distribution of weapons seen in the less detailed indices, so that even in the simpler simulations it is possible to direct attackers of a single type against targets of a single type. One may then be assured that all relevant target and warhead parameters have been taken into account and not glossed over in averages; that targeting plans can be sophisticated enough to match weapon characteristics to target properties so as to use the most effective attackers; that fratricide effects are taken into consideration; and that an attack can be optimized on any of several desired measures. Our tools for policy analysis then become one or more of a number of figures of merit based on the outcome of a hypothetical nuclear exchange, rather than measures based simply on the aggregate characteristics of the arsenals of weapons. Outcome or effects measures thus inherently take into account any asymmetries between sides, whether in weapons technology, military doctrines, or the political structures that produce those doctrines. Many such asymmetries would be neglected or misread when using the simpler and less accurate indices. For example, counting warheads neglects the traditionally more advanced technologies, and thus higher accuracies, of the United States, or the fact that in the past the United States has always had harder military targets. Similarly, counting warheads or EMT tends to draw attention away from the fact that value targets in the United States are fewer in number, larger, and more concentrated than those in the Soviet Union, a situation which implies that assured destruction capabilities require U.S. warheads to be more numerous and Soviet warheads to be larger.

A number of prices, however, are paid for the increased degree of realism afforded by using nuclear exchange models. Measures of results are not always as readily understood and as easily communicated, particularly to the uninitiated, as the simpler indices, because the simulation results depend crucially on large sets of assumptions about the planning and execution of nuclear exchanges. One is always faced with a question of tradeoffs between increased realism versus increased time, cost, and calculational complexity. Even moderate-sized nuclear exchange models require extensive computer programming. The larger models require permanent staffs of programmers for development and maintenance, and must be run on extremely large computers. Although a measure like total throw-weight available in an arsenal may be politically salient, the accurate planning of attack scenarios and of programs to counter them requires detailed analysis of the way in which an exchange actually would be fought, and that analysis requires resort to nuclear exchange models.

In order to carry out a nuclear exchange analysis, one must gather a good deal of information about the characteristics of weapons and targets, and about (actual or hypothetical) attack/targeting plans. One incidental benefit of that process may be an improved understanding of the ranges of (a) uncertainty about performance parameters and (b) ambiguity in attack plans. Once those problems have been resolved, however, and given the outcome of an hypothetical exchange, the results may be assessed using any of a number of measures. The unique benefit of exchange modelling is that it provides a framework in which one can obtain meaningful expectations for numbers of weapons and targets surviving the exchange at any point in the war scenario, e.g., after a first strike or after a retaliatory counterforce strike. It is not clear how one could speak of "expected surviving" weapons without such a simulation. With an exchange model, however, one can obtain the numbers of expected surviving weapons by type, such as missiles, bombers, ICBMs, submarines, and so on. Measures of expected surviving aggregate characteristics, such as numbers of warheads, total megatonnage, and throw-weight also can be obtained. Composite measures may also be used in evaluating the residual force after a nuclear exchange, yielding such measures as expected surviving or residual EMT or CMP.

A number of somewhat more sophisticated calculations may also be performed on the characteristics of a residual force or on the properties of a set of targets destroyed in an exchange. It may be instructive to examine what effect a nuclear exchange would have on the relative surviving arsenal size or relative capabilities of the two sides. This is only one of a number of instances in which a fairly complex index may be calculated from the results of a nuclear exchange. Groover et al. (1978) developed a Relative Force Size (RFS) index as an effect measure for the number of times a given arsenal could destroy a specified set of targets to some expected level of destruction. It was used by Secretary of Defense Harold Brown (1978, 1979, 1980) as a summary measure of U.S. ability to survive a Soviet first strike and retaliate, either at a day-to-day level of readiness or under a "generated alert." Brown (1980, 87) also used U.S. warheads expected to survive a Soviet first strike as another effect measure, displayed annually over a ten-year period, and surviving warheads and EMT expected under the two different alert conditions. Each of these measures requires nuclear exchange modelling in its calculation. Given such measures, one can also compare the expected residual forces and force characteristics of the two sides after exchanges carried out under comparable targeting doctrines. Brown (1980, 125) displayed surviving warheads and EMT in this manner for the period 1979–1989, recording shifts between U.S. advantage and Soviet advantage. While still crucially dependent on the assumed attack plans and weapons characteristics, such comparisons provide one of the more readily grasped displays of the results of exchange modelling. They also provide clear visual presentation of the results of alternative policy choices by either government, as seen in Brown's display (1980, 125) of the alternative impacts if the Soviets did or did not choose to equip the new type of ICBM allowed them under SALT II with MIRVs.

A final and extremely valuable use to which exchange models may be put is evalution of the *range of uncertainty* in the hypothetical outcomes. Unfortunately, such uses are almost never seen. One of the rare open-literature examples in print is by Steinbruner and Garwin (1976, 152 and 165), who present not only mean values, but 95 percent confidence limits for the expected numbers of silos destroyed in attacks on ICBM forces. Given reasonable assumptions about the form of the probability distributions reflected in such aspects of missile performance as the fall of warheads about a point target, each such stochastic event can be simulated repeatedly and the results aggregated to obtain probability distributions for summary measures of the exchange results. As will be seen in the analysis of ICBM vulnerability in Chapter 5, it appears more and more as if the end of the 1980s could bring an era in which each side has perhaps 20,000 ICBM warheads, yet neither can expect more than about five percent to survive a first strike. In a world of such small expected survivabilities, the range of uncertainty in attack expectations must be far more important than ever before, so that increased attention to that range seems both appropriate and necessary.

AN EXAMINATION OF THREE NUCLEAR EXCHANGE MODELS

Before one can perform any policy assessments based on attack simulation, one must have an appropriate nuclear exchange model (hereinafter, NEM). Many such models have been written, but each must perform at least some of the general functions shown in Table 4.3, and often additional functions. While in principle each of these functions can be carried out by

TABLE 4.3 Functions in Nuclear Exchange Modelling

Record weapon and target properties (arsenals)
  Store in retrievable form
  Accept updates for corrections and exchange results
Allocate attackers to targets
  Widely varying degrees of detail may be allowed
  Allocations may be fixed by preprogrammed scenarios
Calculate the effects of defenses
Calculate the effects of attackers that survive defenses
  Properly performed at the level of individual attackers and individual targets
Aggregate the results of individual hits
Optimize the results of the attack
  A wide variety of measures may be used for assessment
  Optimization takes place in the allocation of attackers to targets
Store results of the attack for possible subsequent strikes
  Update arsenals (facilities lists)
Assess the results of the strike
  Many different measures may be used
  Results may be input to subsequent strikes in preprogrammed multistrike scenarios
Conduct subsequent strikes (if desired)
  May be preprogrammed in multistrike scenarios
  May be conducted at operator's option
Assess results of multistrike scenarios (if appropriate)

a human operator using a minimum of computational assistance, usually at least some are programmed for calculation by a digital computer; and the greater the extent of such programming, the greater the level of detail that can be accommodated. Numbers and performance parameters of weapons in the arsenals must be recorded and updated to reflect the results of any attack. Attackers must be allocated to their respective targets in any strike. Effects of each attacker must be calculated, and if there is a defense, its effect must also be computed. Results of all the individual attackers and defenders must be aggregated to obtain the surviving arsenals and target sets. In many NEMs, an attack can be optimized by iterating the process of attack allocation and calculation so as to come as close as possible to a performance goal based on some outcome measure. Subsequent strikes may be allowed at the operator's option, or may be programmed as part of a fixed war scenario: for example, countervalue retaliation after a counterforce first strike, under an assured destruction doctrine. In either case, it is usually desirable to provide for storing data about the arsenals that result after a strike. After each strike, as well as at the conclusion of the simulation, the results may be assessed according to any number of figures of merit, either automatically or at the operator's discretion.

Different nuclear exchange models may be distinguished by the extent to which each function is programmed for automatic calculation, as opposed to being left flexible for choice through operator intervention. NEMs may also be distinguished by the level of detail allowed in the performance of each function. At one extreme, weapons may be divided into a small number of significant major classes, e.g., Minuteman II and Minuteman III ICBMs. At the other extreme, missiles may be listed as individual weapons having distinct geographic locations that limit the range to which they may be launched, with consideration being given to which individual targets lie within the "footprint" of possible warhead separations for a MIRVed missile. Similarly, targets may either be divided into major classes, or disaggregated as far down as the level of individual geographic locations. Defenders may or may not be allowed; and defense against bombers, for example, may take a number of forms. Attack results may be calculated against many types of targets, including hard-point and soft-area targets, and may include blast, radiation, and fallout effects. Alternatively, only one class of targets, such as hard-point locations, might be allowed, and only a dominant mode of destruction such as blast overpressure considered.

There is also some range of argument about the exact form of algorithm to be used in calculating each of these: for example, whether a hard point target lying within one CEP of a blast of appropriate size is to be considered destroyed and a target outside undestroyed (according to a so-called "cookie cutter" distribution), or whether a probability distribution having P_k decreasing smoothly with distance from the blast center is used (which clearly would be more realistic). The allowed degree of optimization of attack and defense varies greatly from one NEM to another. So does the flexibility to allow more than one strike. Some models allow any number of attacks, with the results after each strike being stored for possible use as input data for a subsequent attack. Other models allow only one or more preprogrammed scenarios of one or more strikes each. Finally, the summary measures used to assess results vary considerably from one NEM to another.

The three subsections which follow comprehend a brief consideration of three nuclear exchange models that span the range of variations set out above. The Arsenal Exchange Model (AEM9, first subsection) features a moderately high level of aggregation and several preprogrammed scenarios. The Strategic International Relations Nuclear Exchange Model (SIR NEM D12, second subsection) allows for almost total disaggregation to the level of individual weapons and targets, with very detailed modelling of nuclear-weapons effects and complete flexibility for multiple strikes. Both AEM and SIR NEM have seen extensive use in the defense analysis community. Finally, the author's model (NEMATODE 2.2, third subsection) provides for flexible multiple strikes and a fairly high level of aggregation, and can be run on relatively small computers. The properties of these three models are summarized in Table 4.4.

TABLE 4.4 Comparative Properties of Three Nuclear Exchange Models

Model	Arsenals	Scenarios	Allocations (Method)	Weapons & Targets	Defenses	Optimization	Assessment Measures
Arsenal Exchange Model (AEM9)	Two sides only; read in from cards or tape	Preprogramed, choice of (1) CV (2) CF/V; CF/V; (3) CF; CF/V; CV w/optimum reserve force (4) CF; CF/V; CV w/optimum reserve targets	Weapons are designated to either value or force targets; Most powerful weapons are targeted first; No attackers launched if minimum P_k is not exceeded.	Missiles (ICBMs, SLBMs); Bombers; FOBS; Value Targets	Area and Terminal; ABM; ASM; SLBM defended by SABMIS; ICBM defended by AABMIS; Defenders not attackable as separate targets.	Yes; Max returned value. Can optimize force, given budget (!) Only one side can optimize in any given run.	Destroyed & Surviving Weapons, warheads, cities, population percentage; EMT.
Strategic International Relations Nuclear Exchange Model (SIR NEM D12)	Two sides; read in from tape; modified arsenals stored for later strikes (optional)	Flexible, Modular	Down to individual warheads & individual targets; As many as 600 map cells.	Missiles (ICBMs, SLBMs); Bombers; Value Targets	ABMs; Aircraft; AAMs.	Target damage optimized in allocations.	Facility value surviving; fractions destroyed by different effects; average dosages received.
NEMATODE 2.2	Two sides; any number of stored facilities lists, on disc; modified arsenals may be stored for later strikes (optional)	Flexible, Modular	Up to 10 types of attackers; Up to 10 types of targets; Uniform allocation within each cell of 10 × 10 matrix; set interactively by operator.	Missiles (ICBMs, SLBMs); Value Targets	ABMs grouped by target type.	No (informal)	Surviving weapons; Calculations based on changes in arsenals.

TABLE 4.4 Comparative Properties of Three Nuclear Exchange Models (continued)

Model	Subsequent Strikes?	Computer Operation Model(s)	Major Users & Programmers	Weapons Effects	Other Limitations	Level of Aggregation
Arsenal Exchange Model (AEM9)	Up to two (preprogrammed)	Batch; Control and data inputs from cards; oriented to user operation.	USAF; Martin Marietta	Blast	No cross-targeting; Defenses are either whole-country or one-target; Single-value objective function; No geography; No range limits; No footprints; No collective or collateral damage; No defense suppression; Discrete time intervals; Defense interactions; No fratricide.	Attacker *type*; Individual value targets.
Strategic International Relations Nuclear Exchange Model (SIR NEM D12)	Yes; Results of previous strikes are storable.	Batch; Control cards, data and output tapes; Operated by highly skilled resident programmers.	USACDA; Academy for Interscience Methodology. Originally developed from BEACON family done for USAF.	Blast; Radiation; Thermal; Fallout	Discrete time intervals	Individual attackers and targets.
NEMATODE 2.2	Yes; Results of previous strikes are storable.	Interactive; All stored info on disc; Oriented to user operation.	Author	Blast	No geography; No range limits; No collective or collateral damage; No defense suppression; Discrete time intervals.	Attacker *type*; target *type*; Up to 10 types of each.

The Arsenal Exchange Model (AEM9)

The Arsenal Exchange Model (AEM) features a moderate level of aggregation, preprogrammed scenarios, attack optimization, and a fair degree of flexibility in planning exchanges and force compositions. Originally programmed by Martin Marietta Corporation for the United States Air Force, the model has seen extensive use in DOD in recent years and is currently maintained by Scientific Applications, Incorporated. The detailed comments which follow refer to version 9 (AEM9), which was current in 1969–1970. The basic structure of the model is shown in Figure 4.1, and is seen to parallel the sequence of NEM functions given in Table 4.3 quite closely.

AEM9 is run in batch mode from either card or tape input; the program consists of some 13,200 Fortran statements divided into more than twenty overlays, and requires a computer of moderate size (about 170,000 words octal) for operation. Four preprogrammed scenarios are allowed: (1) a single pure countervalue (CV) strike; (2) a mixed counterforce (CF) and CV strike (CF/V) followed by a CF/V response; (3) CF attack, CF/V response, and CV counterresponse, with reserve forces optimized; and (4) a CF; CF/V; CV strike sequence with reserved targets optimized. Weapons allowed are missiles (ICBMs, SLBMs, and FOBs) and bombers, as individual types; value targets are considered as being of a single type but with parameters that can be varied to allow different areas to each of a large number of such targets, so that major individual value targets can be modelled. Only blast effects are considered. Both area and terminal defenses are allowed, but defenders cannot be attacked as separate targets under a strategy of defense suppression. If area defenses are present, they protect the entire country, and both area and terminal defenses may include ABMs and ASMs. SABMIS defense of SLBMs and AABMIS defense of ICBMs are also permitted. Optimization of attacks is allowed, although only to one side at a time. Value returned to the attacker is optimized, and the program will not allow weapons to be launched unless they have at least a certain minimum probability of destroying a target of some minimum worth (either as a value target or as a weapon potentially capable of retaliation). Weapons must be designated as being targeted at either force or value targets, and will be launched first at the most powerful force targets. It is possible to optimize the strategic force to be purchased given some budget constraint, a particularly intriguing capability for an aerospace contractor to program. Principal measures used for assessment and for summarizing the results of strikes include numbers of destroyed and surviving weapons, warheads, cities, and population percentages. EMT is also reported and used for internal assessments, such as deciding the value of a warhead for purposes of attack allocation.

AEM9 is subject to a number of inherent limitations in addition to those noted above. Cross-targeting by launching warheads from different missiles at the same target is not allowed. Defenses are inherently either

FIGURE 4.1 Structure of the Arsenal Exchange Model (AEM9)

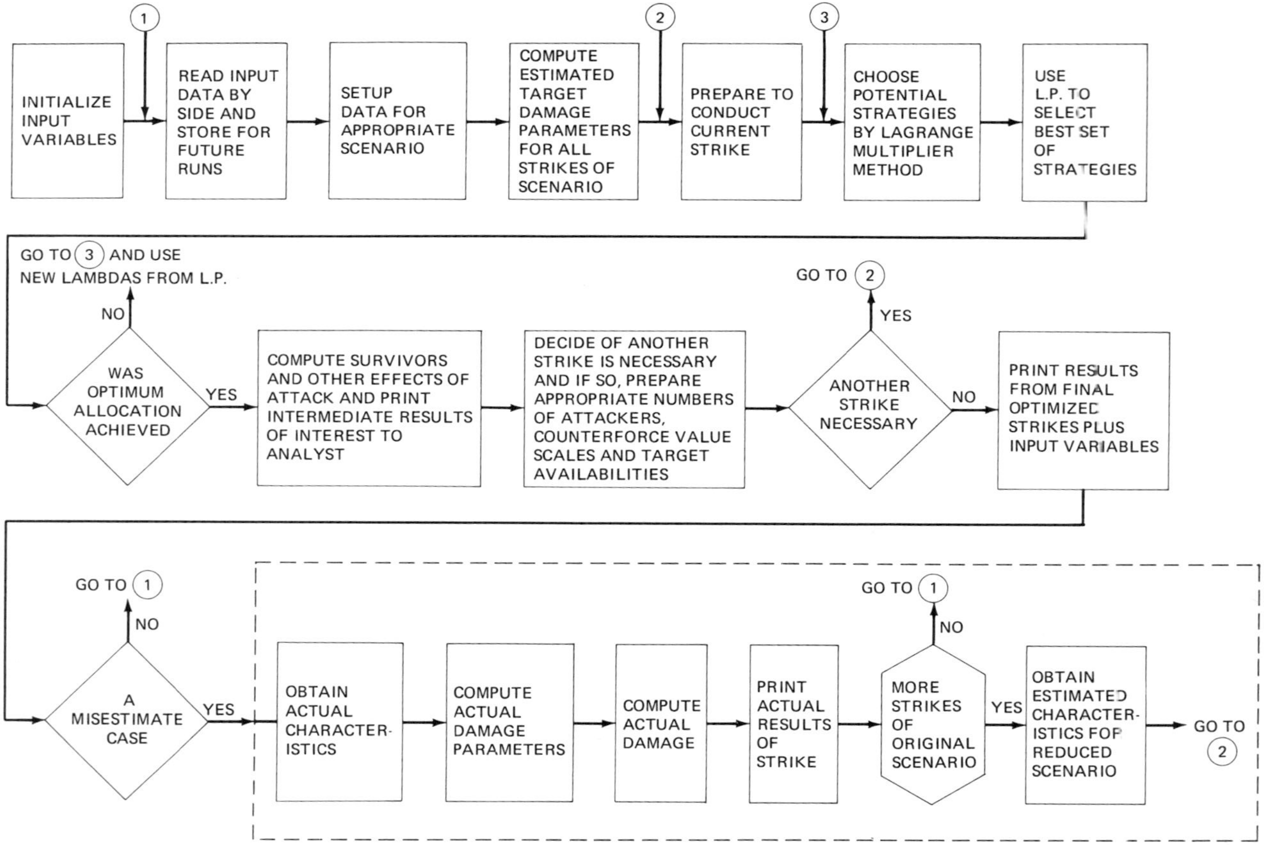

SOURCE: Groover, Garrison, and Cotsworth (1971, unnumbered page)

whole-country or one-target. The objective function is single-valued. Geography, missile footprints, range limits, and collective or collateral damage are not permitted. Time intervals are discrete, which forces one side's entire strike to be completed before the other side's response can begin. Defenders of different types may interact, and defense suppression is not allowed. The two most serious limitations, however, are probably the facts that scenarios are strictly limited and that fratricide is totally ignored. No flexibility is provided for considering sequences of strikes other than the four noted above. No provision for strikes consistent with an assured destruction (AD) doctrine was even provided in the earlier versions of AEM; it was added about 1970. Even more seriously, there are no inherent limits on the number of warheads that may be allocated to a single target, so long as additional warheads would have nonnegligible probabilities of destroying their targets. By thus ignoring fratricide, the model may considerably overstate the capability of a group of warheads to destroy a hard-point force target.

The Strategic International Relations Nuclear Exchange Model (SIR NEM D12)

The Strategic International Relations Nuclear Exchange Model (SIR NEM) is probably the most flexible and most highly detailed or disaggregated such model ever written, and evinces a radically different programming philosophy from that embodied in AEM. Through its greater complexity, SIR NEM overcomes all of AEM9's limitations except the discrete time intervals. SIR NEM is in fact an evolving family of models and has been under development for years, starting with the BEACON family of models sponsored by the United States Air Force, Systems Command, Andrews Air Force Base. Development in recent years has been by the Academy of Interscience Methodology (AIM) under contracts from the United States Arms Control and Disarmament Agency (USACDA). The great differences in programming philosophy between AEM and SIR NEM are reflected in their differing modes of operation. While AEM is designed to be operated by a user who has gained familiarity with a reasonably brief operating manual, SIR NEM is run by the small but highly skilled staff of resident programmers also charged with the continuing development of the model. Their offices are located within the Control Data Corporation computer facility in Rockville, Maryland, close to Washington, where they can have periods of exclusive (dedicated) use of a large and secure computer. By the mid-1970s SIR NEM had evolved to version D12, which consisted of more than 22,650 Fortran statements and CDC system commands in 15 overlays divided into three major files, and required dedicated use of a large (circa 360,000 words octal) computer. Inclusion of specific CDC system commands yielded improved efficiency over earlier versions, at the cost of further limiting the set of installations at which the model could be run.

SIR NEM's input and output formats reflect the expectation that a group of experts will interface between the model and the users of its product. Two nation-states are assumed; data is read to and from tape under control inputs entered on cards, and the highly detailed arsenals are modified to reflect the results of strikes conducted. Program structure is flexible and modular, with one strike conducted at a time and the results stored for possible use as input to subsequent strikes. All types of missiles and bombers are allowed, as are a wide variety of defenses against both missiles and bombers, many types of penetration aids, and use of satellite and other reconnaissance means. Detail is allowed down to the level of individual attackers and targets. Geography, range limits, missile footprints, collective and collateral damage, cross-targeting, defense suppression, and fratricide are all either automatically included or taken into account at operator discretion. Up to 600 individual map "cells" are allowed to take account of geographical effects. Blast, thermal, radiation, and fallout effects of nuclear weapons are modelled, making SIR NEM particularly well suited for the study of collateral damage to value targets and populations. Allocations of attackers to targets are optimized to maximize target damage. Principal assessment measures included in the outputs are the individual facility (weapons arsenal) values surviving, the fractions destroyed by blast, the fractions surviving blast but destroyed by thermal effects, and the fractions destroyed by radioactive fallout after surviving blast and thermal effects. Also, the average dosages of the three effects for each facility and the total survival and destruction information for the facility type are printed. Calculation of other and more highly aggregated summary measures is left to the operators after a run.

Because SIR NEM includes the full range of nuclear-weapons effects against populations and other value targets, it saw considerable use by USACDA during the "retargeting" debates of the mid-1970s, when the number of civilian casualties to be expected in the event of a Soviet first strike against U.S. ICBMs was hotly debated in the Congress. By including almost every known or anticipated weapons effect and weapons type, and by allowing extremely fine detail, SIR NEM is presumably the most complete and accurate NEM ever written. The costs of that completeness and accuracy are those naturally attendant upon complexity: the need for a very large computer of a specific make, and for the interpretive intervention of expert staff who alone are fully aware of the complete workings of the model. This restriction of full knowledge to a select "priesthood" implies that the only fully informed users of the model's analytical product will be its programmer/operators and those few user-agency officials who have worked with those agencies through a long period of the model's evolution. It also makes the product susceptible to the prejudice reflected in the remark of a 1970s USACDA official to the effect that "It is my belief that those of us in this business can do intuitively, in moments, everything that the models can do" (Anschutz, 1972). That view, of course, is in distinct contrast to the positions of other researchers on the value of operations analysis, such as the economist William Baumol's view (1972, 4) of the value of optimality analysis:

> . . . an analysis which is specifically designed to look for optimal decisions, crude and approximate though it may be, is very likely to do much better than the workable but relatively arbitrary rules of thumb of obscure origin that play so prominent a part in business practice.

A Small But Flexible Model: NEMATODE 2.2

The author's nuclear exchange model NEMATODE 2.2 is the latest version in an evolving family of models designed to avoid both the inflexibility of AEM and the great cost and complexity of SIR NEM, while providing a useful tool for analysis of strategic weapons policy options. It is an interactive two-nation model programmed in Fortran, modular in structure to allow for flexibility of scenarios, and divided into three overlays or program divisions for efficient operation. The small first overlay receives user commands and controls access to the two main overlays. The first of those two major divisions handles data storage, retrieval, and manipulation, while the second handles the exchange calculations and assessment. Data is stored on disc in facility lists of up to 10 types of weapons and/or targets for each of two sides. The program is run one strike at a time; two facility lists are selected from those on disc and are used as input to an allocation matrix which records the possible blast effects of different weapons types on different targets. After an allocation has been made, the results are calculated and displayed in an assessment matrix, and the facility lists in memory are automatically updated. The updated lists may be saved on disc or used as input to a subsequent strike.

The program was designed to allow a moderate level of aggregation while providing for low running cost. Since up to 10 weapons types are allowed in each facility list, it is usually possible to represent each major weapon–warhead combination separately. Depending on whether a facility list has been designated as the attacker's or the defender's, a weapon type may be either an attacker (with the obvious exception of value targets included in the facility list) or a target. Targets may be defended by ABMs or SABMIS, with parameters adjusted to reflect area or terminal defenses, although this may require some redefinition of target types. For example, if some fraction of MX missiles were to be defended by LoAD ABMs, that fraction would have to be declared a type separate from the undefended MXs. Only missiles (ICBMs and SLBMs) and value targets are included at this time, and only blast effects are modelled. More than one RV may be targeted at a silo, and RVs of different types may be targeted at the same silo. Allocations of attackers targets are made in a 10 × 10 matrix; within each cell of the matrix a number of attackers may be directed at a number of targets, and the effects of such multiple attacks are automatically calculated. Fratricide effects may be included by limiting the number of attackers per target, a choice made by the operator at the time allocation matrix entries are made. Parameters included in the facilities lists are target type (weapon or value target); launcher type (ICBM or SLBM); quantity; reliability; duty factor or availability for time-urgent launch; grouping factor or number of weapons per aim point (e.g., 16 SLBMs are lost when one Polaris/Poseidon submarine is destroyed); number of RVs per launcher, and their accuracy (CEP) and explosive yield; quantity, reliability, and success rate of ABMs and SABMIS, if any; and hardness of silos or other target types against destruction by blast.

Some of the limitations seen in AEM remain in NEMATODE. In particular, discrete time intervals are assumed, and geography, range limits, missile footprints, collective and collateral damage, and defense suppression are excluded. On the other hand, cross-targeting is allowed, defenses may be allocated somewhat more flexibly, and fratricide may be taken into account quite easily. No automatic optimization routines are included, although they could readily be added. Since the operator must enter many allocation decisions interactively, it is also possible to optimize the allocations informally according to fairly complex objective functions with a bit of side-calculation best carried out on a portable calculator.

The only assessment measures automatically provided are the numbers of surviving and destroyed weapons and targets, on a cell-by-cell basis for each allocation cell and as totals by weapon type and target type. Other indices of results must be calculated from those basic data. The primary advantages of this model are that it avoids both the major inflexibilities of some much larger models such as AEM9, and the great cost and complexity of others such as SIR NEM. NEMATODE was used to carry out a large set of calculations on the import of various policy alternatives for use in dealing with the problem of ICBM vulnerability, as reported and discussed in Chapter 5, and that policy study may best provide for assessment of the utility of the model. Readers desiring more detailed information about the model are encouraged to contact the author. In the next two sections we turn to examining the utility of strategic "balance" measures in assessing and managing strategic weapons programs.

USING "BALANCE" MEASURES TO ASSESS STRATEGIC WEAPONS PROGRAMS

In the section "Strategic 'Balance' Measures" we considered a typology and assessment of measures for the strategic "balance." For the remainder of this chapter we shall direct attention specifically to the application of outcome/effects measures of strategic balance, with particular concern for the ways in which such measures might be used to improve the assessment and management of strategic weapons programs. As noted above, nuclear exchange models (NEMs) and measures derived from them have been used by the armed services, in work done under contract for USACDA, and in recent Annual Reports of the Secretary of Defense. To the extent that NEM-based measures are more complete and more accurate than alternative measures, we should expect them to help promote more efficient and objective strategic program decisions.

In principle, strategic weapons program management can be schematized in the steps outlined for the United States in Figure 4.2. Through a variety of overt and covert means the United States maintains observations of Soviet strategic weapons programs and capabilities. The raw data thus obtained must then be interpreted and assessed, and in those processes lie many opportunities for the loss of objectivity. Because intelligence information is seldom complete, the known bits must be fitted together to paint a coherent picture; and even if we had a complete picture, it would still be subject to differing interpretations, depending on what *intent* was assigned to an opponent. Assessment of capabilities must be based on our knowledge of such factors as past actions, doctrinal assumptions, economic capacity, and political stability, and on the degree of uncertainty in our estimates of these factors. Yet it has become a commonplace that analysts and decision makers interpret information about an opponent's actions in terms of preexistent "images" of that opponent's intent (Holsti, 1962; Jervis, 1970, 1976), so that the same facts may be subject to widely varying interpretations by different analysts. Recall in this connection our discussion of the "essentialist," "mechanist," and

FIGURE 4.2: A Schematic of United States Strategic Weapons Program Management

Observations of Soviet
Programs and Capabilities
↓
Interpretation
(A Filtering Process)
↓
Assessment
(In light of history, doctrinal
assumptions, et cetera)
↓
Program Option Generation
↓
Program Adoption
and Implementation
↓
U.S. Capabilities
(which vary with doctrine)

- This is one half of a feedback control process, with a similar schematic applying to the Soviet Union.
- There is a related chain of events leading to the adoption of strategic doctrine; see Chapters 2 and 3.

"cyberneticist' positions (in Chapter 1, the section "Ideologies and Values") as examples of three important but strongly contradictory images of overall Soviet policy and the consequent possibilities for U.S.–Soviet cooperation.

Like any scientific endeavor, intelligence interpretation and analysis may be viewed as building process theories. Analogously, the greatest pitfall to be risked is that known facts may fit an incorrect theory. It is common in intelligence analysis, for example, to infer an opponent's intent from capability, and to interpret capability very conservatively, in the way most dangerous to oneself ("worst-case analysis"). Yet if intent were to be inferred from capability, the Soviets should have feared a massive U.S. first strike in the 1950s, when the USSR lacked any significant intercontinental nuclear delivery capability—although we know that at that very time many individuals in the United States feared a Soviet first strike! Naturally, there is some range of uncertainty in any intelligence estimate, a fact that led Secretary of Defense McNamara in 1965 to institutionalize a process for considering the "greater-than-expected (GTE) threat" (Freedman, 1977, 85–86). While it may appear conservative to respond to the GTE threat, it also implies a consistent pattern of overreaction which is at least inefficient and expensive, and at worst will trigger an excessive counterreaction and increase the risk of the very war one seeks to avoid. It has been argued, for example, (Snow, 1981) that the massive Soviet strategic military buildup of the late 1970s resulted from a continuing reaction to having been caught in a vulnerable position at the time of the 1962 Cuban missile crisis, with the buildup being extended by bureaucratic momentum.

The interpretation and analysis of Soviet programs and capabilities, combined with many factors of U.S. internal and bureaucratic politics, lead to the generation of program options to meet perceived threats and bureaucratic goals. After passing through a stage of program adoption and implementation, which is itself protracted and continuing, always building on the history of what has already been agreed, the process ultimately leads to U.S. strategic weaponry in place. Exactly what the capabilities of those weapons are, of course, depends on the precise strategic doctrine adopted. As already suggested in Chapter 2, and as will be seen again in the ICBM vulnerability case analyzed in Chapter 5, it is never possible to divorce strategic capabilities from strategic doctrine.

The process of strategic weapons program management schematized in Figure 4.2 is, in fact, one-half of a feedback control process (Baugh, 1977a) through which the programs of the two superpowers interact and influence one another. Both sides of that process are rich in ties to internal politics, influences from other governments, and superpower interactions outside the strategic weapons regime, relations which were sketched in Chapter 3. In addition to these relations, analysis and interpretation of the other superpower's strategic capability and intent play crucial roles in determining each side's weapons programs. The quality and reliability of projections in planning is crucial, because the processes of design, development, and deployment of the weapons are quite protracted. Additionally, the very process of *deciding to develop* a new weapon may be almost as protracted (consider the extended history of efforts to procure a manned bomber as successor to the B-52, extending through the B-70 and B-1 programs for some two decades) and the lifetimes of the deployed weapons are considerable. One is constantly in the position of having to plan to meet a threat expected to materialize in perhaps a decade, using weapons that will probably take at least that long to reach IOC, without being able to forecast when some crucial technological breakthrough may occur. Beyond these presumably "objective" technological–military considerations, a political shift in interpretation of the strategic climate may be imposed at any time in respose to the pressures of other events, as, for example, the beginning of the SALT I negotiations was delayed for about a year to protest the Soviet and Warsaw Pact invasion of Czechoslovakia which began one day before agreement to begin SALT talks was to have been announced (Barton and Weiler, 1976, 177).

The role of nuclear exchange models in these decision processes lies in assessment, yet is still constrained by the quality and completeness of observations (both open and clandestine) of an opponent's capabilities; by the agreed interpretation of those observations; and by the time-lags imposed on any implementation of strategic plans. For example, a truly radical shift in intelligence interpretation occurred in the "Team A, Team B" approach adopted late in the Ford administration, and led to a great increase in estimates of Soviet military spending. While NEMs may lead to more accurate measures than the alternatives considered in the section "Strategic 'Balance' Measures" their use is still limited by the interpretive filter of presumed intent.

One of the most serious implications of misinterpretation may be cycles of overestimation and underestimation of an opponent's capability and/or intent; there is some evidence to suggest that the U.S.–Soviet strategic weapons regime has seen just such historical cycles. Bottome (1971, 54–58) notes that from December of 1959 to September of 1961 the range of publicly quoted estimates of the expected number of Soviet ICBMs for 1961–1962 fell from 1,000–1,500 to 35–52; the disappearance of the missile gap that played so prominent a role in the 1960 election was indeed dramatic. Consider next Freedman's (1977, 102) study of the numbers of Soviet ICBMs for the period 1961–1970, as shown in Figure 4.3. The figure shows the actual number of operational Soviet ICBMs, the number projected by the United States in its National Intelligence Estimates (NIEs) for mid-1967 each year from 1961 through 1967, and similar NIE projections for mid-1970, made annually from 1964 through 1969. The 1967 estimate was initially and finally about correct, yet fell steadily for three years to a low in 1964 before rising for another three years. This may be

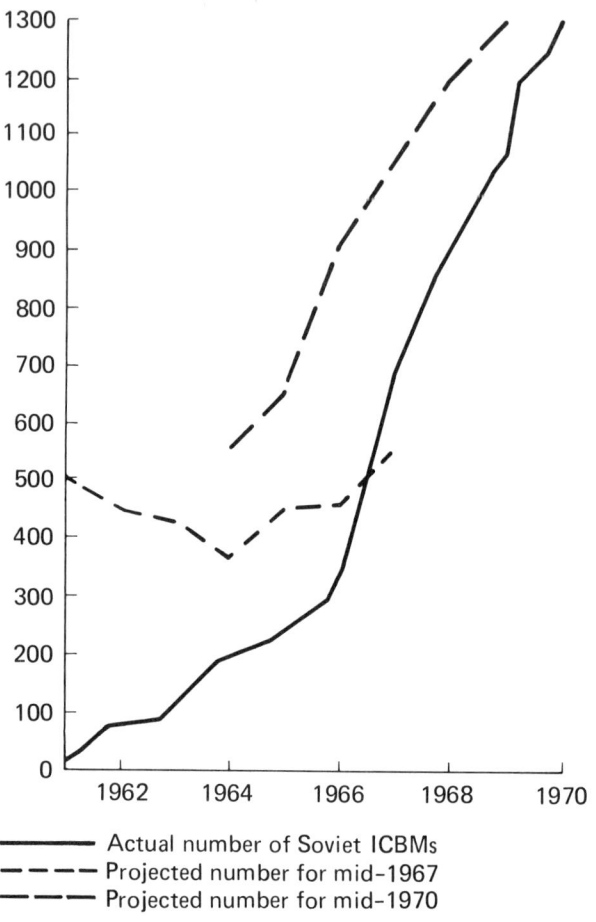

FIGURE 4.3 Actual Numbers of Soviet ICBMs Versus U.S. Projections, 1961–1970.

The solid line shows actual numbers of Soviet ICBMs by year from 1961 through 1970. The lower broken line shows U.S. projections of the Soviet ICBMs expected in mid-1967, as made in the National Intelligence Estimates (NIEs) each year from 1961 through 1967. The upper broken line shows the NIE estimates for Soviet ICBMs expected in mid-1970, as made each year from 1964 through 1969.
SOURCE: Freedman (1977, 102).

interpreted partly as an overreaction by the United States to its having overestimated Soviet ICBM capabilities during the "missile gap" fears of 1957–1961. Yet the Soviet buildup which began in 1966 was not foreseen, so that the U.S. estimate for 1970 rose steadily over a period of six years to more than double its initial value, as more and more evidence about the scope of Soviet ICBM building was accumulated.

On balance, Bottome's and Freedman's evidence suggests that there has been periodic overestimation and underestimation by the United States of Soviet strategic weapons building. Recalling the several inflection points in the historical trends of U.S. and Soviet ICBM quantities as shown in Figure 2.3, one might speculate whether both sides suffered the same estimating difficulties. This seems unlikely, since there is much more open information about strategic weapons developments in the United States than in the Soviet Union. Yet even if only one side is subject to cycles of over- and underestimation, the "lead" according to various measures of the strategic "balance" is likely to shift periodically from one side to the other, quite aside from such long-term trends as Soviet development of effective strategic parity with the United States. (Again, recall Chapter 2.) Cycles in estimation may lead to cycles in building, which in turn may lead to cycles in the other side's reaction, possibly triggering a counterreaction. Evidence of such cycles, using total ICBM warheads as a measure, can be found in Figure 4.4 (Squires, 1982b). Again, we see several inflection points between the years 1960 and 1967 as new missiles were deployed on

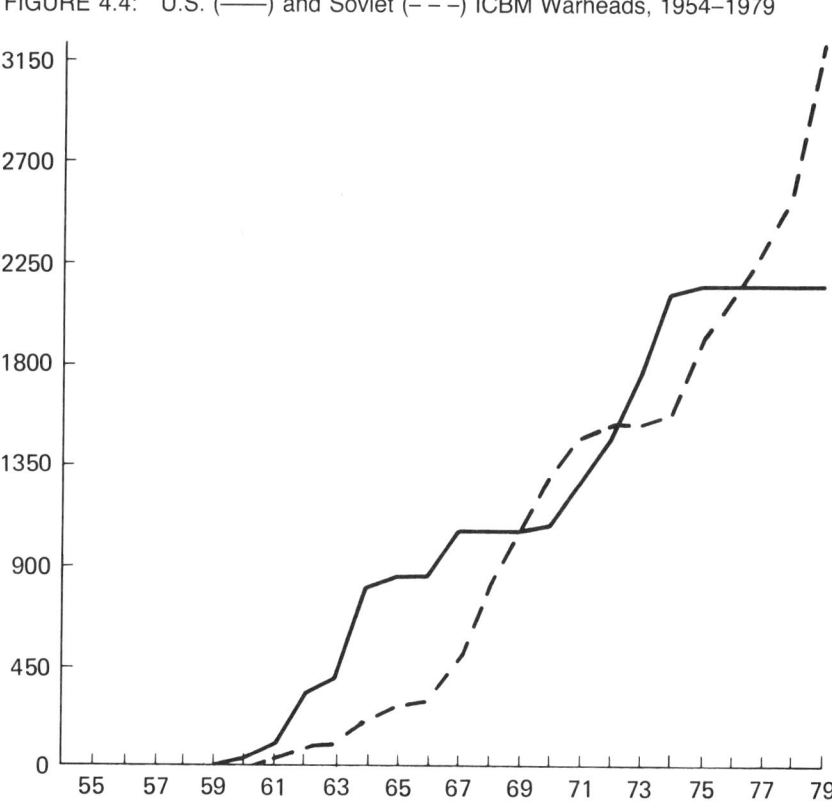

FIGURE 4.4: U.S. (———) and Soviet (– – –) ICBM Warheads, 1954–1979

SOURCE: Squires, 1982b.

both sides; but we also see major inflection points for the United States in 1970 and for the Soviet Union in 1974 as MIRVing programs were begun, leading in both cases to substantial increases in total ICBM warheads. Between 1967 and 1976 the "lead" in numbers of ICBM warheads is seen to shift back and forth with a period of about three years.

While Figure 4.4, based on counting ICBM warheads, might suggest a continuing "race" between the United States and the USSR which one side might be able to "win" by mounting sufficiently large missile-building or MIRVing programs, application of an output/effect measure from a nuclear exchange model yields a very different picture. Figures 4.5a and 4.5b show total U.S. and Soviet warheads together with Squires' (1982b) AEM9 calculations of the numbers of warheads expected to survive a first strike. These figures present a striking illustration of the development of ICBM vulnerability in the U.S.–Soviet strategic regime. U.S. expected survivability is almost 100 percent until 1967 and still great until 1975, while the initially high Soviet expected survivability begins to decline after 1970. By 1979 there are great differences between total warheads and the fractions expected to survive, despite the rapid increase in the numbers of Soviet RVs. This case provides a trenchant illustration of the way in which outcome/effect measures can cut through the fog of sometimes illusory "bean counting" measures to the underlying strategic developments—in this case, that both sides are suffering a major shift in their capabilities, driven by almost inexorable technological improvements in ICBMs and their associated MIRV and RV systems.

Outcome/effects measures also bear an interesting relationship to the long-standing efforts of political scientists and others to construct mathematical models of the patterns by which governments spend money to acquire weapons, usually referred to as "arms race models." Most of the best-known such models include an action–reaction process (ARP) as a major cause of arms spending, as discussed in Chapter 3. Perhaps the best-known family of such models was developed by the late Lewis Fry Richardson (1960), in both two-nation and many-nation versions. These are deterministic, continuous, differential equation models. Most are linear, and all involve a reaction process according to which armaments are purchased at least partly because potential adversaries are purchasing arms. Most tests of these models have assumed that arms racing occurs in expenditures, and the models have been converted to difference equation form so that the parameters could be estimated using time series budget data. Many such tests have been performed (Smoker, 1963a, 1963b, 1964, 1965; Gillespie, Zinnes, Tahim, and Schrodt, 1976; Gillespie, Zinnes, Schrodt, Tahim, and Rubison, 1977; Schrodt, 1978). In addition, many investigators have suggested modifications of the basic models (Caspary, 1967; Brito, 1972; Brito and Intriligator, 1973, 1974, 1977a, 1977b, 1981; Intriligator, 1975; Simaan and Cruz, 1977; Zinnes, 1976), while continuing to apply the models to arms expenditures. With the exception of Richard-

FIGURES 4.5a and 4.5b: U.S. and Soviet Total ICBM Warheads (Upper Curves) and ICBM Warheads Expected to Survive a First Strike (Lower Curves), 1959–1979

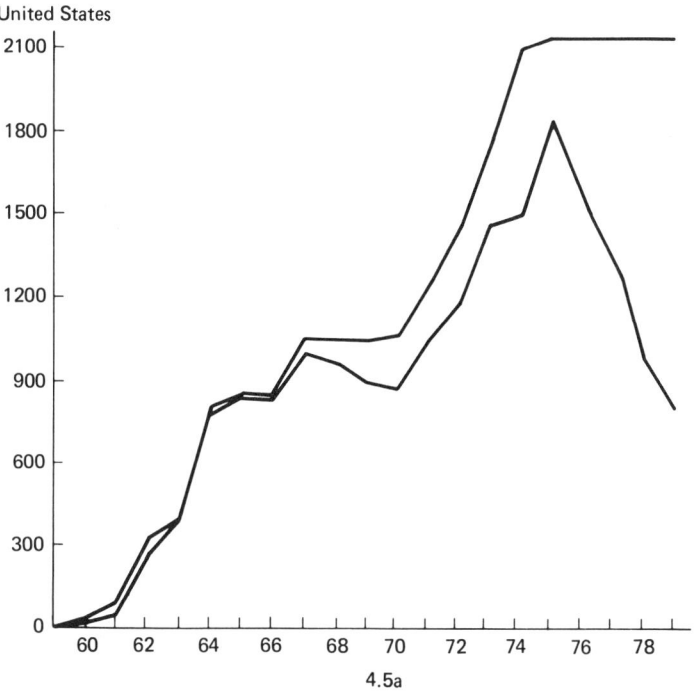

4.5a

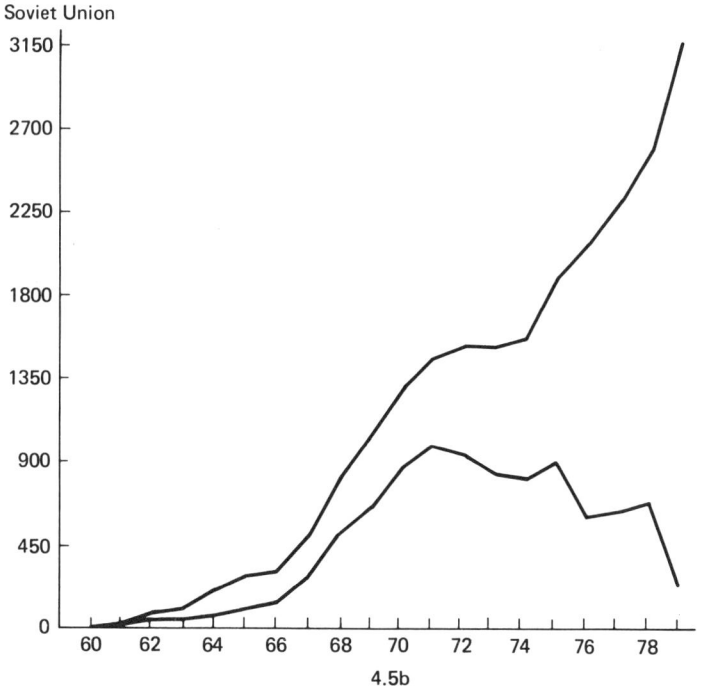

4.5b

SOURCE: Squires, 1982b.

son's classic test on the pre-World War I arms race (1960, 31–34), for which we have excellent historical evidence that the decision makers actually perceived themselves to be engaged in an arms race that had a high probability of leading to war if it were not otherwise terminated, most of these tests have been relatively unsuccessful. The Richardson models, which are forms of the general linear model familiar to econometricians, generally indicate that the best predictor to a nation-state's military spending is its spending in the previous time period. Reaction effects are thus found to be rather limited, despite the professed belief of some political leaders, including former Secretary of Defense McNamara (1967b) and Senator Edward Kennedy, in the existence and importance of such reaction processes.

In his doctoral dissertation, however, Squires (1982b) has married arms race models of the Richardson type with strategic weapons effects measures derived from the AEM9 model, interpreting the crucial arms race variables not as arms expenditures, but as various measures of the strategic balance in the U.S–Soviet regime. In so doing, he has avoided all of the problems usually associated with the use of arms-expenditure measures. Having used several different strategic-balance measures and applied a number of different lags, he finds a number of combinations which indicate that the U.S.—Soviet strategic weapons regime, over the period 1954–1979, moved in a bounded manner toward a position of stable equilibrium in a Richardson system. By implication the decision makers involved recognized the nature of the system in which they found themselves and manipulated their actions so as to maintain security while avoiding any outbreak of strategic war. One of the best (and unlagged) fits used the log of total lethality (K) as the strategic-balance measure. This author has some difficulty in holding that decision makers consciously optimized the log of total K. However, one could argue that since lethality is a rough measure of area-destruction capability, linearizing the inherently logarithmic K measure yields an approximate measure of ability to carry out some targeted amount of area destruction. Because officials since the time of McNamara have held that the United States must maintain the capability to ride out a first strike and retaliate in order to destroy some percentage of Soviet value targets, the log of total K expected to survive a first strike is one measure of ability to carry out the required retaliation. In the following section we turn to a further consideration of the possible uses of NEMs in managing strategic weapons programs.

USING "BALANCE" MEASURES IN MANAGING STRATEGIC WEAPONS PROGRAMS

Given the analyses of Chapter 3 and the previous section, assessment of one's own and one's opponent's capabilities will play a crucial role in the strategic weapons planning process. For that assessment we need to know capability, doctrine, and intent. Having the best possible strategic measures will improve our assessments of capability; and NEMs and other outcome/effects measures will be best. Yet the use of NEMs will not tell us what the stopping point of a building program will be, although it may tell us where that program "ought" to go, depending on the balance between technical and political considerations in setting the program end goal. And NEMs will never tell us an opponent's intent, although they can certainly tell us which intents are *feasible* at any given time.

However, within the framework of these limitations, one could consider the uses of NEMs in designing an optimally efficient strategic weapons program. Rather than simply designing such programs for political saliency, one could proceed through a series of steps, as follows: (1) First, set an appropriate strategic doctrine geared to one's ends, the ranges of means considered acceptable and feasible, and the constraints imposed by the capabilities of other governments. (2) Next, determine the forces required to implement that doctrine, given the nature and capabilities of the opponent's forces. (3) Then project your own and your opponent's forces into the foreseeable future. (4) Finally, decide upon the requisite weapons programs. Under the best of circumstances, such a program will provide an optimally efficient strategic weapons program, within the limitations imposed by one's resources and acceptable strategic doctrines. As always, of course, there will be powerful domestic bureaucratic and political pressures to maintain and expand existing programs and to launch new ones, and powerful pressures may be mobilized in support of those aims. (See, for instance, Ball, 1981.) Again, as before, the size of the arsenal which one must have to meet contigencies is powerfully influenced by assumptions about an opponent's intent.

Nonetheless, presuming a desire for stability in the strategic weapons regime, a program of the type outlined here might lend itself somewhat more readily than the procedures of the past to cooperative U.S.–Soviet measures to stabilize the regime, minimize costs, and reduce the risks of war through arms control and arms reduction measures. Such possibilities are considered in detail in Chapter 6. We turn first, however, to an illustration of the use of a nuclear exchange model in policy analysis, devoting Chapter 5 to a detailed examination of U.S. options for the 1980s in dealing with the problem of ICBM vulnerability.

5
ICBM Vulnerability and Its Solutions

INTRODUCTION

> It has been decisively shown that the ICBM element of the U.S. strategic triad is becoming increasingly vulnerable to a Soviet attack.
>
> House Armed Services Subcommittee report, 1978

> Vulnerability of the land-based missile forces, to paraphrase Wolfgang Panofsky, is far more a state of mind than a physical condition; but, nevertheless, it is an extremely important state of mind, worthy of the most exacting analysis.
>
> Steinbruner and Garwin, 1976

This chapter is devoted to a detailed examination of a single policy problem of the 1980s, in light of the doctrinal and policy analyses of the previous chapters. That problem is "ICBM vulnerability," and the examination includes the study of a number of proposed solutions to that vulnerability. In theory, land-based missiles have become vulnerable to a disarming first strike because the accuracy of attack is outstripping the passive defense capability of fixed targets, while active defenses remain essentially prohibited by the SALT I ABM Treaty. The increases in accuracy result from an inexpensive technological "creep"—what is feasible to develop will be developed, so long as it is not too costly—driven by a prisoners' dilemma fear that even if we do not pursue a possible new development, our opponents *may* pursue it to our detriment. Increasing missile accuracy also has strong ties to strategic doctrine, as discussed in the section, "The SALT I Aftermath" since it is argued that a more accurate missile might be useful in a limited nuclear exchange based on Damage Limitation (DL) doctrine. Under some competing doctrines such as Assured Destruction (AD), however, accuracy increases are seen as highly destabilizing and as raising the chances of first strike use or nuclear escalation in a time of crisis. (See the sections, "Evolution of Strategic Doctrine" and "A Plethora of Doctrines," Chapter 2.)

Several methods have been suggested for solving the vulnerability of land-based missiles: constraining numbers of missiles and warheads; making missiles mobile and thus unlocatable; adding active (ABM) or passive defenses; and adopting deceptive basing modes to disperse missiles among multiple aim points (MAP) or multiple protective shelters (MPS), thus causing the number of targets to exceed the number of warheads available for attacking them. This last scheme was the one proposed by the Carter administration for deployment of the MX missile by the United States. Alternative forms of these solutions are discussed below and assessed using a nuclear exchange model. In the absence of warhead limits such as those set in SALT II, it is not clear that any scheme of MX deployment or any of a number of alternative programs will necessarily solve the ICBM vulnerability problem either for the United States or for the Soviet Union. Yet for other reasons arising in the political process, the MX and some other new strategic weapons will probably be deployed whether or not the SALT/START process leads to new arms control agreements.

The following sections of this chapter cover the origin of the ICBM vulnerability problem; some proposed solutions; methods used in considering the theoretical nuclear "balance" in the 1980s, based on a quantitative analysis of the expected outcomes of possible attacks over the period 1971–1991 under several alternative scenarios; and evaluation of a number of claims that have been made regarding ICBM vulnerability and solutions for it, drawing on the results of the quantitative analysis. This last section includes consideration of the impacts of SALT limitations; deployment of new ICBMs in MPS and "dense pack" basing modes; U.S. deployment of additional Minuteman IIIs (first subsection); MPS basing of Minuteman IIIs (second subsection); the impact of "fractionating" ICBM payloads into very large numbers of small but accurate RVs in an attempt to overcome MPS deployments (third subsection); ABM defense of ICBMs (fourth subsection); and the impact of highly accurate SLBMs, such as the Trident II or Trident D5, on ICBM vulnerability (fifth subsection). The final section of the chapter comprehends a summary discussion of the different proposals and some reflections upon the roles of strategic doctrine, the SALT process, and the politics of action and reaction in arms building, in the light of this case.

THE PROBLEM: ACCURACY IMPLIES VULNERABILITY— AND PERHAPS INSTABILITY

Under SALT we have attempted to freeze *portions* of a technology while leaving other portions uncontrolled, often ignoring the danger that technological pressures to develop whatever can be conceived may exceed our political abilities to manage the result. Indeed, it appears that over the past decade a number of technology shifts with profound political consequences have occurred in part because their monetary costs were so low that they attracted little or no attention in the normal political processes. (See Shapley, 1978, and in Chapter 2, the section "What Drives Doctrine?") The most serious of these technology shifts is the increase in strategic missile accuracies.

The 1972 SALT I agreements imposed some quantitative but very few qualitative limitations; quantities of launchers were limited, but the number of warheads or reentry vehicles (RVs) that could be placed on a single missile was not limited, and no restraints were placed on testing or upgrading RVs. The 1979 SALT II agreements set out a complex series of limits, with closer balances than SALT I on most quantities, and with some qualitative limits expressed in quantitative form. These latter included a 1982–1985 ceiling of 1250 MIRVed missiles and/or heavy bombers, limits on the number of RVs per missile, and some constraints on the testing and deployment of new types of launchers and RVs (U.S. Department of State, 1979). Yet these limitations are not sufficient in themselves to prevent or undo the vulnerability of land-based missiles.

ICBM vulnerability arises because accuracy of attack is outstripping the passive defense capability of fixed targets. Simply put, nobody has been able to conceive a way in which to harden a target sufficiently to withstand the explosion of even a small nuclear device some 100–300 feet away, when the target could actually lie within the blast crater. In an earlier age of less accurate ballistic missiles, roughly from 1960 into the mid-1970s, one could plan for a mutual assured destruction (MAD) scenario in which one would ride out a first strike and then assess the damage, confident that a sufficient number of missiles would survive to wreak overwhelming retaliation on the attacker in a second strike. Any first strike would thus be irrational, and presumably would be deterred. However, the proliferation of warheads with ever-increasing accuracy undermines the rideout assumption, and raises the possibility of a first strike that would disarm all targets in known locations.

For the United States this problem is usually referred to as "Minuteman vulnerability," and most analysts have accepted at least since the mid-1970s that in the early 1980s the Minuteman ICBM force would become vulnerable to almost complete destruction by a hypothetical Soviet first strike (Gray, 1977, 1; Brown, 1979, 15 and 116–117; Wilson and Kaiser, 1979; Marsh 1979). Indeed, in the summer of 1980 Secretary of Defense Harold Brown indicated that, "that [Soviet] potential has been realized or close to it" (Wilson, 1980b, 15A). If thus perceived as vulnerable, the ICBM force (which has always been considered the most flexible and best-controlled leg of the strategic triad) may lose its utility, whether for deterrence, escalatory response, limited exchanges, or employment in major wars in modes other than as a first-strike or launch-on-warning force.

Both the United States and the Soviet Union have carried out extensive deployments of multiple warheads (MIRVs), thereby substantially increasing the numbers of available RVs while leaving the numbers of missiles fixed. At the same time accuracies have been substantially upgraded. Accuracies are usually expressed as "circular error probable" (CEP), the radius of a circle within which half of the warheads launched at a single target would be expected to fall. (The true error pattern, however, is an elliptical probability distribution with normally distributed density.) Programs already well underway in the United States promise accuracies in the range of a 300-foot CEP by the mid-1980s, and recent indications are that the Soviets are at most a few years behind, and perhaps almost "tied" with the United States (Gray, 1977, 11; Robinson, 1978). Other recent sources suggest that the increase in accuracies during the late 1970s was not quite as rapid as had been anticipated by Gray. SIPRI (1980, xxxv) indicated CEPs of already deployed Minuteman IIIs as 350 meters (about 1150 feet), with CEPs of 200 meters (about 656 feet) expected for Minuteman IIIs equipped with the new Mark-12A RV, which began to be deployed in the fall of 1979. Aviation Week (1980b, 67, 69) indicated a CEP of 0.14 nautical miles (about 850 feet) for newly deployed Soviet SS-18 and SS-19 ICBMs, with the accuracy of the Mk 12A-equipped Minuteman III "about that of" the Soviets. Downey (1976, S16212) had indicated an "early 1980s" CEP of 0.1 nm (about 608 feet) for the Minuteman III with Mark 12A. By 1982, Secretary of Defense Weinberger was publicly crediting the Soviets with higher accuracies (Halloran, 1982c). It appears that the consensus of these varied sources is that the state of the art as of about 1980 was a CEP in the range of 650 to 850 feet for the newest ICBMs on both sides, with the United States possibly enjoying a slight lead over the Soviets. As will be seen below, those accuracies are sufficient to yield U.S. ICBM vulnerability to a theoretical first strike using the larger Soviet warheads.

The development of such theoretical vulnerability was foreseen many years earlier, long before the SALT I numeric limits were set, and was a major issue in the ABM debates during the Johnson and early Nixon administrations. Albert Wohlstetter (1970, 2252), for example, spoke about late-1970s Minuteman vulnerability to a Soviet strike with SS-9s (which by 1980 had been almost entirely replaced with the more capable SS-18). Throughout those ABM debates, challenges were offered to the vulnerability calculations (see, e.g., Chayes and Wiesner, 1969) and to the practical feasibility and credibility of such an attack (on a number of grounds)—yet few analysts denied that indefinite increases in accuracy must eventually lead to at least the theoretical possibility of a disarming first strike against land-based missiles.

As will be shown below, investing in Multiple Protective Shelter (MPS) basing as a solution to the ICBM vulnerability problem without at the same time setting limits on the numbers of RVs per missile may reverse the vulnerability (for the United States) or delay its onset by at most a few years (for the USSR). At the same time, however, such MPS basing would increase fallout and collateral damage should war occur, raise costs and the threat of a cost spiral, increase the uncertainties of verification, and threaten to undermine the SALT/START process. ICBM vulnerability under MX/MPS has all the problems that exist with Minuteman vulnerability. One could be left with few options except to shift from rideout doctrine to such alternative doctrines as launch on warning or launch on assessment or launch through attack; the destabilizing character and other limitations of such doctrines were examined in the section "A Plethora of Doctrines" in Chapter 2. (For a contrasting view arguing the virtues of launching a portion of the ICBM force under attack, see Garwin, 1979.)

A further aspect of ICBM vulnerability is that investment in a new generation of missiles known to be vulnerable by the time of full deployment may raise fears, heightened or lessened according to the general international political climate, of an intent to make a first strike. Such fear inspired by the other side's vulnerability has been seen in both the United States and the Soviet Union at different times over the past two decades. With or without MPS or MAP, if the land-based missiles are perceived as being vulnerable, it may invite attack and thus destabilize the regime of mutual deterrence.

Other analysts, however, have seriously questioned the feasibility of a massive and effective disarming first strike against land-based missiles. Such questions have been raised on both political and technical grounds. The key political argument is that even the destruction of all land-based missiles would leave a massive residual force of SLBMs in submarines that were at sea at the time of the attack, plus alert bombers that were able to take off before their bases were struck. Under MAD doctrine the expectation that such a force would survive should deter attack, but the doctrine assumes that one would be willing to accept the probable loss of one's major cities in a counterretaliation, and would not be self-deterred from retaliating by that prospect. If one were actually faced with having to pay such enormous costs after a disarming strike against part of one's deterrent forces, many analysts fear that the only rational response would be to make political concessions. A different political argument made against the idea that ICBM vulnerability is critical is that a threat to launch one's ICBMs on warning of an attack would pull the fangs of any such threatened attack. In effect this proposal would counter the destabilizing situation of ICBM vulnerability by adoption of a destabilizing doctrine about ICBM use.

Still other analysts have challenged the idea of ICBM vulnerability on technical grounds. Their questions go beyond the usual considerations of warhead numbers, yield, and accuracies, or target numbers and hardness. Instead, they center around the uncertainties in extrapolating from limited tests under ideal conditions to full-scale use under operational conditions. It is important to note that we have absolutely no data about massive use of ICBMs under wartime conditions. As Steinbruner and Garwin (1976, 141) observe,

> The United States has never fired an intercontinental range missile at a target in the Soviet Union, has never exploded a nuclear warhead at the end of an intercontinental missile flight, has never fired a strategic missile on 15 minutes warning from an operational silo randomly chosen, and has never fired more than a very few missiles simultaneously or in close coordination. As far as can be known from the public record the Soviet test program has been similarly restricted.

The United States fires such missiles only on test ranges; a small number of operational ICBMs are removed from active silos and test-fired on the Western Test Range from Vandenburg Air Force Base each year; only the Soviet Union conducts test firings from operational silos (some 40–50 firings annually) (Brennan, 1979). Launchings of more than one missile at a time by either superpower are extremely rare. Even if the transition from such limited test launches to massive wartime firings could be made successfully, random errors would imply some range of uncertainty about any attack outcome. As the numbers of RVs per missile increase, an ICBM survival rate of even five to 10 percent would leave a truly formidable force available for retaliation.

Under actual operational conditions, performance is likely to be degraded below test levels in several ways. Steinbruner and Garwin (1976, 148–149), for example, cite degradations in boost phase reliability and warhead reliability; reduction in accuracy caused by interference between warheads (fratricide); mistiming in the attack plan and in execution of that plan; and greater-than-anticipated hardness of targets. Steinbruner and Garwin are among the few writers to take the *range* of uncertainty into account. The introduction of random errors and performance degradation moves the conventional analysis much closer to a realistic projection, yet most of the SALT II debate, like the ABM debates before it, was conducted in terms of the more conventional measures, such as numbers of missiles, numbers of warheads, throw-weight, accuracy, and hardness.

SOME PROPOSED SOLUTIONS TO ICBM VULNERABILITY

Strategic planners have proposed to meet the developing ICBM vulnerability problem by removing ICBMs from the category of fixed targets, using schemes to make them at least somewhat mobile. Nor is true mobility a new idea. Deception in location is inherent in SLBMs, and there was an early proposal to shuttle Minuteman ICBMs around the country on railroad cars, a plan with both technical and arms control problems, chiefly those of providing adequate security for the missiles, protecting them against vibrational damage from constant movement, and allowing adequate and credible verification of the numbers deployed. Many other forms of mobility have been proposed; see Gray (1977, 18–24) for nine such forms. The Carter administration's plan for MX deployment announced in September of 1979 called for a "racetrack" version of horizontal multiple protective shelters (MPS) (Walsh, 1979).

Under MPS or other forms of multiple-aim-point (MAP) basing, the number of possible missile storage and launch points is significantly greater than the number of launchers. Not knowing which of the launch points contains a missile, an attacker is forced to target each possible launch point in order to be assured of destroying every missile. In a strategic weapons regime with equal numbers of missiles having equivalent characteristics on each side, w warheads of reliability r per missile, and s shelters per missile, a surprise attack could not be disarming unless w exceeded s. Since r can never exceed unity, a successful attack would require that the number of warheads per missile exceed the number of known points from which one of the victim's missiles could be launched. Whether this could be achieved would depend on the relative costs of proliferating warheads and/or missiles versus increasing the number of shelters per missile—and also on agreed limitations on any of these quantities, plus the willingness of the governments to entertain the necessary expenditures. (See Richelson [1979] for a brief discussion of vulnerability and verification problems associated with MPS basing as the ability to detect the location of a missile in a group of shelters varies.) Any deviations below perfect missile reliability and 100 percent probability of destroying each target with a single RV would require a further increase in the ratio of warheads to shelters. It is routine to assume that such deviations require launching more than one warhead at each target—which immediately raises the questions of how many are needed and how quickly they can be fired. The atmospheric disturbance from one explosion could divert a later RV from its intended target, and the radiation and electromagnetic pulses produced could disable another incoming warhead. Such interference effects between RVs aimed at the same target are denoted as "fratricide," and it is fairly commonly accepted that such effects limit any short attack to no more than two RVs per target.

Building on the concept of fratricide, the Reagan administration by mid-1982 leaned heavily toward an alternative MX basing mode denoted "dense pack" (Halloran, 1982b). Under that plan, 100 MX missiles would be clustered fairly tightly in an area of some 10 to 15 square miles. Fratricide effects would be relied upon to ensure that although some silos might be lost to a first-wave attack, not all 100 could be destroyed in any reasonably short strike. It is not clear, however, to what extent the same fratricide effects would prevent launching any of the MXs; dense pack basing could thus help guarantee Soviet ability to execute a pindown of the MX force. Perhaps even more ominously, Halloran (1982b) notes that "in the cluster plan, the MX silos would be defended by interceptor missiles that would attempt to destroy or deflect incoming Soviet warheads several hundred miles in space." Deploying more than 100 such ABM interceptors, of course, would require abrogating or renegotiating the 1972 SALT I ABM Treaty, and the dense pack announcement was accompanied by a number of calls for just such changes. Despite its ABM accompaniment, however, dense pack basing arose in part in reaction to the great environmental and local resistance aroused by MPS basing, and in part to the persistent suspicion in Washington that MPS plans were too complex to be practical.

The Carter administration's MPS plan called for some 23 moderately hardened horizontal shelters per missile, each able to withstand a pressure increase (blast overpressure) of 600 to 1000 pounds per square inch (PSI), as compared to the 2000 PSI of current Minuteman silos. It was first proposed to locate the shelters some 7000 feet apart around an oval "racetrack" of roadway; later plans called for a two-thirds-filled hexagonal pattern of shelters with an average spacing of about 6000 feet between shelters connected by a linear road pattern. Missiles could be moved periodically by a transporter and could be launched from a separate launch vehicle at any point in the system. This 1980 version of the MX basing system was designated the loading dock, or separate transporter and mobile launcher (STML) system. By 1980 the originally planned quick-dash capability between shelters had been deleted. Plans incorporated cooperative measures designed to make Soviet verification of the number of missiles feasible; heavy vehicle access to the road network would be blocked after missile installation, and two ports on each shelter could be opened to allow satellite verification that there was only one missile per group of shelters (Walsh, 1979; Griffiths, 1979; *Aviation Week*, 1980d).

Under the 1980 plans, the United States would have deployed some 200 MX missiles, with flight tests beginning in 1983, IOC in 1986, and full operation by 1989 (Bruce Smith, 1980). As shown in the following discussion, such a deployment would alter the strategic balance in some interesting ways. Yet while the Department of Defense held that MPS-based MX missiles would be "highly survivable," it still appears that the vulnerability problem cannot be postponed indefinitely by MPS basing without limitations on the number of RVs available to attack the MPS bases (Brown, 1979, 119). Moreover, the MPS basing proposal raises a series of problems that cannot all be answered readily and optimistically. There are strong indications that it may be more costly to proliferate shelters than to proliferate RVs to shoot at them. The argument hinges on the cost of building shelters or silos plus the necessary transporters and launch vehicles, and cost estimates vary by at least a factor of three. Congressman Bob Carr (1978) estimated a cost-exchange ratio unfavorable to the defender by factors of 1.25 to 1.75 to 1. Using Defense Department cost figures to estimate the incremental cost of an MX missile at 12 million dollars and of a vertical shelter at 1 to 1.5 million dollars and assuming deployment of up to 30 small (55-KT yield) but highly accurate RVs per

MX, a missile costing 12 million dollars could reliably destroy at least 15 shelters costing 15 to 21 million dollars. Horizontal shelters, however, would be less costly than vertical shelters.

An MPS program would appear to have real potential to stimulate a new reaction spiral of spending, both for multiple shelters and for increased numbers of warheads with improved accuracies to shoot at them, ending with a strategic weapons regime having no greater crisis stability than the present regime. Soviet statements to the effect that they do not intend to give up a position of essential equivalence with the United States (e.g., Brezhnev, 1977, 1981) suggest that the Soviet ICBM vulnerability that would result from the MX program (see the assessment in the two sections following) would probably trigger a major Soviet response. If both the United States and the Soviet Union undertook massive MPS programs, the resulting strategic weapons regime would have more RVs and more targets, but land-based missiles could still be vulnerable to a first strike. The only apparent strategic benefit of such a shift would be to reduce vulnerability to attack from a third power unable to deploy enough RVs to saturate the MPS systems—but no third power appears to be acquiring the potential to threaten even the present number of aim points in either the United States or the USSR, at least before 1990 (Washington Post, 1978). In the meantime, a new spending spiral could greatly exacerbate the fears of both superpowers, limit the chances for further arms control agreements, and possibly increase the risk of war.

Whatever the risk, under MPS the severity of a major war might well be increased, because multiplying aim points increases the numbers of RVs that must be targeted, and thus promises increases in both direct and collateral damage, even if RVs are made smaller and more accurate. By thus raising the costs of war we probably decrease the chance for limited response. This danger was recognized in a letter sent to President Carter by 51 House members in 1978, questioning among other things the ". . . advisability of deploying a great sponge of targets in the U.S. designed to absorb Soviet warheads . . ." (Wilson, 1978). Few states are likely to want massive MPS target complexes. While it is some years since the United States has deployed a new missile field, the serious public opposition in both Wisconsin and Michigan during the 1970s to construction of the Seafarer VLF communications complex appeared to be based almost as much on fear of attack as on fear of environmental damage. The original plans to deploy MX/MPS only in Utah and Nevada were modified in 1980 to provide a more extensive deployment, largely because of public opposition in the target states. Later, when the Reagan administration scrapped the MPS plan, the move was greeted with widespread public and political support in the affected western states (Lescaze and Wilson, 1981).

Concern for the combination of Minuteman vulnerability and the potential problems of MPS basing has spurred support in some quarters for the alternative of deploying ABMs or other terminal defenses. As already noted, ABMs were strongly advocated by many supporters of dense pack MX basing. At the very least, ABM deployments promise another cost spiral, with a serious possibility that all terminal defenses can be overcome by sufficient warhead proliferation. All the questions of the ABM-versus-MIRV controversy are raised anew, and the efficacy of terminal defenses remains debatable (Chayes and Wiesner, 1969; York, 1973, 159–222). Perhaps even more seriously, abrogation or weakening of the 1972 SALT I ABM Treaty and the 1974 Protocol would represent a great reversal in the already troubled field of U.S.–Soviet arms limitation agreements and could undermine any prospects for further agreements.

Even if some SALT II or START agreement allowing MPS basing can be obtained, extremely serious verification problems are raised, further threatening to undermine the arms limitation process. Up to now it has been possible to verify quantitative limits on numbers of launchers with high reliability and accuracy through remote-sensing "national technical means of inspection" (NTM), primarily satellite photo-reconnaissance. In the absence of on-site inspection, however, verification of *qualitative* limitations has been much more problematic. One possible solution is to rely on other means of intelligence, such as espionage. Another is to rely on indirect schemes such as counting all missiles of a type that has ever been tested with multiple warheads as being MIRVed. Clearly, the verification of qualitative limits has been less direct and less reliable than verification of quantitative limits. Yet MPS basing would throw a shadow of doubt over even quantitative limits; explicitly hiding *which* aim points contain missiles implicitly allows hiding *how many* contain missiles. Indirect means of intelligence must be relied upon to assure that allowed numbers are not exceeded. Heretofore, missile silos have been counted as "launchers" for purposes of SALT limitations. Fitting MPS basing into SALT or START would require a change, perhaps redefining launchers as the transport cannisters for missiles. Such a change in definition would have the advantage that it would eliminate some of the ambiguity surrounding the ability to enforce SALT launcher limitations upon silos which can be rapidly reloaded with cold-launched missiles.

Despite assurances from the U.S. Arms Control and Disarmament Agency that verification is possible (Oberdorfer, 1978), and despite plans to open the verification ports on each shelter at a prearranged time when a reconnaissance satellite is overhead (and later reshuffling missiles among shelters), basic questions remain: Are U.S. officials confident of their ability to verify Soviet missile quantities in an MPS basing scheme? And if not, can they expect the Soviets to trust a U.S. MPS scheme? Complete certainty seems to require unlimited on-site inspection; and the refusal of the Soviets thus far to entertain such a scheme has spared the United States the problem of deciding whether it can tolerate such inspection. Even given on-site inspection one might ask whether carefully designed statistical sampling of aim points would be politically saleable, e.g., to the U.S.

Congress. It has been suggested in general terms by such analysts as Paul Wolfowitz (1978) that the United States should not preclude any deployment scheme that can be verified by means *that it would be willing to accept*; but this formulation contains very great stumbling blocks for the SALT/START process.

It has also been suggested that MX/MPS vulnerability may be avoided by setting a limit on the number of RVs which may be mounted on a single missile, as agreed in SALT II. Clearly, limiting RVs and missiles while permitting mobility and unlimited numbers of aim points per missile can allow the proliferation of enough aim points per RV to assure that a sufficient number of missiles—or, given many aim points, even most missiles—would survive an attack to present a highly credible retaliatory threat. Such a deterrent system would then be stable in the MAD sense. However, the number of RVs per launcher is one of the more problematic quantities to verify. While it is possible in principle, the stakes may be greater than for almost any other verification issue. A possible long-term solution was raised by the Scowcroft Commission's 1983 recommendation to develop a new light single-warhead "Midgetman" ICBM (Cannon, 1983b). Replacement of known MIRVed types of missiles with known non-MIRVed types would take some time, but could lead to a strategic weapons regime much more stable against disarming first strikes. The change, however, would also require at least tacit U.S.–Soviet cooperation and some assurance that MIRVed missiles were actually dismantled.

Closure does not seem to have been achieved on such questions as the following: Can either side mount a disarming first strike against land-based missiles, even in theory? If so, how soon? Can MPS basing cure theoretical ICBM vulnerability? And, if so, for how long and under what conditions? Whether or not MPS basing would accomplish those aims, would dense-pack basing do so, and could it work without an added ABM defense? To assess these questions, attention is directed in the following sections to a number of different hypothetical attack scenarios spanning the period 1971–1991, and to their implications for the SALT/START process and for strategic planning.

ASSESSING THE PROBLEM AND PROPOSED SOLUTIONS: MEASURING THE STRATEGIC "BALANCE" IN THE 1980s

In order to gain additional information about the claims made regarding possible disarming attacks, a number of different hypothetical attack scenarios against land-based missiles, spanning the period 1971–1991, were studied. The scenarios were run using the author's interactive nuclear exchange model, NEMATODE 2.2 (described in Chapter 4, in the section "NEMATODE 2.2") which allows a mathematical simulation of the hypothetical attacks. The physical outcomes possible under different policy programs may then be studied by policymakers, as they are discussed in

TABLE 5.1 Facilities Lists Used in Assessing a 1981 Soviet Anti-ICBM Strike

ICBM Type	Quantity[1]	Warhead Yield[2]	Silo Hardness (PSI)[3]	Reliability[4]	Accuracy (CEP), nm[5]	Duty Factor[4]
The United States						
Titan II	54	9 MT	300	80%	0.5	85%
Minuteman II	450	1.5 MT	1000	85%	0.3	90%
Minuteman III	375	3 × 170 KT	2000	90%	0.1	95%
Minuteman III w/Mk12A RV	175	3 × 350 KT	2000	95%	0.1	98%
The Soviet Union						
SS-9	18	18 MT	300	80%	0.5	80%
SS-11	580	1.5 MT	300	80%	1.0	80%
SS-13	60	1.0 MT	300	80%	1.5	80%
SS-17	150	4 × 5 MT	2000	85%	0.5	85%
SS-18	248	8 × 2 MT	3500	85%	0.14	85%
SS-19	300	6 × 550 KT	3500	85%	0.14	85%

[1] Quantities used are drawn largely from International Institute for Strategic Studies (1980), SIPRI (1980), and predecessor documents from both sources for earlier years. Both sides are assumed to have followed SALT II limits at least through 1981. Soviet quantities for later years, used in the study of additional attack scenarios, are based on the author's extrapolation using the above sources and such additional sources as the official 1979 quantities released by both sides under terms of the SALT II Treaty (See *Aviation Week and Space Technology* [1979b]). Soviet and U.S. quantities likely under various possible building and arms control schemes are discussed more fully in the text.

[2] Explosive yields of RVs in kilotons (KT) or megatons (MT) of TNT equivalent are drawn from IISS (1980), SIPRI (1980), and Colin S. Gray (1977, 32–35). All missiles of any given type are assumed to carry the maximum number of RVs permitted for that type under the SALT II agreements; see United States Department of State (1979, 35). Where several models of a missile have been tested, yields used are the largest that the missile's throw-weight will allow for the number of RVs carried. Warhead improvements assumed in later years are discussed in the text.

[3] Silo hardness is the increase in atmospheric pressure (overpressure) that would be required to disable the missile, expressed in pounds per square inch (PSI). U.S. values and those for the earlier Soviet types are from SIPRI (1980) and Thomas Downey (1976). The value of 3500 PSI for the latest Soviet SS-18 and SS-19 silos is from *Aviation Week and Space Technology* (1980b). It is assumed that neither side will make much effort to improve the hardness of silos housing older types of missiles such as Titan IIs or SS-11s.

[4] Reliability is the probability that a missile will function correctly from launch through accurate war-head detonation(s). Duty factor is the percentage of time that a given missile is available for launch on short notice, recognizing that some missiles will be undergoing service or movement at any given time. For the scenarios in which attack effectiveness is limited by the number of warheads available, the attacker's surviving ICBM's are only those that were not available for launch. All reliabilities and duty factors are drawn from Downey (1976). These are rather problematic parameters, difficult to estimate and seldom mentioned in the literature. It may be remarked that Downey has proved to be a valuable source on some other parameters which have been disputed and then resolved in his favor. See, for example, Walter Pincus (1979).

[5] Accuracy is given as CEP (circular error probable) in nautical miles (nm). This is the single most critical parameter in determining the ability of an RV to destroy a silo. Accuracies

have been in some dispute in the last few years, but it is clear that they are improving and that Soviet CEPs used to be substantially underestimated. No substantial improvement in the accuracies cited by Downey (1979) for Titan II, Minuteman II, and SS-9 through SS-17 is assumed. The concensus of SIPRI (1980, xxxv), *Aviation Week* (1980b, 67, 69), and Downey is that the best U.S. accuracy in 1981 with the Mk12A RV is 0.1 nm.; *Aviation Week* gives 0.14 nm for the best 1981 Soviet accuracy. It is expected that both sides will achieve further improvements in accuracies; for the U.S., they rely on using the Mk12A RV with the Advanced Inertial Reference Sphere (AIRS) and new on-board computers, as planned for the MX missile.

this and the next sections. The model includes parameters for launcher type and quantity, reentry vehicles per missile, explosive yield and accuracy of those RVs, silo hardness, and numbers and performance parameters of any active ABM defense. Summary figures for the scenarios studied are given in the following section.

The NEMATODE 2.2 model is one of the class of exchange effects models discussed in the section "Outcome/Effects Measures," (Chapter 4). By using an exchange model one automatically takes account of the facts that the results of an attack depend on the allocation of particular types of RVs to particular types of targets, and that our picture of the results can be blurred by applying aggregate measures to entire arsenals. Given the considerable differences in capabilities of different types of missiles, it may be both arbitrary and somewhat misleading to use the *numbers* of surviving missiles and surviving RVs as figures of merit, but those measures are frequently cited. (See, e.g., Brown, 1979, 114–117.) Moreover, there is some evidence that decision makers strive to maintain goals expressed in terms of expected surviving RVs or missiles after riding out an attack (Saaty, 1968, 24; Squires, 1982a, 1982b).

The scenarios presented depend crucially on the parameter values entered in the "facility lists" of available weapons and their characteristics. Those lists were constructed from values in a number of open-literature sources, extrapolated to levels probable under SALT II or other possible policy options; refer to the source notes for Table 5.1, which follows. Derivation of the results of a hypothetical attack requires three operations: (1) Missile quantities and performance parameters appropriate to the date and to the policy options being studied must be determined, so that suitable facility lists can be prepared; (2) Specific numbers of attackers must be allocated to specific types of targets to yield an efficient attack; and (3) The results of the attack must be compiled. Consider this process in detail for a 1981 Soviet attack against U.S. ICBMs, presuming that both sides followed SALT II limitations on the numbers of missiles and warheads, according to their public pledges. The facility lists used in this attack simulation are summarized in Table 5.1, which includes citations to the sources used and assumptions made. Many of the sources used and parameter values adopted are common to the facility lists used in other simulated attacks discussed in the next section.

TABLE 5.2   Allocation of Weapons and Assessment of the Attack;
1981 Soviet Anti-ICBM Strike

TARGETS:		Titan II	Minuteman II	Minuteman III	Minuteman III/Mk12A	
Quantity		54	450	375	175	Total 1054
RVs:		54	450	1125	525	Total 2154
Attackers:						Attackers Not Used[2]
SS-9, -11, -13, -17						808
SS-18	SSPK:[1]		0.886	0.685	0.685	38
(210 of 248	Launched:		72	94	44	
available)	Total RVs:		576	752	352	
	Silos killed:		356	310	145	
SS-19	SSPK:[1]	0.892	0.573			228
(255 of 300	Launched:	18	54			
available)	Total RVs:	108	324			
	Silos Killed:	51	85			
Surviving Missiles:		3	9	65	30	Total 107 (10%)
Surviving RVs:		3	9	195	90	Total 297 (14%)

[1] Single Shot Probability of Kill (SSPK) is the probability that a single warhead (RV) will destroy its target. Reliability of the launchers and RVs is taken into account before calculating and aggregating the results.

[2] Missiles either not needed in the attack or unavailable to use in the attack, according to the duty factor.

Table 5.2 shows the crucial cells in the matrix of weapons allocations and attack results for this hypothetical 1981 attack. Given larger numbers of ICBMs and more warheads per missile, the Soviets require only a fraction of their ICBM force. To utilize the most effective Soviet warheads, all 210 available SS-18s and 72 of the 225 available SS-19s are launched. Fratricide effects are assumed to limit the attack to two RVs per target. In every case two RVs are allocated to each target, presumably cross-targeted from different missiles to increase attack reliability. By using 21 percent of their ICBM force with 42 percent of their total ICBM RVs, the Soviets are able to destroy 90 percent of the United States ICBM force and 86 percent of U.S. ICBM RVs.

Whether or not these results are to be interpreted as indicating a condition of U.S. ICBM vulnerability may be debated. They certainly rely on achieving test-range levels of performance from the entire fifth of the Soviet missile force utilized in the hypothetical attack. Moreover, many analysts believe that the 297 U.S. ICBM RVs expected to survive would constitute a very credible deterrent, even without reliance on the bomber and submarine legs of the strategic triad. It also should be emphasized that the results reported here are the mean values of probability distributions; even if performance is not degraded by operating under wartime conditions, the attacker cannot do as well as the expected value more than half the time. No ABM defenses of missiles were assumed in the scenarios that were run, except those discussed later, in the section "LoAD ABM Defense of ICBMs," although abrogation of the SALT I ABM Treaty would allow such defenses. Furthermore, the United States is preparing to test some ABM options for MX that would still fall within the framework allowed under the terms of that treaty, (Robinson, 1979d; Aviation Week, 1979b) and is considering others, e.g., LoAD and space-based lasers, which probably would require ABM Treaty abrogation. Significant features and results of the various attack scenarios considered are discussed in the following section.

EVALUATION OF THEORETICAL ATTACK SCENARIOS

All of the hypothetical attack scenarios were run in a manner similar to the example considered in the preceding section. They involved a single strike of ICBMs (and, in a few cases, some SLBMs) against ICBMs, targeting two RVs against each possible launch point, up to the total number of RVs available with at least a 10-percent chance of destroying their targets. Attackers were allocated first to destroying missiles with the largest numbers of RVs and/or most effective RVs, beginning with missiles housed in the hardest silos. Since many of the MPS schemes examined had far larger numbers of targets than RVs, and the probability of destroying a warhead was much greater when attacking a hard point silo known to contain a missile, minimizing surviving RVs often led to leaving many of the multiple protective shelters unattacked. Results were assessed primarily according to two figures of merit: expected number of surviving ICBMs, and expected number of surviving ICBM RVs.

The base year for these studies was 1981. Cases from 1971 and 1976 were also examined to give some indication of shifts in the strategic balance over the prior decade, and detailed studies were carried out for the decade 1981–1991 under a number of different possible arms limitation and building programs on both the U.S. and Soviet sides. An overview of the range of possibilities and an idea of the different perspectives afforded by using different figures of merit can be gained through consideration of Figures 5.1 and 5.2. In 1971 the United States could have destroyed about 22 percent of Soviet ICBMs in a first strike, while the Soviets could have destroyed about 12 per cent of U.S. ICBMs. Both attacks would have been limited by the number of RVs available to launch, and the disparity in expected results is due both to higher U.S. accuracies (smaller CEPs) and to the fact that deployment of MIRVs on Minuteman III missiles had already begun. The larger number of U.S. warheads offset the larger number of Soviet ICBMs, and each side would have expected about 1100 RVs to survive attack.

FIGURE 5.1 Expected Percentages of ICBMs Destroyed in First Strikes, 1971–1991

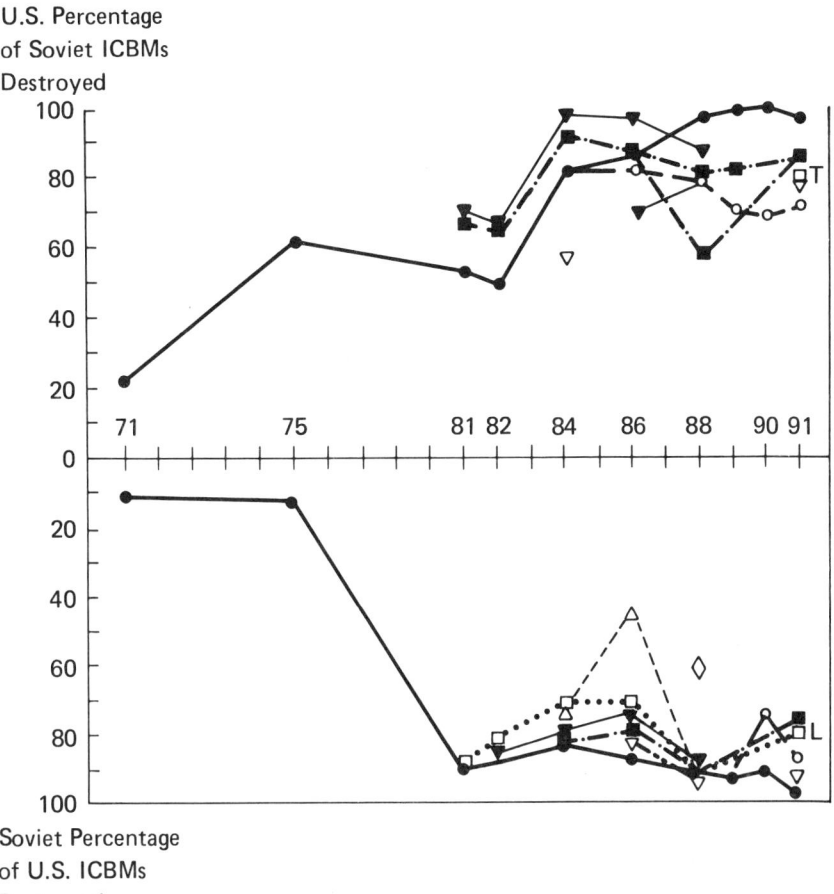

Legend:
- ●——● No MPS
- ○— —○ MPS
- ■-·-·-■ Extra Minuteman III, No SALT
- ▼——▼ Extra Minuteman III, SALT Limits
- □·····□ MM III in MPS, No SALT
- △----△ MM III in MPS, SALT Limits
- ▽-··-▽ U.S. follows SALT, U.S.S.R. does not
- ◊ MM III in MPS, Extra MM III, No SALT
- L LoAD ABM Defense of some silos
- T Trident II or Trident D5

By 1976, however, the strategic balance as measured either by expected surviving ICBMs or by expected surviving RVs had undergone dramatic shifts, which are perhaps better illustrated by the RV measure.

FIGURE 5.2 ICBM RVs Expected to Survive a First Strike Under SALT Limitations

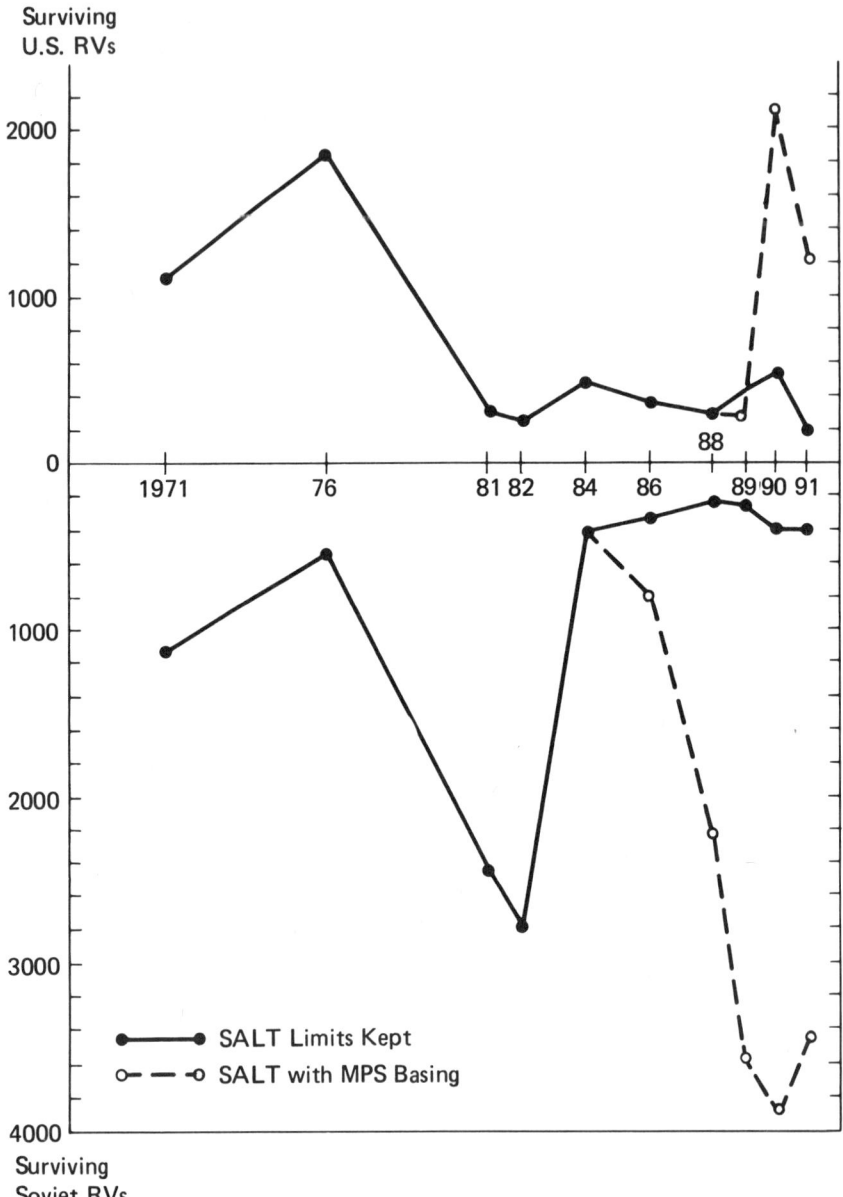

As its MIRVing program continued, the U.S. attack was no longer limited by available warheads, and was expected to destroy about 62 percent of Soviet ICBMs, leaving only about 550 surviving RVs. The Soviets' MIRVing program, however, was just getting under way, and their accuracies

had not yet improved significantly, so that a Soviet attack was only expected to destroy about 13 percent of U.S. ICBMs, leaving some 1850 surviving RVs. Yet if the shift from 1971 to 1976 was dramatic, the shift over the next five years was opposite but equally dramatic. As the Soviets built more MIRVs and increased accuracies, they could take advantage of their larger and more numerous ICBMs. By 1981, as seen in detail in the previous section, they could have expected to destroy about 80 percent of U.S. ICBMs and about 86 percent of RVs, using only 21 percent of their ICBMs and 42 percent of their RVs, while leaving the United States only some 300 ICBM RVs. The United States, by contrast, using smaller RVs against Soviet silos of recently increased 3500 PSI hardness, could only have expected to destroy some 53 percent of Soviet ICBMs, while the larger number of Soviet missiles and the major Soviet buildup in MIRVed types over the previous several years would have left them with some 2500 surviving RVs.

By 1981 the Soviets are seen to have gained a theoretical capability to destroy the vast majority of U.S. land-based missiles, a capability which neither side had in the 1970s, and one not matchable by the United States until at least 1984. As accuracies increase, the Soviet lead in warhead yield translates into very high kill probabilities for one RV against one silo, and the limiting factor in an attack becomes the reliability of an individual missile/RV combination. For example, if that reliability were 85 percent and errors were randomly distributed across launchers and targets, even if the single-shot kill probability were unity, 15 percent of silos would survive the first RV launched against them and 15 percent of those, or 2.25 percent, would survive both RVs. Since it is assumed that fratricide effects limit the attack to two RVs launched at each silo, destruction of the last remaining ICBMs would require a capability to determine exactly which silos had survived so that more missiles could be retargeted at them, a so-called "shoot-look-shoot" capability not assumed in the scenarios analyzed here.

The 1981 U.S. attack is still warhead limited, a fact arising from past decisions on both sides regarding the size and number of ICBMs, and from the numerically unequal ceilings set in SALT I. It is assumed that neither side had much capability to deviate from SALT II limits in 1981. The dramatic shifts in capabilities over the decade 1971–1981 resulted from building programs based on similar technologies but starting at different points in time and from different historical and technological bases of numbers and sizes of ICBMs, degree of miniaturization, and fraction of strategic weaponry comprised of ICBMs. That the Soviet lead in size and numbers of ICBMs would eventually translate into an advantage in destructive effect as missile accuracies increased could have been (and was) predicted years in advance. Similarly, the brief period of relative U.S. advantage in the mid-1970s, based on greater numbers of RVs, was entirely foreseeable and may even have triggered the Soviet MIRVing program. We now know that the Soviets began extensive development of a new generation of ICBMs, including the MIRVed SS-17, -18, and -19, shortly after SALT I was ratified.

The patterns illustrated in Figures 5.1 and 5.2 are quite consistent with the concept of a reaction-process model for strategic arming, in which each side strives for a certain level of capability but the system is subject to substantial lags due to the bureaucratic and technological inertias of starting and stopping programs. In this interpretation, taking expected surviving RVs as the better figure of merit, the last time that there was effective balance between the United States and the Soviet Union was about 1971. Yet at that time the United States had already begun a MIRVing program, and by the time that 550 of the 1000 Minuteman missiles had been MIRVed, an advantage had been gained. Soviet leaders motivated only by the survival interests of their own state still would probably want to restore the approximate strategic balance, and would be likely to launch fairly sizable building programs if they were unsure just how far U.S. accuracy improvements would go and how many U.S. missiles would eventually be MIRVed. (For a more thorough consideration of such reaction processes in strategic arming, see Squires, 1982b.)

For the period 1981–1991, Figure 5.1 indicates an envelope or range of possibilities under a number of strategic weapons development and deployment programs that have been suggested for both sides, with and without SALT II, START, or some similar arms limitation agreement. The corresponding effects of those policy choices on expected numbers of surviving RVs are illustrated in Figure 5.2 and in Figures 5.3 and 5.4, following. The 1981 base case was taken as starting point in deriving the programs studied, and it was assumed that some U.S. moves would be taken to attempt to reduce ICBM vulnerability. In most of the scenarios studied, the United States was assumed to be the policy initiator and the Soviet Union to follow or anticipate with countering moves. Facility lists used were based on assumptions about the probable reactions of each side to the other's moves. Thus, for example, one would not assume that one side would follow SALT-type limitations on missile quantities if the other were pursuing a vigorous new missile building program; and an MPS deployment by one side would likely be matched by an MPS deployment by the opponent. In some cases in which Soviet building programs are already under way, they can deploy such new developments as MPS basing at least as rapidly as the United States. It was assumed that U.S. and Soviet missile performance parameters, such as CEP, would be essentially equivalent by 1991.

Almost all the policy combinations considered lead to a Soviet capability to destroy 70 percent to 90 percent of U.S. ICBMs in the period 1981–1988, and 80–95 percent in 1988–1991, with the United States able to destroy 50–70 percent of Soviet ICBMs in the period 1981–1983 and 60–95 percent or more in 1984–1991. U.S. capabilities generally exhibit

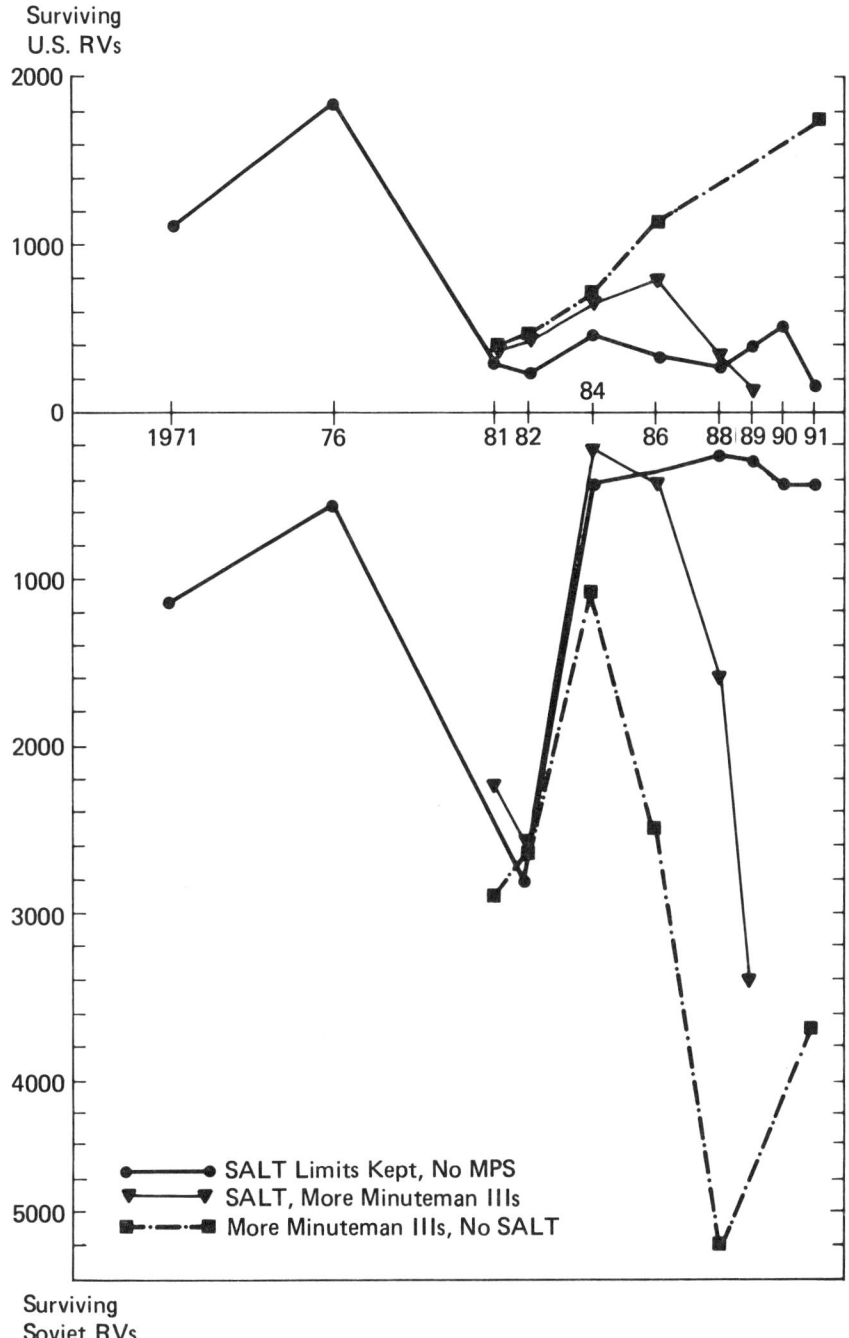

FIGURE 5.3 ICBM RVs Expected to Survive a First Strike; Additional Minuteman IIIs Deployed by the U.S.

176 / *The Politics of Nuclear Balance*

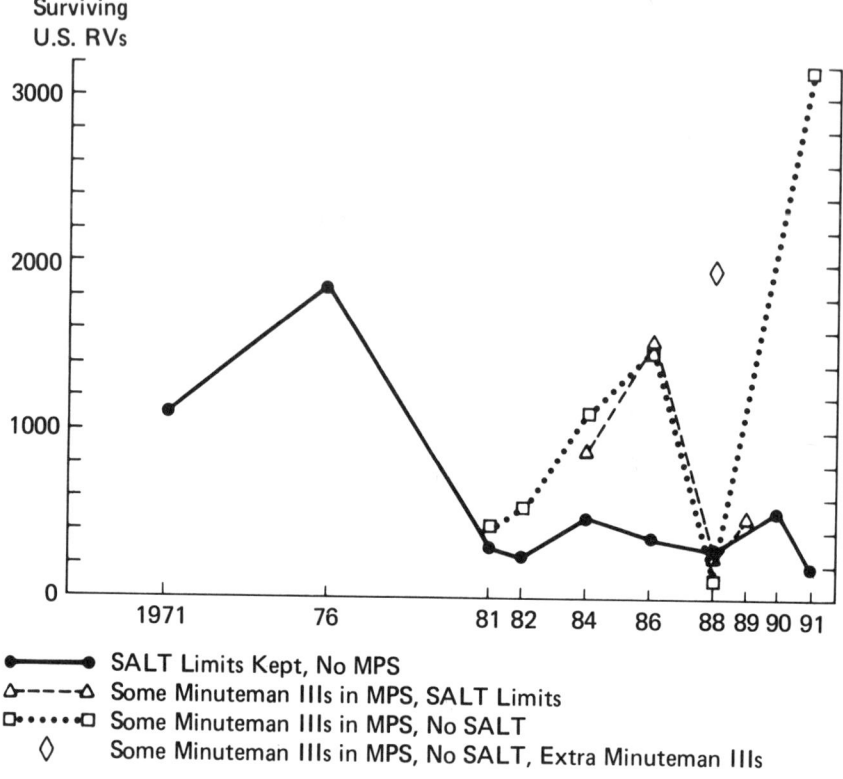

FIGURE 5.4 United States ICBM RVs Expected to Survive a First Strike; Some Minuteman IIIs Deployed in Multiple Protective Shelters

●———● SALT Limits Kept, No MPS
△----△ Some Minuteman IIIs in MPS, SALT Limits
□·····□ Some Minuteman IIIs in MPS, No SALT
◊   Some Minuteman IIIs in MPS, No SALT, Extra Minuteman IIIs

a wider range of variation, because they are based on smaller numbers of missiles, smaller warhead yields, and (on average, even after any MX deployment) fewer RVs per missile. Yet even 10-percent ICBM survival may lead to extremely large numbers of RVs expected to survive attack. Two general policy options are illustrated in Figure 5.2, both based on limitations on numbers of ICBMs and numbers of RVs per missile being maintained at approximately SALT II levels over the decade. If neither side deploys any ICBMs in MPS basing schemes, and neither adopts a substantial ABM defense of ICBMs, both sides will be able to destroy over 95 percent of the other's ICBMs by the mid-1980s. Expected RVs surviving will fall to a 1988 low of about 300 per side, then rise slightly as newer types of missiles are deployed in harder silos. In this scenario the SSPKs are so high that almost all surviving missiles result from the combination of missile reliability limitations with fratricide limits on the number of RVs that can be launched at a single silo.

If both sides were to deploy some missiles in MPS basing schemes, however, the picture alters drastically. A new Soviet ICBM is assumed with a 1984 IOC and MPS basing in 20 shelters of 1000 PSI hardness per missile, about 100 such missiles being deployed each year after an initial 50 in 1984. The U.S. MX missile program is assumed to be further behind, yielding a 1986 IOC with 10 missiles, and 50 or more new missiles per year thereafter, using 23 shelters of 600–1000 PSI hardness per missile. The Soviet lead in numbers of total RVs means that the U.S. MPS effort has no real impact before 1990, whereas the Soviets MPS effort already more than doubles their expected surviving RVs by 1986. U.S. expected surviving RVs are actually lower under MPS in 1989, since the MPS shelters are much softer (600 PSI) than the alternative hard point silos (3000 PSI) and the Soviets have enough RVs to attack and destroy all 4600 MX shelters. By 1990, however, more MX shelters have been built and the Soviets no longer have enough RVs to attack all of them, so expected surviving U.S. RVs rise dramatically. Soviet surviving RVs at the end of the decade exceed U.S. surviving RVs due to the Soviet Union's larger numbers of ICBMs and of RVs per missile (although both the MX and the new Soviet ICBM are assumed to have 10 RVs), while the drop from 1990 to 1991 is due to anticipated accuracy improvements. By 1991 each side could expect significantly more than 1000 surviving RVs under SALT II limits and MPS basing.

Similarly, expectations may be altered if one or both sides adopt dense pack basing for some fraction of ICBMs. The survivability of those missiles depends critically on fratricide effects, and the details of those effects are not readily assessed from open-literature information. If the plan works, it should assure the survival of a formidable deterrent force (i.e., it should provide an assured destruction (AD) retaliatory capability.) Additionally, dense pack basing appears to offer the promise of providing an AD capability less expensively and with fewer new missiles than would be required under MPS basing schemes. However, it remains suited to a narrower range of doctrines and attack scenarios than MPS: missiles in the dense pack are less capable of withstanding a limited attack than missiles in an MPS basing mode, and are more susceptible to pindown by a controlled slow sequence of incoming warheads. Thus, dense pack basing is no universal cure for other imbalances in the strategic weapons regime. Finally, deploying MX missiles in Minuteman silos contributes nothing to reducing ICBM vulnerability beyond a marginal addition to the number of expected surviving warheads, since those silos are already vulnerable and would surely be the first ones attacked. Deployment of new Minuteman IIIs in additional silos would actually add more expected surviving warheads.

Deploying Additional Minuteman IIIs

Given the apparent imbalance in ICBM vulnerability between the United States and the Soviet Union, and also given the years needed for development of the MX missile with its larger number of warheads (regardless of basing mode), one suggestion raised in 1980 was that the United States deploy additional Minuteman IIIs. One hundred fifty or more could be drawn directly from stores of spares (*Aviation Week*, 1980b), and additional Minuteman IIIs could be built quickly by reopening the production line. Even if SALT II limitations on numbers of missiles and numbers of MIRVed missiles continued to be followed, the number and accuracy of U.S. RVs available could be raised by replacing older, unMIRVed Minuteman IIs. This would not reduce U.S. ICBM vulnerability, but it would increase the number of RVs expected to survive a Soviet first strike and would increase U.S. ability to attack the Soviets. Presuming that the new missiles were installed in new or rebuilt hardened silos, it would also slightly decrease overall ICBM vulnerability. As seen in Figure 5.1, this plan would immediately raise expected U.S. capability by some 10 to 15 percent of Soviet ICBMs destroyed and decrease Soviet expected destruction of U.S. ICBMs by three to five percent, although those differences would be diminished by around 1990. The effect of maintaining SALT II limits on both sides while the United States deployed additional Minuteman IIIs would be favorable to the United States, since it is assumed that without SALT II the Soviets would deploy still more missiles having larger average numbers of RVs per missile than the Minuteman III. If SALT II limits were followed, by 1984 the United States could destroy some 95 percent of Soviet ICBMs in a first strike, while the Soviets could only destroy some 80–84 percent of U.S. ICBMs, so that the ICBM vulnerability situation of 1981 would be brought much closer to a balance, and slightly into the United States' favor.

The effect of these programs on the numbers of ICBM RVs expected to survive attack is shown in Figure 5.3. Both U.S. and Soviet numbers are higher without SALT limitations, since both sides can deploy larger numbers of missiles. Numbers of expected U.S. surviving RVs rise immediately from about 300 to approximately 400 in 1981 and rise steadily to almost 1800 in 1991 without SALT, while falling after 1986 if SALT limitations are maintained. With or without SALT, however, it is assumed that MX and the new Soviet ICBMs are deployed in MPS basing modes, with IOCs in 1986 and 1984, respectively. This replacement of older ICBMs with a more effective type is responsible for the 1986–1988 downturn in U.S. expected surviving RVs under SALT, as the fraction of Soviet ICBMs that are highly effective is increased. Under SALT the MX causes a similar downturn in Soviet expected surviving RVs between 1988 and 1991, although the always larger numbers of Soviet ICBMs lead to very high numbers of RVs—generally over 3500 expected to survive—by the late 1980s. As seen before in Figure 5.2, surviving U.S. RVs under SALT fall below those predicted in the non-SALT base case for 1989, when Soviet RVs still outnumber U.S. shelters, because the 600 PSI MX shelters can be destroyed while not all of the alternative 3000 PSI hard silos can be neutralized. A year or two later this situation is reversed and MPS basing leads to more expected survivors, as additional MX shelters begin to exceed the numbers of available Soviet RVs. Overall, the option to deploy more Minuteman IIIs, whether accompanied by SALT II limitations or not, is seen to be a short-term way for the United States approximately to double its number of expected surviving RVs in the early and middle 1980s.

Deploying Minuteman IIIs in Multiple Protective Shelters

An alternative or supplementary short-term option is to deploy at least some Minuteman IIIs in multiple protective shelters (MPS). For example, enough new silos could be built to have three launch points for each of some number of Minuteman IIIs, a much simpler MPS basing plan than those proposed for the MX. The impact of such a proposal on expected surviving missiles is shown in Figure 5.1, and its effect on expected surviving RVs is shown in Figure 5.4. U.S. capabilities under this proposal are the same as those analyzed in the preceding section. Soviet capabilities to attack U.S. ICBMs would be significantly reduced during the period 1984–1988, however, with the Soviets expected to be able to destroy some 70–74 percent of U.S. ICBMs in 1984. If SALT II limits were followed, that percentage would drop to about 45 in 1986, when the number of aim points would become significant relative to the available warheads, and before the new ICBM would become a major part of the Soviet arsenal. By 1988 that transient advantage would be reversed, and the steady increase of accuracies and numbers of RVs per missile would restore Soviet capabilities to destroy U.S. ICBMs to about the 1981 level, regardless of whether or not more Minuteman IIIs were deployed and regardless of the basing mode adopted. In the period 1984–1986, however, using the MPS basing mode for the extra Minuteman IIIs would raise the expected number of surviving U.S. warheads by some 300–400. Questions have been raised, however, about whether additional vertical hard silos for MPS deployment of Minuteman could be considered as conformable to SALT I limitations on the numbers of launchers; on the face of the issue, it would appear that they could not.

Although the percentage of ICBMs destroyed is higher without SALT limitations, absolute numbers of both U.S. and Soviet surviving RVs are higher. For the United States this non-SALT margin is moderate through the early 1980s, and substantial at the end of the decade. The drop in expected surviving U.S. RVs around 1988–89 is due to a transient Soviet advantage as new Soviet missiles replace less effective older types more rapidly than the U.S. deploys the MX. All these scenarios assume that MX and a new Soviet ICBM will be deployed beginning in the mid-1980s, with larger numbers of such deployments if SALT limits are not followed. The transient Soviet advantage in 1988 could be neutralized if the United

States were to deploy some 700 additional Minuteman IIIs (see the isolated point in Figure 5.4), although such a deployment would be quite expensive and time-consuming to plug a gap of short duration. Moreover, shifts of as little as a year in the deployment plans of either side could significantly reduce that transient gap. Similarly, if the United States were to adopt MPS basing for MX and increase the number of shelters above the initial 23 per missile, the new shelters might begin to come on line in the late 1980s, further alleviating the problem indicated in Figure 5.4.

Fractionation of Payloads to Counter MPS Basing

It has been suggested (see, e.g., Downey, 1976) that one way to overcome MPS basing modes may be to place larger numbers of highly accurate RVs on the same number of ICBMs. For example, if an MX warhead of yield 350 kilotons and 0.05 nm CEP would have a 0.993 expectation of destroying a shelter hardened to 1000 PSI, a maneuverable RV (MaRV) of yield 55 KT and 0.02 nm CEP would have better than a 0.999 expectation of destroying that same shelter. The MX missile would have throw-weight sufficient for some 30 such RVs, increasing by a factor of three the number of shelters that the MX force could attack. Similarly, it appears on the basis of throw-weights that the anticipated new Soviet ICBM could carry about 30 similar warheads, and the SS-18 perhaps 24. In the absence of SALT limitations on the numbers of RVs per missile, such "fractionation" of payloads could raise the number of warheads to the same approximate level as the numbers of shelters. As long as the warheads could be made sufficiently accurate, it would not be necessary to have as many as two RVs per shelter, and the attack would be limited primarily by the reliability of the attacking missiles. Those reliabilities are generally rising, and there seems to be general agreement that the necessary MaRV accuracies could be achieved by the end of the 1980s, if not before (Gray, 1977, 32–34).

The results of two general fractionation scenarios are shown in Table 5.3. In the first it is assumed that payloads of the U.S. MX and the Soviet new ICBM and SS-18 are fractionated with MaRVs, and that the United States has begun deployment of SLBM RVs accurate enough (CEP = 0.05 nm, yield = 350 KT) to be usable as counterforce weapons. (See also the discussion in the section, "Accurate Counterforce SLBMs.") Because of the close relationship between fractionation and MPS basing, it is also assumed that both sides have moved to quite extensive use of such basing modes, with the United States deploying 416 MX in 12,000 shelters of 1000 PSI hardness and 1000 Minuteman in 3000 silos of 3000 PSI hardness, and the Soviets deploying 528 of their new ICBMs in 10,560 shelters of 1000 PSI hardness. Because of the larger numbers of Soviet ICBMs and their higher average number of RVs per missile, the Soviet attack is fratricide limited while the U.S. attack is warhead limited. Whichever side attacked, the United States would be expected to emerge with fewer remaining ICBMs and fewer RVs. The United States could expect to destroy some

TABLE 5.3 LoAD, Trident Counterforce, and Fractionation (1991)

Scenario	Attacker	LoAD ABM Defense	Attackers RVs	Attackers Targets	Attack Limiting Factor	Percent of ICBMs Destroyed	ICBMs Left U.S.	ICBMs Left USSR	Percent of ICBM RVs Destroyed	ICBM RVs Left U.S.	ICBM RVs Left USSR
Fractionation and TD5/CF											
MX/FRAC/MaRV + TD5/CF No SALT	U.S.		15,771	14,990	W	96%	38	101	94%	159	967
MX/MM3MPS New ICBM + SS-18/FRAC/MaRV	USSR		30,120	15,054	F	99%	14	1,535	99.4%	42	5,056
MX/FRAC/MaRV SALT limits	U.S.		13,827	11,280	(W)	99.7%	90	4	99.7%	193	28
MX/MM3MPS New ICBM + SS-18/FRAC/MaRV	USSR		22,614	15,070	(W)	99.2%	8	162	99.7%	24	1,278
LoAD ABM Defense of 220 MX											
SALT base case	USSR	No LoAD	8,938	12,620	W	80%	209	162	66%	1,990	1,278
		LoAD	8,938	12,620	W	72%	302	162	50%	2,920	1,278
		Change				−8%	+93		−16%	+930	
NoSALT	USSR	NoLoAD	13,990	15,054	W	83%	249	909	67%	2,369	2,006
		LoAD	13,990	15,054	W	79%	315	909	57%	3,106	2,006
		Change				−4%	+66		−10%	+737	
No SALT, FRAC/MaRV on both sides	USSR	No LoAD	28,710	15,054	F	99%	14	1,590	99.4%	42	9,094
		LoAD	32,542	15,054	W	94%	81	909	90%	712	5,262
		Change	+3,832			−5%	+67		−9%	+670	−3,832
SALT limits on missiles only; FRAC/MaRV on both sides	USSR	No LoAD	22,614	13,720	W	99.2%	8	162	99.8%	24	3,090
		LoAD	22,614	13,720	W	95%	43	162	97%	454	3,090
		Change				−4%	+35		−3%	+430	

Attack scenarios were run with the author's interactive computerized nuclear exchange model, NEMATODE 2.2. No more than two RVs per target were allowed, in order to represent fratricide limits to the number of warheads that could be delivered accurately and exploded within a short period of time. All attacks were designed to destroy first the opponent's most threatening missiles, those with MIRV's and high accuracy. The "Limiting Factor" on destruction is labeled in each case as either "F" (fratricide limit of two RV's per target) or "W" (exhaustion of the attacker's available alert warheads before reaching the fratricide limit). Even in massive attacks some missiles are left to the attacker, since not all missiles are ever on alert and available to be launched at a given moment.

96 percent of Soviet ICBMs and 94 percent of ICBM RVs, but the Soviets would expect to emerge with almost 1000 RVs, about six times as many as the United States. If the Soviets were to attack, however, they could expect to destroy 99 percent of U.S. ICBMs and more than 99 percent of U.S. ICBM RVs, while having about 1,350 ICBMs and more than 5,000 ICBM RVs left. Thus the U.S. first strike would be almost self-disarming, while the Soviet first strike would leave a formidable surviving deterrent. Comparison of these results with those shown in Figures 5.1 through 5.4 suggests that this fractionation of highly accurate warheads could overcome many of the advantages otherwise claimed for MPS basing, and that the Soviets' larger missile sizes and quantities would work to their advantage.

The second general fractionation scenario studied was the perhaps improbable combination of payload fractionation with SALT-like limitations on the numbers of missiles. In this scenario both the U.S. and Soviet attacks would be warhead limited, but essentially all MPS-based missiles would be destroyed. Well over 99 percent of both ICBMs and RVs would be destroyed in either attack, and expected numbers of surviving missiles would be exceedingly small. Under such circumstances the range of uncertainty associated with any attack becomes exceptionally important. In either case the attacker would expect to emerge with more missiles and more RVs than the victim. This set of expected outcomes is more favorable to the United States than those expected in the absence of limitations on missile quantities, but it could be argued to be destabilizing because of the attacker's favored position.

LoAD ABM Defense of ICBMs

One method which has been suggested for gaining leverage against Soviet superiority in numbers of ICBMs and RVs, and which might also offer some benefits in attempting to counter payload fractionations, is the deployment of an active ABM defense for at least some U.S. ICBMs (*Aviation Week*, 1980e, 1980b). The Army's Ballistic Missile Defense Systems Command intends to demonstrate a preprototype of such a system, dubbed "LoAD" for Low Altitude Defense, by the mid-1980s. The system would use a very-high-speed, nuclear-armed interceptor missile as one key element in a transportable terminal defense system which could be housed in an MX MPS missile shelter. Under attack conditions several LoAD interceptors and a small phased-array radar would be moved out of their shelter. The interceptors would defend the nearby shelter that housed the MX missile, but would not be fired at warheads targeted at other shelters in that MX complex. Unlike the earlier U.S. Sentinel and Safeguard ABMs, the LoAD interceptors would be autonomous, relying on electrooptical sensors and on-board data processing so as to be independent of ground-based radar after launch. Several interceptors could thus be launched in rapid succession if needed to counter a dense attack. Because the interceptions would take place at relatively low altitudes well within the atmosphere, decoys and other penetration aids would probably already have been filtered out by their passage through the atmosphere, simplifying the tracking and discrimination tasks of the ground computer. The LoAD system could also evolve into the lower tier of a two-altitude missile defense system similar to Sentinel or Safeguard. Yet radiation from explosions of incoming warheads and from the LoAD interceptors' own warheads is still seen as a major obstacle to the correct functioning of the system in a wartime environment, as well as an extremely serious political and human cost.

Deployment of more than 100 such LoAD interceptors or deployment beyond a single ICBM field would violate the existing 1972 SALT I ABM Treaty and its 1974 Protocol. Nonetheless, any widespread perception that the United States is disadvantaged relative to Soviet ICBM capabilities, and/or an inability to reach some SALT II or START limitations on missile quantities, could increase pressure to abrogate the ABM Treaty and proceed with LoAD deployment. Even in early 1981 it was being suggested that the United States might take the opportunity of the 1982 five-year review point to abrogate the treaty or request Soviet agreement to weakening of its restrictions. As dense pack basing of MX gained favor, the case for LoAD or some alternative ABM defense grew even stronger, as noted earlier (Halloran, 1982b).

The LoAD preprototype development effort was strongly endorsed by the House Armed Services Committee in 1980 (*Aviation Week*, 1980a). With MX in the Carter administration's proposed MX-MPS deployment mode, an attacker would have to target one or more RVs at each of 23 shelters to be sure of destroying a single MX missile, and the multiple of shelters per missile would rise to about 29 to one by 1991 under suggestions that MX be expanded to a force of 416 missiles in 12,000 shelters (*Aviation Week*, 1980b, 67). The defense, on the other hand, would require only perhaps six LoAD interceptors per MX, which might lead to a cost ratio favorable to the defense. If each LoAD could achieve a 60 percent kill probability against a single incoming warhead, each MX could be protected against several warheads with fairly high assurance, depending primarily on the timing of attack and defense. Results of four Soviet first-strike scenarios are shown in Table 5.3, each given with and without LoAD defense. In each case it was assumed that the United States would deploy 416 MX in 12,000 shelters. IOC for the LoAD system was assumed to be 1989, with enough deployed by 1991 to defend 220 of the MX missiles. The LoAD interceptors were assumed to have a 90-percent reliability and a 60-percent kill probability.

Under the base case assumptions if SALT limitations were continued to 1991, a hypothetical Soviet attack would be limited by the numbers of available Soviet warheads; only about 71 percent of U.S. aim points could be attacked. Presuming an attack first against the harder Minuteman III silos and then against as many as possible of the 12,000 MX shelters, the

Soviets could expect to destroy some 80 percent of U.S. ICBMs and 66 percent of ICBM RVs, leaving the United States with perhaps half again as many ICBMs and ICBM RVs as the Soviet Union. LoAD defense of 220 MX would raise the surviving numbers on the U.S. side by about half, although even without that defense the United States would expect to have almost 2,000 surviving RVs, which should be a highly adequate deterrent. Without SALT limitations, the numbers of resulting RVs surviving on the two sides are remarkably similar. Although the Soviets would expect to have about three times as many surviving ICBMs as the United States, they would be mostly older and less effective types, leaving the United States with a margin of 3:2 in RVs and a higher margin in recent model RVs. The remaining scenarios assume that ICBM payloads are fractionated in the same manner discussed in the previous section. In all such cases, the Soviet Union's larger numbers of missiles and larger throw-weights translate into larger numbers of ICBMs and RVs after the attack. Without SALT II limits or LoAD, the United States would expect over 99 percent destruction of its ICBMs and ICBM RVs, while the Soviets would expect over 1,500 ICBMs and over 9,000 RVs surviving. Clearly, this scenario represents an extreme case of U.S. ICBM vulnerability. With the LoAD defense, however, U.S. expectations are raised by a crucial 67 MX missiles, leaving over 700 RVs, a presumably adequate deterrent under AD doctrine. If missile quantities are constrained to SALT-like levels but fractionation is permitted, the results are similar, although the numbers of surviving missiles and RVs are smaller on both sides.

Overall, these results suggest that LoAD would not be necessary to ensure a sizable U.S. surviving deterrent in 1991 *unless* fractionation were to occur. In fact, without fractionation the United States would expect to emerge from a Soviet first strike with more RVs than the Soviets, and a LoAD defense would simply raise that margin further. The cases with fractionation are more problematic. If the United States had to depend solely on ICBMs for its deterrent, then LoAD would appear to be necessary to assure enough surviving RVs; and, even then, the Soviets would expect to have about seven times as many surviving ICBM RVs. These results, however, are based on protecting only 220 of 416 MX with LoAD; a LoAD deployment to protect all the MX would be expected to yield more balanced numbers of surviving RVs. The results suggest, however, that LoAD can be foregone so long as fractionation does not occur; and both these limitations could be maintained either through SALT or through tacit bargaining.

Highly Accurate SLBMs for Counterforce Use

If land-based ICBMs are becoming vulnerable to overwhelming first strikes, one might look to the other legs of the strategic triad to preserve a post-attack deterrent. If the post-attack forces are to have a significant counterforce capability, that capability might be assured by deploying highly accurate SLBMs. Such a capability is clearly sought by some segments of the U.S. military community. In 1980 Vice Admiral Charles H. Griffiths, Deputy Chief of Naval Operations for Submarine Warfare, stated that "there is no question that the U.S. needs a strong strategic warfighting capability with a requirement to diversify that capability to provide hedges against failures" (*Aviation Week*, 1980c, 92). While U.S. SLBMs circa 1980 had significant countervalue attack potential, their accuracy/yield combinations were not great enough to attack hard point targets with high probabilities of success. Indeed, it had once been argued that this fact gave assurance to the Soviets that the Polaris program was intended only as a survivable deterrent and not as a first-strike force. When the first Trident submarine became operational in 1982, it carried Trident I missiles each equipped with eight Mk.4 RVs and W76 warheads; the Mk.4 has a current CEP of about 1,500 feet (0.25 nm) and the W76 has a yield of about 100 kilotons (*Aviation Week*, 1980c, 91; IISS, 1980; SIPRI, 1980). Against a silo hardened to 1000 PSI this combination would have an SSPK of only 0.082, and against a silo hardened to 3500 PSI its SSPK would be 0.031. Thus, while still a formidable countervalue weapon, the Trident I with the Mk.4/W76 loading would be almost totally ineffective as a countersilo weapon, although it could be useful in a counterforce role against softer military targets.

Strategic warfighting in the 1980s, however, is usually assumed to require a countersilo capability, and the Navy and its supporting industrial contractors are working on several approaches to improving fleet ballistic missile (SLBM) systems to provide that capability. One approach is to upgrade the accuracy of the Trident I's stellar inertial navigation unit, which is expected to reduce CEP from 1500 feet to approximately 750 feet (0.12 nm). Another approach is to utilize telemetry data from the satellite Global Positioning System (Navstar) to locate the missile's position in three dimensions to within some 70 feet or better at any time during its flight. Tests of this system were scheduled to begin on the Western Test Range by 1982 (*Aviation Week*, 1980f). A lengthened Trident I would be capable of carrying eight RVs to 6000-nm range, rather than the present 4000 nm, while holding accuracy to a 750-foot CEP. A larger Trident II or D5 missile would be able to carry more and/or larger warheads up to 6000 nautical miles. The Trident I or C4 missile retrofitted in Poseidon submarines was constrained in size to fit the launch tubes of that submarine series, while the D5 can be larger because it will be carried only by Trident submarines. The D5 could carry the Mk.12A RV already in use on Minuteman III ICBMs, with a W78 warhead of 335-kiloton yield. Eight Mk.12As could be carried up to 6000 nm, or 10 Mk.12As for shorter ranges, with 750-foot CEP at 6,000 nm (*Aviation Week*, 1980c). Finally, terminally guided maneuverable RVs (MaRVs), on which some development work has already been done, may well be capable of CEPs less than 300 feet.

Decreasing Trident CEPs to 0.1 nm would raise the SSPK of the Trident I against a 3500-PSI silo to 0.178, and against a 1000-PSI silo to 0.414, which is high enough to have some utility against MPS deployments. With the larger Mk.12a/W78 RV/warhead combination, the Trident II would be expected to achieve SSPKs of 0.364 against 3500-PSI silos, and 0.709 against 1000-PSI silos. Two such RVs cross-targeted from different missiles would have a very high probability of destroying a 1000-PSI MPS shelter. If different approaches to accuracy improvements were to be employed concurrently and CEPs reduced to 0.05 nm, the Trident I would achieve an SSPK against 1000-PSI targets of 0.882, while the Trident II would achieve SSPKs of 0.837 against 3500-PSI targets and 0.993 against 1000-PSI targets. Such accuracies would give the Trident II a countersilo capability essentially equivalent to that of the best land-based ICBMs, over intercontinental ranges, and with the added benefit of protective mobility. One may easily surmise that such a development is the Navy's long-range solution to the problem of ICBM vulnerability. As noted by *Aviation Week* (1980c, 91),

> [The Navy] is convinced it can produce a fleet ballistic missile combining improved accuracy and increases in payload/yield sufficient to destroy hardened targets at ranges up to 6,000 naut. mi. [including] silos for Soviet intercontinental ballistic missiles . . . [and] plans to achieve the same accuracy now possible only with fixed land-based ICBMs launched from presurveyed sites.

An advanced development program planned to cost in excess of half a billion dollars through Fiscal Year 1983 was begun in 1980, with plans for engineering development to start in 1983 and IOC in 1989 (*Aviation Week*, 1980c, 91).

The first of the fractionation scenarios summarized in Table 5.3 assumes a 1989 IOC for a counterforce-capable Trident D5 with 350 KT yield and 0.05 nm CEP, with six Trident submarines so equipped by 1991. In the scenario reported in Table 5.3 only three of the submarines were assumed to be on station and available, providing 72 SLBMs with a total of 576 RVs. While those RVs do not make a major contribution to an attack against 14,990 separate aim points, they do achieve SSPKs of 0.993 against 1000-PSI ICBM shelters, and deployment of substantial numbers of such SLBMs clearly would affect the strategic balance. Such deployments also have interesting implications for a post-attack environment, in which they might well be almost the only surviving missiles with a significant countersilo capability. If it were possible to preserve satellite detection systems and communicate effectively with the submarines in that environment (both rather problematic propositions), the SLBM force could provide a formidable shoot-look-shoot countersilo capability.

IMPLICATIONS OF ALTERNATIVE SOLUTIONS TO THE ICBM VULNERABILITY PROBLEM

ICBM vulnerability, at least by some definitions, is already an accomplished fact. Yet its seriousness is determined by political perceptions. Questions about the numbers of missiles that would probably be destroyed or the numbers of warheads that would be expected to survive attack can be answered with some assurance, despite continuing arguments about the range of uncertainty inherent in such estimates. Whether such measures are interpreted as indicating ICBM vulnerability depends crucially both on which measures of strategic balance are accepted and on which strategic doctrines are employed. The political component of strategic doctrine encompasses the general missions to be performed under different eventualities, including the extent to which an ability for ICBMs to ride out an attack is required, and the approximate number of RVs that must be assured of surviving such an attack. If, for example, 400 RVs are expected to survive a first strike and doctrine states that only 200–300 RVs are required to provide a force sufficient to deter any such attack, ICBM vulnerability probably would not be judged to exist. Yet the political component of strategic doctrine may also specify requirements on the strategic balance, and may stipulate that it is unacceptable for an opponent to be able to make an attack in which he would expect to emerge with a greater damage capability (i.e., more unused missiles and/or RVs) than his victim. The existence or nonexistence of ICBM vulnerability at any given time thus depends critically both on measures and on perceptions which are subject to rapid change. Moreover, even if the figure of merit chosen to measure the strategic balance remains the same, its value is subject to relatively quick shifts that depend on complex interactions between the policy choices made by both governments.

If, for example, ICBM vulnerability is taken to mean that 90 percent or more of one side's ICBMs could be destroyed in a first strike, then the United States clearly was vulnerable by 1981. Alternatively, if ICBM vulnerability is taken as meaning that fewer than 200 ICBM RVs would probably survive such an attack, the United States was not vulnerable. Moreover, protections against ICBM vulnerability could be taken to include the SLBM and bomber legs of the strategic triad, for surely the United States could mount a serious counterattack with such forces, particularly if that attack were directed against countervalue targets. An assured destruction mission is thus not in significant doubt by any measure of the strategic balance, although the survival of enough forces to mount a counterforce retaliation against very hard targets may be called into question. Whether it is ever possible to conduct massive first strikes successfully may still be argued, although the range of uncertainty inherent in any such attack could also limit one's confidence in having sufficient surviving forces. Finally, if being able to emerge from a first strike with at least as many surviving missiles and/or RVs as one's attacker is a goal, then the United States must again be seen as vulnerable by 1981.

As seen in the preceding figures and tables, the strategic balance indicated by these several measures is subject to very great changes over the decade 1981–1991, to rapid shifts over periods as short as two years, and to a wide range of possibilities regarding U.S. or Soviet "advantage," depending on the combinations of policies chosen by the two governments about such options as arms limitations, new ICBMs, increases in warhead sizes and accuracies, ABM defenses, silo hardening, and multiple protective shelter (MPS) or other alternative basing schemes. All such future possibilities are affected by the historical background of available technologies, strategic doctrines, arms limitation agreements, and mixes of strategic forces between the different legs of the triad. In particular, almost every measure of the strategic balance in the 1980s is affected by the prior existence of larger Soviet throw-weights, larger numbers of Soviet ICBMs, and different historical timings of the U.S. and Soviet MIRVing programs. The shifts in the balance seen over the previous decade appear to reflect an action–reaction process in which each side attempts to maintain some position relative to the other, subject to the constraints of uncertain prediction of the opponent's plans, long lifetimes for whatever forces are acquired, and long lead times in developing and deploying new strategic forces. The potential of these interactions to lead to cyclical shifts in the strategic balance is obvious. Such shifts appear to have occurred over the decade 1971–1981, and to be quite possible over the decade 1981–1991.

If two otherwise competing governments agree to place limits on the use of *portions* of a strategic weapons technology, it seems inevitable that they will continue to compete in the areas not constrained. The prisoners' dilemma fear of an opponent's potential new developments, the desire to remove some of one's uncertainties by seeking a position of advantage, and natural bureaucratic incentives to maintain and expand programs to their full potential will all act as pressures to explore every unconstrained strategic weapons option. The limitation of ICBM and ABM quantities in SALT I left an unconstrained MIRVing race; and while that race led to temporary U.S. advantage in the middle 1970s, it also set the stage for a shift to Soviet advantage in the early 1980s, and to calls for some U.S. response. While the temporary U.S. advantage in MIRVs offset larger numbers of Soviet missiles at the time of SALT I, it could never be more than transitory. Indeed, since it was once argued that the major reason for MIRVing was to overcome possible ABM defenses through saturation, a strong case could be made for combining an ABM ban with a MIRV ban, and such a combination was seriously considered in the early stages of the SALT I negotiations (Barton & Weiler, 1976, 182–187; Gerard Smith, 1980). Having failed to make that crucial connection, however, and having proceeded with massive MIRV deployments, neither side was left in a good position to return to the possibly more stable world of missiles armed only with single warheads. Nonetheless, such a return was suggested by the Scowcroft Commission's 1983 proposal for development of a new single-warhead light ICBM (Cannon, 1983b). That return would require the verifiable replacement of MIRVed missiles with such new light ICBMs on both sides, including verifiable destruction or dismantling of the MIRVed types.

If the United States were to deploy additional Minuteman III missiles while continuing development of the MX, it could match Soviet levels of ICBM destruction by 1984, and if neither side proceeds with MPS basing, each could expect to destroy over 95 percent of the other's ICBMs in a first strike by the mid-1980s, leaving as few as 300 ICBM RVs to the victim. Those 300 RVs should suffice for an assured destruction mission, even if not augmented by SLBMs and bombers. Moreover, the U.S. program of SLBM accuracy improvements should help assure that even a counterforce retaliation mission could be carried out with high assurance after riding out a first strike. Yet while presumed to be highly survivable, that SLBM counterforce deterrent will not be available in significant force before 1990. In the meantime, debate over the shape of an MX system continues, with strong arguments still being made about the workability of MPS basing schemes. Even in the face of other development programs, MPS basing appears to offer assurance of large numbers of surviving RVs by 1990. Without the MX program, however, the United States could be at a serious disadvantage even if the Soviets limited their efforts to accuracy improvements and refrained from deploying a new large ICBM. Dense pack basing may offer the promise of moderate ICBM survival at lower cost than MPS, but with a higher degree of uncertainty (due to dependence on fratricide effects) and reduced operational flexibility (due to the possibility of pin-down).

If the United States were to deploy additional Minuteman III missiles starting in 1981, while continuing to maintain SALT II limits by withdrawing equivalent numbers of Minuteman IIs from the arsenal, its hard-target kill capability against Soviet silos would be raised by some 10–15 percent immediately. Raising the total number of ICBMs and foregoing SALT limits would raise this capability still further, and if the new missiles were housed in new, harder silos, expected ICBM losses under a Soviet attack would be reduced by three to five percent. This scheme appears to offer a way for the United States approximately to double its expected number of surviving ICBM RVs in the early and middle 1980s. Building additional silos so as to be able to deploy Minuteman IIIs in any of three aim points each would offer only marginal advantages over deploying more Minuteman IIIs in single silos, in terms of either ICBMs or RVs expected to survive attack; compare Figures 5.4 and 5.3. Again, the United States would measure slightly better without SALT than with SALT.

If both sides were to fractionate the payloads of their larger ICBMs into large numbers of highly accurate MaRVs, the results would be somewhat mixed. The Soviets would still be advantaged by greater numbers of large ICBMs, and would expect to emerge with more ICBMs and more RVs in every scenario except the rather improbable case of a U.S. strike in a world that featured MaRV fractionation but SALT II limits on numbers of ICBMs. While there are serious questions about whether anticipated MaRV accuracies could be maintained in an environment in which many of the terrain features necessary for terminal guidance could easily have been destroyed, fractionation might well cause the U.S. government to attempt to increase its number of ICBMs in order to assure enough surviving RVs. Clearly, fractionation with MaRVs *could* overcome widespread MPS basing, with the dispersion of missiles among many aim points being countered by substantial increases in the numbers of RVs per missile. The proposed LoAD ABM defense system for MX would not appear to be needed *unless* fractionation were to occur, in which case it would assure a significant survivable deterrent. LoAD could offer the United States even stronger assurance than an increase in its numbers of ICBMs— but both LoAD and fractionation could either result from or ensure the complete breakdown of the SALT/START process.

Some of these suggested policy options would not have significant impact before the early 1990s, and many uncertainties cloud our picture of that period. The decade 1981–1991 will see two U.S. presidential elections and has already seen the passing of Leonid Brezhnev as Soviet leader. Such changes could easily promote doctrinal shifts on both sides, but it is too early to evaluate the full impact of Yuri Andropov's succession to power. Additionally, although the lead times to develop, test, and deploy new strategic weapons are quite long and have tended to grow still longer as costs have risen, we are less certainly able to predict our precise achievements using new technologies the further into the future we attempt to make such predictions. For example, while ICBM CEPs in the range of 300 feet (about 0.05 nm) by 1980 were being predicted about 1977, the 1980 consensus on the best CEPs achieved proved to be only about 0.1 nm.

Overall, it appears that a "window of vulnerability" opened about 1980–81 for the United States, if that "window" is interpreted as the ability of an opponent to destroy upwards of 90 percent of fixed land-based missiles in a "disarming" first strike. By the mid-1980s the same window will open for the Soviet Union. If the window is interpreted as an *imbalance* in such hypothetical first-strike capabilities, it opened for the United States about 1980–81 and will close in the mid-1980s, even without an MX program. Finally, if the window is interpreted as an inability to maintain some minimum assured destruction retaliatory force against such a hypothetical attack, then no such window has yet opened for either superpower, nor is it likely to.

The answers to the fundamental questions whether ICBM vulnerability exists, and whether it matters if it does exist so long as there are other legs to the strategic triad, depend critically on which measures of the strategic balance are accepted, and upon the political component of strategic doctrine that determines what *values* of the crucial measures are perceived to be critical. If, as suggested earlier, there has existed a cyclical action–reaction process of misperception, overestimation and underestimation, building and counterbuilding programs motivated by desires to achieve or maintain critical values on one or another measure of the strategic balance, the development of procedures to manage and control that cyclical process could redound to the benefit of both governments. In the following chapter we turn to an exploration of the possibilities and probabilities of such institutional developments, and some indicators for determining which policies are actually being pursued.

6

A Future for Arms Control? Structure, Indicators, and Prospects for the 1980s

INTRODUCTION

The lesson of history is: When a war starts, every nation will ultimately use whatever weapon has been available. That is the lesson learned time and again. Therefore, we must expect, if another war—a serious war—breaks out, we will use nuclear energy in some form.

Q. What do you think is the prospect, then, of nuclear war?

I think we will probably destroy ourselves, so what difference will it make? Some new species will come up that might be wiser.

I think from a long-range standpoint—I'm talking about humanity—the most important thing we could do is start in having an international meeting where we first outlaw nuclear weapons to start with, then we outlaw nuclear reactors, too.

Q. Do you think that's realistic in a world with the Soviet Union?

I don't know.

> Excerpts from the "farewell" Congressional testimony of Admiral Hyman G. Rickover, 28 January 1982. Questions from Senator William Proxmire. (*The New York Times*, 1982)

These excerpts from the preretirement thoughts of the "father of the nuclear navy" capture many of the dilemmas of contemporary strategic weapons management, including the unprecedented destructive capabilities now available, which have led to an unprecedented level of danger to civilization as we know it; the widespread belief that somehow it "ought" to be possible to resolve those dangers; and the pervasive pessimism about the political chances of obtaining such a resolution. Indeed, the management of the strategic weapons regime over the past two decades demonstrates what seems on the surface to be a major paradox: weapons quantities and destructive capabilities have moved almost monotonically upward during a period in which the numbers and scope of arms control agreements expanded significantly. Moreover, neither governments nor publics appear to enjoy even the limited sense of security perceived 20 years ago.

Seeking to reverse the increase in nuclear arms, or even to stabilize at present levels without ever resorting to their use, requires actions without any parallel in history. As suggested by Admiral Rickover, governments *in extremis* have always utilized their most powerful weapons. The underlying reason why we should be especially concerned at *this* point in history is that the levels of destruction—both directly through blast and radiation, and indirectly, through radioactive fallout, fire, and the disease and chaos which would follow the disruption of societal infrastructures—are so great, and the weapons delivery systems so rapid and far-reaching, that no government can remain unconditionally viable (recall the first section of Chapter 1), and the life of every individual on the planet is potentially at risk in a major nuclear exchange. While opinions on these issues are often far more emotional than expert, even the most optimistic analysts have some doubts about the survivability of governments and the quality of life following a nuclear exchange, and most would grant that there is at least a possibility of destroying life as we have known it on the planet.

This situation arose in a classic case of the "prisoners' dilemma": The U.S. government began a nuclear weapons development program when it became evident to physicists that it *might* be possible to build such a bomb, and both physicists and political leaders were rightly concerned about the dangers should the Nazis develop it first. Once the weapon had been developed, the physicists found to their dismay that the weapon was to be fitted into the existing political–military command structure (i.e., it was to be used like any other weapon). As we came to realize just how powerful a weapon had been created, we began to search for political mechanisms to regulate that danger. Thus far the regulation has been relatively unsuccessful, for a variety of reasons, most of which are political in nature but highly constrained by the physical possibilities. Since the 1940s the original prisoners' dilemma of entering the nuclear era has been compounded by the recurring prisoners' dilemma every time some new technological development or possibility threatens/promises potential advantage. Given the stakes, arms control measures to limit or reduce the risks of war seem at least desirable, if not imperative. Therefore we must ask whether the development of nuclear weapons is reversible, and, if not, whether it is controllable. Irreversible changes are known to occur in many physical and biological systems; perhaps this is an instance of an irreversible change in a technopolitical system (that is, a system which lies at the interface of technology and politics).

At its heart, science is puzzle-solving, the unraveling of the processes by which the physical and social worlds function. Once a solution to a particular puzzle is found, it may be expanded or superseded by a more comprehensive solution, but it will not be lost; only dying civilizations forget their science. As a civilization we cannot *unlearn* the possibility and technique of building nuclear weapons. Moreover, as long as at least one government—or, potentially, even a group consisting of a few key individuals—expects relative advantage from possessing such weapons, we cannot readily make massive reductions in the strategic arsenals already on hand. Therefore, if we wish to reverse the nuclear weapons acquisition process, or even bring it into long-term stability, *we shall have to devise new political institutions for the management of the strategic weapons regime*. Ideally, those institutions must be capable of providing absolute assurance to all that a technology already widely known will be so regulated that no government or group can ever utilize it for political advantage. More realistically, those institutions must reduce the risks of arms control to levels less than those inherent in continuing without such controls.

An analogue—and a possible model—of this interaction between war risk and control risk is provided in the branch of topological mathematics developed in the 1970s and known as "catastrophe theory" (Thom, 1972, 1975; Zeeman, 1976, 1977). This branch of mathematics deals with discontinuous and divergent phenomena, and takes its name from the abrupt changes in behavior that sometimes result from gradual changes in driving forces or motivations. It has been said to be particularly applicable to social phenomena because it can represent multivalued situations such as confrontations in which one individual will fight while another will flee. A simple physical example of a system exhibiting such divergent behaviors consists of a soda straw clamped at one end and pushed along its axis from the other end. As one pushes harder and harder, the straw is placed under increasing compression; yet sooner or later it will buckle, projecting in one direction or another. The factor determining which direction the straw buckles may be almost undetectable, perhaps a slightly off-centered push or a minute imperfection in the straw itself.

An application of catastrophe mathematics to conflict behavior is schematized in Figure 6.1, which represents a three-dimensional behavior surface of differing war policies under varying levels of threat and cost. This behavior surface is folded in the pattern called the "butterfly catastrophe," and the projection of the fold lines onto the threat/cost plane below the behavior surface is called a "bifurcation set" that divides the plane into regions each of which corresponds to one *or more* behaviors. For costs greater than BF and threats lower than AFD, policy calls for surrender; the combination of high threat (greater than AG) with low cost (below BGE) calls for attack; in the "pocket" AGCFB negotiation is possible; but for cost/threat products outside EGCFD, *either* attack or surrender is possible, depending on the path followed to reach the present location on

FIGURE 6.1 Behavioral Surface for War Policy

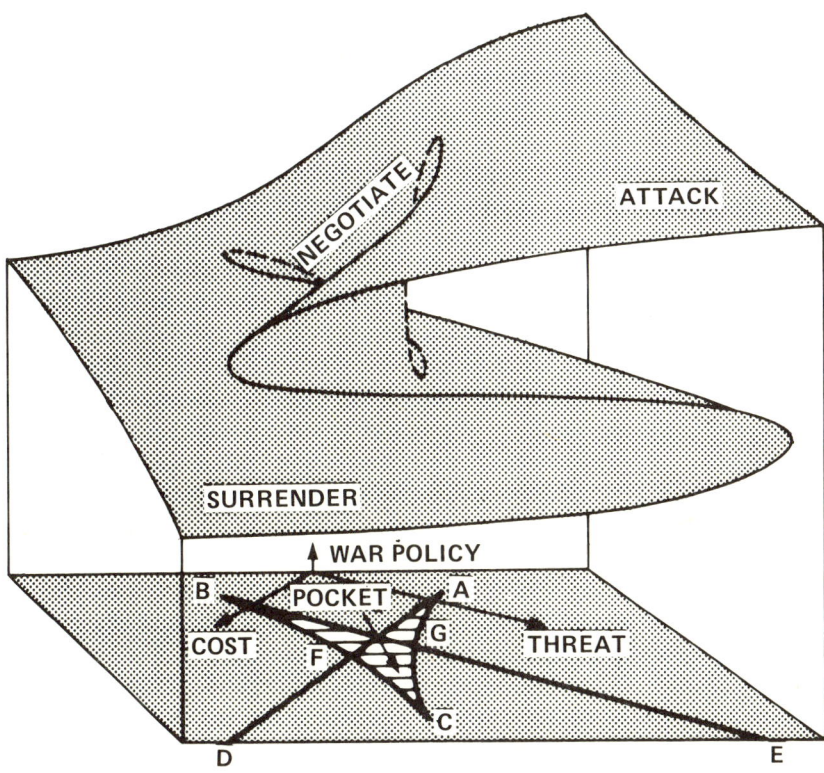

This behavioral surface for war policy follows the "butterfly catastrophe" (after Zeeman). The surface is controlled by four parameters, two of which are here held fixed and two of which are interpreted as cost and threat. The bifurcation set is a complex curve with a "pocket" in the middle. On the behavior surface above the pocket is a sheet that provides a compromise negotiation option. If both threat and cost are sufficiently high, the only behaviors allowed are attack or surrender; the intermediate behavior is possible only within a narrow range of relatively low costs and threats.

the behavior surface. This model thus demonstrates several properties common to other catastrophe models: (a) the behavior is bimodal in part of its range, and can jump suddenly from one mode to the other; (b) in that range of bimodal behavior, there is an inaccessible zone on the behavior axis, in this example the zone between attack and surrender; and (c) behaviors following only slightly different paths away from the low-cost, low-threat corner can diverge to attack, surrender, or negotiation.

The catastrophe–theoretic model is, of course, only suggestive, and Figure 6.1 represents only a single government's policies, while a full description of a strategic weapons regime would require at least two military strength in hopes of deterring attack. Governments may engage in arms buildups in order to obtain a more favorable outcome should war occur, particularly if they believe that war is likely and that deterrence will ultimately fail. A state may engage in arms racing in order to increase its diplomatic weight, either through direct use of military force in coercion or by extracting political concessions through threats of such coercion. Arms racing may serve the vested interests of domestic military–industrial complexes and their political allies. States may build arms in order to preserve or enhance a degree of dignity or prestige believed appropriate or necessary to their positions in the world. They may engage in arms races because having another government act as an external "pacer" serves deeply entrenched bureaucratic and programmatic interests (Gray, 1974a). Significant new arms programs may be advanced in hopes of the elusive strategic "breakout" so sought after yet so feared if achieved by other governments. Finally, new technological possibilities tend to exert the "pull" of solving a previously uncracked puzzle as well as the "push" of fear born in the prisoners' dilemma.

In the prenuclear age the denial and punishment functions of almost all weapons were closely related; the same weapons that could be used to wreak punishment on the population and military forces of an opponent could be used to deny victory by defending one's own population and forces. With the decline of nation-state viability brought about by (a) the tremendous increase in destructive power and (b) the general lack of any adequate defense in the nuclear age, denial and punishment have been decoupled. Strategic nuclear arms may be used to attack an opponent's population centers or military forces, but do not themselves provide a direct defense against such attacks on one's own territory.

That decoupling between denial and punishment is compounded by the continuing debate between counterforce (CF or countermilitary) and countervalue (CV or counterpopulation) targeting of nuclear weapons. Given that the CF or damage-limiting mission is much more difficult to perform and calls for potentially much larger numbers of weapons, while a CV deterrent mission can be performed with a few hundred nuclear weapons as long as they are assuredly secure against any preemptive destruction, adoption of a strategic doctrine of deterrence and preparation for a CV retaliatory strike can be viewed as a form of arms limitation. Thus the strategic doctrine adopted has far-reaching implications for the prospects of arms control, and it is not unreasonable to consider "deterrence as arms control" (Morgan, 1981). Yet, as Morgan has suggested, additional problems may be posed by assigning this task to the military; the biases inherent in the military profession have tended, even in times when deterrent doctrine was clearly ascendant, to promote weapons escalation and to maintain a general hesitancy in controlling or deescalating arms.

In addition to the denial–punishment decoupling, it has become common to speak of a decoupling of military forces into nuclear and "conventional" arms. Despite the use of nuclear weapons on Hiroshima and Nagasaki during the period of U.S. nuclear monopoly, and despite the fact that the line between the explosive power of the very largest conventional weapons and the very smallest nuclear weapons has become quite blurry, there is a clearly perceived "nuclear threshold." Maintaining that threshold depends far more on its political saliency than on its technological or military significance. Its political saliency is *very* great, backed up in part by doubts whether any war which crosses the threshold can remain limited, and whether the threshold itself, once crossed, would forever cease to be viewed as significant.

The nuclear threshold, of course, is rather akin to the poison-gas threshold in World War II; both sides were prepared to fight such a war, but neither wished to initiate it. Insider accounts suggest that threats of nuclear escalation have been made in a number of conventional and limited wars as far back as Korea (Ellsberg, 1981), raising some question about how salient the nuclear threshold has been to top political leaders. Yet the persistent tendency to view that threshold as significant does suggest that one particular route to arms control may be to lay even greater emphasis on the nuclear threshold, perhaps by encouraging "no-first-use" declarations.

Such an emphasis would raise a number of doctrinal problems, however. NATO has long relied on the threat of nuclear response to a Warsaw Pact attack on western Europe, while Soviet declaratory doctrine has regularly denied the possibility of limited nuclear war, and has tended to stress the use of all available types of weapons in any general war. The United States has consistently declined to pledge no-first-use of nuclear weapons, although in April 1982 several former key officials including former Secretary of Defense Robert McNamara urged the adoption of such a pledge, making them the highest-ranking current or former U.S. government officials ever to take such a position (Hedrick Smith, 1982).

In both the denial–punishment and nuclear–conventional decouplings, the *ambiguities* in strategic doctrine become an important complicating factor. In the debates between CF and CV targeting the issue of the feasibility or infeasibility of limited nuclear war has been raised time and time again without ever being resolved. NATO doctrine has depended for years on a rather ambiguous threat of nuclear escalation in response to an attack on western Europe, a threat ambiguous both because of the likely levels of destruction and because of NATO's probable political disarray in attempting to reach such a decision. Also within NATO, an issue about regional decoupling has been raised, questioning whether the Soviet Union would limit its nuclear responses to European states if it were struck by U.S. nuclear weapons based in Europe and/or under NATO control.

In all these instances it appears that ambiguities in strategic doctrine may imply serious instabilities in the strategic weapons regime, manifested as incentives for preemption or first strikes, and based on the difficulty that an ambiguous doctrine may not be sufficiently credible to deter such attacks. If NATO doctrine relies upon a threat of nuclear escalation that is not believed by the Soviet Union, over time it may help lead to the very imbalance of conventional forces that could invite a Warsaw Pact attack in some time of crisis. If the United States promotes such a NATO nuclear-escalation policy out of a belief that U.S. nuclear forces in Europe and/or under NATO control can be decoupled from strategic nuclear forces based in the United States itself, it could help promote Soviet escalation to a heartland-to-heartland nuclear exchange. Such an exchange might also be encouraged by incentives inadvertently structured into the forces deployed by one or the other superpower, for example in the form of land-based missile forces highly vulnerable to a disarming first strike.

The advent of nuclear strategic weapons, described above and in the first section of Chapter 1 as leading to an increase in destructive power so great as to prevent any government from attaining unconditional viability, has raised the stakes in the game of international strategy in some additional ways. The combination of vast increases in the destructive capabilities of single weapons with truly high-speed intercontinental delivery systems has greatly quickened the potential pace of a nuclear war relative to that of a conventional war. Indeed, the increase in firepower even at the conventional level has led to a quickening of the pace of war, provided that adequate numbers of troops and supplies of materiel are maintained. The pace of conventional conflicts has also been quickened by the improved means of rapid command communication which were developed partly in response to the need to act quickly in the event of nuclear war. Probably the best examples of both the firepower and the communications effects upon the pace of war are found in the 1973 Yom Kippur war, long noted for its great speed and mobility and for its very rapid depletion of materiel. This great increase in the pace of war implies very serious problems of command, communication, and control (C-cubed), a lack of time for reflection during the course of battle, and a consequent need for extremely creative and thorough contingency planning. In turn, that need subjects the political and policymaking processes to demands so extreme that they may never be met fully. Indeed, Vincent Ostrom (1973) has pointed out the theoretical impossibility of anticipating every contingency, particularly as one tries to project further and further into the future.

The higher stakes attendant on more destructive means of warfare also imply that the range of uncertainty in outcomes is increased. Thus the expected results of any policy are somewhat ambiguous, providing a strong incentive to "hedge" weapons requirements upward. This case is itself somewhat ambiguous, however, since the same concern about the uncertain outcome of a potential conflict could also provide an incentive to lower the stakes or take measures to stabilize the system. Perhaps the best one can say at this time is that the uncertainty of outcomes, itself very little addressed in the literature of strategic debates, can be either an arms race or an arms control incentive to different decision makers, depending on their individual proclivities to accept or to minimize risk.

Disincentives to Arm

With this last partial exception, the incentives discussed thus far are all "pushes" upward on arms levels. What can be said about the other three categories of constraints identified above, including the "pulls" of the status quo and the disincentives to disarm or control arms levels? Let us begin by considering the disincentives to arm. Spending in the military sector entails opportunity costs, the social costs of foregone opportunities to spend resources on alternative private or public goods. The point is basic and is familiar as the classic choice dilemma between "guns versus butter" beloved of economists. Both the risk of war and the severity of war risked also *may* be disincentives to arm; yet one must immediately raise the caveat that arms are often and traditionally thought to lead to security ("si vis pacem, para bellum"). Whether additional numbers of nuclear arms lead to greater levels of security depends partly on the strategic doctrine adopted, as discussed in Chapter 2; the common concept of "overkill" makes sense if one holds that deterrence will work, but is meaningless if one is unsure that deterrence will be effective, and thus concerned that some weapons must be assured of surviving any possible attack.

A final disincentive to arm may be found in the point noted earlier, that rapidly rising levels of nuclear armament have not been accompanied by any concomitant increase in perceived security levels. Indeed, it is not clear that either public or governmental perceptions of security against nuclear attack are any greater today than in the middle 1950s. Given that situation, and the clear perception that a nuclear war today could easily be far more destructive than one that might have occurred three decades ago, it may well be reasonable to assert that the contemporary strategic weapons regime has failed to provide "true" security, so that it should be radically revised.

Incentives to Disarm

The incentives to disarm are largely the same as the disincentives to arm, including opportunity costs of arming and the risk and severity of potential war. Additionally, one might cite such social benefits as greater availability of financial resources for alternative social projects, utilization of natural resources in ways more conducive both to the social good and to economic growth, and a greater concern for our stewardship of the planet as the heritage of generations yet unborn. Finally, when recalling the prisoners' dilemma that tends to promote arming, it should be recalled that the prisoners' dilemma is a *mixed*-motive game of strategy. Just as there is an individual incentive to gain at the expense of an opponent, there is an

FIGURE 6.2 The Decision to *Reduce* Existing Arms as a Prisoners' Dilemma

	"Their Decision" Reduce	"Their Decision" No Reduction
"Our" Decision — Reduce	Jointly Optimal Outcome Probable Gains for Both Lower Costs, Unless Offset by Other New Programs Problem: Maintaining "Balance"	Possible Advantage "Breakout" Possible Preemption Incentives (to Either or Both) Important *Dynamic* Elements Possible Loss
"Our" Decision — No Reduction	Possible Loss Possible Preemption Incentives (to Either or Both) Important *Dynamic* Elements Possible Advantage "Breakout"	Status Quo Continued Competition Extension of Present Dangers

incentive to cooperate for social and (smaller) individual gain, partly to promote long-term cooperation in repeated play. Such cooperative play is found frequently in experimental settings (e.g., Rapoport and Chammah, 1965); the requisite conditions are discussed more fully in the following section.

Disincentives to Disarm

Just as the dynamic that tends to push governments into developing new weapons as they become technologically feasible was interpreted as a prisoners' dilemma, the decision to *reduce* levels of existing arms presents a prisoners' dilemma. The basic structure of this interaction is set out in Figure 6.2. If neither side chooses to reduce arms, the status quo obtains, arms competition continues, and the dangers inherent in the present are extended both into the future and, most likely, into new areas of arms competition over time, in keeping with the previous analysis of upward biases on arms levels and capabilities. If both sides choose to reduce arms levels, the jointly or socially optimal outcome is *probably* obtained, depending on the exact structure of the strategic weapons regime and on the actions of any relevant third powers. Both sides can obtain lower costs and risks, presuming that the arms control agreement is appropriately structured and that the savings are not siphoned off into some new and offsetting weapons program. Given the survival dynamic inherent in bureaucracies, this last assumption actually is a fairly big one. Moreover, there may be major problems in measuring and maintaining the strategic "balance" during a program of arms reductions; both sides must believe that the outcome does not create any new imbalance.

It is in the remaining two outcome cells that the mixed-motive character of this interaction is manifested. Depending on the speed and magnitude of arms reductions and on their overall significance in the strategic weapons regime, if one side reduces while the other side does not, a highly imbalanced situation might result. Presumably such a situation could arise only through cheating by one side or through a major—and perhaps ill-conceived—unilateral reduction. Such an imbalance could promise major gains to one side and threaten major loss to the other. It would also cause important dynamic elements to enter the calculations of decision makers; a government might be encouraged to strike preemptively either while it held an advantage or before its expected disadvantage worsened.

This structure, which is symmetric in that both governments see the same range of choices and possible outcomes, is that of the classic prisoners' dilemma. Since the fear of possible loss in an unmatched arms reduction is likely to appear more perilous than the dangers inherent in continuing the status quo, a minimax player (who seeks to avoid the worst thing that could happen) will choose not to disarm. Movements to the mutually cooperative outcome cell, in which mutual arms reductions take place, can occur only if the fundamental dynamic of the prisoners' dilemma can be overcome.

Solutions that mitigate the prisoners' dilemma, whether the dilemma of new weapons "push" or existing weapons "pull" on strategic arsenals, may be classified into several categories. These include promotion of communication and trust-building between the participants; external enforcement threats or actions, either from participants or from some player otherwise external to the game; and a recognition of the inherent advantages of the mutually cooperative outcome cell as an equilibrium superior to the minimax equilibrium (here, the status quo), a solution suggested by a metagame analysis of the dilemma. (See Saaty, 1968, 94–100, or Howard, 1971, 44–49.)

Arms control moves thus occur within a complex framework of incentives and disincentives to arm or disarm that put decision makers under strong cross-cutting pressures. While there may be little disagreement about the factuality of those incentives and disincentives, there may be significant disagreements over their weighting according to importance. To one individual, for example, the single most salient consideration about a new nuclear weapons program may be that it contributes to the danger of destroying the heritage of succeeding generations, while to another individual the key consideration may be the perceived role of that weapons program in deterring the Soviet Union from adventures like the 1979 invasion of Afghanistan or similar acts seen as being encouraged by any perceived U.S. nuclear disadvantage. Against this background of incentives and disincentives, the following section is devoted to a review and examination of the major arms control accomplishments of the post-World War II period.

POST-WORLD WAR II ARMS CONTROL ACCOMPLISHMENTS

Although the numbers and destructive capabilities of nuclear weapons held by the superpowers have risen steadily since the dawn of the nuclear era, numerous agreements have been reached either between the United States and the Soviet Union, or on broader multilateral bases, to restrict the types, numbers, deployment areas, qualitative characteristics, and possible proliferation of nuclear (and a few other types of) weaponry. A brief review of these major steps in contemporary arms control sets the stage for an examination, in the next section, of the political principles embodied in the agreements reached to date; those agreements are summarized in Table 6.1.

The "Open Skies" and "Bomber Bonfire" proposals, made in the middle of the Eisenhower presidency and rejected by the Soviet Union, were important precursors of the SALT agreements of the 1970s. Open Skies would have opened about half of the United States and all of the European USSR to overflights by reconnaissance aircraft in order to allow verification of arms control undertakings; the Bomber Bonfire would have scrapped moderate numbers of obsolescent aircraft at a time when, as discussed in Chapter 2, in the Section "Bombers and First-Generation ICBMs," the United States enjoyed overwhelming superiority in numbers of intercontinental bombers. Although neither of these U.S. proposals ever moved far into negotiation with the Soviets, each embodied significant features later incorporated into the SALT agreements and other arms control proposals and negotiations of the 1970s. Both would have been *bilateral* U.S.–Soviet undertakings. Open Skies would have relied on what have come to be known under SALT as *"national technical means of inspection"* (*NTM*)—use of one state's high technology means of reconnaissance to determine the other state's activities, without on-site ground inspections or the intervention of any third parties in support of inspection. The "Bomber Bonfire" would have represented a *destruction of selected weaponry*, chosen to cause the least diminution of remaining capability; this is precisely the sort of weapons destruction incorporated in a limited way in SALT II and proposed in some other arms control negotiations.

Another precursor of later proposals and agreements was the Antarctic Treaty of 1959, under which that never-yet-fortified continent was declared to be a military-free zone in perpetuity. Like the Treaty for the

TABLE 6.1 Major Steps in Contemporary Arms Control

	Dates
"Open Skies" and "Bomber Bonfire" proposals	1955
Moratorium on Atmospheric Nuclear Testing	1958–1961
Antarctic (Military-Free Zone) Treaty	1959
Hot Line Agreement (Revised 1971)	1963

Limited Nuclear Test-Ban Treaty
  Only underground tests allowed
  France and China continue to abstain
	1963

Outer Space Treaty Prohibits orbiting weapons of mass destruction	1967
Treaty for the Prohibition of Nuclear Weapons in Latin America	1967–1968

Nuclear Nonproliferation Treaty (NPT)
  Defines classes of sovereignties (weapons and nonweapons states)
  Numerous significant nonsignatories
	1968

Seabed Arms Control Treaty	1971
Agreement updating Hot Line for satellite technology	1971
Nuclear Accidents Pact (U.S.–USSR)	1972
Agreement on Prevention of High-Seas Incidents (U.S.–USSR)	1972

Biological Weapons Convention
  Disarmament, Destruction, and Prohibition
  Significant loopholes remain
	1972

SALT (U.S.–Soviet *Strategic Arms Limitation Talks*)
  First tentative contacts
  Originally planned opening of negotiations
  Negotiations opened
  First agreements (SALT I) signed and ratified
    ABM Treaty (Still in force; Amended by Protocol in 1974)
    Interim Agreement on Strategic Weapons
      Expired 1977
      Subsequently followed tacitly by both sides
  Protocol amending and strengthening ABM Treaty
  Vladivostok Accords (Guidelines for SALT II agreement)
  SALT II Agreements signed (to expire in 1985)
    Withdrawn from submission for U.S. Senate ratification
	
	1965
	1968
	1969
	1972
	
	1974
	1974
	1979
	1979

Threshold Nuclear Test-Ban Treaty (U.S.–USSR)
  Set 150-kiloton limit on size of underground tests
  Not ratified by U.S. Senate
  Terms tacitly observed by both sides
	1974

Peaceful-Nuclear-Explosions (PNE) Treaty (U.S.–USSR)
  Set 150-kiloton limit on size of peaceful underground explosions
  Provides for limited on-site inspections
  Not ratified by U.S. Senate
	1976

Convention Banning Modification of the Environment
  32 signatory governments, including U.S. and USSR
  Prohibits military or hostile use of modifications
  Not ratified by U.S. Senate
	1977

Prohibition of Nuclear Weapons in Latin America and the Seabed Arms Control Treaty of 1971, it constituted an agreement to *refrain from engaging in acts of militarization not yet taken.*

The first major arms control agreement of the nuclear era was the Limited Nuclear Test-Ban Treaty of 1963. Generally considered one of the few lasting accomplishments of the Kennedy administration, it was preceded by a series of preliminary partial agreements, as well as unilateral and reciprocal moves by the United States and the Soviet Union. Prompted by growing public concern about the dangers of radioactive fallout from atmospheric nuclear and thermonuclear weapons tests in the 1950s, the two superpowers entered into negotiations in 1958, beginning with an eight-nation Geneva conference of scientific experts in July and August of that year. A series of unilateral moratoria on nuclear testing announced by one or another of the three nuclear powers of the time (the United States, the USSR, and Great Britain) was extended from time to time while the test-ban negotiations seemed to be progressing, and eventually ran from November of 1958 until September of 1961.

Almost two more years of argument and negotiation were to follow, however, before the signing of the Limited Test-Ban Treaty in August of 1963. As early as April of 1957, when the Soviet Union first proposed separating the question of nuclear testing from other arms control and disarmament issues so that it could be settled without delay, there was substantial agreement on the desirability of ending the production of radioactive fallout, as well as on the detectability of nuclear tests in the atmosphere, underwater, and in outer space out to very considerable distances from the earth. Almost the only sticking point was whether small underground tests could be conducted clandestinely, with what degree of consequent advantage, and, thus, what means of inspection should be provided to prevent violations of a comprehensive ban on testing. After five years of negotiation the ultimate solution was to define the problem area out of the treaty by limiting the ban to atmospheric, underwater, and space explosions. The Soviets' final position on inspection presaged their position later in the SALT negotiations: each government should verify the adherence of others to the treaty by means of its own inspection systems deployed on its own territory (i.e., by NTM) (York, 1973, 107–125).

The major deficiencies of the Limited Test-Ban Treaty (LTBT) were evident even at the time it was being negotiated and signed; the treaty was neither universal nor comprehensive. First, since no government could be compelled to adhere to the ban, it was not universal. While the established nuclear powers, the United States, the Soviet Union, and Great Britain, would no longer contribute to the fallout problem, other states such as France and China could and would argue that they were placed at a disadvantage relative to the states possessing accumulated nuclear test results, and would abstain from the ban, conducting atmospheric tests for years to come. Second, because the ban was not comprehensive, it did not freeze the state of the art in nuclear weapons development even for the governments adhering to the limited test ban. While it is true that new weapons can be designed as extrapolations of older, tested models, the range of uncertainty about performance is increased as the extrapolations are extended further and further. Thus, eventually, the inability to test new nuclear-weapons designs must act as at least a partial brake on their construction and deployment, so that a comprehensive test ban should ultimately slow the escalation into new models.

While U.S. and Soviet negotiators came close to agreement on a comprehensive nuclear test ban in the late 1970s, the continuing failure to enact a comprehensive ban could be interpreted as a hedge by the adherents of the Limited Test-Ban Treaty against the danger that holdout states which continue nuclear testing may eventually develop weapons more sophisticated than their own. Yet noncomprehensiveness also provides a loophole for the proliferation of weapons to new nuclear powers. India, which signed the LTBT but not the Nonproliferation Treaty (NPT), provides a case in point.

The Nuclear Nonproliferation Treaty (NPT) of 1968 is an unusual document in that it divides states into the two distinct—and supposedly fixed—groups of nuclear weapons states and non-weapons states. In return for promises by the former to work for meaningful disarmament, the latter pledge not to acquire nuclear weapons by any means, including transfers from weapons states. The obvious problem is holdout states, who include most of the potential new nuclear powers. Further, there is the problem of states that might acquire nuclear weapons and then ask to be accepted into the privileged group in return for signing the NPT and pledging not to help still more states become nuclear powers. While such a change of status is prohibited under the terms of the NPT, the United States has found it difficult to decide to cut off shipments of reactor fuel to India, thus far the only NPT nonsignatory state to develop nuclear weapons. Unfortunately, while the NPT divided the world "irreversibly" into two groups of states, the development of nuclear weapons appears to be a process even less reversible than a treaty.

The 1967–68 Treaty for the Prohibition of Nuclear Weapons in Latin America is also subject to some of these same problems. Like the Antarctic Treaty, it proposed to prevent the spread of (a class of) weapons to an area into which they had not yet been introduced. And like the NPT, it was subject to the danger of holdouts, so that by the early 1980s there were growing concerns that states such as Brazil or Argentina might "go nuclear." Also subject to the holdout problem was the Seabed Arms Control Treaty (SACT) of 1971, which prohibited placing weapons of mass destruction on "the seabeds, the ocean floor and in the subsoil thereof" (York, 1973, 128). Of course, that treaty provided yet another example of agreement to refrain from deploying nuclear weaponry in areas not already affected. By the early 1980s, as the search continued for some

ICBM basing mode less vulnerable than the traditional fixed silos on land, schemes for seabed emplacement that would violate SACT were being proposed.

The early 1970s saw several new arms control agreements, most of which were related to the early SALT negotiations between the United States and the Soviet Union. A 1971 agreement updated the Hot Line Agreement of 1963 to replace transoceanic cables with more secure satellite-based communications links. A 1972 U.S.–Soviet agreement sought to reduce the dangers of accidental nuclear war. Another 1972 U.S.–Soviet agreement sought to limit the dangers of escalation from incidents on the high seas, many of which have occurred over the years. Finally, the Biological Weapons Convention of 1972, which involved wide international membership even though the United States and the Soviet Union were the technological leaders in such weaponry, was a true disarmament measure, calling for the destruction of "microbial or other biological agents, or toxins" and their delivery systems, and prohibiting them in the future (York, 1973, 128). Unfortunately, that Convention has proved to have a number of loopholes, one of which is the class of binary nerve gases.

Certainly the extended U.S.–Soviet Strategic Arms Limitation Talks (SALT) process must be seen as one of the most significant arms control undertakings of the nuclear era. The first tentative suggestions at the presidential level for serious nuclear arms control or reduction talks can be traced back to 1965. By 1968 an agreement to begin such negotiations on a bilateral basis had been reached; the agreement was to have been announced on the day following the Soviet/Warsaw Pact invasion of Czechoslovakia. In what may ultimately prove to be the most fateful instance of political "linkage" ever to be invoked in strategic arms negotiations, the United States delayed the SALT talks in protest of the Czech invasion. Negotiations did not begin until more than a year later; by that time the United States had begun to deploy multiple warheads (MIRVs) on some of its ICBMs, essentially dooming any chance of negotiating a ban on MIRV systems. Without the widespread deployment of accurate multiple-warhead missiles, the problem of a hypothetical disarming first strike, or "ICBM vulnerability," which so filled strategic debates by the late 1970s, could not have arisen.

The SALT negotiations which actually began late in 1969 have led to a series of agreements, although the momentum of SALT I seems to have been gradually lost, leading to ever more protracted negotiations and ever-increasing difficulties in reaching and implementing agreements. The SALT I agreements completed and signed in Moscow in April of 1972 included both an ABM Treaty which is still in force, and an Interim Agreement freezing the maximum numbers of ICBMs, SLBMs, and missile-carrying submarines (SSBNs) for five years. The symmetry-of-weapons problem was solved in the ABM Treaty by allowing two ABM sites per side, one to protect the national capital and one to protect an ICBM field, since the Soviets had built a Moscow site and the United States was building two ICBM-field sites. The Interim Agreement froze quantities at levels either already reached or about to be reached through building programs already funded. Two years later the ABM Treaty was amended and strengthened by a Protocol which cut the number of sites to one per side; this was done recognizing that the Senate had voted down funding for a Washington site and that the Soviets had not built an ICBM-field site. The ABM Treaty, as strengthened by the 1974 Protocol, essentially pledged each side to build virtually no ABM defense, and many in the United States believed at the time that it marked a joint acceptance of mutual assured destruction (MAD) strategic doctrine. The reasons for the falsity of that assumption are discussed in detail in Chapter 2.

Later in 1974, the Vladivostok Accords set guidelines for a SALT II agreement that would extend limits to the numbers of strategic bombers and MIRVed ICBMs. As in the SALT I Interim Agreement, the limits set were equal to or greater than deployments already planned, so that at best one could claim that a "cap" had been set on strategic arming. Working out the details of SALT II, however, proved to be an extremely lengthy and difficult process; the treaty signing was delayed until June of 1979, with the treaty to expire in 1985. By the end of 1979, in the face of serious Senate opposition, the Carter administration had withdrawn the treaty from submission for ratification, even before the Soviet invasion of Afghanistan threw a still deeper shadow over U.S.–Soviet relations. Throughout the long SALT II negotiations process and up to the time of this writing, both sides continued to adhere informally to the limits set by the treaties (IISS, 1981). Such tacit adherence, however, is unlikely to extend to Soviet dismantlement of missiles in excess of the post-1982 SALT II limits. By 1981 President Reagan, seeking to mark a political break with the negotiations of the past and the SALT agreements he had opposed, called for meaningful arms reductions through a new set of negotiations designated by a new acronym, START, for STrategic Arms Reduction Talks. Although the START talks began in the summer of 1982, the Reagan administration continued to promote a major U.S. strategic buildup.

The rather dubious prospects of START agreements in the early 1980s also seem to extend to a lack of widespread enthusiasm in the U.S. political system for several other arms control agreements of the middle and later 1970s. These include the U.S.–USSR Threshold Nuclear Test-Ban Treaty of 1974, which set a 150-kiloton limit on underground tests; the U.S.–Soviet Peaceful-Nuclear-Explosions (PNE) Treaty of 1976, which set the same 150-kiloton limit on PNEs and was precedent-setting in that it allowed a limited number of on-site inspections; and the 1977 Convention Banning Modification of the Environment, which prohibited military or hostile use of environmental modifications, and which was signed by 32

TABLE 6.2: Features Commonly Seen in Arms Control Agreements

Negotiating Mechanics
  The More Governments Negotiating, the Less Agreement
  The Broader the Scope of Negotiation, the Less Agreement
  Secret Negotiations Are More Effective than Open Negotiations
  Strong Emphasis on Ideas of "Parity"
  Parity Defined Around Salient Points
  Tacit Adherence to Unratified Treaties and Agreements
  Some Significant Agreements Are Entirely Tacit
  A Few Unilateral Initiatives Have Induced Reciprocation

Political "Prices" of Agreement
  No Destruction of Existing Weapons
  Allow Programs Already Funded to Run to Completion
  Prohibit Only Acts Not Yet Undertaken
  "Packages" of Arms Control and New Weapons Programs
  Uncontrolled Weapons Heavily Exploited
  Difficulties in Obtaining U.S. Ratification

Technopolitical Constraints on Agreement
  Most New Technology Introductions Have Proved to be Irreversible
  Quantitative Limits More Easily Verified than Qualitative Limits
  Any Change May Destabilize the Strategic Weapons Regime
  Static Limits Heighten Incentives for New Developments
  Banning Future Technologies is Extraordinarily Difficult

governments. Each of these agreements continues to be observed tacitly by the signatories, but none has been submitted for U.S. Senate ratification, because of beliefs within each of the recent administrations that opposition would be too severe. In the following section we turn from this summary to a consideration of the political patterns evinced in the major arms control agreements of the nuclear era.

POLITICAL PATTERNS IN ARMS CONTROL AGREEMENTS

The political patterns evinced in arms control agreements of the post-World War II period are synopsized in Table 6.2, in which they have been grouped according to the categories of negotiating mechanics, political "prices" of obtaining agreement, and technopolitical constraints on agreement.

The patterns of negotiating mechanics are reminiscent of Schelling's classic essay on bargaining (1960, Chapter 2). As the number of governments represented in negotiations increases and as the scope of issues bargained increases, agreement becomes ever more difficult. One need only contrast the accomplishments of the (bilateral) SALT negotiations with those of the Eighteen Nation Disarmament Conference. Secret negotiations seem to be much more effective than open negotiations, because the results can be presented as a package with offsetting gains and concessions, helping to prevent any buildup of political opposition to particular parts of the package. This is an especially significant consideration in the United States' political system, and is exemplified by contrasting the fates of the SALT I and SALT II agreements. The SALT I negotiations were conducted with very few "leaks" about the tentative structure of agreements, and the resulting set of agreements was presented to the Congress by President Nixon as a coherent package in which each of the major concessions to the Soviet Union could be argued as being offset by some Soviet concession. In contrast, the SALT II negotiations were much more protracted and were accompanied by many leaks of major details. Indeed, by the year before formal signing, most of the details of the ultimate agreements had been published (Burt, 1978). This permitted strong domestic political opposition to build within the United States against *specific* details of the planned agreements well before SALT II could be presented as a package, and contributed strongly to its downfall.

Concepts of parity and salient points have also played important roles in arms control negotiations. Although the Nixon administration argued that it was justifiable in SALT I to allow more missiles to the Soviet Union than to the United States because the latter had larger numbers of warheads and on-station SSBNs, the Congress imposed the Jackson Amendment on the SALT I instrument of ratification, stating that

> ... the Congress recognizes the principle of United States–Soviet Union equality reflected in the anti-ballistic missile treaty, and urges and requests the President to seek a future treaty that, inter alia, would not limit the United States to levels of intercontinental strategic forces inferior to the limits provided for the Soviet Union . . . (York, 1973, 273)

Regardless of how its military significance may have been perceived, and despite its often very weak relationship to truly sound measures of the strategic "balance," in this instance numeric equality clearly was perceived by many in the U.S. Congress as a *politically* salient measure of nuclear parity.

As already noted, the SALT process has also featured several instances of tacit adherence to agreements reached but not yet formally ratified by both sides. When the President is politically ahead of the Senate, this may be a very constructive development; and as already mentioned, several of the arms control agreements reached in the mid-1970s have never even been submitted for ratification. As the Senate becomes increasingly the domain of idiosyncratic and single-issue candidates, achieving any sort of arms control accords may require reliance on such mechanisms as executive agreements and tacit adherence to unratified treaties. Moreover, this process could be extended into the domain of unilateral moves intended to induce reciprocation without ever engaging in formal negotiations. Some of the atmospheric nuclear test moratoria of the 1958–1961 period had exactly this nature, as did mutual restraint from the use of poison gases in World War II. At least within the U.S. political system, however, it is unclear just how far a President could take such processes without Congressional approval.

The political "prices" of obtaining arms control agreements acceptable within the United States' political system are all clearly demonstrated in the SALT I case. Of all the agreements listed in Table 6.1, only SALT II and the Biological Weapons Convention require any destruction of existing weaponry, and the limited dismantlements envisioned under SALT II are unlikely to occur without ratification. Under SALT I and such other agreements as the Vladivostok Accords, weapons-building programs already funded have been allowed to run to completion; to do otherwise would be to incur much higher political costs within the government agencies having stakes in the programs, as is clearly indicated by classical theories of bureaucratic politics. For the same reasons, it has been common practice to prohibit only actions not yet taken. Consistent with that principle, part of the process of winning support for arms control agreements has been to present them in a "package" which includes new weapons-building programs in all the areas *not* constrained. SALT I presents a particularly dramatic case of this sort of bargaining within the United States, as discussed in detail in Chapter 1, in the subsection, "Bureaucratic and Programmatic Pressures."

Finally, we come to the class of technopolitical constraints on arms control agreements. As discussed in the introduction to this chapter, additions to our collective store of knowledge are essentially irreversible, which is the fundamental reason why new technological introductions tend to be irreversible. New technological applications that prove to be effective tend to remain in active employment until they are displaced with newer and still more effective applications. Thus, for example, the battleship was replaced by the aircraft carrier, which in turn is probably doomed by modern missiles; and nuclear weapons have been largely supplanted by thermonuclear weapons of still higher explosive yield. In this technopolitical constraint lie two radically different possible paths out of the contemporary nuclear arms control dilemma. The first path is into new types of weaponry that promise to be more "effective" but hold out the hope of less potential damage to the planet and its populations; certain scenarios for the development of a large-scale space-warfare capability, such as Graham's (1982) High Frontier program, hold that potential. The second path is suggested by the nuclear "freeze" movement of the early 1980s: in a way far more significant than that of the unilateral nuclear disarmament movement in Britain during the 1950s, the freeze activists suggest that governments should back away from nuclear weapons because their danger level is so high that they cannot realistically prove to be politically or militarily *effective*. The merits and problems of these two divergent paths are considered in detail in the following section.

A very different sort of constraint on arms control agreements has been posed by the essential inability of the superpowers to reach political agreements allowing on-site inspection. The consequent reliance on NTM verification has proved much more conducive to quantitative than to qualitative limitations. The classic instance is the SALT formula of counting ICBM launchers; when it was desired in SALT II to limit the numbers of MIRVed ICBMs, the only formulae that could be devised were to count as MIRVed either all missiles in certain ICBM fields or all missiles of types that had ever been tested with MIRVs. The latter formula was adopted, on the logic that it was unreasonable to deploy missiles with untested reentry vehicles. Yet it is clear that such formulations are at best imperfect and uncertain. Fundamental physical constraints make it easier to count the numbers of weapons than to verify their performance capabilities or other qualities; yet the extent to which those constraints are allowed to impede arms control agreements is a political issue, and as such is in principle subject to being changed.

Another physical constraint which tends to inhibit political change is the fact that any change whatsoever carries some danger of destabilizing the strategic weapons regime. The gradual introduction of ICBM MIRVs with high accuracy raised the problem of ICBM vulnerability, which threatened to undermine MAD doctrine and raised the danger of an increased incentive to carry out a first strike, particularly a preemptive attack in some time of crisis. Other new weapons developments or refinements carry similar dangers of destabilization, as expressed in discussions about the attractions and dangers of strategic breakout. Yet downward shifts also carry dangers of destabilization. In the event of extensive disarmament, as the numbers of nuclear arms held by the two superpowers were lowered, the potential payoffs to a small degree of cheating would increase markedly, and the potential dangers posed by the possession of even small numbers of nuclear weapons by third parties would increase. To the extent that strategic doctrine calls for an assured retaliatory capability, the lower the levels of armaments the greater are the required security levels of the remaining forces.

Additionally, selective and static limits on arms tend to promote vigorous development of unconstrained attributes and technologies. The failure to ban MIRVs under SALT I is the classic contemporary case; after limiting the numbers of ICBMs, both sides pushed ahead rapidly with the development and deployment of new multiple-warhead loadings for those missiles, as well as with the development of new models of missiles to replace older units. The result was a substantial increase in the technical and destructive capabilities of both sides *while operating under the terms of a major arms control agreement*. Unless the highest and best-developed weaponry has reached a point of technological stagnation—a point which is always difficult and therefore dangerous to determine—the setting of any static limit, as on the numbers of missiles, is a formula for the *increase of capabilities* as technological advances increase the capabilities of the fixed quantities of weapons. Although it would no doubt be quite difficult politically to achieve, one might envision seeking arms control agreements that fix the *capability* of the two sides. Such agreements might be possible using performance-capability measures of the type discussed in Chapters 4 and 5, although they would require more effective and probably more intrusive means of verification than NTM.

Finally, it tends to be extraordinarily difficult to ban future technological developments not yet realized or, perhaps, even envisioned. The SALT I ABM Treaty provides an example of an attempt to ban future ABM technologies by defining them functionally. In Article II the parties agreed that:

> For the purposes of this Treaty an ABM system is a system to counter strategic ballistic missiles or their elements in flight trajectory, *currently consisting of* . . . (italics added)

and in Article V they pledged that:

> Each Party undertakes not to develop, test, or deploy ABM systems or components which are sea-based, air-based, space-based, or mobile land-based. (York, 1973, 260–261)

Less than 10 years after the ABM Treaty was signed, as new technological possibilities opened for such developments as space-based laser ABMs, calls were being heard in the United States either to abrogate the treaty or to interpret it as allowing such developments. (See, for example, the discussion in the section, "Exotic Weapons," in Chapter 1). Despite such problems, however, in the absence of some effective international enforcement body, functional definitions of the types of weaponry to be eschewed may be the most effective formula for preventing a relentless escalation into new technologies.

Given these considerations about the patterns of political and technological constraints evinced in arms control agreements achieved over the past two decades, we turn in the following section to the examination of a number of scenarios for possible arms control developments in the 1980s, together with some indicators of the policy paths actually being followed.

SCENARIOS AND INDICATORS FOR ARMS CONTROL IN THE 1980s

What sorts of arms control moves are in prospect for the 1980s? Given the lessons of the past two decades, what sorts of breakthroughs might be envisioned that could lead to greater progress in constraining or reducing nuclear armaments, and with what probabilities could we anticipate such developments? What indicators might be used to identify the policy developments in progress? Table 6.3 sketches some initial answers in the form of a wide range of possible (and not always mutually exclusive) scenarios, together with a number of suggested indicators.

TABLE 6.3 Some Scenarios and Indicators of Policies Pursued

Scenario	Indicators
1 Expanded Competition	Further breakdown of SALT/START process
	Budget increases (nuclear weapons)
	New programs (expanded MX, Trident, etc.)
	Exotic weapons programs (laser ABM, etc.)
2 Nuclear/Conventional Decoupling	Nuclear "freeze" moratorium
	Budget increases (conventional weapons)
	Conventional arms sales increases
	Expansions of RDF, surface Navy, etc.
2a Dropping of "Linkage"	U.S. and Soviet actions, statements
	Maintaining START talks
	(Primarily a U.S. political problem)
3 GRIT Extensions	Unilateral proposals
	Unilateral moves
	Significant departures from past practice
	European IRBM "zero option"
	Modifications of existing European IRBM deployments
3a Perceptual Shifts in Conflict Resolution	Key writings
	Opinion poll data
	Congressional action on nuclear "freeze"
	Related political actions
4 Deterrence Through Space-Based Weaponry	Budgetary and program actions
	Space-based ABM systems
	Expanded manned orbital programs
	Antisatellite weapons programs
5 Major Strategic Defense	ABM systems of any type
	Significant civil defense programs
	Large-scale evacuation programs
5a Defense plus Unilateral Arms Reduction Moves	Strategic defense indicators
	plus
	GRIT extensions indicators
6 Supremacy or First Strike Capability	Declaratory policy of "margin"
	Substantial budget increases
	Major moves into new weapons types

While the scenarios listed in Table 6.3 are very general in character, they describe distinct policy thrusts. Each scenario could encompass a wide variety of specific weapons building and/or arms control or reduction programs of varying scope. The suggested policy indicators are, of necessity, comparably broad and diverse. Scenarios are listed approximately in order from most probable to least probable, although the logic of the ordering undoubtedly requires some discussion. Their relationships to the various possible outcomes in the prisoners' dilemma game of arming and disarming are given in Figure 6.3. Clearly, most of the arming scenarios fall into the mutually uncooperative (lower right) outcome cell in Figure 6.3, while most of the disarming or arms control scenarios fall into the mutually cooperative (upper left) cell. This is consistent with past experience. Under

Figure 6.3 Scenarios in Arming and Disarming
(Scenario Numbers Refer to Table 6.3.)

	Soviet Union Disarm	Soviet Union Arm
United States Disarm	(2) Nuclear/Conventional Decoupling (2a) Dropping "Linkage" (3) GRIT Extensions (3a) Perceptual Shifts in Conflict Resolution (5a) Strategic Defense with Mutual Arms Reductions	(5a) Strategic Defense with U.S. Arms Reductions
United States Arm	(6) Supremacy or First Strike Capability (Possibly leading to expanded competition?)	(1) Expanded Competition (4) Deterrence Through Space-Based Weaponry (5) Strategic Defense with New Arms

SALT I, for example, the United States and the Soviet Union cooperated in the quantitatively constrained areas while competing vigorously in such unconstrained areas of qualitative improvement as MIRV deployments. Not all policy scenarios are quite so readily classified, however; the greater the degree of unilateral initiative or action involved, the more difficult it becomes to classify a scenario into a single outcome cell in Figure 6.3.

Some scenario calling for continued and expanded competition between the two superpowers seems most likely in the early 1980s, given the virtual breakdown of the SALT process late in 1979. Such a scenario would represent political "business as usual." From the strategic bargaining standpoint, of course, it also represents the risk-averse minimax solution to the prisoners' dilemma. Although both sides continued to observe the SALT II limits tacitly, and although President Reagan called for new START talks, and eventually for substantial reductions, the climate of U.S.–Soviet strategic discussion worsened steadily in the early 1980s as Reagan continued to call for a U.S. "margin of safety" over the Soviets. At the same time the Soviets made it clear that, having achieved what they perceived to be parity or essential equivalence, they had no intention of ever again becoming the strategic inferior of the United States. Despite the opening of START negotiations in the summer of 1982, it would be entirely consistent with the past history of strategic arms building and limitation for both sides to pursue extensive new arms-building programs well into the late 1980s before any serious new arms control agreements are reached. Among indicators that might be watched are further increases in the strategic arms budgets and, less critically, the general military budgets of both sides, or any open eschewing of desire to intensify the START negotiations. Particularly significant forms of budget increases would include new weapons programs such as large-scale MX deployments, any type of ABM program, an acceleration in the pace of Trident submarine construction, or any of a variety of exotic weapons development programs.

Curiously, the next most likely scenario appears to be a (probably mutually) cooperative outcome in which significant decoupling occurs between nuclear and conventional weapons, allowing for at least a nuclear freeze and possibly for substantial reductions in nuclear arms. With the stalling of the SALT II treaty and with President Reagan's calls for increased military spending, by 1982 the growing movement for a freeze (at least) in nuclear deployments had become the only active arms control movement influencing Washington. That movement was given considerable impetus by the Kennedy-Hatfield resolution for formal endorsement (Miller, 1982), and by the call by Robert McNamara, McGeorge Bundy, George Kennan, and Gerard Smith for the United States to adopt a "no first use" pledge (Hedrick Smith, 1982). The chief criticisms of the freeze concept are that only the United States is subject to such grass-roots movements; that it therefore threatens to strip the United States of any bargaining leverage in negotiating with the Soviets, who are not subject to such popular pressures; that it mistakenly considers the simple numbers of nuclear weapons to be the primary danger, without taking the dynamics of potential crises and conflicts into account; and that it ignores the requirements of deterrence, especially the security of the deterrent force. The chief criticism of the no-first-use pledge is that it would rob NATO of the deterrent effect heretofore provided by the always-ambiguous threat to escalate to nuclear weaponry in response to a conventional Warsaw Pact attack on western Europe.

These two sets of criticisms are consistent in their implications about a nuclear/conventional weapons decoupling, which makes them consistent in what they imply about indicators that such a policy is being pursued, for both policies speak directly only about nuclear weapons. And both threaten to create situations in which, barring some fundamental shift in the way in which international politics is carried out, conventional weapons and forces would have to be expanded to maintain deterrence. It is therefore logical to predict that the adoption of either policy would lead to increases in the budget for conventional military forces. Moreover, given that strategic weapons typically absorb only about one-tenth of the United States' military budget, these policy changes could easily lead to increases in total military spending. One therefore might look for signs of increases in significant components of conventional forces, such as the surface Navy, the Rapid Deployment Force, or the Military Air Transport Command, as accompaniments of any major shift to decouple nuclear from conventional forces and to depend more heavily on the latter. If reliance on threats of nuclear escalation and nuclear "umbrellas" over allied states is lessened, increases probably will occur in transfers of conventional weapons through overseas sales and gifts.

One particularly significant policy shift by the United States that would do much to facilitate a decoupling of nuclear from conventional weaponry issues would be the downgrading of "linkage" politics. The fateful role of linkage between SALT and the 1968 invasion of Czechoslovakia has already been discussed. A similar problem occurred in 1979 when the fate of SALT II ratification, already doubtful, became linked to the December Soviet invasion of Afghanistan. Again in 1981–82 linkage was raised between the imposition of martial law in Poland and the opening of START talks, although the talks did begin in 1982. Since the 1973 Yom Kippur war it has become clear that the Soviet Union finds it far easier than does the United States to maintain negotiation channels and some degree of cooperation on strategic weapons issues while continuing to exploit targets of opportunity by all means short of strategic war. This fundamental difference in interpretation of the meaning of "détente" is unlikely to change over time. Such interactions are subject to the constraint of the least common denominator; the United States can either play by Soviet rules that limit cooperation to the strategic sector, or not play at all, and lose the advantages of strategic cooperation. In the game-theoretic sense, breaking linkage means agreeing to cooperate on nuclear issues while continuing to compete at the subnuclear level. Such breaking of linkage should sometimes work to U.S. advantage, as it did in 1972, when the Soviets wanted a SALT agreement badly enough that they did not attempt to apply pressure about U.S. escalations in Vietnam.

Linkage is, of course, primarily a U.S. political problem, and it became more severe under the Reagan administration than it was under President Carter, due to a general increase in the rhetoric of confrontation. Future U.S. and Soviet actions will provide the best indicators of any change in reliance on linkage. One encouraging sign was the opening of START talks, despite Soviet actions bearing on the advent of martial law in Poland. Another sign would be maintaining such talks on a serious, productive, and ongoing basis. If the nuclear freeze movement gains additional influence in the United States, it will undoubtedly pressure the administration to engage more seriously in strategic arms reduction negotiations, regardless of opportunities or temptations to cite linkage concerns as reasons for postponing such talks.

A somewhat less likely set of scenarios calls for major initiatives by one or the other of the superpowers, making significant departures from past practice in order to induce a response in kind that would allow major progress in actual arms reductions. Such initiatives are here classified as extensions of Charles Osgood's (1962) classic proposals for Graduated Reciprocation in Tension-reduction (GRIT). Substantial acceptance of the nuclear freeze initiative by the United States could be interpreted as consistent with GRIT, as could President Reagan's 1981 "zero option" proposal regarding European-based IRBMs, provided that it was considered a serious proposal. Osgood's formulation, however, calls for a sequence of unilateral moves by each side, the sequence being continued as long as responsive moves sufficient to avoid any serious disadvantage to either side are forthcoming. Such a sequence is thus probably best classified as mutually cooperative in the arming/disarming game of strategy. Adoption of such a program by either side should be obvious, although occasional proposals such as the "zero option" or the Soviet counter offer could be seized upon as initial steps upon which such a program might be built even if not originally so intended. Such a program would, of course, be a substantial departure from the past practice of both superpowers, and would much more likely be the policy output of a "cyberneticist" decision maker than an "essentialist." (See Chapter 1, "Ideologies and Values.") Given that the Reagan administration inclines toward the essentialist view, at least in its declaratory policy, the prospects for such initiatives in the middle 1980s do not appear promising.

One development that could materially increase the chances of such initiatives, however, would be significant and widespread shifts in political and, especially in the west, public perceptions of the strategic weapons regime's inherent dangers. The movements in support of a nuclear test ban in the 1950s and early 1960s provide prototypes; public and media combined to bring pressure on politicians to negotiate some agreement that would solve the fallout problem. Moreover, in the Kennedy administration sentiment to stabilize the arms race must have been at least somewhat affected by the resounding public rejection of the 1962 attempt to win support for a broad, nationwide program of fallout shelter construction. The nuclear freeze movement in the United States and western Europe in the early 1980s is the first mass public arms control movement in two decades to even begin to compare in scope with the antitesting movement; and its goal, if accomplished, would have much more far-reaching consequences both for the strategic weapons regime and for the conduct of international politics.

If the freeze movement is even moderately successful, it will have succeeded in bringing about a significant and widespread shift in opinions. One indicator of such a shift would be the widespread sale and acceptance of such writings as Jonathan Schell's apocalyptic book *The Fate of the Earth* (1982). Another indicator may be the extent and origins of critical responses to such writings. Max Lerner, for example, criticized Schell for his single-minded focus on the terror aspect of nuclear weaponry, stating that:

> What Schell fails to realize, enthralled as he is by his eschatology, is that no plan for averting a nuclear holocaust is worth anything if it doesn't acknowledge the deeply flawed nature of man and his institutions.

He continues, stating:

> The full impact of the "extinctionist" antinuclear movements will be felt in the democracies, not in the Soviet Union. (1982, 28)

In evaluating that impact, one should follow both key writings and poll data wherever available. Several early 1982 polls indicated up to 70-percent support for a nuclear freeze. A March 1982 *Los Angeles Times* nationwide poll, for example, yielded freeze support by 57 percent to 37 percent. It also indicated some very disquieting trends in public thinking. Twenty-nine percent said that they believed the United States capable of initiating a nuclear war, as against 63 percent believing the same of the Soviet Union; and 57 percent opposed the NATO policy of using nuclear weapons to stop a Soviet conventional-weapons invasion of western Europe. Fifty-three percent said that they would not "want to survive an all-out nuclear war" and, no doubt far more seriously for the prospects of stabilizing the strategic weapons regime, 55 percent said that they found the subjects of nuclear weapons and strategic warfare so depressing that they would rather ignore them (Scheer, 1982).

The freeze movement, of course, might be interpreted as an attempt to shock people out of such depressive apathy by insisting that their views can have political impact. Beyond poll data, one might look for evidence of success for the freeze and related movements in Congressional statements and actions. The growth of the movement in 1981–82 was aided, almost paradoxically, by fears heightened by President Reagan's repeated and insistent calls for major increases in military spending, including new strategic weaponry, prior to any further arms-control negotiations.

The remaining scenarios sketched in Table 6.3 are both more speculative and less likely, and beginning to implement them might well take considerably longer. Nonetheless, they mark some alternative paths along which the strategic weapons regime might evolve in coming decades, with widely varying prospects for arms control and, perhaps, for peace. One competitive scenario on which opinions would doubtless be highly divided, although it certainly gained some support in the Reagan administration and in the Congress, is to move strongly into building space-based deterrent and defensive systems. Such systems include both orbiting counters to Earth-based weapons, such as laser ABM systems, and weaponry designed to carry out hostilities between orbiting weapons systems, beginning with antisatellite devices. Congressional calls for such exotic weapons programs have already been discussed in Chapter 1. Among the advantages that might be claimed for such developments are the possibility of an effective defense against ballistic missiles; a bureaucratically effective way to buy the U.S. Air Force out of its current mission to operate land-based ICBMs by giving it a substantial new mission, thus solving the problem of ICBM vulnerability and helping stabilize the strategic weapons regime against the danger of disarming first strikes; promotion of an expanded manned space program with its attendant economic and technological spinoffs; the possibility in the longer range of moving at least a small fraction of the human race to locations off the surface of the Earth, thus reducing the danger of extinction through major war; and the possibility of redirecting attention to such a degree that any major military confrontation would take place off the surface of the planet, with far less loss of life than in any conflict fought with current types of strategic weapons. This last possibility would return the planet to a contemporary analogue of the situation in Europe prior to the French Revolution, when most wars were fought by small professional armies, with the primary impacts on the general populations being the economic costs of preparing for such conflicts and the political realignments that followed.

Each of the putative advantages of such a scenario, however, has vigorous critics. Serious challenges have been raised to the concept of space-based ABM systems, particularly lasers, on technical grounds (see, for example, Tsipis, 1981) as well as on the political ground that they would violate the SALT I ABM Treaty. Moreover, the development of an ability to attack missiles that rise above the Earth's atmosphere would likely produce renewed competition in intraatmospheric weapons. Further, the political and technical significance—or reality—of ICBM vulnerability has been strongly criticized (see, for example, Steinbruner and Garwin, 1976). The technological spinoffs of the space program have been conspicuous mainly in the realm of microelectronics and in the use of satellites for communications and weather forecasting. Yet advances in space technology have also come under attack on the ground that they are used first for military purposes, so that additional advances are likely to promote the arms race even further. Vincent Helman (1983), drawing on Congressional Research Service classifications of space launches as "primarily civil" or "primarily military" in orientation, reports that over the period 1957–1981, 338 of the 778 U.S. launches (43 percent) were primarily military, while 949 of the 1397 Soviet launches (68 percent) were primarily military. He also reports that both the U.S.–Soviet quantitative imbalance in numbers of space launchings, and the fraction devoted to primarily military missions have shifted further in favor of the Soviets; for the decade 1972—1981, 70 of the 233 U.S. space launches (30 percent) were primarily military, while 609 of the 889 Soviet launches (75 percent) were primarily military. These data lend additional support to the assertion that the Soviets are devoting considerable efforts to developing a near-earth military space capability. The use of all societies' latest and highest technologies in support of military efforts is not, of course, a new phenomenon in history.

Naturally enough, the economic spinoffs of such efforts are also criticized, and by the early 1980s, as the economic impacts of the Reagan tax-cut programs began to unfold, a vigorous Congressional debate had developed over whether the United States could afford further increases in defense programs at the expense of cuts in social services and further increases in the soaring federal deficit. And, finally, those who would urge massive cuts in military spending and in nuclear arsenals would argue that their programs offer far better chances for the long-term survival of the human race than would an expansion into space for any motive. The key indicators of any serious movement into space weapons are likely to revolve around Congressional hearings and budgetary actions, together with the statements of interested and influential parties in government and industry. Space-based ABM systems and antisatellite weapons would be logical first steps. Certain types of manned orbital programs could also play such roles, which is why some of those opposed to further military buildups have criticized the United States' space shuttle program. The shuttle actually provides a good example of a technology that can be exploited either for peaceful or warlike purposes, but it *is* a logical prelude to any expanded space program. More generally, the development of any capability to keep humans in orbit on an extended and continuous basis, unless strictly limited to scientific and manufacturing pursuits, would presage the development of an expanded space military capability—which is still not necessarily tantamount to a space warfare capability.

A different speculative scenario would be to utilize major moves into strategic defense as a means to allow substantial and unilateral reductions in strategic arms. Such a scenario could encompass mutual cooperation or unilateral U.S. moves in the face of Soviet noncooperation. If an effective ballistic missile defense could be mounted from orbit, for example, maintaining deterrence would no longer require massive numbers of missiles. According to bureaucratic–political theories, of course, only very great pressures could bring about the abandonment of major present missions, which is the primary argument why this scenario is quite unlikely. Indicators that such a policy was being pursued would include those already considered under both strategic defense and GRIT extensions. Under such a policy, a civil defense program need not imply any first strike intent.

A final and least likely scenario would be for the United States to strive openly and consciously to achieve a first strike capability against the Soviet Union. Note, particularly in the light of the discussion of strategic doctrines in Chapter 2, that this is not the same as acquiring nuclear superiority over the Soviets. Barring some major technological breakthrough, such as a highly effective ballistic missile defense, no strategic breakout is foreseeable. Yet that breakout continues to draw yearning attention from some, and it is difficult to prove that any ABM system or population-evacuation program exists solely as a defensive measure. A cause for greater concern may be that some in the West have criticized such systems as MX as being inherently first-strike weapons, ignoring the fact that the slow increase in missile accuracies that brought about the ICBM vulnerability problem is the root cause of the attendant destabilization of the strategic weapons regime's deterrent basis. Any real shift to a first-strike or supremacy program would have to entail substantial budget increases for new weaponry and major moves into new types of weapons, and almost certainly would be accompanied by shifts in declaratory policies. One may still worry, though, about just what attaining a "margin of safety" in strategic weaponry means to different decision makers.

CONCLUDING REMARKS: THE PROSPECTS FOR ARMS CONTROL

Over the past decade the management of strategic policy has become an increasingly important issue in U.S. domestic and foreign policy, and in the mid-1980s both the United States and the entire strategic weapons regime stand uncertainly at a cusp of decision. Moreover, the probable future course has become much less certain since Ronald Reagan's election to the presidency in 1980. On one side stand those who argue the dangers inherent in nuclear weapons and the risk that they are uncontrollable, who perceive that the strategic weapons regime is vastly overbuilt and consequently dangerous almost beyond imagining, and who therefore call with increasing political potency for a nuclear weapons freeze to be followed by substantial disarmament. As this group gains political impact, it puts the president under increasing pressure to modify his policy stands, at least superficially and reactively. On the other side stand those who have been more or less in the political ascendency throughout the nuclear era, for whom fear of the Soviet Union exceeds their fear of nuclear weapons, who perceive the United States to be at a current strategic disadvantage, who call for substantial new strategic weapons programs to redress that imbalance, and who point to almost 40 years of successful management of the strategic weapons regime to bolster their claim that business more or less as usual can be continued indefinitely.

This clash of positions results in part from serious disagreement on the nature, measurement, and significance of the nuclear strategic "balance." That balance is ambiguous because there is no agreement either within or between nation-states on how it is to be measured. The lack of agreement arises in part from technical and methodological issues in policy assessment, but it arises much more strongly from the fact that the doctrines for the use of strategic weapons are themselves ambiguous. Those ambiguities, in turn, exist because we have never fully resolved the political questions about what to do with the weapons we already have, let alone the weaponry we can envision. Severe disagreements exist about both means and ends, and are reflected in the contemporary debate within the United States over further arming versus disarming. While such disagreements are traditionally at the heart of politics, in the nuclear weapons case the set of available solutions is very much constrained by the history of previous actions.

The evolution of the nuclear strategic weapons regime rests on two fundamental propositions. First is the combination of extreme destructive capability with reliable and prompt intercontinental delivery systems. This combination has meant that in a world of many nation-states, no single state can have unconditional viability. Each is open to attack from any other possessor of the weapons and delivery systems, so that the world power ordering is reminiscent of Morton Kaplan's (1957) "unit veto" system. The second fundamental proposition is the essential irreversibility of the knowledge that such weapons systems can be built. The combination of these two propositions means that, no matter how strongly the fear of war may drive peoples and governments toward disarmament, a countervailing fear of possible cheating will tend to drive them away and toward further arming, or at least toward maintaining the status quo. Additionally, this interaction takes place against the background of a great unanswerable question: deterrence *may* have worked to prevent war since 1945, but we can never prove it.

These difficulties are further compounded by the dangers of nuclear weapons proliferation to still more states. Since 1960 France has built an independent striking force (the "force de frappe") capable of carrying out minimum deterrent (MD) strikes against the Soviet Union. Construction of such a force was seen as a logical response to the decreasing credibility of a U.S. "nuclear umbrella" as Soviet strength grew. But well before the year 2001, given present building programs, France will be able to threaten far more than MD against the European USSR. This suggests that the acquisition of nuclear weapons by states with fairly strong economies threatens to lead to significant increases in the ranks of "major" nuclear powers by the end of this century, a development which would greatly complicate the achievement of substantial nuclear arms control, let alone disarmament. Thus the achievement of such controls, no matter how difficult the task may seem today, is not likely to become any easier in the future.

Because of the proliferation problem, bilateral superpower arms control as we have known it in SALT is at best a stopgap measure. And while it is undoubtedly true that most of our politics consists of stopgap measures, the achievement of truly effective arms control will require the development of some new political institutions. The problem of balancing off the risks of control against the risks of war is unlikely to disappear; but more effective control institutions must shift the balance of risks. This is likely to require more intrusive means of inspection than the national technical means (NTM) thus far accepted. It may also involve defining arms limits functionally, so that weapons capability or effect measures are employed. Such measures, of course, require increased agreement within and between governments on the desirability of control and on the means of measuring weapons effectiveness. Yet, as we build agreement on the technical questions of evaluation, the crucial questions increasingly become those of the political management of the perceived strategic balance.

Agreement on those questions might be achievable through radical change, e.g., through agreement on general nuclear disarmament. But our political institutions, especially at the international level, tend to evolve incrementally. A more probable but still hopeful path thus would appear to be the building of eventual comprehensive strategic weapons control through a series of small cooperative steps beginning from the status quo. From our experimental and theoretical knowledge we can anticipate that cooperative solutions to the prisoners' dilemma game of strategic arms and arms control may be found through such means as building communication and discussion between the players, emphasizing that play is repeated over long periods of time, and that the long-term benefits of cooperation thus can far exceed the short-term benefits of conflict. The game is played, of course, in the absence of any external enforcer, which heightens our concern about the dangers of proliferation.

The prevalence of incremental political processes at both national and international levels militates against the achievement of comprehensive nuclear arms control through any single step. Yet the stakes are sufficiently high, even in the short run, that it may be possible to stimulate serious dialogues about the issues, both within the United States and internationally, and out of those dialogues to reach agreement on arms control measures much more far-reaching than any yet attained. Whatever path is followed, the technical face of the strategic weapons regime will change significantly by the year 2001; how different the political face appears will depend on our collective inventiveness and perseverance.

References

Allison, Graham T. 1971. *Essence of Decision: Explaining the Cuban Missile Crisis*. Boston: Little, Brown and Company.
Alsop, Stewart. 1962. Our New Strategy: The Alternatives to Total War. *Saturday Evening Post*, 1 December.
Anschutz, Eric E. 1972. Personal communication dated 17 March.
Aviation Week and Space Technology. 1979a. Missile Defense Gains Support. 22 October: 14–17.
———. 1979b. U.S., U.S.S.R. Strategic Arms Compared, 25 June: 22.
———. 1980a. House Unit Backs Low-Altitude ABM Effort. **112**, 24 (16 June): 220.
———. 1980b. Soviets Nuclear Arsenal Continues to Proliferate. **112**, 24 (16 June): 67–76.
———. 1980c. Trident Missile Capabilities Advance. **112**, 24 (16 June): 91–100.
———. 1980d. MX Basing Decisions Clear Way for Design Advances. **112**, 24 (16 June): 132–134.
———. 1980e. Demonstration Planned for MX Defense System. **112**, 24 (16 June): 220–221.
———. 1980f. Telemetry Data Vital to Trident. **112**, 24 (16 June): 102–103.
Axelrod, Robert. 1979. The Rational Timing of Surprise. *World Politics* **31**, 2 (January): 228–246.
Baker, John C., and Berman, Robert P. 1974. Evaluating Counterforce Strategy. *The New York Times*, 22 February: 33.
Ball, Desmond J. 1974. *Deja Vu: The Return to Counterforce in the Nixon Administration*. Santa Monica: The California Seminar on Arms Control and Foreign Policy.
———. 1977. The Conterforce Potential of American SLBM Systems. *Journal of Peace Research* **14**, 1: 23–40.
———. 1981. *Politics and Force Levels: The Strategic Missile Program of the Kennedy Administration*. Berkeley: University of California Press.
Barbieri, William. R-1314. RAND Memorandum on Counter-Military Potential.
Barton, John H., and Lawrence Weiler, eds. 1976. *International Arms Control: Issues and Agreements*. By the Stanford Arms Control Group. Stanford, Calif: Stanford University Press.
Baugh, William H. 1977a. Response to Sudden Shifts in a Two-Nation Arms Race. *Behavioral Science* **22**, 2 (March): 69–86.

———. 1977b. Is There An Arms Race? Alternative Models of Slow Growth Processes. In *The General Systems Paradigm: Science of Change and Change of Science*. Washington, D.C.: Society for General Systems Research: 445–450.

———. 1978. Major Powers and Weak Allies: Stability and Structure in Arms Race Models. *Journal of Peace Science* **3**, 1 (Spring): 45–54.

Baumol, William J. 1972. *Economic Theory and Operations Analysis*. Englewood Cliffs, N.J.: Prentice-Hall.

Bellany, Ian. 1973. The Essential Arithmetic of Deterrence. *Journal of the Royal United Services Institute for Defence Studies*, **118** (March): 28–34.

———. 1979. More Arithmetic of Deterrence: Throw Weight, Radioactivity and Limited Nuclear War. *Journal of the Royal United Services Institute for Defence Studies*, **124** (June): 35–38.

Blalock, Hubert M., Jr. 1969. *Theory Construction: From Verbal to Mathematical Formulations*. New York: Macmillan.

Bottome, Edgar M. 1970. *The Missile Gap: A Study in the Formulation of Military and Public Policy*. Cranbury, N.J.: Fairleigh Dickinson University Press.

———. 1971. *The Balance of Terror: A Guide to the Arms Race*. Boston: Beacon Press.

Boulding, Kenneth E. 1962. *Conflict and Defense: A General Theory*. New York: Harper and Row.

Brams, Steven J. 1976. *Paradoxes in Politics: An Introduction to the Nonobvious in Political Science*. New York: Free Press.

Braybrooke, David, and Lindblom, Charles E. 1963. *A Strategy of Decision: Policy Evaluation as a Social Process*. New York: Free Press.

Brennan, Donald G. 1979. SALT II: Strategic Considerations. Presentation at a seminar for West Coast alumni of the National Security Education Seminars, "David at the End of an Inoperative Slingshot?" Portland, 19 May.

Brezhnev, Leonid I. 1977. The Great October Revolution and the Progress of Mankind. Radio Moscow (live) November 2; also in *Pravda* and *Izvestiva*, 3 November.

———. 1981. Remarks in response to President Reagan's goal of military superiority. Week of 26 January.

Brito, Dagobert L. 1972. A Dynamic Model of an Armaments Race. *International Economic Review*, **13**: 359–375.

———, and Intriligator, Michael D. 1973. Some Applications of the Maximum Principle to the Problem of an Armaments Race. *Modeling and Simulation*, **4**: 140–144.

———. 1974. Uncertainty and the Stability of the Armaments Race. *Annals of Economic and Social Measurement*, **3**: 279–292.

———. 1977a. Strategic Nuclear Weapons and the Allocation of International Rights. In *Mathematical Systems in International Relations Research*, eds. John V. Gillespie and Dina A. Zinnes, pp. 199–215. New York: Praeger.

———. 1977b. Nuclear Proliferation and the Armaments Race. *Journal of Peace Science*, **2**: 231–238.

———. 1981. Strategic Arms Limitation Treaties and Innovations in Weapon Technology. *Public Choice*, **37**, 1: 41–59.

Brodie, Bernard, ed. 1946. *The Absolute Weapon: Atomic Power and World Order*. New York: Harcourt, Brace and Company.

Brody, Richard A. 1968. Deterrence. In *International Encyclopedia of the Social*

Sciences, ed. David L. Sills, Vol. 4, pp. 130–133. New York: Macmillan Company and The Free Press.

Brown, Harold. 1978. *Department of Defense Annual Report, Fiscal Year 1979*. Washington, D.C.: U.S. Government Printing Office.

———. 1979. *Department of Defense Annual Report, Fiscal Year 1980*. Washington, D.C.: U.S. Government Printing Office.

———. 1980. *Department of Defense Annual Report, Fiscal Year 1981*. Washington, D.C.: U.S. Government Printing Office.

Brown, Thomas A. 1976. Missile Accuracy and Strategic Lethality. *Survival*, **18** (March-April): 52–59.

———. 1977. Number Mysticism, Rationality and the Strategic Balance. *Orbis* **21** (Fall): 479–496.

Burke, James. 1978. *Connections*. Boston: Little, Brown and Company.

Burt, Richard. 1978. The Scope and Limits of SALT. *Foreign Affairs* **56**, 4 (July): 751–770.

———. 1980. Study Says a Soviet Move in Iran Might Require U.S. Atom Arms. *The New York Times* 2 February: 1, 4.

Cannon, Lou. 1982. Reagan Urges MX 'Dense Pack' In Wyoming. *Washington Post* 23 November: A1, A8.

———. 1983a. President Seeks Futuristic Defense Against Missiles. *Washington Post* 24 March: A1, A13.

———. 1983b. Silo Basing Backed for MX Missile. *Washington Post* 12 April: A1, A6.

Carr, Bob. 1978. Dissenting views in U.S. Congress, House, Committee on Armed Services, Subcommittee on Intelligence and Military Application of Nuclear Energy. *SALT II: An Interim Assessment: Report of the Panel on the Strategic Arms Limitation Talks and the Comprehensive Test Ban*, 95th Cong., 2nd Sess. 23 December: 46.

Carter, James Earl. 1980. National Security Policy. Address before the American Legion, Boston, 21 August. Washington, D.C.: U.S. Department of State, *Current Policy No. 214*.

Caspary, William R. 1967. Richardson's Model of Arms Races: Description, Critique, and an Alternative Model. *International Studies Quarterly*, **11:** 63–88.

Central Intelligence Agency, National Foreign Assessment Center. 1978. A Dollar Cost Comparison of Soviet and US Defense Activities, 1967–77: A Research Paper. Washington, D.C.: Central Intelligence Agency.

Chayes, Abram, and Wiesner, Jerome B., eds. 1969. *ABM: An Evaluation of the Decision to Deploy an Antiballistic Missile System*. New York: New American Library.

Church Committee. 1976. *Select Committee to Study Government Operations with Respect to Intelligence Activities, Final Report, Book 1: Foreign and Military Intelligence*. Washington, D.C.: U.S. Government Printing Office. 26 April. Report 94–755.

Collins, John M., and Cordesman, Anthony H. 1978. *Imbalance of Power: An Analysis of Shifting U.S.–Soviet Military Strengths* [by Collins] and *Net Assessment Appraisal* [by Cordesman]. San Rafael, California: Presidio Press.

Committee on the Present Danger. 1978. Where We Stand . . . Summaries of Policy Statements 1976–1977. Washington, D.C.: Committee on the Present Danger.

Congressional Record. Washington, D.C.: U.S. Government Printing Office.
Covault, Craig 1980. Antisatellite Weapon Design Advances. *Aviation Week and Space Technology* **112**, 24 (16 June): 243–247.
———. 1981. Proposed Delay in Shuttle at Vandenburg Cut 50%. *Aviation Week and Space Technology* **115**, 8 (24 August): 22–24.
Crecine, John P. 1970. *Defense Budgeting: Adaptation to Organizational Constraints*. Santa Monica: Rand Corporation.
Cypher, James. 1974. Capitalist Planning and Military Expenditures. *The Review of Radical Political Economics* **6**: 1–19.
Daniel, Clifton. 1955. Moscow Air Show Unveils 4-Jet Transport Airliner. *The New York Times* 4 July: 1, 2.
Davis, Lynn E. 1976. *Limited Nuclear Options: Deterrence and the New American Doctrine*. London: International Institute for Strategic Studies, Adelphi Paper Number 121.
———. and Schilling, Warner. 1973. All You Ever Wanted to Know About MIRV and ICBM Calculations But Were Not Cleared to Ask. *Journal of Conflict Resolution*, **17** (June): 207–242.
Davis, Otto A., Dempster, M. A. H., and Wildavsky, Aaron. 1966. A Theory of the Budgetary Process. *American Political Science Review* **60**: 529–547.
Defense Monitor **6**, 6 (August) 1977. The $100 Million Mobile Missile: The MX and the Future of U.S. Strategic Forces. Washington, D.C.: Center for Defense Information.
———. **9**, 5 (June) 1980. American Strength, Soviet Weakness. Washington, D.C.: Center for Defense Information.
Doder, Dusko. 1982. Soviets Said to Consider Faster Nuclear Missile Launch in Crisis. *Washington Post* 11 April: A5.
Donley, Michael B., ed. 1979. *The SALT Handbook*. Washington, D.C.: The Heritage Foundation.
Downey, Thomas L. 1976. How to Avoid Monad—and Disaster. *Foreign Policy* **24** (Fall): 172–201. A more complete form is given under the title "How to Avoid Monad," *Congressional Record—Senate*, 20 September, S16210–S16218.
Drell, Sidney D. 1979. SUM. *Arms Control Today* **9**, 8 (September): 1–8.
———, and Garwin, Richard L. 1981. Basing the MX Missile: A Better Idea. *Technology Review* **83**, 6 (May/June): 20–29.
Dulles, John Foster. 1954. Policy for Security and Peace. *Foreign Affairs* **32**, 3 (April): 353–364.
Ellsberg, Daniel. 1981. Nuclear Weapons: Will We Use Them? *Current* **233** (June): 35–43.
Enthoven, Alain C. 1968. Hearings before the Senate Preparedness Investigating Subcommittee of the Committee on the Armed Services, 1 May. Washington, D.C.: U.S. Government Printing Office: 118.
Ermarth, Fritz W. 1978. Contrasts in American and Soviet Strategic Thought. *International Security* **3**, 2 (Fall): 138–155.
Fain, Tyrus G., Plant, Katherine C., and Milloy, Ross, eds. 1977. *The Intelligence Community: History, Organization, and Issues*. New York: R. R. Bowker Company, Public Documents Series.
Foster, William Z. 1972. Testimony on the FY 1973 Defense Department RDT & E Program before the House Armed Services Committee, 29 February: 1–13, 14, 15.

Freedman, Lawrence David. 1977. *U.S. Intelligence and the Soviet Strategic Threat*. Boulder, Colo.: Westview Press.
Friedberg, Aaron L. 1981. A History of the U.S. Strategic 'Doctrine'—1945 to 1980. *Journal of Strategic Studies* **4**, 1 (March): 37–71.
Futrell, Robert Frank. 1971. *Ideas, Concepts, Doctrine: A History of Basic Thinking in the United States Air Force 1907–1964, II*. Maxwell Air Force Base: Aerospace Studies Institute (June).
Galbraith, John Kenneth. 1967. *The New Industrial State*. New York: Penguin.
Garthoff, Raymond L. 1978. Mutual Deterrence and Strategic Arms Limitation in Soviet Policy. *International Security* **3**, 1 (Summer): 112–147.
Garwin, Richard L. 1979. Launch Under Attack to Redress Minuteman Vulnerability? *International Security* **4**, 3 (Winter): 117–139.
Gelber, Harry G. 1974. Technical Innovation and Arms Control. *World Politics* **26**, 4 (July): 509–541.
George, Alexander L., and Smoke, Richard. 1974. *Deterrence in American Foreign Policy*. New York: Columbia University Press.
Getler, Michael. 1980. Carter Directive Modifies Strategy for a Nuclear War. *Washington Post*, 6 August: A10.
———. 1981. Reagan's Nuclear Strategy Criticized. *Washington Post*, 4 October: A1, A14.
Gillespie, John V., Zinnes, Dina A., Tahim, G. S., and Schrodt, Philip A. 1976. A Sensitivity Analysis of a Perceptual Arms Race Model. In Patrick J. McGowan, ed., *Sage International Yearbook of Foreign Policy Studies*. Beverly Hills, Calif.: Sage Publications.
———, Zinnes, Dina A., Schrodt, Philip A., Tahim, G. S., and Rubison, R. M. 1977. An Optimal Control Model of Arms Races. *American Political Science Review* **71**: 226–244.
Glasstone, Samuel, ed. 1977. *The Effects of Nuclear Weapons, Third Edition*. Washington, D.C.: U.S. Government Printing Office.
Graham, Daniel O. [L. Gen. USA (Ret.)] 1982. *High Frontier: A New National Strategy*. Washington, D.C.: High Frontier.
Gray, Colin S. 1972. The Arms Race is About Politics. *Foreign Policy* **9** (Winter): 117–129.
———. 1974a. The Urge to Compete: Rationales for Arms Racing. *World Politics* **26**, 2 (January): 207–233.
———. 1974b. Rethinking Nuclear Strategy. *Orbis* **17**, 4: 1145–1160.
———. 1977. *The Future of Land-Based Missile Forces*. London: International Institute for Strategic Studies, Adelphi Paper No. 140.
Griffin, Larry J., Devine, Joel A., and Wallace, Michael. 1981. Monopoly Capital, Organized Labor, and Military Expenditures: Military Keynesianism in the United States 1949–1976. *American Journal of Sociology*, Special Edition.
Griffiths, David R. 1979. MX Flexibility Allows Doubling Shelters. *Aviation Week and Space Technology* **112**, 24 (16 June): 16–18.
Groover, Paul L., Garrison, W. V., and Cotsworth, W. L. 1971. *The Arsenal Exchange Model Handbook, September 1969; Revisions to Sections 4 and 5 and Appendix A, February 1971*. Atlanta, Ga.: Martin-Marietta Corporation.
———, Kownacki, Edward J., Prukop, Joseph P., and Jilli, Margarita J., 1978. *Assumptions and Rationale Used to Calculate an Arsenal's Relative Force Size (RFS)*. Springfield: Scientific Applications.

Halloran, Richard. 1982a. Aides Say Reagan Favors a Cluster of 100 MX Missiles. *The New York Times* 20 May: A1.
———. 1982b. Pentagon Rejects Airborne MX Plan. *The New York Times* 23 June: A14.
———. 1982c. Weinberger Says Soviet Now Tops U.S. in Missiles' Accuracy of Aim. *The New York Times* 15 April: A1.
Halperin, Morton 1972. The Good, the Bad, and the Wasteful. *Foreign Policy* 6 (Spring): 69–83.
———, with the assistance of Clapp, Priscilla, and Kanter, Arnold. 1974. *Bureaucratic Politics and Foreign Policy*. Washington, D.C.: The Brookings Institution.
Head, Colonel Richard G. 1978. Technology and the Military Balance. *Foreign Affairs* 56, 3 (April): 544: 563.
Helman, Vincent M. 1983. Prospects for International Cooperation in Space Activities Between the United States and Other Launching Countries/ Organizations. Presentation to the Continuing Regional Colloquium on International Affairs, School of International Studies, University of Washington, 14 January.
Hitch, Charles, and McKean, R. 1961. *The Economics of Defense Spending in the Nuclear Age*. Cambridge: Harvard University Press.
Holsti, Ole R. 1962. The Belief System and National Images: A Case Study. *Journal of Conflict Resolution* 6: 244–252.
———. and George, Alexander L. 1975. The Effects of Stress on the Performance of Foreign Policy-Makers. In Cornelius P. Cotter, ed., *Political Science Annual: An International Review; Volume Six—1975*. Indianapolis: Bobbs-Merrill: 255–319.
———. North, Robert C., and Brody, Richard A. 1968. Perception and Action in the 1914 Crisis. In J. David Singer. ed., *Quantitative International Politics: Insights and Evidence*. New York: The Free Press: 123–158.
Hoopes, Townsend. 1969. *The Limits of Intervention: An Inside Account of How the Johnson Policy of Escalation in Vietnam Was Reversed*. New York: D. McKay Company.
Hornblower, Margot, and Wilson, George C. 1983. Recommendation on MX Basing 'Has a Chance' for Hill Approval. *Washington Post* 12 April: A7.
House Armed Services Subcommittee. 1978. U.S. Congress, House, Committee on Armed Services, Subcommittee on Intelligence and Military Application of Nuclear Energy, Staff Study, *Land-Based ICBM Forces Vulnerability and Options*, 95th Cong., 2nd Sess, 5 October, HASC Report No. 95–69.
House Joint Resolution 566. 1980. Withdrawing the United States of America from the Treaty on the Limitation of Anti-Ballistic Missile Systems, and the Interim Agreement, Protocol, and Agreed Interpretations to the Treaty, signed on May 26, 1972.
Howard, Nigel. 1971. *Paradoxes of Rationality: Theory of Metagames and Political Behavior*. Cambridge, Massachusetts: The MIT Press.
Ing, Dean. 1981. Personnal communication.
International Institute for Strategic Studies [IISS]. 1980. *The Military Balance 1980–81*. London: International Institute for Strategic Studies.
———. 1981. *The Military Balance 1981–82*. London: International Institute for Strategic Studies.

Intriligator, Michael D. 1975. Strategic Considerations in the Richardson Model of Arms Races. *Journal of Political Economy* **83**: 339–353.

Jackson, Henry M. 1971. The Strategic Balance: The Future of Freedom. Address before the American Society of Newspaper Editors, Washington, D.C., 15 April. *Vital Speeches of the Day*, **37**, 16 (1 June): 482.

Jervis, Robert. 1970. *The Logic of Images in International Relations*. Princeton, N.J.: Princeton University Press.

———. 1976. *Perception and Misperception in International Politics*. Princeton, N.J.: Princeton University Press.

———. 1979. Deterrence Theory Revisited. *World Politics* **31**, 2 (January): 289–324.

Kahn, Herman. 1960. *On Thermonuclear War: Three Lectures and Several Suggestions*. Princeton, N.J.: Princeton University Press.

———. 1965. *On Escalation: Metaphors and Scenarios*. New York: Praeger. (Hudson Institute Series on National Security and World Order).

Kanter, Arnold. 1972. Congress and the Defense Budget: 1960–1970. *American Political Science Review* **66**: 129–143.

Kaplan, Fred. 1982. Missile Envy: Bigness is Beside the Point. *The New Republic*, Issue 3,534 11 October: 13–14.

Kaplan, Morton A. 1957. *System and Process in International Politics*. New York: John Wiley and Sons.

Kaufmann, William W. 1954. *The Requirements of Deterrence*. Princeton University: Center of International Studies, Memorandum Number Seven, 15 November.

———. 1964. *The McNamara Strategy*. New York: Harper and Row.

Kennan, George M. 1947. The Sources of Soviet Conduct. (Written under the pseudonym "X"), *Foreign Affairs* **25**, 4 (July): 566–582.

Kintner, William R., and Pfaltzgraff, Robert L., Jr., eds. 1973. *SALT: Implications for Arms Control in the 1970s*. Pittsburgh: University of Pittsburgh Press.

Klass, Philip J. 1980. Ballistic Missile Defense Tests Set. *Aviation Week and Space Technology* **112**, 24 (16 June): 213–218.

Kolkowicz, Roman. 1971. Strategic Parity and Beyond: Soviet Perspectives. *World Politics* **23**, 3 (April): 431–451.

Kramer, Gerald. 1971. Short Term Fluctuation in US Voting Behavior, 1896–1964. *American Political Science Review* **60**: 131–143.

Kuenne, Robert E. 1966. *The Polaris Missile Strike: A General Economic Systems Analysis*. Columbus: Ohio State University Press.

Kulish, Yu. 1972. Untitled comments, pp. 212–215 of "Strategic Forum: the SALT Agreements." *Survival* **14**, 5 (September/October): 210–219.

Kupperman, Robert H. 1975. Personal communication, 10 April.

Laird, Melvin R. 1972. Testimony in *Hearings Before the Committee on Foreign Relations of the United States Senate: Strategic Arms Limitation Agreements*. Washington, D.C.: U.S. Government Printing Office, 19, 20, 21, 26, and 28 June and 20 July, 1972. See especially pages 60–64, 94–99.

Langer, Albert. 1977. Accurate Submarine Launched Ballistic Missiles and Nuclear Strategy. *Journal of Peace Research*, **14**, 1: 41–58.

Lawrence, W. H. 1953. U.S. Lacks Evidence Soviet Can Deliver a Hydrogen Bomb. *The New York Times* 21 August: 1, 3.

Leestma, David. 1972. [Then of the Weapons Evaluation and Control Bureau,

U.S. Arms Control and Disarmament Agency] Personal communication, 17 April.

Lerner, Max. 1982. Visions of the Apocalypse. [Review of Jonathan Schell's *The Fate of the Earth*], *The New Republic*, Issue 3, 511 28 April: 26–29.

Lescaze, Lee, and Wilson, George C. 1981. Reagan Asks for 100 MXs, 100 B1 Bombers. *Washington Post*, 3 October: A1, A12.

Lindbeck, A. 1976. Stabilization Policies in Open Economies with Endogenous Politicians. *American Economic Review* **66**: 1–19.

Loftus, Joseph A. 1961. Gilpatric Warns U.S. Can Destroy Atom Aggressor. *The New York Times*, 22 October: 1, 6.

Luce, R. Duncan, and Raiffa, Howard. 1957. *Games and Decisions: Introduction and Critical Survey*. New York: John Wiley and Sons.

Marsh, Alton K. 1979. Salt Verification Fears Begin to Ease in Senate. *Aviation Week and Space Technology*, 30 July: 18–19.

McNamara, Robert C. 1961. Testimony before the Committee on Armed Services, House of Representatives, 23 February.

———. 1962. Remarks at the Commencement Exercises. University of Michigan, 16 June: 4.

———. 1963. Testimony before the House Subcommittee of the Committee on Appropriations, *Hearings on Department of Defense Appropriations for 1964, Part I*: 340–341. Washington, D.C.: U.S. Government Printing Office.

———. 1964. Posture Statement delivered before a combined session of the Senate Committee on the Armed Services and the Senate Subcommittee on Department of Defense Appropriations on the FY 1965 Defense Budget, January: 31–32.

———. 1967a. Testimony before a combined session of the Senate Committee on the Armed Services and the Senate Committee on Appropriations, 25 January.

———. 1967b. Excerpts from a speech, 18 September, before UPI editors and publishers, announcing the decision to deploy a "light" ABM system. *Washington Post*, 19 September; A10, and *The New York Times*, 19 September: 1, 16.

Middleton, Drew. 1980. U.S. Stressing Expansion of Ability to Put Units in Iran to Fight Soviet. *The New York Times* 3 February: 10.

Miller, Judith. 1982. 139 in Congress Urge Nuclear Arms Freeze by U.S. and Moscow. *The New York Times* 11 March: A1, A12.

Morgan, Patrick M. 1977. *Deterrence: A Conceptual Analysis*. Beverly Hills: Sage Library of Social Research, Volume 40.

———. 1981. Personal communication, 6 November.

Neustadt, Richard E. 1960[1976]. *Presidential Power: The Politics of Leadership* [*with Reflections on Johnson and Nixon*] New York: John Wiley and Sons.

Newhouse, John. 1973. *Cold Dawn: The Story of SALT*. New York: Holt, Rinehart and Winston.

The New York Times. 1953. The Text of President Eisenhower's Address Before the United Church Women. 7 October: 3.

———. 1954. Text of Dulles' Statement on Foreign Policy of Eisenhower Administration. 13 January: 2.

———. 1982. Excerpts From Farewell Testimony by Rickover to Congress. 30 January: 3.

Nincic, Miroslav, and Cusack, Thomas R. 1979. The Political Economy of US Military Spending. *Journal of Peace Research* **16,** 2: 101–115.
North, David M. 1980. Survivability Key to Trident Program. *Aviation Week and Space Technology*, **112,** 24 (16 June): 101–106.
Oberdorfer, Don. 1978. Warnke: SALT Doesn't Preclude 'Shell Game' Idea. *Washington Post* 25 August: A6.
Office of Technology Assessment. 1981. Small Submarine Basing of MX. In *MX Missile Basing*. Washington, D.C.: Office of Technology Assessment: Chapter 5 (pp. 165–214).
Osgood, Charles. 1962. *An Alternative to War or Surrender*. Urbana: University of Illinois Press.
Ostrom, Charles W. 1977. Evaluating Alternative Decision-Making Models: An Empirical Test Between an Arms Race Model and an Organizational Politics Model. *Journal of Conflict Resolution* **21:** 235–266.
Ostrom, Vincent. 1973. *The Intellectual Crisis in American Public Administration*. University: The University of Alabama Press.
Oxford English Dictionary, The Compact Edition. 1971. New York: Oxford University Press.
Payne, Fred A. 1977. The Strategic Nuclear Balance: A New Measure. *Survival* **20** (May/June): 107–110.
Peck, Merton J., and Scherer, Frederic M. 1962. *The Weapons Acquisition Process: An Economic Analysis*. Boston: Harvard University, Graduate School of Business Administration, 1962.
Perry, Robert L. 1966. The Mythography of Military R & D. Santa Monica: Rand Corporation Paper P-3356.
———. 1977. The Faces of Verification: Strategic Arms Control for the 1980s. Santa Monica: Rand Corporation Paper P-5986.
———. 1979. The Interaction of Technology and Doctrine in the USAF. Rand Corporation Paper P-6281.
Pike Committee. 1975. *Select Committee on Intelligence, Hearings: U.S. Intelligence Agencies and Activities. Part I: Intelligence Costs and Fiscal Procedures*. Washington, D.C.: U.S. Government Printing Office. 31 July, 1, 4, 5, 6, 7, & 8 August.
Pincus, Walter. 1979. U.S. Downgrades Soviet ICBM Yield. *Washington Post*, 31 May, A1.
Pipes, Richard. 1980. Soviet Global Strategy. *Commentary* **69,** 4 (April): 31–39.
Pitman, George R. 1969. *Arms Races and Stable Deterrence*. Los Angeles: University of California, Security Studies Paper Number 18.
Portland Oregonian. 1982. Note regarding departure of the U.S.S. Ohio. 28 September: B8.
Pranger, Robert J., and Labrie, Roger P., eds. 1977. *Nuclear Strategy and National Security: Points of View*. Washington, D.C.: American Enterprise Institute for Public Policy Research.
Rapoport, Anatol. 1966. *Two-Person Game Theory: The Essential Ideas*. Ann Arbor: University of Michigan Press.
———. 1970. *N-Person Game Theory: Concepts and Applications*. Ann Arbor: University of Michigan Press.
———, and Chammah, Albert M. 1965. *Prisoner's Dilemma: A Study in Conflict and Cooperation*. Ann Arbor: University of Michigan Press.

Ravenal, Earl C. 1980. Personal communication, 29 August.
Raymond, Jack. 1958. 500-to-5,500-Mile Missile is Approved for Air Force. *The New York Times* 28 February: 1, 3.
Reagan, Ronald W. 1980. Speech before the American Legion, Boston, 20 August.
———. 1982. Nationwide televised address, 22 November, reported in Cannon (1982).
Richardson, Lewis F. 1960. *Arms and Insecurity: A Mathematical Study of the Causes and Origins of War*, Nicolas Rachevsky and Ernesto Trucco, eds. Pittsburgh: The Boxwood Press, and Chicago: Quadrangle Books.
Richelson, Jeffrey T. 1979. Multiple Aim Point Basing: Vulnerability and Verification Problems. *Journal of Conflict Resolution*, **23**, 4 (December): 613–628.
———. 1980. Evaluating the Strategic Balance. *American Journal of Political Science* **24**, 4 (November): 779–803.
Riker, William H. 1962. *The Theory of Political Coalitions*. New Haven: Yale University Press.
———. 1980. Implications from the Disequilibrium of Majority Rule for the Study of Institutions. *American Political Science Review* **74**, 2 (June): 432–446.
Robinson, Clarence A., Jr. 1978. Soviets Boost ICBM Accuracy. *Aviation Week and Space Technology*, 3 April: 14.
———. 1979a. SALT May Allow 3 New Soviet Missiles. *Aviation Week and Space Technology*, 25 June: 21–24.
———. 1979b. USAF Commands Push Stretching 155 F-111's. *Aviation Week and Space Technology*, 24 September: 16–19.
———. 1979c. MX Racetrack Questioned in Congress. *Aviation Week and Space Technology*, 12 November: 17–19.
———. 1979d. U.S. to Test ABM System With MX. *Aviation Week and Space Technology*, 19 March: 23–26.
Rosen, Steven. 1973. *Testing the Theory of the Military–Industrial Complex*. Lexington, Mass.: Lexington Books, D.C. Heath.
Rosenberg, David Alan. 1979. American Nuclear Strategy and the Hydrogen Bomb Decision. *The Journal of American History* **66**, 1 (June): 64.
Rowen, Henry S. 1975. Formulating Strategic Doctrine. In Commission on the Organization of the Government for the Conduct of Foreign Policy, Volume 4, Appendix K: *Adequacy of Current Organization: Defense and Arms Control*. Washington, D.C.: U.S. Government Printing Office: 220.
Rummel, Rudolph. 1976. Will the Soviet Union Soon Have a First-Strike Capability? *Orbis* **20** (Fall): 579–594.
Russett, Bruce M. 1963. The Calculus of Deterrence. *Journal of Conflict Resolution* **7**: 97–109.
———. 1970. *What Price Vigilance? The Burdens of National Defense*. New Haven: Yale University Press.
Saaty, Thomas L. 1968. *Mathematical Models of Arms Control and Disarmament: Application of Mathematical Structures in Politics*. New York: John Wiley and Sons.
Sarkesian, Sam C. 1972. *The Military–Industrial Complex: A Reassessment*. Beverly Hills: Sage Publications.
Scheer, Robert. 1982. Nuclear Arms Freeze Favored by 5–3 Margin. *Los Angeles Times* 21 March: 1, 21, 22.
Schell, Jonathan. 1982. *The Fate of the Earth*. New York: Knopf.

Schelling, Thomas C. 1960. *The Strategy of Conflict*. New York: Oxford University Press.

Schlesinger, James R. 1974. Testimony before the Subcommittee on Arms Control, International Law and Organization of the Senate Committee on Foreign Relations, Hearing on U.S. and Soviet Strategic Doctrine and Military Policies, 4 March. (Top secret hearing held on 4 March; sanitized and made public on 4 April.)

Schrodt, Philip A. 1978. Statistical Problems Associated with the Richardson Arms Race Model. *Journal of Peace Science 3*: 159–172.

Shapley, Deborah. 1978. Series on "Technology Creep and the Arms Race" in *Science*, consisting of "ICDM Problem a Sleeper," **201** (22 September): 1102–1105; "A World of Absolute Accuracy," **201** (29 September): 1192–1196; and "Two Future Arms Control Problems," **202** (20 October): 289–292.

Sibley, Bruce. 1977. *Surviving Doomsday*. London: Shaw and Sons.

Simaan, M., and Cruz, Jose B., Jr. 1977. Equilibrium Concepts for Arms Race Problems. In *Mathematical Systems in International Relations Research*, John V. Gillespie and Dina A. Zinnes, eds., pp. 342–366. New York: Praeger.

SIPRI (Stockholm International Peace Research Institute). 1974. *World Armaments and Disarmament: SIPRI Yearbook 1974*. Cambridge, Mass.: The MIT Press.

———. 1980. *World Armaments and Disarmament: SIPRI Yearbook 1980*. New York: Crane, Russak and Company.

———. 1982. *World Armaments and Disarmament: SIPRI Yearbook 1982*. London: Taylor and Francis Ltd., and Cambridge, Mass.: Oelgeschlager, Gunn and Hain, Inc.

Smith, Bruce A. 1980. MX Missile Performance, Throw Weight Improved. *Aviation Week and Space Technology* **112**, 24 (16 June): 122–131.

Smith, Gerard. 1980. *Doubletalk: The Story of the First Strategic Arms Limitation Talks*. Garden City, N.Y.: Doubleday.

Smith, Hedrick. 1982. 4 Former Officials Urge West to Drop First-Strike Plan. *The New York Times* 8 April: 1, 8.

Smoke, Richard. National Security Affairs. In *Handbook of Political Science, Volume 8: International Politics*, Fred I. Greenstein and Nelson W. Polsby, eds., pp. 247–362. Reading, Mass.: Addison-Wesley.

Smoker, Paul. 1963a. A Mathematical Study of the Present Arms Race. *General Systems Yearbook* 8: 61–76.

———. 1963b. A Pilot Study of the Present Arms Race. *General Systems Yearbook* 8: 61–76.

———. 1964. Fear in the Arms Race: A Mathematical Study. *Journal of Peace Research* **1**: 55–64.

———. 1965. Trade, Defense and the Richardson Theory of Arms Races: A Seven Nation Study. *Journal of Peace Research* **2**: 161–176.

Snow, Donald M. 1980. Lasers, Charged-Particle Beams, and the Strategic Future. *Political Science Quarterly* **95**, 2(Summer): 277–294.

———. 1981. *Nuclear Strategy in a Dynamic World: American Policy in the 1980s*. University: The University of Alabama Press.

Squires, Michael L. 1980. Personal communication, 3 September.

――――. 1982a. Modeling the U.S.–Soviet Arms Competition, 1954–1979. Paper presented at the annual meetings of the International Studies Association, Cincinnati, 26 March.

――――. 1982b. *A Quantitative History and Analysis of the U.S.–Soviet Strategic Arms Competition 1954–1979.* Unpublished Ph. D. Dissertation, Department of Political Science, Indiana University.

Steinbruner, John D., and Garwin, Thomas M. 1976. Strategic Vulnerability: The Balance between Prudence and Paranoia. *International Security* **1**, 1 (Summer): 138–181.

Talbott, Strobe. 1979. *Endgame: The Inside Story of SALT II.* New York: Harper and Row.

Tammen, Ronald L. 1973. *MIRV and the Arms Race: An Interpretation of Defense Strategy.* New York: Praeger.

Thom, Rene. 1972. *Stabilite Structurelle et Morphogenese; Essai d'une Theorie Generale des Modeles.* Reading, Mass.: W. A. Benjamin.

――――. 1975. *Structural Stability and Morphogenesis; An Outline of a General Theory of Models.* Translated, as updated by the author, by D. H. Fowler. Reading, Mass.: W. A. Benjamin.

Tsipis, Kosta. 1974a. *Offensive Missiles.* Stockholm: SIPRI Stockholm Paper No. 5 (August).

――――. 1974b. The Calculus of Nuclear Counterforce. *Technology Review* (Oct/Nov): 34–47.

――――. 1975a. Physics and Calculus of Countercity and Counterforce Nuclear Attacks. *Science* **187**, 4175 (Feb): 393–397.

――――. 1975b. The Accuracy of Strategic Missiles. *Scientific American* (July): 14–23.

――――. 1975c. Response to Walsh, *Science* **190** (12 Dec.): 1119.

――――. 1981. Laser Weapons. *Scientific American* **245**, 6 (December): 51–57.

Tufte, Edward. 1975. The Determinants of the Outcome of Midterm Congressional Elections. *American Political Science Review* **64**: 812–826.

――――. 1978. *The Political Control of the Economy.* Princeton, N.J.: Princeton University Press.

Tullock, Gordon. 1965. *The Politics of Bureaucracy.* Washington, D.C.: Public Affairs Press.

United States Department of State. 1979. *SALT II Agreement.* Washington, D.C.: Selected Documents No. 12A, Department of State Publication 8984.

Van Cleave, William R., and Barnett, Roger W. 1974. Strategic Adaptability. *Orbis* **18**, 3 (Fall): 655–676.

Von Neumann, John, and Morgenstern, Oskar. 1944. *Theory of Games and Economic Behavior.* Princeton, N.J.: Princeton University Press.

Walsh, Edward. 1979. Carter to Deploy MX in Utah, Nevada. *Washington Post* 8 September: A1.

――――, and Goshko, John M. 1980. SALT II Temporarily Scrapped. *Washington Post* 4 January: A1.

Walz, Jay. 1952. Experiments for Hydrogen Bomb Held Successfully at Eniwetok; Leaks About Blast Under Inquiry. *The New York Times* 17 November: 1, 2.

Washington Post. 1978. China May Now Have ICBMs. 1 September: A14.

――――. 1980. Campaign Notes. 2 October: A3.

Weinberger, Caspar W. 1981. Testimony on Strategic Weapons Proposals, Part 1,

before the Senate Foreign Relations Committee. 3 November: 3–55.
Willrich, Mason, and Rhinelander, John B., eds. 1974. *SALT: The Moscow Agreements and Beyond*. New York: The Free Press.
Wilson, George C. 1978. 51 Representatives Write Carter, Challenge Missile Holes Proposal. *Washington Post*, 23 September: A11.
———. 1980a. A Buildup in U.S. Forces: Reagan Advisors Urge More for Defense. *Washington Post* 16 June: A1, A4–5.
———. 1980b. Change in Nuclear Target Policy Not a Radical One, Brown Says. *Washington Post*, 21 August: A1.
———. 1981. Gen. Jones Doubtful on MX Plan. *Washington Post*, 6 October: A1, A12.
———, and Kaiser, Robert G. 1979. Carter Decides to Build MX Mobile Missile. *Washington Post*, 8 June: A1.
Wohlstetter, Albert. 1970. On the Counterforce Calculations of Some Prominent ABM Opponents. Testimony before the Committee on Armed Services, *U.S. Senate, Authorization for Military Procurement, Research and Development, Fiscal year 1971, and Reserve Strength, Part 3*: 2251–2264.
Wolfe, Thomas W. 1979. *The SALT Experience*. Cambridge, Mass.: Ballinger.
Wolfowitz, Paul W. 1978. Personal communication, 29 June.
———. 1970. The Proposal to Launch on Warning. In *U.S. Senate, Committee on Armed Services, Authorization for Military Procurement, Research and Development, Fiscal Year 1971, and Reserve Strength, Hearings, Part 3, 91st Congress, 2nd Session*. Washington, D.C.: U.S. Government Printing Office. 2278–2282.
York, Herbert F. 1973. *Arms Control: Readings from Scientific American*. New York: Freeman.
Zeeman, E. C. 1976. Catastrophe Theory. *Scientific American* **234**, 4 (April): 65–83.
———. 1977. *Catastrophe Theory: Selected Papers*. Reading, Mass.: Addison-Wesley.
Zimmerman, William. 1974. Choices in the Postwar World. In *Caging the Bear*, Charles Gati, ed. Indianapolis: Bobbs-Merrill.
Zinnes, Dina A. 1968. The Expression and Perception of Hostility in Prewar Crisis: 1914. In J. David Singer, ed., *Quantitative International Politics: Insights and Evidence*. New York: The Free Press.
———. 1976. *Contemporary Research in International Relations: A Perspective and a Critical Appraisal*. New York: The Free Press.

Glossary

A Compendium of Terms in Strategic Weaponry, Doctrine, and Arms Control

Debates and writings about the strategic weapons regime, strategic weaponry and doctrine, and arms control have long been characterized by terminology that tends to intimidate the uninitiated and outdistance those who do not follow new developments assiduously. However, the structure of related terms, abbreviations, and acronymns usually is straightforward; with relatively little use, that structure becomes both familiar and mnemonically helpful. Accordingly, in preparing this glossary the author has sought to emphasize that structure while preparing a simple and internally consistent set of definitions. Another goal has been to provide comprehensive coverage of terms used in the strategic weapons regime, strategic weapons and doctrine, assessment measures, and arms control. Words and abbreviations appear intermingled in strict alphabetic order; numbers appear before letters. In the relatively rare cases of terms or usages peculiar to this volume, any disagreement with the usages of others is indicated. A list of sources consulted in preparation of this glossary follows the list of terms.

AABMIS   Airborne anti-ballistic missile system.

ABM   Anti-ballistic missile (system): A defensive weapon system to destroy offensive missile re-entry vehicles (RVs). The ABM systems explicitly discussed in the SALT I ABM Treaty comprise three major types of components: interceptor missiles, launchers, and radars; all three are limited by the treaty. The radars are used to track incoming RVs and guide interceptor missiles from the launchers.

ABM Treaty   Formally titled the "Treaty between the United States of America and the Union of Soviet Socialist Republics on the Limitation of Anti-Ballistic Missile Systems," signed in Moscow on 26 May 1972. Together with the Interim Agreement on limitation of offensive missiles, it forms the package known as the SALT I agreements. The ABM treaty entered into force on 3 October 1972 and is of unlimited duration, although reviews are provided at five-year intervals. By most interpretations, it limits new types of systems to intercept ballistic missile warheads, as well as the types developed by 1972. The original treaty limited each side to two ABM deployment areas of up to 100 launchers and interceptors, one area to protect the national capital and one area to protect an ICBM field. A Protocol to the Treaty signed in 1974 further restricted each side to a single ABM deployment area.

Accidental war Hypothetical situation in which nuclear war would occur as a result of some unauthorized or accidental event, rather than as a result of conscious decision by political authorities.

ACDA The United States Arms Control and Disarmament Agency (also USACDA). A small agency housed within the U.S. Department of State, with reporting lines both to State and to the President. ACDA has played a major role in such negotiations as SALT.

ACIS Arms Control Impact Statement: A statement required to accompany proposals for new weapons systems, in which the effect of their deployment on arms control efforts is assessed.

Active defense Systems, such as ABMs or interceptor aircraft, designed to interdict and destroy incoming strategic weapons before they reach their targets.

AD Assured Destruction: A situation in which one has confidence of being able to absorb (ride out) any likely attack and emerge with sufficient remaining forces to mount a devastating retaliation. Also, a strategic doctrine calling for such a capability. AD has played some role in U.S. strategic targeting policy at least since 1962.

AEM The Arsenal Exchange Model. See Chapter 4.

Aggregate The SALT II Treaty set quantitative limits on several aggregates of weapons. These included an initial ceiling of 2,400 on the aggregate of ICBM launchers, SLBM launchers, heavy bombers, and ASBMs; an aggregate sublimit of 1,320 MIRVed ICBM launchers, SLBM launchers, ASBMs, heavy bombers equipped to carry ALCMs with a range greater than 600 kilometers; an aggregate sublimit of 1,200 on launchers of MIRVed missiles; and a limit of 820 MIRVed ICBM launchers through 1985.

Air-breathing forces Bomber and cruise missile forces, the only leg of the triad which does not consist of ballistic missiles.

AIRS The Advanced Inertial Reference Sphere: Central component of an advanced inertial guidance system developed by the United States in the late 1970s. Designed to reduce accuracy errors caused by gyroscopic drift, it is a 10.3 inch diameter sphere containing inertial navigation components and floated without gimbals in a neutrally buoyant state in a highly controlled thermal environment. Scheduled for deployment on the MX missile.

Air-to-Surface Ballistic Missile (ASBM) A ballistic missile launched from an aircraft at a target on the earth's surface. Under SALT II, considered to be such a missile with a range greater than 600 kilometers.

Use of such missiles may allow aircraft to "stand off" outside the range of antiaircraft defenses and attack their targets with relatively invulnerable ballistic missiles, thus considerably extending the useful life of the aircraft as strategic weapons platforms.

Air-to-Surface Missile (ASM) A missile launched from an aircraft at a target on the earth's surface. In contrast to ASBMs, not a ballistic missile. This type includes air-launched cruise missiles (ALCMs).

ALCM Air-Launched Cruise Missile: A pilotless subsonic aircraft capable of travelling long distances at low altitudes with high accuracy when launched from a bomber or cruise missile carrier (CMC).

Anti-ballistic Missile Treaty See ABM Treaty.

Area defense Defense of a large geographic area, such as a city, as contrasted with the defense of a particular point, such as an ICBM silo.

Arms freeze An agreement, either formal or tacit, to limit one or more types of armaments at the level of actual deployments at some time.

ARP Action–reaction process or phenomenon: A hypothetical process, often associated with the name of Lewis Fry Richardson, according to which arms race phenomena are explained as reactions by one party to the actions of the other(s).

ASAT Antisatellite, as in antisatellite warfare.

ASBM carrier A bomber or other aircraft equipped to carry ASBMs and launch them while in flight. Under SALT II, such aircraft are counted as heavy bombers.

ASM Air-to-Surface Missile.

Assured Destruction (AD) The capability to inflict unacceptable damage on an attacker even after absorbing his first strike attack. If both sides in a strategic weapons regime possess AD capability, they are said to possess a mutual assured destruction (MAD) capability.

Assured Survival Designation of the program, circa 1982, of those proposing an extensive strategic defense (ABM) system; chosen for its political contrast with "assured destruction." See High Frontier.

ASW AntiSubmarine Warfare: Systems designed to destroy subsurface combatant vessels.

AWACS Airborne Warning And Command System: A system comprising a flying command post with "look-down" radar and other communications gear, capable of performing a crucial role in a "look-down, shoot-down" defense against aircraft and cruise missiles.

B-1 Proposed U.S. intercontinental bomber to replace the B-52 bomber force. Deployment of a version with limited supersonic capability was deferred by the Carter administration in 1977; deployment of a simplified version was proposed by President Reagan in 1981.

B-52 Subsonic U.S. intercontinental bomber, first deployed in 1955 and subsequently greatly modernized.

Back channel Secret contacts between individual officials that circumvent the usual channels of communication between or within governments.

Negotiation of SALT I depended crucially on details worked out in a back channel between Henry Kissinger and high Soviet officials in Washington and Moscow, much to the frustration of U.S. SALT negotiatiors; in the last few days before signing, negotiations were in progress simultaneously in Moscow and Helsinki.

Backfire NATO designation for the Soviet TU-26 variable-wing supersonic bomber, which entered service in 1974. Although deployed to operational units with theater and naval strike roles, its characteristics fall between those generally attributed to heavy bombers and those of medium bombers. Given disagreement about whether its unrefueled range allows intercontinental capability, it was the subject of bitter argument in the U.S. SALT II debates, in which treaty opponents argued that it should have been counted as a strategic bomber.

Ballistic missile Any missile designed to follow the trajectory which results when it is acted upon predominantly by gravity and aerodynamic drag after thrust is terminated. Typically, much of their flight path lies above the atmosphere and thrust is terminated after a very brief period during which the missile is steered by a self-contained inertial guidance system.

Bargaining chip An actual or projected weapons system the purpose of which is, at least in part, to gain some concession in arms control negotiations in response to actual or threatened deployments.

Bear NATO designation for the TU-95 Soviet turboprop intercontinental bomber, first flown publicly in 1955.

Bison NATO designation for the MYA-4 Soviet turbojet intercontinental bomber, first flown publicly in 1955.

Blast overpressure The increase in atmospheric pressure caused by the detonation of a nuclear or thermonuclear weapon; measured in pounds per square inch (PSI).

Bomber An aircraft designed to deliver bombs or missiles; see also ASBM Carrier, Cruise Missile Carrier (CMC), and Heavy Bomber.

BOT Balance of Terror: Term used by some analysts to describe the mutual possession of second strike capabilities by the United States and Soviet Union.

BMD Ballistic Missile Defense, consisting of active, e.g., ABM, and passive elements.

BMEWS Ballistic Missile Early Warning System: U.S. radar network in Greenland, Scotland, and Alaska, deployed in the early 1960s, to give about 20-minutes warning of Soviet missiles incoming by polar routes.

Bomarc U.S. Air Force surface-to-air antibomber missile, now obsolete.

Breakout Escape from mutual assured destruction (MAD) into a new situation of strategic advantage or first strike (FS) capability, through some new weapons development.

Bureaucratic Politics (BP) A model of arms spending according to which programs grow steadily and incrementally over time.

Bus On a MIRV-equipped ballistic missile, the postboost vehicle, which carries low-thrust engines and control and guidance equipment for maneuvering after the initial boost so as to dispense multiple warheads on trajectories leading them to different targets.

Capability The potential power capacity, particularly military, under a government's control. While capability need not imply intent, it is so interpreted under worst-case analysis.

Catalytic war A hypothetical major war between the superpowers, caused either purposely or inadvertently by some act of a lesser power.

CBW Chemical–biological warfare.

CD Civil Defense; used both for such a program and for doctrine calling for such a program.

CEP Circular Error Probable: Fundamental measure of the accuracy of missiles attacking point targets. It is the radius of a circle about the target point, within which half of the warheads launched at the target are expected to land.

CF Counterforce.

CF/V Counterforce and/or countervalue.

Checkhov NATO designation for a large, modern phased-array radar under construction in the Moscow area during the SALT I negotiations, and believed to be a part of the Moscow ABM defense system.

CIA United States Central Intelligence Agency.

Circular Error Probable CEP.

CMP Counter-Military Potential: Also lethality or K; a composite measure of the ability of a missile force to destroy a set of hard-point targets; subject to several aggregation problems; see Chapter 4, "Composite Measures."

Cold Launch A technique for ejecting a missile from a silo or submarine launch tube by low-pressure gas. The missile's first-stage rocket motors ignite only after it has cleared the silo or water surface. This technique allows the usable diameter of an ICBM to be increased up to 50 percent by reducing internal shielding requirements and gas-escape passages, or, alternatively, it allows silo diameter to be reduced, making hardening easier. Perhaps even more significantly, the technique may permit the rapid reloading of launch silos with new missiles, since cold launches produce far less damage and chemical contamination of launch silos than do hot launches, in which the missile's engines are fired while still inside the silo.

Collateral damage Damage inflicted as a secondary effect of military action. In the context of missile exchange calculations, collateral damage usually refers to losses of civilian lives and property attendant upon attacks on military targets.

Composite Measures A class of measures of the capability of a total strategic arsenal, produced by calculations or transformations upon simple counts of the weapons or their characteristics according to simple theories, in order to overcome some of the difficulties of aggregating the properties of individual weapons across entire arsenals. Compare effects measures.

Conditional viability A situation in which a nation-state could be destroyed, but the nation-state with that capability refrains from doing so. If that restraint occurs because it would not pay to attack, the conditional viability is said to be secure. If the potential attacker refrains even when it would pay to attack, the potential victim is said to have only insecure conditional viability. See Chapter 1, first section.

Controlled response Early Kennedy administration doctrine aimed at keeping the level of nuclear exchange low enough to allow damage limitation in a war-fighting environment. See also flexible response.

Cooperative measures Arms control measures, either voluntary or negotiated, taken by one side to enhance the other side's ability to verify compliance with the provisions of the agreement.

Correlation of forces A Soviet phrase describing military, political, economic, and psychological factors bearing on the world situation, often in the context of claims that the correlation is shifting in favor of the Soviet Union and its allies.

Counterforce Attack or policy of targeting attack against the military forces of an opponent, presumably to remove the means of retaliation. Contrast with countervalue attacks on industrial and population centers.

Cross-targeting Attack-planning tactic of assigning warheads from more than one missile to strike a given target, in order to minimize the effects of any missile malfunctions.

Cruise missile A small pilotless jet aircraft or guided missile with a flight path remaining within the atmosphere. Its attributes include low cost relative to ballistic missiles, difficulty of interception due to its very low altitude flight path, and high accuracy due to its terrain-matching (TERCOM) guidance system. Different versions allow ground launch (GLCM), air launch (ALCM), or launch from submerged submarines (SLCM).

CSCE Conference on Security and Cooperation in Europe, which produced the Helsinki accords.

Cruise Missile Carrier (CMC) An aircraft equipped for launching cruise missiles. SALT II limitations apply to CMCs equipped for cruise missiles having ranges greater than 600 kilometers.

Cruise missile range Under SALT II, the maximum distance that can be flown by the missile in its standard design configuration until fuel exhaustion.

CTBT Comprehensive Test-Ban Treaty: A proposed agreement to ban all nuclear testing. It would extend the limits of the Limited Test-Ban Treaty of 1963 to include low-level underground explosions. In theory, a CTBT would eventually slow or stop the development and deployment of new nuclear weapons, since they could not be tested.

CV Countervalue.

CVL Countervailing: The Carter administration's version of flexible response or damage limitation strategic doctrine.

Cyberneticist Also cybernetic view: A predisposition to interpret the foreign-policy moves of other governments as being manipulable, in the sense that we may be able to evoke desired responses by sending the correct signals. Compare essentialist and mechanist.

Damage Limitation (DL) A term denoting measures taken or doctrine adopted to lessen the effects of enemy attack; may include such things as counterforce preemptive attacks, active defense including ABM systems, and passive defense including civil defense systems.

Data Base In SALT II the United States and the Soviet Union agreed on a Memorandum of Understanding listing, for each side, the numbers of strategic offensive arms subject to the Treaty limitations. It was to be periodically updated through the SALT Standing Consultative Commission (SCC).

DDR&E In the U.S. Department of Defense, the Director of Defense Research and Engineering.

Deep-cut arms reductions Significant decreases in strategic arsenal sizes.

Defense The military act of defending against an enemy attack, as contrasted with deterrence, which is the prevention of such an attack. Prior to the nuclear era, the same military forces tended to provide both deterrence and defense; those functions have now been somewhat separated or decoupled.

Deliberate concealment Measures such as camouflage, use of converings, encryption of test telemetric information, or other means of limiting one side's ability to verify compliance with an arms control agreement through national technical means (NTM). Under SALT II the United States and USSR agreed not to use deliberate concealment measures, although compliance with that agreement has been disputed.

Delivery system The vehicle, such as an aircraft or missile, that delivers a weapon to its target.

Delta-I, -II, -III Modified and enlarged versions of the Soviet Y-class nuclear submarine (SSBN). IOC's of the three versions were in 1972, 1973, and 1977, respectively.

Dense Pack A basing scheme for the MX missile, announced by the Reagan administration in 1982, under which the missiles would be clustered closely, relying on fratricide effects to limit the ability of attackers to destroy a significant fraction of the force.

Deployment Putting weapons and forces in place for military utilization. See also IOC.

Depressed trajectory Flight path of a ballistic missile fired at a much lower angle than the normal minimum-energy trajectory. Firing on a depressed trajectory reduces both the missile's flight time and the warning time of line-of-sight radars, thus increasing the threat to systems that depend on warning time for their security, such as alert bombers or dash-mobile ICBM systems.

DET Weapons Directed Energy Transfer Weapons: Weapons relying on the directed transmission of energy, such as the light beam from a laser or a beam of charged or neutral particles from a particle beam weapon, to destroy a target, for example by heating and disabling an ICBM warhead in flight above the atmosphere.

Deterrence A strategy intended to convince an opponent that the costs and risks of aggression severely outweigh any benefits to be gained. Although often thought of as a product of the nuclear age, deterrence is an ancient military concept. Compare with defense.

Deterrence-only The strategic school of thought that holds the only utility of nuclear weapons to be their deterrent effect.

Deterrence-plus The strategic school of thought that advocates planning for actual use of nuclear weapons, as well as for their deterrent role. Note that this need not imply any desire for war nor any intent to resort to first use of nuclear weapons.

Detente A general relaxation of tensions, especially as applied to U.S.–Soviet relations in the early 1970s.

Development The process from laboratory research through engineering and field testing, by means of which a new weapons systems is prepared for production and deployment.

DEW Distant Early Warning system or DEW Line, a radar system across northern Canada and Alaska, built in the 1950s to warn of Soviet transpolar bomber attack.

DIA Defense Intelligence Agency: Organized under President Kennedy in 1961–62 to consolidate Army, Navy, and Air Force intelligence forces.

DL Damage Limitation.

DM Doomsday Machines: A family of hypothetical machines devised by Herman Kahn. The ultimate deterrent device, they would destroy the planet upon warning of an attack.

Dog House NATO designation for a large phased-array Soviet radar. A Dog House radar tracks incoming reentry vehicles for the Moscow ABM defensive system.

Dyad A strategic force structure with two "legs," as contrasted with the present triad. Abandonment of land-based missiles in response to ICBM vulnerability would be the most likely move to a dyad.

Effects Measures Outcome Measures: The simulated results of nuclear exchanges in actual war outputs. Relative to simple counts ("bean counting") and composite measures, they overcome most aggregation problems of assigning multiple attackers to multiple targets.

EMP ElectroMagnetic Pulse: A brief, intense burst of electrical and magnetic fields from an exploding nuclear weapon; it can destroy or impair the performance of electronic equipment, including communications gear, computer memories, and some missile guidance systems.

EMT Equivalent MegaTonnage: A composite measure of the surface blast damage that a nuclear weapon or force of weapons could inflict. See Chapter 4, the section, "Composite Measures."

Encryption The encoding of communications for the purpose of concealing information. In SALT II, the encryption of certain missile test data was prohibited. See also deliberate concealment.

Enhanced-radiation warhead A fission–fusion warhead with blast effects reduced and initial neutron production increased, relative to earlier warhead types. Also popularly called neutron bomb.

Escalatory process Hypothesized sequence in which an initial use of nuclear weapons would lead to a general nuclear exchange between the superpowers' zones of interior or heartlands.

Essential equivalence Force level policy enunciated by former Secretary of Defense Schlesinger, according to which U.S. and Soviet strategic arsenals should have roughly equal capabilities, although not necessarily equal numbers of weapons in all classes. See Chapter 2, the section "1974 ff.: The SALT I Aftermath," and compare with parity.

Essentialist One who is inclined, as set out by William Zimmerman (1974), to describe Soviet foreign policy behavior as "flowing naturally from the nature of totalitarianism." Contrast with mechanist and cyberneticist.

EW Index Equivalent Weapons Index: A composite measure, due to Payne (1977), allowing for soft-point, soft-area, and hard-point targets. See the section "Composite Measures" in Chapter 4.

Explorer I First U.S. earth satellite, weighing 30.8 pounds, placed into orbit January 1, 1958 by an Army Jupiter C missile.

Ex post–ex ante Dilemma in strategic planning posed by the fact that a strategy optimal for deterrence might be highly undesirable should deterrence fail. This objection has been raised against MAD doctrine.

External environment Factors outside the domestic control of a nation-state that influence strategic doctrine.

Facilities List In a nuclear exchange model, the list of weapons and their characteristics, and/or targets and their characteristics, on one side. An exchange is then modelled between two such lists.

FB-111H So-called "stretched" version of the FB-111 fighter–bomber, proposed as an alternative to the B-1 bomber or as a stop-gap measure until some new strategic bomber could be developed.

FBS Forward-Based Systems: A Soviet term referring to U.S. weapons such as aircraft based in Europe or on aircraft carriers so as to have sufficient range to deliver nuclear weapons against Soviet territory. In a major Soviet concession, such systems were excluded from the SALT I and II definitions of strategic offensive weapons.

Firebreak See nuclear threshold.

First Strike An attempted surprise attack, presumably against an opponent's nuclear forces in order to prevent retaliation.

First-strike capability The capacity to launch an effective preemptive strike, depriving an opponent of the ability to retaliate.

First-strike strategy The intention to launch a first strike before absorbing an attack.

Fission The simplest type of nuclear reaction, in which the nuclei of unstable elements are split to form the nuclei of lighter elements, releasing substantial amounts of energy.

Fission–fusion Two-step nuclear reaction in which a fission "trigger" initiates a fusion reaction, joining nuclei of hydrogen and tritium to form heavier helium nuclei, with an energy release substantially greater than that of a pure fission reaction. Such a reaction is the basis of "hydrogen" and "enhanced radiation" ("neutron") bombs.

Fission–fusion–fission The nuclear reaction sequence in the largest "hydrogen" warheads; a fission trigger ignites a fusion reaction, the heat and emitted neutrons of which trigger a second fission reaction.

Fixed ICBM Launcher A nonmobile launcher, whether hardened or "soft," for an ICBM. The most familiar form of fixed launcher is a hardened ICBM launch silo.

Flexible Response (FR) A policy initiated in the Kennedy administration to give the United States nonnuclear military-response options to perceived aggression. FR policy called for a substantial buildup of U.S. conventional and counterinsurgency forces.

Flight-Test Under SALT II, an actual launch of of a missile (as opposed to a static test) for any purpose, including development, demonstration, and crew training. Such launches were limited by the treaty.

FOBS Fractional Orbital Bombardment System: A system devised by the Soviets for placing an ICBM warhead into orbit around the earth, then bringing it down to earth. Since the warhead does not complete one full revolution around the earth, the Soviets interpret it as not violating the Outer Space Treaty prohibition against orbiting weapons of mass destruction. A FOBS system requires greater energy and has lower accuracy than a purely ballistic missile trajectory, but it offers a lower trajectory and can follow longer flight paths, e.g., avoiding the conventionally expected north polar route.

Force de Frappe The French medium-range hydrogen bomber force on which development work was begun under the de Gaulle regime. Designed to provide an independent deterrent force against the Soviet Union, the force was begun under the belief that the U.S. nuclear "umbrella" was becoming less and less credible as the Soviets gained in nuclear strength.

FR Flexible Response.

Fractional Orbital Bombardment System FOBS.

Fractionation Division of a missile's payload into several warheads. Equipping a missile with MIRVs is one example, although the term is used here to designate very large increases in the number of warheads per missile, up to perhaps 24–30. SALT II limited fractionation to a maximum of 10 warheads per missile.

Fratricide The phenomenon whereby nuclear warhead explosions create so much local turbulence, suspended debris, and EMP that other warheads incoming toward the same or nearby targets are diverted, damaged, or destroyed.

Freedom to mix The concept, as embodied in SALT II, that each side is free to determine the composition of its overall total strategic delivery systems, within the various aggregate limits and sublimits set by agreement.

FS First Strike.

Functionally Related Observable Differences (FRODs) The means agreed on under SALT II for distinguishing between aircraft capable of performing SALT-limited functions such as heavy bombing or carrying cruise missiles with ranges over 600 kilometers, from aircraft not so equipped.

Galosh NATO designation for the Soviet ABM system deployed around Moscow. Roughly equivalent to the U.S. Nike-Zeus system, 67 Galosh launchers were built before work was stopped on the project.

Game of Strategy A situation characterized by actors who interact, who have certain definable options or strategies open to them, whose choices jointly determine the outcome of the interaction, and who receive definable costs and/or benefits as the payoffs of the outcome.

GET Greater-than-Expected Threat: Method of Defense Department estimating developed under Secretary of Defense McNamara during the Kennedy administration; it involves planning to meet enemy capabilities projected beyond the National Intelligence Estimate.

GKO (Soviet) State Committee of Defense.

GLCM Ground-Launched Cruise Missile.

Golf(G)-Class Submarine NATO designation for a first-generation Soviet diesel-powered ballistic missile submarine carrying two or three SLBMs, with IOC in 1960.

GOSPLAN (Soviet) State Planning Committee.

GRIT Graduated Reciprocation In Tension-reduction: A scheme devised by the psychologist Charles Osgood (1962) under which a confrontation is progressively deescalated by each side unilaterally making small moves as long as the other side makes some appropriate response.

Ground Alert An alert system under which a certain number of long-range bombers is kept in constant readiness on the ground, capable of takeoff within 15 minutes or less after receipt of an attack warning.

Ground-Launched Cruise Missile (GLCM) A cruise missile capable of launch from ground installations or vehicles.

GRU Main Intelligence Directorate of the Soviet General Staff.
Hardening Protection with concrete, earth, and other means so as to withstand the heat, radiation, and (especially) blast effects of nuclear attack. The term is most commonly applied to missiles housed in underground concrete silos fitted with armored blast doors.
Hard-target Counterforce A strategic doctrine and capability designed to destroy hardened military targets, especially missile silos and command-and-control installations.
Headroom Issue The argument that the larger numeric limits allowed to the Soviets under SALT I would allow the Soviets to catch up with or surpass the United States once they matched U.S. technology; see Jackson amendment.
Heavy (Ballistic) Missile Large ICBMs, including Modern Large Ballistic Missiles and Older Heavy Ballistic Missiles, as recognized under SALT. The SALT I Interim Agreement prohibited converting launchers for light ICBMs or older heavy ICBMs into launchers for modern heavy ICBMs. Because the Soviets would not agree to a definition of "heavy" in SALT I, the United States made a unilateral definition as an ICBM greater than 70 cubic meters in volume. Under SALT II both sides agreed that heavy missiles would be those with launch-weight or throw-weight above those of the Soviet SS-19 ICBM. The only current heavy ICBMs are the 308 Soviet SS-18s, and many opponents of SALT III argued against continuing to allow the Soviets this class of missiles prohibited to the United States.
Heavy Bomber Aircraft in the categories limited under SALT II, including such bombers as the B-1 and B-52, future bombers capable of carrying out similar missions, and bombers capable of carrying cruise missiles with ranges over 600 kilometers or carrying ASBMs.
Hen House NATO designation for a large, phased-array Soviet radar type deployed on the periphery of the USSR for early warning of missile and air attacks.
High Frontier A comprehensive proposal (Graham, 1982) for a major U.S. space exploitation and military space program, including a several-tier strategic defense (ABM) system geared to achieving "assured survival."
Hot Line The Washington–Moscow crisis communications link, first established in 1963 through undersea cables and revised in 1971 to use satellite links.
Hotel (H)-Class Submarines NATO designation for a first-generation Soviet nuclear-powered ballistic missile submarine (SSBN) carrying three SLBMs, with IOC in 1960.
HSD Hard Site Defense: An ABM defense designed specifically to protect ICBM silos or other hardened facilities from nuclear attack.
IA Interim Agreement on offensive strategic weapons under SALT I.
IAEA International Atomic Energy Agency: Charged under the Nuclear

Nonproliferation Treaty (NPT) with monitoring safeguards against the diversion of nuclear materials to weapons use; chronically short of the staff and funding required for comprehensive monitoring.

ICBM Vulnerability Susceptibility to destruction in a counterforce attack, a situation brought about by the slow increase in ICBM warhead accuracies. See stability.

Inertial Guidance The basic guidance system for ballistic missiles; a fully self-contained system which senses accelerations of the missile in three dimensions and compares those movements with a preprogrammed flight path in order to control corrections made during the boost phase and during release of reentry vehicles.

InterContinental Ballistic Missile (ICBM) A land-based fixed or mobile rocket-propelled vehicle capable of delivering a warhead to intercontinental ranges; under SALT such ranges exceed 5,500 kilometers or about 3,000 miles. Once outside the atmosphere, an ICBM follows an elliptical ballistic trajectory. An ICBM consists of a rocket booster, one or more reentry vehicles, possibly penetration aids, and if equipped with MIRVs, a postboost vehicle (PBV) or bus.

Intercontinental Ballistic Missile (ICBM) Silo Launcher A "hard" fixed underground installation, usually of steel and concrete, housing an ICBM and its launch equipment.

Initial Radiation Emission of gamma rays and neutrons at the instant of a nuclear explosion; primary effect of enhanced-radiation weapons.

INR Bureau of Intelligence and Research, in the U.S. Department of State.

Interference Under SALT II each party is to use its own national technical means (NTM) of verification to assure the other side's compliance with the treaty, and each undertakes not to interfere with such NTM. An example of such interference would be attacking or blinding reconnaissance satellites. See also deliberate concealment, NTM, telemetry, and verification.

Interim Agreement (IA) Formally entitled the "Interim Agreement Between the United States of America and the Union of Soviet Socialist Republics on Certain Measures With Respect to the Limitation of Strategic Offensive Arms," signed at Moscow May 26, 1972. Together with the ABM Treaty, it forms the SALT I agreements. The IA entered into force on October 3, 1972 and formally expired five years later. In September of 1977 both sides pledged to continue following the IA's terms pending completion of SALT II negotiations, a pledge later renewed in independent statements after the death of SALT II.

Internal Environment Domestic factors influencing the formulation of strategic doctrine, as contrasted with the external environment.

Intrusive Monitoring The right of inspection to determine violations of agreements, usually by on-site methods and often without prior approval of inspection. Accepted in a limited form under the Peaceful Nuclear Explosions Treaty, but not yet under SALT or START.

Invulnerability Goal of protecting forces from being destroyed by a counterforce attack. Measures to promote invulnerability include hardening, dispersal of forces, mobility, and concealment.

IOC Initial Operational Capability: The date on which a weapons system is first deployed or capable of being deployed, after the completion of research and development and the establishment of a production capability.

IRBM Intermediate Range Ballistic Missile: A ballistic missile with a range of some 1,500 to 3,400 miles.

ISA International Security Affairs (U.S. Department of Defense).

J-5 Directorate Group in charge of plans and policy under the director of the Joint Staff, U.S. Department of Defense.

Jackson Amendment The stipulation, attached by the U.S. Congress in its ratification of the SALT I agreements, that succeeding arms control agreements should seek, inter alia, equal numeric limits for both sides.

JCS U.S. Joint Chiefs of Staff.

Joint Statement of Principles The Joint Statement of Principles and Basic Guidelines for Subsequent Negotiations on the Limitation of Strategic Arms, one of the three parts of the SALT II agreements. (The other two were a treaty running through 1985 and a protocol running through 1981.) The Joint Statement of Principles set out general objectives for further (SALT III) negotiations.

K See CMP or lethality.

KGB (Soviet) Committee of State Security.

Kiloton A measure of explosive power of a nuclear weapon; equivalent of 1,000 tons of TNT. The Hiroshima bomb had a yield of approximately 14 kilotons.

Launch Under SALT II definitions, a launch is a missile flight for any purpose, but does not include so-called pop-up tests, which are tests of the launcher and ejection mechanisms. See also flight-test and launcher.

Launch On Warning (LOW) The launching of missiles following detection and warning of a attack in progress but before the attacking warheads reach their targets. Variants of LOW have been proposed as a solution to ICBM vulnerability, on the argument that the ICBMs could be fired before they would otherwise be destroyed.

Launch-Weight The weight of a fully loaded missile at the time of launch; includes the aggregate weight of all booster stages, the post-boost vehicle (PBV), and payload. See heavy missile and throw-weight.

Launcher That equipment which launches a missile. ICBM launchers are land-based but may be either fixed (silos) or mobile. SLBM launchers are the missile tubes on a ballistic missile submarine (SSBN). An ASBM launcher is the carrier aircraft with its associated equipment.

Launchers for cruise missiles may be installed on aircraft, ships, or land vehicles or installations.

Lethality Often called K or kill-factor, or countermilitary potential (CMP), lethality is a composite measure derived from warhead yield and accuracy. See the section "Composite Measures" in Chapter 4.

Light (Ballistic) Missile Under SALT II, an ICBM other than a heavy ballistic missile (i.e., one with launch-weight and throw-weight not exceeding those of the Soviet SS-19).

Limited Nuclear Options (LNO) Position often associated with former Secretary of Defense Schlesinger, under which nuclear-force usage options short of general war were developed. See also damage limitation and warfighting.

Linkage The concept that progress in SALT or other negotiations should not be allowed by the United States unless overall Soviet foreign-policy behavior is acceptable. Notable instances include the postponement of the first SALT I negotiations from 1968 to 1969 in protest of the invasion of Czechoslovakia, and the shelving of attempts to ratify the SALT II Treaty in 1979, partly in response to the Soviet invasion of Afghanistan.

LOA Launch on Assessment: Launch of missiles, notably ICBMs, on warning of an incoming attack and assessment that the attack is serious enough to pose a major threat to the missiles and/or to the state. Compare with launch on warning and launch through attack (LTA).

LoAD Low Altitude Defense: U.S. ABM system proposed in the late 1970s and given initial Congressional approval for development funding in 1980; often proposed as an adjunct of the MX missile, especially in the dense pack basing mode.

Long Range Aviation (LRA) The component of the Soviet armed forces responsible for operating the Soviet intercontinental bomber force.

Look-Down, Shoot-Down A phrase denoting a combined radar and air-to-air weapons capability for intercepting low-flying aircraft or cruise missiles. Such a capability is intended to overcome the limitations of conventional tracking radars and ground-launched antiaircraft missiles in protecting against such low-level penetration.

LOW Launch On Warning.

LSO Limited Strategic Options: Limited nuclear options (LNOs).

LTA Launch Through Attack: Firing tactics calling for launching missiles after some incoming warheads have arrived, thus precluding the possibility of launching on false warning, but avoiding riding out the complete attack and risking excessive missile losses and a weakened retaliatory capability.

LTBT Limited Test-Ban Treaty: Signed in 1963 by the United States, USSR, and most other governments (but not by France and China), it prohibits nuclear tests above ground, underwater, and in outer space, allowing them underground only.

MAD Mutual Assured Destruction.
Maneuverable Re-entry Vehicle (MaRV) Ballistic missile warhead that can be steered internally or externally after reentering the atmosphere, in order to achieve higher accuracy and/or evade ABM defenses.
Manhattan Project Code name of the World War II research and development project that produced the first nuclear weapons in 1945.
MAP Multiple Aim Points: A version of deceptive basing for land-mobile ICBMs, under which each missile might be in any of a number of silos or shelters. To ensure destroying the missile, an attacker would have to target each such location or aim point.
Mark 12A Re-entry Vehicle Replacement for the Mark 12 RV on a fraction of the Minuteman III ICBM force, beginning in 1979, and planned RV of the MX missile. It features higher accuracy and carries a warhead with an approximately doubled explosive yield.
MARC Modern ABM Radar Complex: Under the SALT I ABM Treaty, a circular area three kilometers in diameter within which ABM radars may be deployed. The MARC concept was introduced by the United States in July 1971 to meet Soviet objections against limiting ABM radars by number and type.
MaRV Manueverable Re-entry Vehicle.
Massive Retaliation (MR) The doctrine formally announced by Secretary of State Dulles in January 1954, under which the United States threatened to retaliate at times and places and with means of its own choosing. MR was an attempt to utilize thermonuclear weaponry to achieve global deterrence at lower cost than a more flexible posture would have required. It suffered immediate credibility problems.
MBFR Mutual and Balanced Force Reductions, the subject of East–West negotiations regarding European forces, begun in 1972.
Mechanist One inclined to interpret the foreign-policy actions of other governments as being dictated by traditional power-balance politics; compare essentialist and cyberneticist.
MD Minimum Deterrent: Doctrine under which one need only credibly threaten the possibility of doing significant damage to any would-be attacker. Typical posture of a new nuclear power. See force de frappe.
Megaton (MT) The explosive equivalent of one million tons of TNT, used as a measure of the power of thermonuclear (hydrogen) weapons.
MICCS Minuteman Integrated Command and Control System: First system of firing and targeting computers for Minuteman ICBMs, housed in control centers hardened to withstand 7,000 PSI overpressure.
Midas An early U.S. strategic warning earth satellite system, first launched in 1961.
Minimum Deterrent (MD) A limited nuclear strike force.
Mininukes Small, low-yield nuclear devices, some with yields lower than those of very large conventional (chemical) bombs.

Minuteman Mainstay of the U.S. ICBM force since the 1963 IOC of the Minuteman I. For a summary of models and deployments over time, see Figure 1.5.

Mirror Imaging The assumption that an adversary does approximately the same things as oneself and/or does things for the same reasons. Belief in mirror imaging is frequently associated with belief in action–reaction phenomena (ARP).

MIRV Multiple Independently targetable Re-entry Vehicle: One of multiple reentry vehicles carried on a single missile, each being capable of striking a different target so long as all targets lie within an elliptical "footprint" some tens of miles across. A MIRVed missile uses a dispensing mechanism or "bus" to maneuver and send each warhead on a separate path to its target, once the missile has ended the boost phase. U.S. Minuteman IIIs carry three MIRVs, Poseidon SLBMs carry 8–14, and the MX is to carry 10 MIRVs, the upper limit allowed under SALT II. Under SALT II, all missiles of any type that has been flight-tested with two or more indepentently targeted RVs are counted as MIRVed.

Missile Gap A perceived gap in ICBM quantities in favor of the Soviet Union, which played a major role in the 1960 U.S. elections. In fact, while the Soviets had more MRBMs and IRBMs at that time, neither side had many ICBMs, and the United States had more ICBMs than did the USSR.

MLBM Modern Large Ballistic Missile: See heavy missile.

Mobile ICBM Launcher Equipment for launching an ICBM, and which can be moved from one location to another. Prohibited under SALT II for the period of the protocol (through 1981); proposed for MX under the Carter administration.

Modernization The process of modifying a weapons system such that its characteristics or components are altered to improve performance capabilities. In general, SALT II permitted many such modifications. See also qualitative limitation.

MOSS NATO designation for a type of Soviet aircraft used for airborne early warning.

MPS Multiple Protective Shelters: A version of deceptive basing for ICBMs, planned for the MX under the Carter administration. See MAP.

MR Massive Retaliation.

MRBM Medium Range Ballistic Missile: A ballistic missile with a range of 600–1,500 miles. The United States has never deployed MRBMs, while the Soviets have deployed 500–600 older MRBMs, mostly targeted on Western Europe.

MRV Multiple Re-entry Vehicle: In contrast to MIRVs, multiple RVs *not* capable of being directed to separate targets. Originally conceived as a means of saturating ABM systems, limited numbers of MRVs

were deployed by both the United States and the Soviet Union.
MSR Missile Site Radar: In the U.S .Safeguard ABM system, an ABM radar designed to provide terminal tracking and guidance for Sprint and Spartan interceptor missiles.
MT Megaton: The explosive equivalent of one million tons of TNT.
MTE Megaton Equivalent: EMT: Measure of the area destructive power of a nuclear weapon, in units of one megaton, compensating for the relatively lower efficiency of using one large warhead relative to many smaller warheads. See the section "Composite Measures" in Chapter 4.
Multiple Independently targetable Re-entry Vehicles MIRVs.
Multiple Re-entry Vehicles MRVs.
Mutual Assured Destruction (MAD) A concept of strategic stability in which rivals are deterred from initiating war by the confidence that each can absorb (ride out) a first strike with enough forces surviving to launch a devastating retaliatory strike.
MX Missile Experimental: U.S. ICBM, currently under development, to carry 10 warheads.
MYA-4 See Bison.
NAC North Atlantic Council: The permanent working group of NATO, with representatives of each NATO member state. The Council meets regularly at NATO headquarters in Brussels.
National Military Command System Designed to establish alternate command center capabilities for the airborne control of U.S. strategic weapons launchings.
National Technical Means (NTM) Methods of unilaterally verifying compliance with arms control agreements through the use of observation satellites and other surveillance instruments. NTM were the only verification means formally accepted in the SALT negotiations.
NATO The North Atlantic Treaty Organization.
Navaho Early (1950s) and relatively unsuccessful U.S. cruise missile.
NAVSTAR NAVigation System using Time And Ranging: A global positioning system of 24 satellites in synchronous orbits (i.e., remaining above fixed points on the earth's surface) providing nearly continuous signals which may be monitored by receivers aboard ships and missiles. Four such signals plus orbital details from the satellites could allow a missile to determine its position to within about 10 meters in three dimensions and thus correct its flight path.
NEMATODE 2.2 The author's nuclear exchange model; see the sections "Three Nuclear Exchange Models" and "NEMATODE 2.2" in Chapter 4.
New Type of ICBM Under SALT II, each side was allowed only one new type of ICBM; specific criteria were established to distinguish a new type from an allowed modification of an existing type.
NCA National Command Authority: The decision-making centers involved in authorizations to utilize strategic weapons.

NIE National Intelligence Estimate: Official U.S. government document expressing the consensus of the intelligence community regarding some subject of interest, e.g., projected Soviet strategic-force levels.

Nike-Ajax Early U.S. surface-to-air (SAM) antibomber defense missile.

Nike-Hercules Successor to Nike-Ajax in 1958, this SAM had a range of 50–75 miles and could reach 100,000 foot altitudes; it carried a nuclear warhead.

Nike-Zeus An early U.S. Army ABM system, nuclear armed. The Spartan portion of the later Safeguard ABM system was an improved Nike-Zeus.

Noncircumvention Under SALT II, both parties undertook not to circumvent treaty provisions through any other state or states or in any other manner. Similar provisions are commonly found in other arms control treaties, for example the Non-Proliferation Treaty (NPT).

NORAD North American Air Defense Command.

NPT Non-Proliferation Treaty: Strongly promoted by the United States and the USSR and signed in 1968, its nonnuclear signatories agree not to produce or acquire nuclear weapons and its nuclear signatories agree not to aid efforts to acquire weapons. It is significant in defining two supposedly permanent classes of states and in not recognizing the acquisition of nuclear weapons by nominally nonnuclear states, such as India. Most prospective nuclear powers have declined to sign the NPT.

NSA The U.S. National Security Agency, which is responsible for monitoring foreign communications and other signals.

NSC U.S. National Security Council.

NSC-68 The first comprehensive planning document on nuclear strategy, developed under the Truman administration.

NSDM National Security Decision Memorandum.

NSSM National Security Study Memorandum.

N*th* Country Problem The additional stability problems created in the global nuclear weapons regime when an additional state (an n*th* country) acquires nuclear weapons.

NTM National Technical Means of verifying compliance with arms control agreements.

Nuclear Threshold The point of escalation at which nuclear weapons are first employed in war; also referred to by some as the firebreak.

Observable Differences (ODs) Under SALT II, externally observable design features used to distinguish between heavy bombers capable of performing SALT-limited functions and those not so capable. See also functionally related observable differences (FRODs).

Older Heavy Ballistic Missile Under SALT I, a large ICBM of a type deployed before 1964, such as the U.S. Titan and the Soviet SS-7 and SS-8 missiles.

OLPAR Other Large Phased-Array Radars: Under the SALT I ABM Treaty, non-ABM-associated radars that are capable of tracking large numbers of incoming ABM reentry vehicles for an ABM defense; minimum distances from ABM installations were stipulated.

OSD   Office of the (U.S.) Secretary of Defense.

Outer Space Treaty   A 1967 international agreement, signed by most of the world's governments, which internationalized outer space and banned the orbiting of "weapons of mass destruction," commonly interpreted to mean nuclear weapons.

PA&E   Program Analysis and Evaluation, in the U.S. Department of Defense.

PAR   Parity in strategic weaponry; also a doctrine seeking/recognizing such parity. A standard for force structure requiring that the sum of military forces and weapons systems be effectively equal to those of an opponent; see also essential equivalence. Additionally, under the U.S. Safeguard ABM program, PAR referred to the Perimeter Acquisition Radar, a powerful radar used for initial detection and long-range tracking of incoming offensive warheads.

Passive Defense   Features of a weapons system or civil defense measure which enable it to survive attack damage; examples include armor plate, mobility, evacuation, planned dispersal, and hardened underground missile silos.

Payload   Weapons and penetration aids carried by a delivery vehicle. In the case of ICBMs, the RVs and ABM penetration aids placed on ballistic trajectories by the main booster and the PBV.

PBV   Post-Boost Vehicle: A set of small rocket engines and controllers allowing a missile to make late-course powered corrections in trajectory for improved accuracy; usually associated with MIRV options, in which case the PBV is referred to as a bus.

Peaceful Coexistence   Public Soviet position that nuclear war is an inappropriate form of East–West competition.

Penetration   The act of passing successfully through defenses in order to reach a target; applied to offensive weapons such as ICBM warheads.

Penetration Aids   Penaids: Devices employed by offensive weapons systems to improve the chances of penetrating defenses; examples include metallic chaff to confuse radars, and dummy reentry vehicles or MaRVs to saturate or evade ABM defenses.

Phased-Array Radar   A modern type of radar which scans an area by means of electronic changes rather than by mechanical movement; relative to mechanically-scanning radars, it is able to handle a heavier signal traffic, and is thus better suited to the demands of ABM defense.

PNET   Peaceful Nuclear Explosions Treaty: Prohibits peaceful detonations above 150 KT except with international observation and inspection, and allows certain on-site inspections.

Point Defense   Defense of a limited geographical area or an individual target such as an ICBM silo; contrast with area defense, as of a city.

Polaris First-generation U.S. missile submarine (SLBM/SSBN) system. Forty-one Polaris submarines were built between 1960 and 1967, each carrying 16 SLBMs. Thirty-one Polaris boats were later converted to carry the MIRVed Poseidon SLBM.

Policy Review Committee (PRC) One of two National Security Council Committees created under the Carter administration; unlike the Special Coordinating Committee, it had a relatively small role in SALT.

Politburo The executive body which acts as the authority for the Central Committee of the Communist Party of the Soviet Union between the biannual meetings of the Central Committee; it is the most powerful Soviet decision-making body.

Political–Business Cycle (PBC) A model of arms spending, according to which such spending is manipulated to promote the interests of officeholders. Compare with the bureaucratic politics (BP) model, with which it is not necessarily inconsistent.

Poseidon Second-generation U.S. SLBM system, MIRVed to carry eight to 14 RVs per missile. Beginning in 1970, 31 of the 41 Polaris SSBNs were structurally modified to carry the Poseidon missile.

Post-boost Vehicle (PBV) See also bus.

PPW Prepositioned Weapons: A seldom-discussed nuclear option under which weapons would be moved through the normal channels of commerce to hiding places in or near their targets during times of nominal peace; in time of war they would be detonated by remote control.

PRC Policy Review Committee.

PRE Preemptive War: A doctrine calling for first strikes against an opponent either when he is thought to be preparing to attack you or in order to deny him that possibility.

Precision Guidance A family of technologies, increasingly developed since the 1970s, which permits an attacking vehicle to home on its target by recognizing some distinctive signature associated with that target. Examples include terrain-following radar/computer systems (TERCOM) in cruise missiles, and bombs or missiles that home on a spot of laser light which another vehicle shines on the target.

Preemptive Strike An attack initiated in anticipation of an opponent's decision to resort to war, which is intended to prevent or reduce the effect of his attack. See also PRE.

Preferential Defense Selective defense of some portion of the silos in a missile field; since an attacker could not know in advance which silos were defended in what strength, he would have to launch a heavy attack against all the silos, thus depleting his strength.

Preventive War Launching of a first-strike attack in the belief that war is inevitable at some time in the future, and can be fought more favorably now than later. Compare with preemptive strike.

Prisoners' Dilemma A classic game of strategy, in which individually risk-averse actions lead to the nearly worst outcome for all parties.

Achieving the joint or social optimum requires communication and/or trust. This game structure has often been used to describe the dilemmas facing governments in decisions regarding new weapons developments and arms control. See the sections "Strategic Weapons Regime Management," (Chapter 1) and "Disincentives to Disarm," (Chapter 6).

PRM   Presidential Review Memorandum.

Production   Manufacturing a particular strategic weapon in volume, following its development and testing.

Proliferation   Acquisition of nuclear weapons by previously nonnuclear states. Often used erroneously to refer to increases in the nuclear weapons stocks of existing nuclear powers.

Protocol   An agreed addition or modification to a treaty: for example, the 1974 protocol tightening the SALT I ABM Treaty limits, or the SALT II Protocol setting certain limits more stringent than those of the Treaty itself, through 1981.

PSI Overpressure   Pounds per square inch above normal atmospheric pressure, used as a measure of target hardness or blast resistance.

PVO   (Soviet) air defense.

Qualitative Limitation   Restrictions on the capabilities of a weapons system, as distinct from restrictions on the numbers of such weapons (quantitative limits). Under SALT II, qualitative limitations were approached in quantitative fashion, for example by limiting the number of RVs on MIRVed missiles and by limiting ALCMs with ranges greater than 600 kilometers.

Quantitative Limitations   Numeric limits on weapons systems in certain categories, as distinct from qualitative limits. Examples in SALT II include the overall ceiling on strategic nuclear delivery vehicles and the various aggregate limits and sublimits.

Rapid Reload   The capability of a launcher to fire a second missile within a short time after an initial firing; cold launch facilitates rapid reload. See also launcher.

Rideout   The process of absorbing (riding out) an attack. Under assured destruction (AD) doctrine, one would first ride out a first strike, then launch a retaliatory second strike.

RV   Reentry Vehicle: That portion of a ballistic missile which houses the warhead and is designed to allow safe reentry through the earth's atmosphere; it is separated from the rocket booster after the boost phase. In a MIRVed missile, a number of RVs are positioned on a maneuvering bus within the booster's protective nose cone.

RDT&E   Research, Development, Testing, and Evaluation: The weapons development process from first conception through implementation, often simplified to R&D.

Residual Radiation   Contamination caused by the return of radioactive byproducts of a fission reaction into the ecosystem.

SA Systems Analysis, in the U.S. Department of Defence.
SA-5 NATO designation for an extensively deployed Soviet high-altitude surface-to-air (SAM) interceptor missile, also called the Tallin missile, once thought to be a possible ABM.
SABMIS Shipborne Anti-Ballistic Missile System: No such system has yet been deployed.
SAC U.S. Strategic Air Command.
Safeguard U.S. ABM system announced by President Nixon in March 1969 to defend ICBM fields; it was a major modification of the Sentinel light city-defense ABM system announced under the Johnson administration. Construction was begun on two Safeguard sites; under SALT I one site was abandoned. The second site was operated briefly before being shut down and dismantled.
SALT Strategic Arms Limitation Talks between the United States and the Soviet Union, begun in 1969
SALT Backstopping Committee (SBC) A National Security Council group established under the Nixon administration and continued through the Ford and Carter administrations, it transmitted guidance on SALT issues and provided support to the SALT delegations.
SALT Working Group NSC staff group supporting the Special Coordinating Committee (SCC) on SALT-related matters.
SAM A surface-to-air interceptor missile for defense against aircraft.
SAMOS Satellite And Missile Observation Satellite, used to monitor Soviet military activity.
SBC SALT Backstopping Committee.
SCAD Subsonic Cruise Armed Decoy: A stand-off weapon designed as a penetration aid for bombers; it carries a nuclear warhead and appears on radar screens as another bomber.
SCC Standing Consultative Commission: A permanent U.S.–Soviet SALT commission established by the ABM Treaty to "promote the objectives and implementation" of the 1972 agreements. It meets regularly and deals with such issues as charges of noncompliance by one side or the other, e.g., by covering missile silos during construction work.
SCC Backstopping Committee An interagency group established under the Carter administration and operated largely by ACDA, to give staff support to the Standing Consultative Commission.
SDF Strength/Distance Function: The function describing the change (usually decline) of usable military or other power with distance from its home base; called "loss of strength gradient" by Boulding (1962).
Sea-Launched Cruise Missile (SLCM) A cruise missile launched from a submerged or surface ship.
Second Strike (SS) A retaliatory attack in response to a first strike.
Second Strike Capability The capacity to absorb (ride out) any likely nuclear first strike and retain sufficient retaliatory capability to inflict

unacceptable damage on the attacker in a second strike. See also assured destruction and mutual assured destruction.

Second Strike Counterforce (SSCF)   As adopted by the United States under Secretary of Defense McNamara in 1962, a doctrine calling for counterforce targeting in second strikes, in order to control escalation and avoid city (countervalue) attacks. Unfortunately, the implied superiority necessary to carry out such a doctrine leads to very great budgetary demands and may be interpreted by an opponent as implying a first-strike intent.

Sensors   Devices used to detect objects or environmental conditions, such as radars and optical systems for detecting and tracking missiles and aircraft.

Sentinel   The first U.S. ABM approved for deployment (by President Johnson in 1967). A light city-defense system, it was superseded by the Safeguard ICBM-defense ABM system announced in 1969, and was never deployed.

Shallow-cut Arms Reductions   Modest decreases in the sizes of nuclear arsenals, at levels that do not significantly decrease overall capabilities.

SICM   Strategic Intercontinental Cruise Missile: A hypothetical but feasible weapon.

Single Integrated Operational Plan (SIOP)   The detailed U.S. contingency plan for strategic retaliatory strikes in the event of nuclear war. The first SIOP was adopted in 1960.

SIOP   Single Integrated Operational Plan.

SIR NEM   A family of highly disaggregated nuclear exchange models developed for ACDA; see the sections "Three Nuclear Exchange Models," and "SIR NEM D12" in Chapter 4.

SLBM   Submarine-Launched Ballistic Missile.

SLCM   Submarine-Launched Cruise Missile.

Special Coordinating Committee (SCC)   One of two NSC committees created under the Carter administration, it replaced the Verification Panel of the Nixon–Ford administrations. Unlike its predecessor, it dealt with non-SALT as well as SALT-related issues. See also Policy Review Committee.

SRAM   Short-Range Attack Missile: A stand-off weapon designed to help bombers penetrate heavy terminal defenses; an SRAM was carried by later B-52s, the B-58, and the FB-111.

SRF   (Soviet) Strategic Rocket Forces.

SS   Second Strike. Also, the prefix for designation of Soviet land-based missiles.

SS-9   Heavy liquid-fueled Soviet ICBM, later replaced by the SS-18.

SS-11   Liquid-fueled Soviet ICBM, the most numerous type in their arsenal at the time of SALT I.

SS-13   First Soviet solid-fueled ICBM, roughly equivalent to the U.S. Minuteman I.

SS-16 Fourth-generation Soviet ICBM, solid-fueled and capable of silo or mobile deployment, with or without MIRV; successor to the SS-13.
SS-17 Fourth-generation Soviet ICBM, successor to the SS-11, deployable with or without MIRV; IOC in 1975.
SS-18 Fourth-generation Soviet ICBM, MIRVable, successor to the SS-9 heavy missile; IOC in 1974.
SS-19 Fourth-generation Soviet ICBM, follow-on to the SS-11 but with four or five times the throw-weight; MIRVable; IOC in 1974.
SS-20 Soviet land-mobile IRBM, comprising the first two stages of the SS-16 ICBM; IOC in 1977. Because it can be converted readily to an SS-16 but is exempt from SALT limitations, it has caused serious concern in the West.
SSBN Nuclear-powered ballistic missile submarine.
SSCF Second Strike CounterForce.
SSKP Single Shot Kill Probability: The probability that a given strategic weapon will destroy its target upon delivery.
SS-N-6 Soviet liquid-fueled SLBM, range 1,300 nautical miles, deployed on Yankee (Y-) class nuclear submarines.
SS-N-8 Soviet SLBM with a range of 4,200 nautical miles, deployed on Delta-I-class nuclear submarines.
SS-NX-17 First Soviet solid-fueled SLBM, employing a PBV and thus MIRVable.
SS-NX-18 Soviet Liquid-fueled SLBM, MIRVable, with a range in excess of 4,000 nautical miles.
Spartan Long-range antimissile missile of the Safeguard system, with a range of about 400 miles and a megaton-range nuclear warhead.
Spectrum Defense The concept that nuclear weapons can be used to deter a wide spectrum of military threats, both nuclear and conventional.
Sprint Short-range antimissile missile of the Safeguard system; range 15–25 miles at altitudes from 5,000 to 100,000 feet; nuclear-armed, with a warhead in the 10-kiloton range.
Sputnik 1 The first artificial earth satellite, launched October 4, 1957 by the Soviet Union.
Stability "Arms race" stability exists when neither side has strong incentives to improve existing weapons systems, introduce new ones, or add to existing force levels. Crisis stability exists when neither side has serious temptations to launch a first strike under crisis conditions, because even under such conditions the advantage inherent in a first strike is minimal. Weapons system stability exists when only weapons deemed to contribute to stability are deployed. Exactly which weapons so contribute and under what conditions, however, are matters of great dispute, which tend to betray the political and doctrinal leanings of the analysts making the proposals.
Standing Consultative Commission SCC.
Stand-off Launch The firing of weapons, such as ALCMs and ASBMs,

from outside an opponent's airspace or terminal defenses; a technique for extending the useful life of aircraft when penetration is difficult.

START STrategic Arms Reduction Talks: Arms control negotiations begun in 1982 between the United States and the Soviet Union, succeeding the SALT negotiations. The acronym START was chosen by the Reagan administration to emphasize the political break with SALT.

Stealth A family of technologies for reducing the probability that an aircraft will be detected by enemy sensors, such as radar; also the designation of a possible strategic bomber utilizing such techniques, to succeed the B-1.

Strategic Delivery Vehicle Under SALT, a bomber or missile capable of delivering a nuclear weapon from the homeland of one party to the homeland of the other.

Strategic Doctrine As defined by Ermarth (1978), "a set of operative beliefs, values, and assertions that in a significant way guide official behavior with respect to strategic research and development (R&D), weapons choice, forces, operational plans, arms control, etc."

Strategic Parity A condition of at least rough balance or equality between U.S. and Soviet strategic nuclear capabilities.

Strategic Power A nation-state's military, economic, and political power or ability to control the course of political–military events. Nuclear weapons systems are considered strategic because of their capabilities to damage or destroy an opponent's political system, economic resources, and military capabilities.

Strategic Rocket Forces (SRF) The missile component of Soviet strategic forces, responsible for operating Soviet ICBMs.

Strategic Sufficiency (SUF) See sufficiency.

Strategic Weapons See strategic delivery vehicle.

Strategic Weapons Regime As utilized in this volume, the complex of strategic arsenals and doctrines held by the United States and the Soviet Union.

Strategy A plan for the use of military forces in war; broader in scope than tactics, the plans for conducting a battle.

Strategic Stability See stability.

Submarine-Launched Ballistic Missile SLBM.

SUF Sufficiency.

Sufficiency Strategic doctrine of the Nixon administration at the time of SALT I, under which rough parity in capabilities was sought but numerical inferiority was acceptable. Other conditions, which were difficult to specify, called for an adequate second-strike retaliatory capability, no incentive for the Soviets to strike first in a crisis, and the capability to inflict urban–industrial losses on the Soviet Union equivalent to what they could inflict on the United States. See also the sections "SALT I and Assured Destruction" and "The Salt I Aftermath" (Chapter 2).

SUM Small Underwater Missile system: A plan proposed by Drell (1979) and Garwin (Drell and Garwin, 1981) for basing strategic missiles in a large number of small submarines which would cruise in the relatively secure waters above the continental shelf. It could be used as an alternative to land-based missiles in curing ICBM vulnerability.

SUPER Superiority: Strategic doctrine calling for greater strategic forces than an opponent, sometimes a "margin of safety." The United States had superiority by virtue of its early nuclear monopoly, and that superiority extended until perhaps 1970. It is not clear that superiority in the contemporary strategic weapons regime necessarily implies a first strike capability.

Swarmjet An ABM concept in the High Frontier proposal, in which many small unguided rockets would be fired from a steerable launcher, to disable by impact an incoming warhead at low altitudes; in effect, it is a nonnuclear shotgun.

Tactics In general, the plans of immediate battlefield actions, or the detailed operational means of pursuing a strategy.

Targeting In strategic warfare, the selection of targets and their assignment to the weapons that are to attack them.

Technological Prisoners' Dilemma The difficulty in limiting research and development of new weaponry in the absence of effective means of verification.

Telemetry The transmission of data by radio; under SALT, the transmission of data on missile tests, not all of which can be encoded. See encryption and deliberate concealment.

TERCOM TERrain COmparison Matching: A guidance method in which sensors compare target-area characteristics such as ground profiles with information stored in a guidance computer to achieve very high accuracy through guiding a weapon in its terminal phase of flight. Applied in cruise missiles, and proposed for ballistic missile MaRVs.

Test and Training Launcher Under SALT II, an ICBM or SLBM launcher at a test range, used solely for test and training purposes.

Test Range Under SALT II, a facility where ICBMs are flight-tested. The two sides agreed that each had two such ranges at the time of the treaty signing, and to notify each other of future additions.

Thor Early U.S. liquid-fueled IRBM, with a range of about 1,750 miles and a payload of 1,500 pounds; deployed in Britain in 1959.

Three-tier Framework The structure of the SALT II accords, consisting of a Treaty, a Protocol, and a Statement of Principles.

Throw-weight The total payload capacity of a ballistic missile or, in MIRVed missiles, of its postboost vehicle (PBV), including all reentry bodies, warheads, and decoys. In general, larger boosters permit greater throw-weight and thus more and/or larger warheads.

Titan Older, large U.S. liquid-fueled ICBM, with IOC in 1962. The 54 Titan IIs were retained past obsolescence because of their contribution to the throw-weight balance.

TNW Theatre Nuclear Weapons: As distinguished from strategic weapons, battlefield nuclear weapons dedicated to use in a particular theatre, usually Europe. See also forward-based systems (FBS).

Triad The fundamental three-element structure of contemporary U.S. and Soviet strategic forces, consisting of ICBM, SLBM, and air-breathing (bomber and cruise missile) legs. Since each element has a different deployment mode, each would have to be attacked somewhat differently, which reduces the chance of a successful preemptive strike against the total strategic force.

Trident U.S. SSBN and its associated SLBM; the first Trident SSBN reached IOC in 1982; it carries 24 missiles rather than the 16 SLBMs of Polaris or Poseidon boats. Trident I or C-4 missiles are being retrofitted to some Poseidon boats, while the Trident II or D-5 SLBM promises both longer range and accuracy sufficient to attack some hard targets. Trident was originally designated Underwater Long-range Missile System, or ULMS.

TTBT Threshold Test-Ban Treaty: A 1974 agreement limiting underground nuclear tests to 150 KT yield or less.

TU-26 See Backfire.

TU-95 See Bear.

Typhoon Soviet SSBN, possibly competitive with the U.S. Trident, first seen under construction in 1978.

ULMS Underwater Long-range Missile System: See Trident.

Unconditional Viability The condition in which a nation-state cannot be destroyed as an independent decision-making center by an attack.

USIA United States Information Agency.

USIB United States Intelligence Board: Submits National Intelligence Estimates (NIEs) to the President or the National Security Council. Members are representatives of the U.S. Air Force (A-2), Navy (Office of Naval Intelligence), and Army (G-2), the director of intelligence of the Nuclear Regulatory Commission, State Department (Assistant Secretary of State), Federal Bureau of Investigation, National Security Agency, and the director of the Defense Intelligence Agency; the USIB is chaired by the Director of Central Intelligence (CIA).

Verification The process of determining, to the extent necessary to adequately safeguard national security, that the other side is complying with an agreement. See NTM (national technical means) and SCC (Standing Consultative Commission).

Verification Panel The senior committee in the Nixon NSC system responsible for U.S. SALT policies. Chaired by Henry Kissinger as the President's Assistant for National Security Affairs, the Panel included the Director of ACDA, the Deputy Secretary of State, the Deputy Secretary of Defense, the Chairman of the JCS, and the Director of Central Intelligence. A Verification Panel Working Group with representatives of those agencies prepared and coordinated detailed studies of specific SALT issues for consideration by the Verification Panel.

Viability The capability of a nation-state to survive attack and remain an independent decision-making center. See also conditional viability and unconditional viability.

Vladivostok Accord An agreement reached between President Ford and General Secretary Brezhnev at a summit meeting in Vladivostok in November 1974. It set ceilings and other terms for a strategic arms treaty to succeed the 1972 Interim Agreement of SALT I; most of those terms were followed closely in the eventual 1979 SALT II Treaty.

VPK (Soviet) Military–Industrial Commission.

War Mobilization (WM) A model of arms spending, according to which a permanent increase ("ratcheting up") in spending occurs whenever there is a war; compare action-reaction process (ARP), bureaucratic politics (BP), and political–business cycle (PBC) models.

Warfighting A strategic doctrine and force structure designed primarily to engage an adversary's military forces and their essential support directly, rather than to punish by threatening industrial and population (value) resources. Damage limitation and flexible response may be seen as elements of warfighting in U.S. doctrine; nonetheless, the Soviets have always stressed warfighting more heavily than has the United States. Both warfighting and assured destruction doctrines, of course, may be adopted in hopes of deterring a would-be attacker.

Warhead That part of a missile or other weapon which contains the nuclear, thermonuclear, or other device intended to inflict damage; often used interchangeably with reentry vehicle (RV), which is actually the part of a missile designed to bring a warhead safely back into the atmosphere to its target.

Weapons System Entity consisting of an instrument of combat, such as a bomber or missile, together with all related equipment, support facilities, and services required to deliver the instrument to its target.

Worst-Case Analysis Analytic method involving finding the most dangerous possible outcome of a situation and planning to counter it. Such analysis may provoke overreaction to an opponent's actual intent. See also greater-than-expected threat (GET).

Yankee (Y)-Class Submarine NATO designation for a second-generation Soviet nuclear-powered ballistic missile submarine capable of carrying 16 SLBMs. Thirty-four Y-class SSBNs were deployed between 1968 and 1974.

Yield The energy released in an explosion. The yield of nuclear and thermonuclear weapons is usually measured in kilotons (KT) or megatons (MT) of TNT required to produce the same energy release.

Zero Option Designation of a 1981 proposal by President Reagan that both NATO and the WTO withdraw all MRBMs and IRBMs from Europe. Given that at the time only the WTO had modern missiles of those types, the proposal was not taken very seriously.

A Note on Sources

Primary sources consulted in preparation of this glossary included Gerard Smith (1980), *Doubletalk*, and Thomas W. Wolfe (1979), *The SALT Experience*. Additional sources consulted include the following; detailed citations will be found in the References.

Edgar M. Bottome (1971), *The Balance of Terror*.

Colin S. Gray (1977), *The Future of Land-Based Missile Forces*.

Robert W. Lambert (1967), *Glossary of Arms Control and Disarmament Terms*.

Donald M. Snow (1981), *Nuclear Strategy in a Dynamic World*.

U.S. Dept. of State (1979), *SALT II Agreement*.

Final responsibility for all definitions and usages, of course, rests with this author.

Index

ABM (anti-ballistic missile), 13–15, 28, 32, 55, 72–73, 82, 164–165, 221–222
ABM Treaty, 13, 15, 18–19, 64, 83–84, 163, 165, 183, 208–209
Accuracy, 78, 129, 156–161
Acquisition process, 87–88
Action-reaction process (ARP) model, 94–98
AD, *see* Assured destruction
AEM9, *see* Arsenal exchange model
Afghanistan, Soviet invasion of, 209, 218
Air Force, 91–92
Air-launched cruise missiles, 31
Aircraft, strategic, 31–32
ALCMs, *see* Air-launched cruise missiles
Andropov, Yuri, 190
Antarctic Treaty of 1959, 204–205
Anti-Ballistic Missile, *see* ABM
Anti-ICBM weaponry, space-based, 32–33
Antisatellite weapons, 33–34
Arms control
　ARP model and, 97
　common features of, 210
　concluding remarks, 223–225
　constraints on, 197
　denial-punishment decoupling, 198
　disincentives to arm, 201
　disincentives to disarm, 202–203
　early 1970s, 208
　future of, 192–225
　future technology and, 214
　incentives to arm, 197–201
　indicators for 1980s, 214–223
　institutionalized, 115–118
　major steps in, 205
　nuclear and conventional decoupling, 199, 217–218
　physical constraints, 213
　political patterns of negotiating, 210–214
　post-World War II, 117, 204–210
　scenarios for 1980s, 214–223
　　continued and expanded competition, 216–217
　　cooperative outcome with decoupling nuclear-conventional, 217–218
　　first strike capability, 222–223
　　major initiatives, 218–219
　　unilateral reduction, 222
　structural constraints, 196–204
　systemic constraints, 196–204
　technology and, 110–113, 212, 214
　unconstrained technologies, 213–214
　See also SALT
Arms expenditure literature, 94
Arms race, 15–18, 95, 100, 152–154, 197–201
　BP model, 100
　disincentives to, 201
　incentives for, 197–201
　models, 152–154
　other rationales for, 18
　prisoners' dilemma, 15–18
　technological drive, 15–18
Arsenal exchange model (AEM9), 138, 141–143, 152
Assured destruction (AD), 6, 12, 15, 57–65, 67, 71, 73, 156–157
Assured detection, 112

269

270 / Index

Assured survival, 83
Attack scenarios, ICBM vulnerability and, 166, 186
  1971–1976, 170–173
  1981 attack by Soviets, 167, 169, 170, 173
  1981–1991, 174
  additional Minuteman IIIs, 177–179
  evaluation of, 170–186
  fractionation of payloads, 180–182
  LoAD ABM defense, 182–184
  Minuteman IIIs in MPA, 179–180
  MPS basing, 176–177
  policy combinations and, 174–177
  simulations of, 134
  SLBM for counterforce, 184–186

Ballistic missile defense, 26–29
Bargaining chips, 93
Battleships, 100
Bear intercontinental bombers, 51
Biological Weapons Convention of 1972, 208, 212
Bison intercontinental bombers, 51
Bomarc A9B antiaircraft missiles, 53
Bomber Bonfire proposal, 204
Bombers, 9, 31–32, 43, 48, 52–57, 91, 93, 99, 114
  B–1, 32, 91, 99
  B–29, 43
  B–36, 48
  B–52, 32, 91
  long-range, 52–57, 114
Breakout, 82–85
Brezhnev, Leonid, 63, 164, 190
Brown, Harold (Secretary of Defense), 70, 135–136, 158
Bureau of Intelligence and Research of State Department, 106
Bureaucratic politics (BP) model, 94, 99–101
Bureaucratic pressures, 18–19
Butterfly catastrophe, 194–195

C4 missile, 185
C–5A transport aircraft, 92
Carter administration, 1, 27, 31, 70, 84, 99, 102, 117, 157, 162, 163, 183, 209, 218
Catastrophe theory, 194–196
Central Intelligence Agency (CIA), 106
CEP *see* Circular error probable
Chinese leaders, 50

Circular error probable (CEP), 159, 185–186, 190
Cities targeted, 47, 53, 72–73, 97, 129
Civil defense measures, 61
Close packing, 103
  See also Dense pack
Cold launch capabilities, 26
Command and control channels, 67–68
Communication channels, 67–68
Composite measures, 123, 128–134
Conditionally viable, 5
Conflictual motivations, 11
Containment, 23, 48, 49, 51
Control risk, war risk and, 194
Convention Banning Modification of the Environment, 209–210
Conventional (nonnuclear) weapons, 7–8
  See also Nuclear-conventional decoupling
Cooperative motivations, 11
Counter-Military Potential (CMP) index, 129–133
Counterforce (CF) strategy, 51, 54–55, 67, 69, 78, 181, 184–186, 198
Countersilo capability, 185–186
Countervailing (CVL) strategy, 70–71, 78, 81
Countervalue (CV) strikes, 54–55, 58, 59, 67, 198
Crisis stability, 119
Cruise missile, 31, 93, 110–111
Cuban missile crisis, 12, 99, 147
Czechoslovakia, Soviet invasion of, 149, 208, 218

D5, 185
Damage limitation (DL), 57, 58, 60, 62–65, 67, 71, 73, 78, 81, 156
Declaratory policy, political role of, 62
Defense, major dilemma of, 9
De Gaulle, Charles, 57
Delivery vehicles, 47–51
Dense pack, 27, 28, 103, 162–163, 177, 189
DET *see* Directed Energy Transfer
Détente, 218
Deterrence, 9, 36–41, 76
  definition of, 37
  development of contemporary theory, 39–41
  doctrines, 9
  mutual assured destruction, 9
  quick trigger finger, 76

strategic doctrine and, 41–42
  types of, 38
  viability and, 39
Directed Energy Transfer (DET)
  weapons, 14, 82
Director of Central Intelligence (DCI),
  103–107
Disincentives
  to arm, 201
  to disarm, 202–203
  paradox of, 12
Disarmament, 201–203
  disincentives, 202–203
  incentives, 201–202
  See also Arms control
Distinct Blasts Index (DBI), 129
DL, *see* Damage limitation
DM, *see* Doomsday machines
DOD budget, 91, 97, 98, 99
Domestic stakes, 12
Dominant, 5
Doomsday machines (DM), 73, 75
Dulles, John Foster (Secretary of
  State), 50

Economic targets, 48
Effects measures, 119–120, 123,
  134–136
Eisenhower administration, 13, 49, 60,
  204
Equivalent megatonnage (EMT),
  128–129
Equivalent Weapons (EW) index, 133
Essential equivalence, 68–69, 164
Essentialist position, 22–23
Europe, 67
Expected surviving weapons, 135–136
Explosive yield, 126–129

F–111 aircraft, 91
FB–111–aircraft, 31, 91
Figures of merit, 123, 128–134
First strike, 26, 58, 160, 175, 176, 178,
  222–223
Flexible response (FR), 60, 61, 71, 73
Flexible targeting (FT), 65–71, 78, 81,
  82
Ford administration, 97, 149
Foreign stakes, 12
Fractionation of payloads, 180–182,
  189–190
France, 57, 224
Fratricide, 27, 103, 131, 133, 146, 162,
  169

Freeze movement, 212, 217, 218–220

Games of strategy, 10–12
  See also Prisoners' dilemma
Graduated Reciprocation in
  Tension-reduction (GRIT),
  218–219
Greater-than-Expected Threat (GET),
  97, 147
Ground zeros, 48
Guns vs. butter, 201

Hard-target kill capability, 133
Hardened silo, 178–179, 185
High Frontier project of Heritage
  Foundation, 82–84
Hot Line Agreement, 119, 208
House Armed Services Subcommittee
  report, 156
Hungary, Soviet invasion of, 51
Hydrogen bomb, 49
Hypothetical attack scenarios, *see*
  Attack scenarios, ICBM
  vulnerability and,

ICBMs (Intercontinental Ballistic
  Missiles), 26–29, 156–191
  CEP and, 190
  first generation, 52–57
  gap in 1960, 54
  historical trends in quantities of, 151
  lethality, 132–133
  Midgetman, 166
  Minuteman, *see* Minuteman
  operational conditions, 161
  SDF, 9
  SALT limit on size, 20
  SALT II, 28–29
  simple counts of, 125–126
  Soviet, 151
  test firings, 161
  U.S. counts, 127, 151
  vulnerability, 26–29, 65, 78, 82, 87,
    103, 108, 156–191
    ABM defense of, 55, 82
    challenge to idea, 160–161
    first strike against, 26, 136, 175,
      176, 178
    LoAD ABM defense of, 182–184
    MPS basing, 159–160
    implications of alternative
      solutions, 187–191
    introduction, 156–157
    proposed solutions to, 161–166

272 / Index

survival of first strike, 136, 175, 176, 178
  See also Attack scenarios, ICBM vulnerability and,
Ideologies, 22–24
Incentives to arm, 197–201
Incentives to disarm, 201–202
India, 207
Indochina, 50, 51
Information, degree of, 11
  See also Intelligence
Initial Operational Capability (IOC), 21
Intelligence, 89–90, 103–107, 147–148
Intelligence community, 105
Intercontinental Ballistic Missiles, *see* ICBMs
Intercontinental bombers, 9
Intercontinental delivery vehicles, 47–51
Interim Agreement, 64, 65, 208
Intermediate-range ballistic missile (IRBM), 92
IOC (Initial Operational Capability), 21
Insecure, 5
Iran hostage crisis, 8
IRBMs (intermediate-range ballistic missile), 92

Jackson amendment, 79, 211
Javits, Jacob (Senator), 19
Johnson administration, 63, 97, 159
Joint Strategic Target Planning Staff (JSTPS), 56

K index, 130–133, 154
Kennedy administration, 59, 60, 206, 219
  See also McNamara, Robert
Kennedy-Hatfield resolution, 217
Kissinger, Henry, 18, 19, 69
Korean War, 49, 51, 93, 99, 102
Khrushchev, Nikita, 56

Laird, Melvin (Secretary of Defense), 19, 97
Land-based ICBMs, vulnerability of, *see* ICBMs, vulnerability
Land-based missiles, disarming first strike against, 160
Launch on assessment (LOA), 72, 75–76
Launch on warning (LOW), 72, 75–76

Launch through attack (LTA), 72, 75–76
Lethality, 130–133, 154
Limited Nuclear Test-Ban Treaty of 1963, 116, 206–207
Linkage politics, 218
LOA (launch on assessment), 72, 75–76
LoAD (Low Altitude Defense), 82, 181, 184, 186, 190
Long-range bombers, 52–57, 114
Loss of Strength Gradient, 5
LOW (launch on warning), 72, 75–76
Low Altitude Defense (LoAD), 82, 181–184, 186, 190
LTA (launch through attack), 72, 75–76

McNamara, Robert (Secretary of Defense), 40, 57–62, 67, 71, 95, 126, 147, 154, 199, 217
MAD, *see* Mutual assured destruction
Maneuverable RV (MaRV), 78, 180, 190
Manned bombers, 31–32, 91, 93
Margin of safety, 64
Massive retaliation (MR), 40–51, 56, 67, 73, 74
MD (minimum deterrence), 55–57, 73, 74
Measures of strategic balance, 119–120, 123–136
Megatonnage, 126–129
Midgetman ICBM, 166
Military-industrial complex model, 102
Military spending, 201
Military targets, 48
Minimum deterrence (MD), 55–57, 73, 74
Minuteman, 20–21, 57, 78, 103, 158, 177–180, 189
MIRVs (Multiple Independently Targetable Reentry Vehicles), 21, 65–69, 78, 103, 111, 152, 159, 166, 188–189
Missile gap, 54, 56, 150
Missile performance parameters, 126–127
Missile warhead, *see* Warheads
Mixed-motive game, 11
Mk12A RV, 78, 185
Mk12A-equipped Minuteman III, 159

Motivation, 11, 95
Multiple Independently Targetable Reentry Vehicles, *see* MIRVs
MPS (multiple protective shelter) basing, 159–160, 162–166, 176–177, 179–180, 189
Multiple warheads, *see* MIRVs
MR, *see* Massive retaliation
Multiple Protective Shelter basing, *see* MPS basing
Mutual assured destruction (MAD), 5, 9, 12, 40, 60, 158, 160, 209
Mutual secure conditional viability, 6
MX missiles, 23–24, 27–28, 30, 99, 102–103, 157, 162–166, 177, 180, 183, 190, 199

National Command Authorities, (NCA), 77
National Intelligence Estimates (NIEs), 103–105, 149
National Intelligence Officers (NIOs), 104
National Security Agency (NSA), 106
National Security Council paper NSC–68, 49
National technical means of inspection (NTM), 204
NATO, 199, 200, 217
Navy, 91–92
NEM, *see* Nuclear exchange models
NEMATODE 2.2, 130, 138, 145–146, 166–168
NIEs (National Intelligence Estimates), 103–105, 149
Nixon administration, 18–19, 63–64, 79, 97, 119, 159
No first use pledge, 217
Nuclear-conventional decoupling, 6–7, 199, 217–218
Nuclear exchange models (NEM), 135–146
  arsenal exchange model (AEM9), 138, 141–143, 152
  comparative properties of, 139
  functions in, 137
  managing strategic weapons programs, 154–155,
  NEMATODE 2.2, 130, 138, 145–146, 166–168
  reaction-process, 174
  in scenarios for attack, 166–170
  strategic international relations (SIR NEM D12), 138, 143–145

Nuclear freeze movement, 212, 217, 218–220
Nuclear missile-carrying submarines, *see* SSBNs
Nuclear Nonproliferation Treaty of 1968, 116, 207
Nuclear threshold, 199
Nuclear weapons acquisition, reversal of, 193–194
Nuclear weapons technology, *see* Technology

On-site inspection, 213
Open Skies arms control proposal, 13, 52–53, 204
Organizational essences, 91
Outcome-effect measures, 123, 134–136, 152
Outer Space Treaty of 1967, 32
Overkill, 201

Pace of war, 200
Paradox of disincentive, 12
Paradox of inducement, 11–12
Parity, 75
Peaceful-Nuclear Explosions (PNE) Treaty of 1976, 209
Personnel for nuclear weapons, 43–44
Poland, 218
Polaris SLBM program, 29, 91, 185
Political aspects of strategic policy, 12–24, 35, 41–42, 77–79, 86–93, 187
  bureaucratic pressures, 18–19
  evolutionary development, 18–22
  ideologies and values, 22–24
  prisoners' dilemma, 15–18
  programmatic pressures, 18–19
  technology as constraint, 12–18
  technology as drive, 15–18
Political-business cycle (PBC) model, 94, 100–103
Policy, intelligence and, 104–107
Poseidon SSBNs, 29, 185
Poll data, 220
Post-World War II, 98–99, 117–204, 210
Power, 5, 6
Power projection capability with distance, *see* Strength-Distance Function
Precedent, 119
Prisoners' dilemma, 15–18, 48, 77, 107–108, 188, 193, 201, 203

274 / Index

Program options, 90
Programmatic pressures, 18–19
Proliferation problem, 224
PSI index, 133

Quick trigger finger, 76

Range of uncertainty, 136
Reaction-process model, 174
Reagan administration, 14–15, 27, 29, 31–32, 80, 81, 84, 99, 102–103, 162–164, 209, 216–222
Reentry vehicle (RV), 81, 111, 166, 178, 184, 185
Residual force, 134–135
Response-time problem, 75–76
Retargeting debates, 65–69
Rideout, 71–73, 75, 76, 80
Roosevelt administration, 17
RV (reentry vehicle), 81, 111, 166, 178, 184, 185

SALT, 10, 79–80, 127, 179, 188, 204, 208–209
  ICBM size, 10
  precursors of, 204
  Soviet heavy ICBM, 127
  unconstrained portions of weapons technology, 188
  verification problems, 79–80
  See also SALT I; SALT II
SALT I, 4–5, 13, 26, 40, 63–65, 103, 116, 117, 149, 158
  aftermath of, 65–69, 110–112
  DET weapons, 14
  first session of, 96
  incentives to arm, 197
  MIRV, 188
  negotiations, 211, 212, 213
  SLBM, 29–30
SALT I ABM Treaty, *see* ABM Treaty
SALT II, 4–5, 27–29, 102, 110, 111, 117, 119, 158, 161, 209
  ICBM, 28–29
  Minuteman III, 178
  negotiations, 211, 212, 213
  SLBM, 29–30
  verification problems, 111–112
Satellite launchers, 53
Schlesinger, James R. (Secretary of Defense), 27, 65–70
Scowcroft Commission, 27, 166, 189
SDF (Strength/Distance Function), 5–9

Seabed Arms Control Treaty (SACT) of 1971, 206, 207–208
Second strike counterforce (SSCF), 57–63, 71
Secure conditional viability, 5, 6, 9
Security levels, perceived, 201
Short-Range Attack Missiles (SRAMs), 31, 91
Simulations of war scenarios, 134
Single Integrated Operational Plan (SIOP), 56
Skybolt, 91
SLBMs (Submarine-Launched Ballistic Missiles), 19, 20, 29–31, 78, 126, 184–186, 189
Small Underwater Missile (SUM), 30–31
Soviet advantage, transient, 179–180
  See also Missile gap
Soviet ICBMs, 111, 113, 127, 150
Soviet invasions, 51, 149, 209, 218
Soviet policy, interpretations of, 22–23, 80, 89–90, 149–151
Soviet SS-N-8, 29
Soviet SS-N-13 SLBM, 29
Soviet SS-20 MRBMs, 111
Soviet space-based systems, 221
Soviet strategic doctrine, 42, 52–53, 55–56, 62–63
Space-based weapons, 14, 32–34, 82, 220–221
Spasm war, 52
Spheres of influence, 5
SRAMs, *see* Short-Range Attack Missiles
SSBNs (nuclear missile-carrying submarines), 29–31
SSCF, *see* Second strike counterforce
Stalin, Joseph, 48
START (Strategic Arms Reduction Talks), 27, 81–82, 117, 209, 216–217
Stealth technology, 31, 32
Strategic Air Command (SAC)
  high-altitude subsonic bombers, 91
Strategic aircraft, 31–32
Strategic Arms Limitation Talks, *see* SALT
Strategic Arms Reduction Talks, *see* START
Strategic (nuclear) balance, 119–120, 122–155, 188
  assessment of, 122–155

See also Nuclear exchange models
  composite measures, 123, 128–134
  figures of merit, 123, 128–134
  introduction, 122–123
  managing strategic weapons programs, 154–155
  measures of, 123–136
  1980s, 166–170
  outcome or effects measures, 123, 134–136
  scenarios for attack, see Attack scenarios, ICBM vulnerability and,
  simple counts of weapons, 123, 125–127
  strategic weapons program assessment using, 146–154
  typology of measures, 124–125
Strategic capabilities, factors influencing, 89
Strategic doctrinal positions
  abbreviations for, 57
  ambiguities, 199–200
  assured destruction, see Assured destruction
  damage limitation (DL), 57, 58, 60, 62, 63
  definition of, 35
  deterrence, 36–42
  dimensions of, 72
  drives, 77–80
  evolution of, 35–36, 43–71, 80
    1945–1949, 43–47
    1949–155, 47–51
    1955–1962, 52–57
    1962–1968, 57–63
    1968–1973, 63–65
    1974–1980, 65–69
    1980–, 70–71, 85
  flexible targeting, 65–69
  future of, 80–85
  general trends in, 70–71
  massive retaliation, 56
  minimum deterrence, 55, 56, 57
  mutual assured destruction (MAD), see Mutual assured destruction
  paradoxes of, 36–37
  plethora of, 71–76
  presidential administrations, see specific administrations
  as problem and solution, 35–85
  roots of, 36–41
  Soviet, 42, 52–53, 55–56, 62–63
  technical and political aspects of, 35, 41–42
  U.S. supremacy and restraint, 43–47
Strategic International Relations (SIR NEM D12), 138, 143–145
Strategic issues
  broadest sense, 10
  definition of, 4–5
  major dilemma, 9
Strategic policy issues, contemporary, 24–34
Strategic policy management, dilemmas of contemporary, 24–34
  ballistic missile defense, 26–29
  exotic weapons, 32–34
  ICBMs, 26–29
  major dilemmas, 9
  SLBMs, 29–31
  strategic aircraft, 31–32
  viability and nature of strategic weaponry, 4–10
Strategic sufficiency, 64
Strategic weapons, definition of, 4–5
Strategic weapons acquisition process, 87–88
Strategic weapons expenditures, 86–121
  See also Strategic weapons regime/program
Strategic weapons regime/program, 44–46, 86–121, 146–155
  action-reaction process (ARP) model, 94–98
  balance measures in assessment of, 146–154
  balance measures in management of, 154–155
  bureaucratic politics (BP) model, 94, 99–101
  concluding remarks, 120–121
  definition of, 10
  evolution of, 90–91, 224
  as game of strategy, 10–12
  interactions between factors, 86–93
  interactive environment influence on, 93–103
  introduction, 86–93
  models, 94–103
  other influences on, 118–120
  political-business cycle (PBC) model, 94, 101–103
  political process regarding, 12–24, 86–93
  technology and, 86–93

U.S., schematic representation of, 147
war mobilization (WM) model, 94, 98–99
Strength/Distance Function (SDF), 5–9
Submarines, 19, 20, 29–31, 78, 91, 126, 184–186, 189
SUM (Small Underwater Missile), 30–31
Superiority, 61, 74, 75
Survival of weapons, 135–136, 175, 176, 178

Tactical Air Command (TAC), 91
Tax cuts, 221–222
Technological creep, 90, 92, 108
Technological forecasting, 118
Technology, 4, 77–79, 86–98
  categories of advantages, 108–110
  arms control agreements and, 110–113, 212
  as constraint, 12–15, 107
  as drive, 15–18
  contrast of U. S. and Soviet approaches, 112–114
  as incentive, 107
  strategy and, 35, 41–42, 107–115
  unconstrained by SALT, 188
Thermonuclear bomb, 48, 49, 77
Thor IRBM, 92
Threshold Nuclear Test-Ban Treaty (1974), 209
Throw-weight, 127
Titan II, 127
Tomahawk, 110–111
Topological mathematics, 194
Treaty for the Prohibition of Nuclear Weapons, 204–206, 207
Trident, 18–19, 29–31, 185–186
TRX, 91
Turbo-prop-versus-turbojet, 114

Uncertainty, 136, 200–201
Unconditionally viable, 5, 6, 9
Unilateral reduction, 222
United Nations, 48
United States Arms Control and Disarmament Agency (USACDA), 147
United States Congress, 9, 156, 211–212, 217
United States Department of Defense, 4–5
  See also specific Secretaries of Defense
United States House of Representatives Joint Resolution 566, 14
United States interpretation of Soviet policy, 22–23, 80, 89–90, 149–151
United States strategic doctrine and policy, 80–85
  See also specific presidential administrations
USACDA (United States Arms Control and Disarmament Agency), 147

Values, 22–24
Vanguard satellite launcher, 53
Verification, 13, 79–80, 111–112, 119, 165–166, 213
Viability, 4–10, 39
Vietnam war, 93, 99, 102, 104–105, 218
Vladivostok Accords, 209, 212

War mobilization (WM) model, 94, 98–99
War risk, control risk and, 194
Warheads, 66, 126–129, 152, 168
Warning time, 76
Weapons, denial and punishment functions of, 198
Weapons counts, simple, 123, 125–127
Weinberger, Caspar (Secretary of Defense), 32
Window of vulnerability, 190
World War II, 17, 54
Worst-case analysis, 95–96, 97

Yom Kippur war (1973), 218, 220

Zero option, 219